Portugal, The Pathfinder

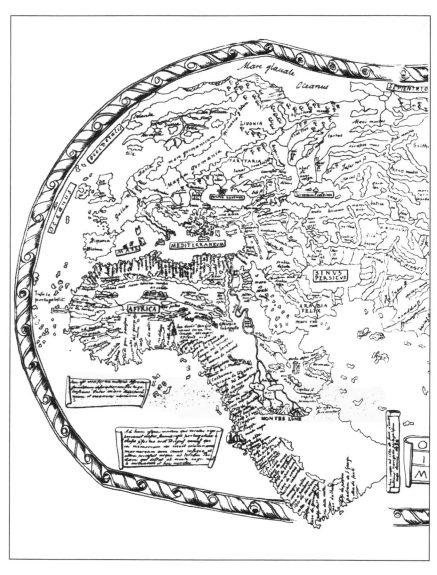

*Map of Henricus Martellus (1489), first to reflect the voyages
of Cāo and Dias*

Portugal, The Pathfinder
Journeys from the Medieval toward the Modern World
1300-ca. 1600

Edited by
George D. Winius

Madison, 1995

Portuguese Series No. 2

ISBN 1-56954-008-X

To Their Excellencies,
The Ambassadors Fernando and Nora de Magalhães Cruz,
who with brilliance and grace have represented their country

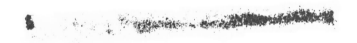

A special publication of the Luso-Brazilian Review
with the financial assistance of the Gulbenkian Foundation,
The Luso-American Development Foundation
and the Portuguese Quincentenary Commission.

Every scholarly book is a labor of love. No one save the author(s) and the editors realize how much work goes into it; when it is finally complete it looks inevitable, and all the sweat, corrections, revisions, lost footnotes, letters, faxes, phone calls and late nights vanish as a dream. This volume was scarcely an exception.

Portugal, the Pathfinder was originally to be a special issue of the *Luso-Brazilian Review* – and it still is. But, in the meantime, it has grown into a textbook of Europe's earliest expansion into the outer world, one we hope will prove of real value to historians, librarians, students and history fans. All of us involved in its creation have been inspired by Portugal, its history and a deep affection for its people. Moreover, we have long been aware that Portuguese history has scarcely received its due; it seems that the more recent European traditions of overseas exploration and colonization by the larger powers, namely the English, French and Spanish, simply elbow it out of the way. In the United States, ignorance of Portugal's contribution to world history is probably due to the early school curricula, which begin history with Columbus and the Pilgrims, and to the university patterns dating from prior to World War I, which feature the "big" cultures – England, France, and Germany, if only because these were on peoples' minds at the moment the university chairs and specialties were allotted. These have tended to dominate our vision to this day, and in effect, to blot out other pictures which should have an equal place.

The authors of this volume were all happy to contribute their work to the project, if only to help correct the imbalance and to show how fundamental the Portuguese have been in creating the world as we know it. But by the same token, it is usually the lot of the foundation-builder that more conspicuous are a structure's windows, walls and roof, all constructed subsequently. What we have striven for is to call attention to that underpinning of modern history too long overlooked, but which has been basic to the world as we know it.

Professor Manuel Villaverde Cabral, of the Instituto de Ciencias Sociais at the Universidade of Lisbon, has provided invaluable assistance to the *Pathfinder* project from the very beginning; without his help in obtaining moneys, this book could never have come into being. All of us involved in it wish to extend to him our appreciation.

The costs of this publication have been fully subsidized by the Gulbenkian Foundation and the Luso-American Development Foundation, with further support from the Portuguese Quincentenary Commission. Without their help this book could not have been produced, and we gratefully acknowledge their indispensable assistance.

In turn, I wish to thank those writers, my good friends all, who have contributed their time and best efforts; they have been both genial and very patient during the *Pathfinder's* long gestation. Then there has been the sage, friendly and generous – but nearly invisible – support of Professor Stanley G. Payne, former editor of the *Luso-Brazilian Review*, who by any criterion is the *Pathfinder's* guiding spirit. My appreciation is also gratefully expressed to his (former) graduate helper, Miss Jenny Pilling, who has guided the work from an assortment of manuscripts into neat printer's proofs, subsequently revised and marked up – and then made neat again. In this, she has been aided by a genial Irish scholar and computer expert, John O'Neill, who shares her unfailing good humor and has displayed much-appreciated patience through all the revisions. Finally, but hardly least, I wish to thank two capable and helpful people responsible for the *Pathfinder's* attractive appearance. They are Ms. Elizabeth Jones, who has cheerfully gone so far beyond duty's call so many times in rescuing my deviations from graphic reality, and Dr. Manuela Mendonça, of the Arquivo Nacional da Torre do Tombo, who called my attention to and furnished the delightful work of the XVI century artist and courtier, Duarte de Armas. Together, we have generated *Portugal, the Pathfinder*, and we hope it will fill a genuine need for years to come.

George D. Winius

Table of Contents

Index to Maps

The recent "Columbus Year" has been equally a curse and a blessing for the Portuguese, an intensely history-minded people. This is because a decisive process of world civilization, the greatest global transfer and mixing of peoples, things, and ideas in history, has been totally represented in the public consciousness by the deeds of a single individual on his portentous voyage under the Castilian flag to a wrong (but afterwards significant) location. Such a malfocus, especially in the United States, is partly the result of cliché-ridden primary- and secondary-school teaching and partly the fault of newsmedia which give no critical thought to almost any centennial. In fact Columbus inaugurated only one part of that enormous process, called by scholars the Expansion of Europe (for lack of a better name). It was not born in Spain, but in Portugal, whose real stardom goes all but unrecognized for having launched that movement which eventually established Western technology and rationalism as norms throughout the entire planet.

It is to be expected that the European expansion would have its victims as well as its beneficiaries – and, among the victims, the American indigenes, or, rather, their descendants, understandably (but somewhat opportunistically) selected Columbus and the quincentennial celebrations as the symbolic object of their ire. In this respect the Portuguese are fortunate that the Portuguese-trained Genoese has served as their lightning rod. For in the United States at least, rather than any rational debate over the merits as well as the evils of the expansion process, the Columbian commemorations frequently became a soap-box for the dissidents – while the commemorators played the willy-nilly role of apologists. All of which was in sharp contrast to the Columbian paeans of self-glorification which have been recorded from 1892!

There was a recent book, called *The Past is a Foreign Country*, whose title alone is enough to suggest that we cannot judge its inhabitants as readily as we do a neighbor who beats his children or in recent memory a Hitler who attempts genocide. One cannot equate the Inquisition with the holocaust of the Nazis, nor should one overlook the positive contributions of a George Washington or a Thomas Jefferson merely because they were slave owners at a time when their societies accepted slavery. Much less can we condemn the whole of European expansion. As in any great process, inevitably the work of the pious, the wicked and the in-betweens, all acting within the spirit of their own times, the great outreach benefitted some and dispossessed – and even enslaved – others, but in the long run it did create One World, thanks to the Western bent for profit combined with applied technology. While no one but a fool could maintain that the process has produced universal happiness, still few among us, including the protesters themselves, might wish to return to the standards of the year 1500 in respect to medicine, transport, communication and even civil liberty. What the protests of the American indigenes really expressed was indignation for their ancestors' treatment rather than the slightest desire to understand the nature of a process that had long since become irreversible, a *fait accompli*. One can only reach the conclusion that the time to study history was not during this centennial.

The original intent was that this volume should appear during 1992, but in light of the foregoing considerations, it is perhaps fortunate that it – and with it Portugal – escaped the maelstrom of that five-hundredth anniversary. For its purpose is less to provoke controversy than to reach historians and other students of history who wish a modern and panoramic view of what the Portuguese accomplished in the two centuries of their explorations and colonization. As the writers of its essays conceive history, geographical reconnaissance is but the merest transient phase of an ongoing activity, namely, the consequent interaction between European peoples and non-European ones, together with its consequences. Perhaps, as the authors see it, the word "discovery" can best be used in the sense of "establishing contact" and we propose that the time span involved in this activity hardly ended with the mere sighting of land and the planting of a flag, as on what became Brazil. For Brazil only became what we know as Brazil after the Portuguese next planted sugar there and began to form societies. Only then did there arise the particular nation we recognize. Nor was

Vasco da Gama's finding of Calicut initially significant as much more than a splendid feat of navigation: it was the contacts that followed his landing over the next century that determined the shape of things to come. Da Gama made India known to Europe, and vice-versa, but he did not, in the usual modern sense of the term, "discover" it.

The twenty essays in this volume have been conceived more or less as chapters in a book and designed to provide a vision not only of the geographical explorations of the Portuguese, but also of their contacts, colonies and commercial and diplomatic activities. Please note that they do not focus on the religious/missionary activities of the Portuguese pioneers explicitly, but that these do figure in the narratives at the appropriate junctures, if because they frequently became (as they were certainly intended to be) important components of the Portuguese outreach.

Most of the essays deal with activities of the Portuguese in the non-European world, but there are three which suggest how experience of the Portuguese expansion was translated into science and into literature: these are Luís Adão da Fonseca's "The Discovery of Atlantic Space," Rebecca Catz's "Consequences and Repercussions of the Portuguese Expansion on Literature," and "Portugal and the Dawn of Modern Science," by Onésimo Almeida. Then of course, there is the one by Harold Livermore which ably explains the Portuguese medieval background to the expansion, a necessary part of any synoptic vision involving it.

The views presented, while hardly unorthodox in light of recent historiography, may be surprising to those whose previous readings on the Portuguese have been confined to the older and more traditional works. Prince Henry, for instance, is no longer presented as a mysterious visionary and intellectual, but as a not particularly studious magnate who was but one among several principals at the inception of the maritime expansion. His navigators did not discover most of the Atlantic Islands, but merely rediscovered them. The *sigilo*, or secrecy, theories of the late Jaime Cortesão are not merely debunked, as has been the fashion for many years, but are put into new perspective: his ideas of prediscovery may be true, or partially so, after all. The actual establishment of the Portuguese in Africa, Brazil, China and India may differ from what one thinks one knows about colonialism: it was only violent in relatively small patches and as in Africa, India and the Far East was largely a matter of collaboration between the Portuguese and their indigenous neighboring rulers (who defined their relationships in treaties not in terms of superior-inferior, but of mutual advantage). It can scarcely be maintained that the Portuguese were altruistic or disinterested colonialists, but they did far less dominating anywhere than fitting in. Portugal in the XV or XVI century had between one- and three million inhabitants and there could not have been much more than ten- or twenty thousand Peninsular-born individuals in Portuguese Asia at any one time; so, anyone who maintains that Portugal, with only a few square miles of territory and some strategic forts, could lord it over that continent (or any other, for that matter) simply is confusing it with Spain in Mexico or Peru or Victorian or Edwardian England in India or Africa. In the XV century, the Portuguese were far more like inquisitive, seafaring opportunity-seekers and in the XVI century, more like skillful manipulators and tightrope walkers. But they did not know how to be dull, and as will be seen, all of them made the best for themselves of what they could find or create.

The essays may be read in sequence, as chapters of a book, or selectively, as reference material. At the end, I have appended a bibliographical essay of primary documents in print to serve as a useful guide to those who might like to delve into some of the raw materials from which this volume was produced. Otherwise, readers may consult the notes which follow each chapter for specific reference materials.

And, finally, I should perhaps add a caveat. In regard to anything so inexact as tracing the history of the medieval oceanic navigations, there are bound to be differences of perception and interpretation, even among scholars who are not otherwise far apart in their philosophies. This is apparent in the articles concerning maritime discovery within this volume – those by Charles Verlinden, Luís Adão da Fonseca, Francis Dutra and Felipe Fernández-Armesto, not to speak of myself. Such variances are normal, when one considers the paucity and often the conflicting indications of the source materials, and the reader must not expect that all of us would necessarily agree on such things as the exact moments in which discoveries were made, or even on the navigators and perhaps even the circumstances involved. (Nearly everything in this arena boils down to informed speculation.) In fact, even if we all were to agree that something had occurred in exactly the same manner at the identical moment, that would not necessarily make our assertion demonstrably true!

One must rather be content to read all the historiography and documentation one can absorb – and to form one's own opinion. On the other hand, the broad conclusion – that Portugal was Europe's great pathfinder to the outer world – is ineluctable.

George D. Winius

Certain books dedicated to the discovery of new lands in the Americas create the impression that the Atlantic Ocean plays a negligible role in the discoveries of the XV century. It is portrayed simply as the empty stage – an horizon taken for granted and disregarded–upon which the founding acts of modern times took place.

In a certain way, this perspective corresponds to that which effectively occurred. Nonetheless, it should be replaced by another perspective, one which better illustrates the change of mentality which was brought about through the influence of the great discoveries.

Two conceptual models

Hence it is interesting to pose the problem in other terms, and not to limit oneself to the question of consideration whether the Atlantic was more–or less–known. It is undeniable that the physical knowledge of the Atlantic space had progressed in the XV century. All the same, that which matters is not so much the comparison between the state of ignorance which surrounded the Atlantic prior to the great voyages of maritime discovery and the knowledge which followed them, as it is the confrontation of parallel conceptual models which governed the one and the other. Radically different, these conceptual models constituted two different visions. It is convenient to consider these for their own sakes, rather than merely to compare them as the one representing an earlier ignorance and a subsequent certainty.

Thus, for example, Vasco da Gama, as compared with Gil Eanes, did not only know much more about the Atlantic, but above all, he knew the Atlantic in a different manner. The nuance is a considerable one. By taking account of it, we permit ourselves to develop two orders of considerations.

It is appropriate, in the first place, to align our ideas with those considerations which permit us to understand the phenomenon of the discoveries at the end of the XV century. The discoveries presuppose a voyage, maritime in this case, and the voyage assumes an essential dimension, the manner in which the voyager conceives his voyage and the space in which this unfolds, the manner in which the navigator conceives his navigation and the art which he applies to navigating, a dimension which I shall call for short *the experience of the voyage*. And in fact, this dimension has been rather forgotten, perhaps because the memory which the time retained of the *voyage of discovery* is rather the *memoir of the discovery* than the *memory of the voyage*. Eanes, Cadamosto, Dias, Columbus, Da Gama, Cabral, Vespucci, all navigators and discoverers of the XV century, are known much more for the importance of the discoveries which they made (whether these be of a cape, of islands, of a route or of a new continent), but much less for the maritime voyage which they conducted. As if the remembrance of the discovery had virtually obliterated and relegated the memory of the voyage to second rank.

Herein lies the second order of consideration, as a consequence of the first. To restore the memory of the voyages leads one to recover the continuity of the different ways in which the voyagers thought about and experienced them.

Under these conditions, it is not simply a question of opposing the medieval and the modern conceptions of the voyage, as that of an imaginary voyage to an imaginary place and that of a real voyage to a real destination. What is important is to disclose the spiritual attitude which ruled each of the visions. To ask oneself how the modern vision of the Atlantic Ocean was formed, or about the genesis of the modern idea of space is finally to ask oneself about the state of the navigators' minds, about their way of considering the maritime spaces upon which they were about to embark. It is said that the great discoveries signal the beginning of modernity. This modernity, however, takes its source from the medieval vision of the voyage and the space in which it could happen. Thus the presupposed continuity manifests itself between the medieval and modern visions of the voyage. And it is certainly the maritime experience of innumerable navigators and discoverers of the XV century, who in the extension of the traditional views of the Middle Ages, actually inaugurated that modernity so often laid claim to by so many others.

The question thus having been posed, according to the conceptions of the Middle Ages and of modern times, of the "experience of the voyage," in order to answer it, it is now useful to determine the elements belonging to the conception of the voyage on the Atlantic Ocean at the beginning of the XV century, at the moment the voyages began. One can, it seems, determine three of them: as we are about to see, each of them has its own genealogy and was nourished by a specific number of real experiences.

The ocean of the Ancients

In the first place, we have the representation of the ocean inherited from the ancient geographers and which has deep Biblical roots. In this perspective, the ocean is the area of the unknown, the hostile and the dangerous. Perceived as an exterior ocean, northern or western, it finished by being assimilated into the maritime space which surrounded the inhabited landmass. Saint Isidore of Seville expressed it succinctly: "The ocean is thus designated by the Greeks and the Latins because, as a circle, it surrounds the Orb; or perhaps because it shines with the color of the purple, *ut caelum*, like the heavens." Medieval cartography, notably such as that represented by maps of the type T/O, show perfectly this exteriority of the Atlantic. These maps, drawn on a circular field, represent the seas as arranged in the form of a T; from which the expression T/O is derived, indicating that the maritime surface is found in the interior of a circle. Besides which, on a great number of these maps, the exterior circle is formed by the representation of an ocean which, in this manner always surrounds the globe. Under these conditions, the exteriority of the Atlantic winds up by becoming marginal. Such is the representation that the Middle Ages made of the ocean, according to the rather bookish sort of knowledge it cultivated, inspired by the Bible and the geographers of late antiquity. Let us take a look at the consequences which followed from this in the vision of the medieval student.

Because of its exteriority, the ocean appeared as a liquid mass, enormous and unique, which surrounded the continents, preventing for this reason all differentiation between Atlantic and Indian Oceans. This lack of differentiation favored the transfer to the Atlantic of all the fantastic and imaginary components which traditionally Europeans projected upon the Indian Ocean. As Pierre d'Ailly wrote at the beginning of the XV century in an allusion which Columbus later did not neglect to underline: "the regions of the Pillars of Hercules and of the Indies are bathed in the same sea."

As for this marginality, it imposed for a long period of time a vision of the Atlantic as a sea opposed to the Mediterranean. This sea, according to ancient geography, assumed an axial dimension at the center of the surrounding lands. A treatise on cosmology of the XIII century, the *Compositione del mondo*, mirrored this idea: in order for the land to be inhabitable, it should: "be constituted in such a way that there should exist, approximately in its center, a large and wide arm of the sea...into which empty all the rivers whose courses are directed towards the center of the land."

Medieval man knew, however, that the Atlantic is an open space, which was distinguished from the Mediterranean, which is a closed one. But concretely, he had great difficulty in imagining this difference. He ended up by projecting upon the Ocean the model of maritime space which actually existed only in his mind: the Mediterranean model. Thus he projected beyond Gibraltar a certain number of purely imaginary elements which were traditionally developed on his own side of the Straits, and he did it the more easily inasmuch as this projection did not deal with a known space, but with a different one, one rather defined through its difference. The ascetic dimension which characterizes the imaginary voyage on the Atlantic (the voyage of St. Brendan, for example) draws its origin from that.

The Meridian Ocean, first Atlantic Space

So here now appears the second of the elements which contribute to the image of the Atlantic voyage at the end of the Middle Ages. This is the maritime liaison between the western Mediterranean and the ports of France, of Flanders and of England, which suggested the form of an ocean existing vertically from the south to the north, with the horizon always defined by a coast situated to the east.

This vision of the Atlantic links back to the Europe of the XI century which endeavoured to surmount the crisis brought about by the disintegration of the Carolingian empire. From these efforts there resulted, among other things, a very different spatial organization from the one the European world knew beforehand. The Europe, which in the classical era had been developed around an interior sea, the Mediterranean, unfolded within a continental interior during the reigns of the Carolingian kings. And it progressively discovered the Atlantic. A discovery accompanied by unpleasant connotations: the Ocean appeared as an unknown space from which the Norsemen appeared in successive waves. Thus with its back turned to the Islamic Mediterranean, European man associated the new maritime space with the idea of suffering: it was an Atlantic where the important thing, above all, was to defend oneself.

This vision was modified between the XI and the XIII centuries from a variety of factors, all connected closely with British history. Shortly after the middle of the XI century (1066), William of Normandy conquered the English throne. Thus was constituted a new maritime space between lands, a second one besides the Mediterranean, the English Channel, a paltry space in its dimensions, but rich in significance: neither as a defense horizon, nor as a frontier of civilization, but as an arc of communication between two territories (Normandy and England), integrated into the same political community. As a result, the English monarchs of William's line, among whom Henry II (1154-1189) was particularly distinguished, extended considerably this new space to along the whole western coastline of the kingdom of France, from Normandy all the way down to Bayonne.

It was thus between the last quarter of the XI century and the last quarter of the XII century, between 1066 (the battle of Hastings) and 1189 (death of Henry II of England), that the first Atlantic maritime zone took form. It was a fragile space, in political and economic terms. Nevertheless, it presented several characteristics which can be detected in men for long in the future: they thought of the space as determined by meridional coordinates, projected vertically along the western coast of France, limited at the top by the North Sea and at the bottom by the northern coast of the Iberian peninsula. Furthermore, it was born of the politic of the English sovereigns, and the image which continentals made of this is connected to the diplomatic and military action which those kings exerted upon the continent of Europe up to the middle of the XIV century.

Under these conditions, two series of events between the end of the XIII and the beginning of the next century were to hold a decisive importance upon the evolution of this Atlantic space in the course of the late Middle Ages. Although different in their nature and in the geographical setting in which they developed, they presented certain very significant common features. The first explains why the Atlantic from the beginning was perceived as a space linked with the European coast. The other was to be correlated with the third of the elements which fashioned the image of the Atlantic at the beginning of the XV century.

The first of the series of events is well known to historians of medieval economy. They were shaped from the end of the XIII century, after the opening of the Strait of Gibraltar to Christian navigational and political supremacy, which permitted the lines of direct communication between Italy and the Flemish and English coasts and inaugurated the framework of the European economy. Communications which had been effected until that time through crossings of the Alps, and along the Rhone, the Seine and the Rhine, thereafter followed as the preferred route the maritime passage through Gibraltar as more rapid and economical. The Atlantic of the XII and XIII centuries, the vertical Atlantic of the western coast of France, of the zone which extended from the Cantabrian shores of the Iberian peninsula to the North Sea, the medieval Atlantic engendered by the English dynasty of the Plantagenets, thereby gained a hitherto unsuspected importance. That which had comprised the framework of English politics, in its sharp decline after the middle of the XIII century, became a geo-economic space, plowed by real maritime routes, that is, regular ones founded on economic, military and political ties. These presupposed and favored commercial exchanges which the economic growth of Western Europe, characteristic of these centuries, made possible: first English, then Castilian wool fed the Flemish textile industry; the wines of Acquitaine, then of the Iberian peninsula, flowed to the northern markets; the cereal grains of the north nourished the south. But these routes also extended to other places: they extended along the southern coasts of the Iberian peninsula and through Gibraltar penetrated into the Atlantic and the Mediterranean, via the English Channel and London, extending northwards to the Baltic Sea, unifying in the same spatial arc all the western coasts of Europe and the western Mediterranean.

The ocean of the latitudes, the second Atlantic space

Thus we arrive at the third element of the medieval vision of oceanic voyaging at the end of the Middle Ages. Here again, an historical event marks it: piratical activity of the Christians in the larger Mediterranean-Atlantic maritime space which extends from Liguria via Morocco to the Canaries and to the Azores, and whose nerve center is the Strait of Gibraltar. This is a Mediterranean space whose representation had an immediate connection to the second series of events which exercised a decisive importance on the history of the Atlantic.

It revolved about events which are among the best known of medieval history, but whose effects on the history of the Ocean have never been sufficiently underlined. It was a question of those conflicts generally known under the title, The Hundred Years War. As is well known, this designation can be misleading, for it allows one to suppose that this was about only a single war which unfolded during all this period, a notion totally at odds with reality. In fact it is necessary to distinguish, for one thing, the system of belligerence which was developed in the course of the XIV century (between 1337 and 1388) and which is currently called "the complex of wars of Crecy," from the battle of the same name. Its cause at that moment was no less than control of maritime communications at the heart of the Atlantic space. For another thing, it is necessary to distinguish the system of belligerence afterwards, from 1415 to 1444, which might be called "the complex of wars of Agincourt": in the years that followed the treaties of Tours, important transformations took place in all Europe (the reestablishment of French hegemony, 1444-1464; in Spain, the predominance of the anti-Aragonese faction, from 1430 to 1453). In this context, the conviction spread within the Iberian peninsula (supported by reasons military, political and economic) that it was of primary importance to create a climate of peace in order to permit the Iberian monarchies to assure themselves of the control, of crucial importance to them, of the Strait of Gibraltar, and through it of the maritime route from the Mediterranean to the Atlantic.

It was in this situation that a new vision of Atlantic space developed. It manifested itself within the context of Atlantic communications already noted, but it clearly differs in other respects. It revolves around a second Atlantic space, in which the dimension of horizontality predominates, a space defined by latitudes. The products which circulated there and the preoccupations which were aroused among those concerned were typically Mediterranean ones. It appeared as a heterogeneous space of bipolar dimension with the Strait joining both areas. The reasoning behind this was given in a study published some years ago, in which I described it as a space which, from the Strait to the Azores to Cape Verde, assumed a triangular form which in turn touched upon a second triangle, the inverse of the first, whose base rested upon an hypothetical line which went from Liguria to the north of Algeria. One might obtain in this manner a space which could be depicted graphically by two inverted triangles, united at Gibraltar.

Within this geometry was situated the piratical activity which was then practiced between the two seas. Obviously, privateering was restricted neither to that epoch nor to that zone. But even so it displays at that period and in that area certain specific characteristics. In fact, it was the privateers who originated numerous voyages of discovery, at least during the first stages. It is essential not to neglect this aspect.

From the medieval vision of the Atlantic to the modern one

One must now recall the vision which people of the late Middle Ages had of the Atlantic: in cultural terms it was an open space, while in terms of maritime experience it already appeared as a space *of secondary importance through its relation to the coast*, as a space conditioned by the coordinates of horizontality. But it might be simpler to address the other facet of the question, the advent of the modern vision of the Atlantic.

It is easy to understand why this beginning cannot be considered as the result of a simple process of substitution: neither the medieval vision nor the modern vision allow themselves to be reduced to a single definition or to a simple way of seeing or thinking of the Atlantic. Concerning the first, the medieval, we have seen how many varied perspectives there were—each of them possessed its own origins and its own dynamic and deserves to be perceived as an element which the discoverers inherited and which determined their way of thinking of the Atlantic. The modern vision of the Ocean was hardly the product of a single stroke, but was constituted little by little, as a product of the actual voyages which the navigators made and of the difficulties which confronted them. The transition from a medieval vision to a modern one was hardly so simple as going from a fantastic to an actual vision of the Ocean. This oversimplification does not consider the subjective understanding, belonging to the medieval, against the objective understanding, proper to modern times.

It seems that, among the elements of the medieval vision of the Atlantic, there are those which are the fruits of the purely imaginary (rooted in the biblical or ancient traditions) and those based on real experience (of captains of merchant vessels on the Flanders route, or of pirate vessels in the seas surrounding the Strait). And it is much the same with the historically modern perspectives. In fact, we return with them to the initial problem posed herein: in regard to what is ordinarily considered as being simply progress in the understanding of Atlantic space, I have rather preferred to talk of a parallel between two conceptually different models.

It is in this sense that the observations which follow must be viewed: they will constitute a rapid inventory of situations in which, starting from a vision inherited from the Middle Ages, a new perception of the Ocean will arise.

In the history of the Atlantic during the XV century, the experience of the oceanic voyage practically evolved during the middle fifty years of the century, according to decisive stages. These are of such importance that, in the last quarter of the XV century, the determining elements of our modern vision of the Atlantic were acquired.

The problematic and difficult experience of returning from more and more distant voyages represents one of the determining stages. Until then, voyages were encompassed by a sea limited and determined by its coastlines. Thereafter, they ventured out upon the open spaces of the Ocean. The texts, beginning with the famous passage of Azurara about Cape Bojador, say this explicitly. Beyond the Cape, the ultimate intrusion of known land upon the immensity of the sea, the navigator is aware of having entered into a new world: the sea and its currents are unknown, just as were the territories bounding it and their black populations.

If the chronicle of the discoveries represents these voyages as the exploration of virtually new domains, those of the west coast of Africa, the navigators themselves experienced them with quite a different vision. They continued, in their first voyages of Atlantic discovery, the traditional experiences of Mediterranean sailors. They projected their voyages as in closed seas, their horizons coastal ones, their navigational method the set course, their obsession the return home. This was the experience of the privateering skippers along the routes leading to Gibraltar, of the western Levant and Mahgreb coasts, which progressively, already in the wake of the expeditions to the Canaries of the XIV century, came to include the northwest coast of Africa in their theater of operations. For these seamen, the Atlantic upon which they moved was above all the frontier space with the Islamic enemy, and they moved about as if in a prolongation of the Mediterranean. Interesting themselves chiefly in gold and in slaves, they were more coastal predators than discoverers. Given to ambushes, to landings and to surprise attacks, they had to assure their own safety through the rapidity of their departures and through flight.

Then they extended their field of action. In this phase, a different cape becomes the symbol: Cape Verde, discovered in 1444, where the equinox began and where the nights and days always had equal length, as we can read in the chronicles of the time. In these places, navigators continued scrupulously to follow the coastline, "without ever losing it from sight," as Cadamosto writes. They came in contact with the great tropical rivers. Until then accustomed to rivers of lesser size, they abruptly came to grips with impetuous currents which made a deep impression upon them; reacting according to the stereotypes of the medieval imagination, remembering Mediterranean rivers like the Nile, they even began to think that they were on the road which would lead them to Paradise. In this oceanic space, on the far side of Cape Verde, to the Gulf of Guinea, the voyaging experience lost very quickly the bellicose character which had typified it more to the north. The spirit of the voyages changed: the engine is now commercial, as Antoniotto Usodimare says, in his famous letter written in 1455, which recalls the first medieval voyages in the mid-Atlantic region towards Flanders and the north and speaks of them rather condescendingly.

In any case, resemblances stop there. Navigators thereafter had totally different experiences of the maritime voyage, as for example through the slowness of the return in comparison to the swiftness of the outward travel, the adversity and the unhealthiness of the climate and the rapid deterioration of the vessels, as Munzer indicates. About the return, for example, one learns what difficulties had to be surmounted: one had to discover the "detour of Guinea," or as it was later called, "the detour of Mina." Having begun to be practiced in systematic fashion around 1435 to 1440, the "detour" is connected to the observation of Polaris above the horizon, about which the earliest testimonies date from soon after mid-century. Although these first testimonies still betray a method of observation which is little developed, it is no less true that they already presuppose a quite different way of experiencing a maritime voyage of the day. They reveal the appearance of a new art of navigation, quite beyond the art of Mediterranean sailing, which would end in the determination of latitude through use of the midday heights of the sun. From thence came a final and particularly important change in the manner of experiencing the voyage at sea and of practicing the art of navigation.

The new mode of navigation in fact departed from that of cabotage along the coasts and marked the beginning of astronomical navigation, all the more necessary in light of the fact that when one descends ever farther towards the south, it becomes impossible to observe the Pole Star. The oldest chronicles, whether Portuguese or not, which signal the use of declinations of the sun, date from 1485-1488. One may thus accept the date 1485 in order to mark the transition from the one to the other of the great methods of experiencing the Atlantic. Basically, there are two ways to consider the horizon: if previously one had kept in view the horizon of the coast, in order to discover the whereabouts of a formidable reef, it was henceforth the heavenly horizon in which to discover the guiding star.

This new experience of oceanic navigation can be envisaged in two forms. It goes beyond the boundaries of the second period of Atlantic voyaging, that of Guinea. The navigator is no longer the Mediterranean mariner who plies between coast and coast. He directs himself according to the stars, and the return voyage ceases to disturb him. Moreover, as with the northward Atlantic voyage, to England and to Flanders, his purpose has become mainly commercial.

But, in another form, political events accelerated this change in his Atlantic vision. These were the Luso-Castilian Treaty of Alcáçovas-Toledo, of 1479-1480, the coming to power of the King, D. João II, in August of 1581, and the construction of the fort at

S. Jorge da Mina, in 1582. Of these, perhaps the Treaty of 1478-1479 was the most significant. This diplomatic accord, which brought an end to the period of strife over the succession to the crown of Castile, also announced the partition of the Atlantic and prefigured the Treaty of Tordesillas: from this start of the 1480s, the Atlantic was henceforth envisaged not as a route or as a coast to explore, but as a space which was not as yet known but which was nonetheless laid claim to.

The discovery of the Atlantic

How was this still unknown Atlantic perceived? The monumental study which Joaquim Barradas da Carvalho dedicated to the figure and work of Duarte Pacheco Pereira provides the answer to this question. The author examines the history of the term *descobrir* and the concept of discovery in Portuguese literature between 1055 and 1567. We will call attention to only one of his conclusions: the term *descobrir*, in the sense of discovery of lands, appeared for the first time in 1472, while the more abstract term for "discovery," *descobrimento*, surfaced in 1486. One would not be very far from the truth in asserting that parallel to the change which affected the experience of the oceanic voyage in the course of the 1480s, this mutation had as its determining component an intellectual dimension. The experience of the Atlantic overflowed the limits of traditional perception: those of coast and route, and the Ocean itself became a space to discover. As one thus considers it, it is a whole new vision, and not simply one more to add to the preceding ones, as if it were merely a question of the banal accumulation of experiences. There is a complete break involved which, produced by its connection with two great previous experiences (that of the Saharan coast and that of Guinea), introduced a vision of an open space, entirely liberated from any relation to the coast and of all dimension of horizontality which the previous experiences both contained. In fact, it is at this point that the modern vision of the Atlantic was born.

This modernization of perception is clearly revealed in the expedition of Bartolomeu Dias in 1487-1488. As I wrote in my little book, *O Essencial sobre Bartolomeu Dias*, "The expedition of Bartolomeu Dias represents a decisive moment which, in the evolutionary process of giving birth to the modern Atlantic, simultaneously implies the rupture of the medieval Atlantic vision. From an Atlantic fantastic, uncertain, nebulous, full of marvels, from a space open towards the west, given access through a horizontal projection of the Mediterranean, with the same mode of navigational cabotage where the island (fantastic or real) held a predominant importance, we move to another Atlantic distinct, anticipated, studied, a space open towards the south along a meridional projection, where the coastal navigation was replaced by astronomical navigation on the high seas according to a route previously determined." In fact, it is indeed there, in the Portuguese voyage to the south, where the great break with tradition was produced, involving an upward step. The break with the coastal tradition is indeed visible when, as a result of his difficulties encountered while sailing along the African littoral at the Angra das Voltas, Bartolomeu Dias decided to steer towards the west, thereby achieving, by his detour in the arc of a circle his entry into the Indian Ocean. Finally, this departure from the horizontal dimension takes leave of the medieval practices and underlines the unique role of the navigator, now figuratively on its maiden voyages. Dias had thus embarked upon what became his decisive task in developing the future Cape route which Da Gama and Cabral would soon follow.

From place to space

The moment has arrived for my conclusion. And I do so while underlining the characteristics of the modern Atlantic which the Portuguese voyagers contributed when travelling towards the south. It is the definition of the Atlantic considered as an ocean with limits, with an almost mechanical function, at least so far as the winds and currents are concerned, and with a unity which its projection into meridional coordinates had rendered possible.

And why had it been possible to come onto this unifying vision of the Ocean, so different from the medieval vision? Because during the last quarter of the XV century the Portuguese had come to replace the idea of a geography dominated by *places* with one characterized in terms of *spaces*. It is here where the fundamental step was taken.

Incapable of thinking of space as a coordinate of reality independent of the objects which occupy it, the men of the Middle Ages did not take account either of distances or of the proportion of their representations; for them, space emanated from things. This is why the medieval Atlantic is chiefly an assemblage of places, maritime ones, differentiated and concrete. It is there that we can place the experiences of the first Henrician navigators who reached Guinea: it was the experience of the discovery of new places.

When, in the course of the same eighth decade of the XV century the Atlantic came to be thought of in terms of *over here and out there*, the mutation was produced: space was henceforth thought of in terms of the bodies which occupied it. This was the vision of space made over into the maritime vision. It was this vision which animated Bartolomeu Dias, Duarte Pacheco Pereira and Vasco da Gama.

It was not by chance that the instruments which permitted the measurement of this space were developed at that very moment. It was thence astronomical navigation. This implies ultimately that the Atlantic is thought of as a grid defined in terms of quantifiable coordinates. This was the meaning of latitude. It was the Ocean in its aspect of extension which was the important thing to grasp. To arrive at the right harbor, one had to employ successive operations involving measurements. For this sea was not simply a matter of the succession of places on a medieval portulan chart.

This is the reason why I think that it was in finding the route to the Cape of Good Hope, in the course of the last quarter of the XV century, that Portuguese navigators definitively put an end to the medieval vision of the Ocean and that at the same time the idea of the Atlantic as quantifiable space dawned upon them, the same vision of space which is common to our modern civilization.

Luís Adão da Fonseca

Note

* This article previously appeared as "La découverte de l'espace atlantique" in *Cadmos: Cahiers trimestriel du Centre Européen de la Culture* no. 53 (1991): 11-25.

The Iberian Peninsula

Portugal and the Prelude to the European Expansion

The Portuguese, rather than any other people, were the pioneers in the great movement of European exploration and expansion. In the space of a century, their navigators opened up the rest of the globe to commerce, to religion, science and study, to European civilization, development, and destruction. The enterprise is conventionally dated from a day in the summer of 1415 when D. João I, accompanied by four of his sons, crossed the Straits of Gibraltar to occupy the ancient port of Ceuta in Africa. Its situation is symbolized by the two keys of its coat of arms: one represents access between Europe and Africa, the other the junction of the Mediterranean with the Atlantic Ocean. From this precarious foothold there ensued the rediscovery and occupation of the Atlantic Isles, the Madeiran and Azorean groups, then uninhabited and thenceforward incorporated into the Portuguese nation, the coastal exploration of West Africa, the discovery of the kingdom of Congo and Angola, the establishment of the trade castle of Mina, the rounding of the Cape of Good Hope, and the discovery of Brazil in 1500. Nearly five centuries have passed, and the Portuguese language now stands with English and Spanish as the most widely spoken tongues of Europe.

Portugal's geographical predisposition for this enterprise is not difficult to explain.[1] It stands at the southern and western extremity of Europe, and it faces the permanent frontier of the sea. Since settled societies began, its inhabitants have looked to the shore to supplement their diet. The high tablelands of the Iberian Peninsula are broken up to form its northeastern frontier and below the Tagus fall away to a level expanse. It appears to turn its back on the *mesetas* of Leon and Castile. Its main centres of population are the two great cities of Lisbon and Oporto, which have arisen at the mouths of the rivers Tagus and Douro. They draw together the inhabitants of the hinterland, but are not navigable beyond the existing frontier. By their agriculture, customs and religion, its people are bound to Europe: its language is perhaps the closest to Latin of any surviving speech. Its climate is that of Southern Europe and is moderated by the proximity of the sea, and its physical landscapes are reduplicated elsewhere on the continent. It has enjoyed political independence or autonomy for nine hundred years, and the human decisions that governed the exploration of the middle Atlantic and the colonization of the islands and of Brazil, and the foundation of a chain of trading-stations stretching from Morocco to Macau were taken in or near Lisbon, not in the land-based capital of some continental empire. The presence of the sea is essential. The long Portuguese coastline is dotted with fishing villages: they were formerly much more numerous. The prerequisite for naval construction has been the existence of timber. Much of Portugal is now covered with pine forests, often the result of reforestation, practised in the thirteenth century and in modern times. But the distance between this kind of natural and human predisposition and the formation and execution of a conscious policy of expansion is very great. Portugal's share of the world's resources of precious metals was probably exhausted in Roman times, when an auriferous belt of quartzite stretching across the Northwest was exploited over a lengthy period. Its very want provided an impetus for expansion, discernible only at intervals during Portugal's early history, but gathering momentum in the later middle ages.

The archeology of Atlantic Europe shows common terms between the peoples of Galicia and Portugal and those of Britain and Brittany, but this is not evidence of direct contact by sea or that pre-Celtic and Celtic adventurers did more than provide material for legend. If the Greeks, who certainly reached the eastern and southern shores of the Iberian Peninsula, explored the Atlantic coasts, they have left little record of the fact. The Phoenicians, who founded Carthage and Cadiz, certainly navigated the west coast of Africa, described in the fragmentary periplus of Hanno: they effectively closed the Straits of Gibraltar for a long period to Greek and other shipping, and they must have colonized the southern and western coast of Portugal, but their records were deleted by the Romans.[2] The annexation of what is now Portugal to the Roman empire began with the defeat of Carthage in the Second Punic War, when Hannibal had wintered troops in the present Algarve. The great hero of the Lusitanian resistance, Viriatus, was murdered in 139 B.C. The mountaineers of the north coast remained unsubdued until the time of Christ. The Roman empire, though it made full use of the Mediterranean, was land-based. Consuls annexed new provinces as commanders of legions: they rarely became illustrious as admirals. The first famous historical figure to visit both Portugal and Britain was Julius Caesar: he used ships to carry his men up the western coast of Portugal, and bestowed on Lisbon the title of Liberalitas Julia. But he did not make the voyage between the two by sea. When Augustus created the province of Lusitania for his veterans, he made their capital inland at Mérida, now in Spain.

The Germanic Partition

By the end of the fourth century, the Roman army was much reduced and Hispanicized, and the administration subordinated to the requirements of the western Prefect, stationed on the Rhine frontier. Germanic peoples, with some others, had already overrun the Danubian provinces and migrated westward into the Franco-German border zone when the defenses collapsed at the end of 406, and northern tribes pushed their way through Gaul into Spain. They were soon assigned land in the western provinces, but the only one of the four peoples concerned to remain permanently in the place was the Sueves, who occupied the region of Oporto and Braga. They were peasants and soldiers who did not disdain to raid or sell their services elsewhere, but who intermarried with the existing population and became in 446 the first Germanic people to acknowledge a Catholic king. The rich concentration of Germanic toponyms found in Oporto and Braga bears witness to their presence, but their language has left as little impression on the Portuguese vocabulary as the Visigothic on Spanish. As northern peasants, they probably built wooden cabins, of which no trace remains. The heavy northern wooden plough is attributed to their influence, and they may have introduced new types of boats. The Sueves had first appeared in western Germany on the Elbe, but one division, the Marcomans or Quads, had moved eastwards into what is now Czechoslovakia and had entered Roman Pannonia, now Hungary. Those who arrived in Portugal may have been from either or both groups.[3] In about A.D. 550 they reappear under king Theodemir, who was converted to Catholicism through the efforts of St. Martin of Dume, a monk born in Pannonia, and perhaps trained in Byzantium.

During its last half-century before the Islamic invasion of the Peninsula in A.D. 711, the Gothic aristocracy which had largely replaced the Roman senatorial families, involved the monarchy in its ambitions for power. Kings confiscated the estates of their enemies, and rewarded their friends, who were in turn replaced by the friends of their successors. The gold coin issued by Leovigild and Reccared was debased. It came from trade conducted largely by foreign merchants dwelling in the ports of Andalusia and eastern Spain. The Sueves of northern Portugal, if not isolated, had only a small share of this activity.

Conquest by Islam

If the Roman Empire of the west had drawn gold from Portugal and Galicia, the eastern empire sent its own treasure to buy the dubious loyalty of barbarian kings. But its relations with the distant west were rudely interrupted by the unexpected eruption of a new land empire. It appeared on the periphery of the Roman world in Arabia, and its founder, the Prophet Mohammed, had died in the same year as St. Isidore. Six years later, his followers conquered Egypt and Syria. Both were the seats of ancient civilizations. In early times Egypt had been in contact with Greece: its port was named after the conqueror Alexander, but it preferred simpler beliefs to the disputatious theology that delighted the Greeks, and was increasingly dissatisfied with a long period of Byzantine anarchy. The Prophet Mohammed had not prescribed any form of government, but only strict observance of personal morality, reinforced by obedience to the law, to be enforced by whoever ruled in God's name, his *vicarius* or deputy, the *khalifa*. The converts, who had found Egypt almost undefended, had been held for a time by the Christians of Carthage. They had then converted the tribes of the North African interior who dwelt beyond the Roman pale and reached Atlantic Morocco by land in 682 A.D., or the 63rd year of Mohammed's *hijra*. The Byzantine governor of Ceuta joined the Visigoths, who closed their southern ports in an attempt to prevent infiltration. They themselves had formerly been a military tribe organized for war, but they had become a clique of landowners ruling villages of serfs, whom they now expected to defend them. One of their parties sought to engage the support of the Muslim governor of Ceuta, who crossed the Straits in five ships, defeated the forces hastily called to oppose them, killed King Roderic, occupied Toledo, and after a lengthy siege of Mérida, received the submission of all the subjects of the Goths.

Islam was checked at the Pyrenees and in Asia Minor. When its first caliphal dynasty was overthrown, its centre moved eastward from Damascus to Baghdad, and it undertook the conversion of Persia and the tribes of Asia. For the first time Europe was girdled by peoples who saw the domination of Italy as oppressive, yet which offered a kind of tolerance to those who had been Christians, Roman or not. Muslims in Spain were at first only a military colony, which took over the barracks of the Visigoths, and restored hundreds of villas to the displaced Visigothic dynasty, though not the title of king. As the caliphate moved eastwards, Spain became a detached province of the Muslim world. Muslim Spain was Roman Spain, and the ancient cities of the Roman provinces became the capitals of the Muslim frontiers. Only Braga in the northwest was sacked and abandoned. The seat of government was moved forward from Seville to Cordoba, and contingents from Syria and Egypt were settled in Andalusia and the Algarve. But some of the Berber peoples who had flocked to Spain in the first flush of conquest found only famine and returned to their own country, vacating much land south of the Douro, which the independent Christians of the north were able to reenter in expeditions but not to reoccupy. The resistance was led by descendants of Gothic families who had taken refuge in the mountains of the Cantabrian coast: their followers were tribespeople who had survived absorption under Romans and Visigoths. Their numbers were small, and their rulers were for a time constrained to pay tribute to the Muslims.

If Islam put an end to the invasion of Europe by nomadic peoples from Asia, it also established the barrier which was eventually broken down by the Portuguese voyages of discovery. The barrier was not complete. Yet increasingly Islam became entrenched in the desire to hold what it had gained, and Christian Europe in that to recover what it thought it had lost. The attempt of Charlemagne to mould the Franks and Germans into a new Roman empire failed for many reasons. Not least among them was his vain attempt to conquer the Spanish Vascones by force, and their reaction in destroying the unity of the Hispanic church, the only institution which might have brought about the replacement of Muslim rule.[4]

The Vikings, Galicia and Santiago

The small corner of the Peninsular northwest had become almost a separate solitude within the isolation of Europe. It had submitted to the Muslim conquest on terms which virtually avoided an occupation: there are scarcely any Arabic toponyms in Galicia and few in northern Portugal. It had not suffered the extensive depopulation caused by the flight or persecution of the Visigoths who settled on the Douro from León to Soria. But it had lost the leadership of its capital at Braga, and the Galicians had at first been reluctant to accept the rule of the Gothic leaders of the Asturias. Charlemagne's intrusion against Pamplona had left them uninvolved, though the attempts of his son Louis the Pious to provoke rebellion against Cordoba brought refugees from Mérida. One of these, Mahmud ibn al-Jabbar, attempted to form a new society between the Muslim south and the Asturian north on the Douro near Oporto, but on his death his followers were absorbed into the existing stock: his name survives in the toponym of Mafamud, south of the city. As the influence of the church of Toledo declined, the Christians of the northwest found a new source of unity in the discovery of the tomb of the Apostle St. James. According to a Byzantine tradition of the fifth or sixth centuries, the Apostles had dispersed to the quarters of the globe assigned to them. It was thought that St. James the Greater had reached Iría in Galicia. Successive Asturian kings rewarded the Apostle with gifts of land in return for his help in gaining victories. In the first half of the ninth century the shrine was removed to its present site at Santiago de Compostela.

The reason for this second migration of the Apostle was probably the appearance of seafarers from Scandinavia, whose long-ships now enabled them to make extensive voyages. They reached the rivers of France, from whose estuaries they plundered undefended cities. In 844 they attacked Bordeaux and Toulouse. They passed on to northern Spain, where the short rivers gave access to no rich capital, but they heard of the prosperity of Seville and found the mouth of the Guadalquivir unguarded. Troops were brought up, and they were defeated in October 844. Viking depredations were repeated at irregular intervals. In about 856 they embarked on an expedition which carried them as far as Morocco and may have lasted three years. They wintered in the *rías* or fjords of southern Galicia, and sacked Iría, taking prisoners for ransom. These raids explain why the supposed remains of St. James were removed inland for safety. The invaders were driven off by a count named Pedro. The inhabitants could not respond at sea but they could defend the mouths of rivers with castles or move inland where they were less likely to be taken by surprise.

The formal reconstitution of the Suevic region is attributed to a Galician count named Wimara Pérez, who restored the territory of Portucale, or Oporto. His equestrian statue stands outside the cathedral of Oporto, and surveys the lower course of the river Douro. His restoration is dated 868.[5] However, the counts of Portucale made their seat not at Oporto but at the inland settlement of Guimarães, in farmland not easily accessible from the sea.[6] Further south, the old Roman city of Aeminium of the Mondego formed the nucleus of another county. It was now known as Colimbria or Coimbra, the site of a former bishopric, transferred to this hill-top stronghold. Access was guarded by the building of Montemór, closer to the sea and commanding its estuary and tilled lands. In 1015 a Viking fleet entered the Minho and sacked Tuy, and sailed up the Ave, being checked at Vermoim, a castle built to protect Guimarães. The saga of King Olaf, who died in 1030, names his battles, and refers to the defence of Santiago by a Count Gonzalo Sanches.

Scandinavian long-ships also invaded Scotland, northeast England and Ireland, and established themselves in western France, where their crews intermarried with the indigenous population, adopted a kind of French speech, accepted Christianity and founded the state of Normandy. From the north they reached Greenland and Canada, where they planted small colonies. They were therefore the first to make the trans-Atlantic voyages of discovery. But their colonies proved too distant to be supplied in times of crisis or too small and too intractable to mingle with their neighbours. They held out for many years, but eventually flickered away, leaving only traces in records of Nordic societies which attracted no attention in an increasingly introspective Europe. Nor does it seem that contemporary Portuguese were infected with their wanderlust. In the course of their raids some Northmen settled on the coast, and may have contributed to the formation of fishing communities such as Povoa de Varzim. But the Asturian kings were immersed in the acquisition of land on their own frontier, and the counts of the northwest lacked the power, means, and knowledge necessary for voyages of discovery. The experiences of the Scandinavians in America were a warning, but not an invitation.

The Reconquest begins

At the end of the tenth century the predominantly agrarian society of the northwest, in common with all the Christian north, was shaken by an invasion from another quarter. The Muslim rulers of Cordoba had assumed the title of caliph and used their wealth to establish an ascendancy in North Africa, where they engaged the services of mercenaries and of Berber tribal contingents to wage "campaigns of omnipotence" against their northern neighbors. In 998 they succeeded in sacking the shrine of St. James and in recovering Coimbra and the cities between it and the river Douro. Their leader, the *hajib* al-Mansur, traversed Portugal with his cavalry but sent his infantry northward by sea from Alcácer do Sal at the mouth of the Sado. Coimbra and the frontier were placed under Berber garrisons, whilst the displaced counts either retired north of the river or submitted.

But this attempt to crush and subject the Christian states was quickly followed by the collapse of the caliphate itself. After al-Mansur's death, still on campaign, in 1002, his successors were unable to reward the forces he engaged, and Cordoba lapsed into anarchy, declaring itself a republic in 1031. The rest of Muslim Spain dissolved into its component parts, soon dominated by half a dozen large cities and their districts, the *taifa*-states. The collapse of the caliphate coincided with a final bout of Viking piracy in 1028. At the same time the old Asturo-Leonese monarchy was replaced by King Sancho García III of Navarre, whose mother was Castilian. The last effective member of the Asturo-Leonese house, Alfonso V, was killed by a bolt from the walls as he attempted to recover Viseu in 1028. Sancho III's second son Ferdinand became the first king of Castile in 1037, and legitimized the seizure of the Leonese empire by his marriage to Alfonso V's daughter, Sancha. Thus the whole north from the ocean to the Pyrenees was brought together under a single hand. The change was probably not welcomed in the West, whose counts had been on close terms with the old ruling house, to which it supplied wives, tutors, and counsellors. Other Portuguese had already shown signs of independence: in 1034 Gonçalo Trastemires of Maia near Oporto had seized Montemór at the mouth of the Mondego. He died soon after, but the place was held by Sisenando Davidiz, a Christian who had spent his youth in Muslim Seville. Castile was distinct in its speech and ways. When Ferdinand bestowed a rudimentary constitution on his realms, he allowed that it should adhere to the customs of his grandfather, but the law of Leon and Asturias applied in Galicia and Portugal, the most populous part of his monarchy. His royal lands were administered by his *maiorini*, administrators and judges vested with great local authority. He retook Lamego in 1057, Viseu in 1058, and finally Coimbra, after a lengthy siege, in 1064. Sisnand Davidiz, who had negotiated its surrender, became its first governor or vizir, *alvazil*, employing the Arabic term, not that of count. It was the first major Muslim city to pass under Christian control, and Ferdinand and his son used Sisenando in their dealings with the Muslims. These were now numerous, for although Ferdinand died before Valencia in the following year, he bequeathed to his sons the right to collect tribute, *parias*, from the *taifa* rulers. This income, paid in gold, far exceeded the revenues of the monarch derived from the produce of the land and usually payable in kind. It also served to raise the ruler above the class of counts, who maintained themselves from the taxes and dues paid by their subjects, in the main rural cultivators. It also sustained a class of military leaders, not dignified by the title of counts, who commanded professional soldiers to enforce payment in the Muslim states. Needless to say, such tributes paid to infidels were illicit under Muslim law and so undermined the legality of the *taifa* rulers who provided them. In his testament, Ferdinand I was able to dispose of the right to collect *parias*, assigning different *taifas* to his three sons.

He also recognized for the first time the separate existence of a kingdom in the west, Galicia and Portugal, which spoke a different language. His eldest son Sancho received his own inheritance of Castile. His second son Alfonso (VI) took Leon and Asturias, the portion of his wife Sancha. His youngest son García was given the new kingdom of Galicia, which had hitherto possessed no capital except the religious centre of St. James and had no treasury, and none of the few institutions with which an agrarian monarchy was then equipped. King García was perhaps too inexperienced to perform the difficult task assigned to him. His reign lasted only five years, 1066-1071. He was then removed by his brothers and spent the rest of his life a captive. But his appointment had aroused desires for autonomy and independence among his subjects which had to be satisfied.

The wealth and power acquired by Ferdinand I gave him and his sons a heightened prominence outside the Iberian Peninsula. The payment of tribute in a feudal world implied subjection, and it appeared that Muslim Spain must shortly submit. Hitherto, the rulers of the north had exercised an uneasy control of an agrarian monarchy struggling to gain control of underpopulated borderlands. The long and desultory conflict now took on a more ideological and impassioned character. Islamic tolerance had permitted Christians to live as separate and tax-paying communities, though not that Muslims should live under Christian or polytheistic rule. The Hispanic church had existed almost in isolation from Rome, with a liturgy and script inherited from Gothic times. In Leon bishops were appointed by the king from his household. Monasteries were set up by the royal and other families, and served them for many purposes: their agrarian activities were essential in the time of war, and all records were written and preserved by them. The monarch attributed his victories to St. James and rewarded his church, but its bishop was usually a member of one of the comital families of Galicia, where the towns were governed by stewards appointed by the bishop. Until the reign of García, the ancient metropolitan capital of Braga had stayed bishopless: its see had now been restored, but its primacy was still unacknowledged.

The ideal of a new Roman world under the rule of Rome, with its hierarchy of archbishops and bishops, and its monasteries freed from secular interference and practising only the liturgy and laws of Rome, was put into execution by the monk Hildebrand, who, after serving as papal legate in France and Germany, became Pope Gregory VII in 1072. His predecessor had been the first pope to send a legate to Spain, whose liturgy was seen to be different, but not heretical: the cult of St. James had been repudiated in Rome. For Gregory the model for the new monasticism was the abbey of Cluny in Burgundy, dominated from 1049 until 1109 by Abbot Hugh, a member of the ruling family of Burgundy. The influence of Cluny had crossed the Pyrenees, and Ferdinand I had received a Cluniac adviser. In his testament he promised Cluny a regular tribute in gold in return for its prayers on behalf of himself and his family. When he died, Cluny approved of the reunification of the three realms under his second son Alfonso VI of Leon who, guided by his sister Urraca, removed both García from Galicia and Sancho II of Castile. When in 1085 he recovered the Roman and Gothic capital of Toledo, Abbot Hugh provided him with a Cluniac archbishop, Bernard, who became also primate of Spain and papal legate there. Abbot Hugh also supplied Alfonso with a second wife, his niece Constance, who became the mother of his daughter Urraca.

The Burgundian influence was perpetuated by her marriage, whilst still a child, to another Burgundian, Count Raymond, who was appointed Count of Galicia: the west thus had a royal countess, if not a king of its own. Raymond proved incapable of holding Lisbon and Sintra, which with Santarém, were extracted from the Muslim ruler of the *taifa* of Badajoz, and in 1096 it became necessary to appoint another Burgundian, Count Henry, his cousin, to be Count of Portugal, as the husband of Alfonso VI's illegitimate daughter Teresa. Thus Portugal became also a royal county, comprising the territory of Portucale, the vizirate of Coimbra and the outpost of Santarém on the Tagus. Under the protection of Archbishop Bernard of Toledo a host of French clergy flocked into the Hispanic church, among them Gerald of Moissac who, with the aid of Count Henry, restored the archbishopric of Braga. Thus by the end of the eleventh century, the west had become two royal counties, not one.

The Almoravid invasions

The Gregorian reform and the Burgundian marriages thus riveted the Iberian Peninsula to the ideal unification of Europe under the auspices of Rome, a Rome which had now incorporated the Germanic north. But the greed of Alfonso VI and others in extracting tribute from the Muslims, combined with his undisguised ambition to take over all the *taifas*, obliged the Muslim rulers to bow to the wishes of their subjects and place themselves in the hands of North Africa, where an Islamic revival had spread beyond the Sahara and mobilized many converts professing a puritanical faith. These were the Almoravids, or revivers of the holy war, who made their capital at Marrakush. When Alfonso VI received the capitulation of Toledo in 1086, they responded to appeals from Spain and sent over a large force which defeated the Christians at Zallaqa, near Badajoz. Alfonso himself was wounded. The *taifas* suspended the payment of tribute. Although the Almoravids returned to Africa, it soon became clear that they could not undertake the defence of Islam without control of supplies and permanent installations in the Peninsula itself. They then proceeded to take over the *taifas* of Seville, Granada, Toledo and Badajoz, being held out of Valencia and Saragossa, by the resistance of the Cid, who held Valencia and its district with his own army until his death in 1099. By their control of Ceuta and the Straits of Gibraltar the Almoravids isolated the western half of the Peninsula from the Mediterranean, and although their efforts to retake Toledo were unsuccessful, they carried the frontier to the level of the Tagus, and rendered it no more than the nominal seat of the Leonese empire and the reformed church.

The Almoravid reform taught the simple customs of the desert. But they governed the supply of trans-Saharan gold, and permitted the cities of Islamic Spain to flourish. The elegant minaret of the Giralda in Seville is testimony to the works of their day. They produced a gold coinage which circulated in the Christian states and perpetuated their name in the *morabatino*, eventually debased into the Hispanic maravedí. They possessed the Balearic Isles, which they reached from the North African ports, but it is not until about 1115 that sea-battles are recorded between their fleets and those of the Christian Spaniards, supported by the Pisans or Genoese. These activities were soon communicated to the west coast, but in the form of freebooting expeditions rather than naval warfare.

Count Raymond of Galicia had died in 1107, leaving the Burgundian claim to his infant son Alfonso Raimúndez, the future Alfonso VII. In the following year the old Emperor Alfonso VI's only son Sancho, whom he had legitimized, perished in battle at Uclés. The succession of his daughter Urraca could not be avoided, and when Alfonso himself died on June 30, 1109, his advisers concluded the marriage of Urraca to the most successful soldier of the day, Alfonso I of Aragon, remembered as "the Battler." The ensuing quarrels need not occupy us here, but the constant strife between Leon and Aragon rendered the pilgrim route to St. James unsafe, and doubtless increased the number of the devout who travelled by sea. The Burgundian cause was dashed by the death of Count Henry of Portugal in 1112, but espoused by Raymond's brother, Archbishop Guy of Vienne, who having become pope at Cluny with the title of Calixtus II, used the authority of his office to have his young nephew Alfonso proclaimed in the place of his mother Urraca. His chief ally was bishop Diego Gelmírez, formerly Raymond's secretary, and now promoted to be the first archbishop of Santiago. Gelmírez acquired great estates for his church in central Galicia, built ships to prey on Muslim commerce in the ports between Lisbon and Seville, and employed captives in the construction of his new cathedral and palace. He possessed the means to mount expeditions and secured the services of a Genoese or Pisan shipwright to design larger vessels for freebooting, but his immediate object was to gain wealth for his own ambitious projects. A Cluniac pope, Urban II, had preached the First Crusade from Burgundy in 1095 and many volunteers had sailed for Byzantium and Palestine to participate in the conquest and defence of Jerusalem, but the exodus was chiefly from southern France, and Urban's successors expressly discouraged adventurers from Spain from leaving their own country whilst it was still in danger.

The first evidence of a voyage of discovery is provided by the Muslim geographer Idrisi, born at Ceuta but writing in the middle of the twelfth century at the Norman court of Sicily. He extols the thriving commerce of Seville, Niebla, and Saltes, where iron was worked, Silves, with its export of dried figs and other fruits, Alcácer do Sal, where many ships were built in the estuary of the Sado, and the Ribatejo. In speaking of Lisbon, he tells how eight men, members of one family, built a trading-vessel, loaded it with water and provisions for a voyage of months, and sailed out southward. They found a reefy shore, and went on for eleven days, when they discovered shallow and foul-smelling waters, and unguarded animals with unsavoury meat on the "Isle of Sheep." They sailed south for twelve more days until they came upon an island with tall, bronzed men, one of whom knew Arabic. Their chief said that his men had sailed out for a month, but found nothing. They were arrested and sent back to sea with their hands tied. They then reached a land inhabited by Berbers who freed them and told them they were at the westernmost edge of the world, called Safi.

This glimpse of exploration is more credible than the legends of Atlantic islands, mysterious landfalls and maritime knights-errant, dear to Celtic folklore. The eight adventurers of Lisbon were not dreamers, but merchants who had prepared an expedition in search of commercial opportunity, which eluded them.

Afonso Henriques and Portugal

In Portugal, Queen Teresa had attempted to restore the limits of Suevic Portugal, which had included Tuy and the borderlands of Galicia, being drawn into an alliance with Gelmírez's Galician enemies. But she could not herself command, and in 1128 she was replaced by her son Afonso Henriques, now approaching twenty, and strongly supported by the Archbishop of Braga and the barons of the Douro valley. His overthrow of his mother and of her Galician allies, who were subjects of his cousin Alfonso VII, is usually regarded as the foundation of Portuguese nationhood, although his mother regularly used the title of queen and he did not assume that of king until Gelmírez was out of the way. His long reign, from 1128 until 1186, certainly assured Portugal's continued existence, which was obtained with the favour of Rome. But although the Portuguese might have established an independent monarchy in Teresa's day, it is doubtful whether it could have survived the buffetings of nine centuries without the conquest of Lisbon. The possession of the great port at the mouth of the Tagus coupled with the reconquest of the Algarve provided the necessary setting for the exploration of the West African coast and the adoption of a deliberate policy of governing the south Atlantic and opening the sea-route to the East.

Soon after he assumed the title of king of the Portuguese, Afonso Henriques made an initial attempt to take Lisbon, using the services of shipmen from Southampton. It was unsuccessful and the circumstances are unknown. But in 1146, when St. Bernard, the founder of the Cistercian reform, began to preach the Second Crusade, addressing the monarchs and peoples of England, Flanders and Lower Germany, the king of Portugal, recently married to Mafalda of Savoy (a house close to the Burgundian reformers) applied to the saint for aid. This took the form of a large force assembled at Dartmouth in May 1147 in some 164 ships, which arrived at Oporto, where the bishop persuaded them to put in at Lisbon. Afonso Henriques had taken Santarém by a surprise attack, and contracted with the crusaders to stay for the siege. It lasted from June until October, when the city capitulated and was sacked by the visitors, who pursued their voyage to Palestine after wintering in the Tagus. Some accepted the king's invitation to settle, and the first bishop of the newly annexed see was Gilbert of Hastings.

The king himself had marched on Lisbon by land, and his naval resources alone would not have sufficed for so distant an undertaking. Coimbra was separated from Lisbon by a thinly populated expanse, the settlement of which was a matter of some moment. The line of the Tagus was defended by the military Orders, particularly the Templars, formed originally to defend the Christian conquests in Palestine. They, rather than the old landed nobility, were charged with manning the new frontier, whilst Cistercian monks, established at Alcobaça and other monasteries, undertook its settlement and agrarian development. Other expeditions of passing crusaders aided Afonso Henriques and his son in gaining a temporary foothold in the Algarve, but it was only in the middle of the thirteenth century that the Portuguese reconquest was completed, as the forces of Leon and Castile, reunited under Ferdinand III, engaged in the conquest of Cordoba and Seville and other places in Lower Andalusia, leaving only Granada under Muslim rule. All idea of restoring the Roman provincial divisions proposed in 1100 had been abandoned in favour of the projection southward of the reconquest, which left Mérida, abandoned by the Muslims, in the hands of Castile and Leon, whilst Portugal retained Évora and Beja. The southern frontier was set at the mouth of the Guadiana, after lengthy negotiations. With few changes it has remained until this day.

The acquisition of land had been the predominant preoccupation of the Peninsular monarchies. In Portugal, the region north of the Douro had been occupied by a land-owning aristocracy which had raised men and founded monasteries in the enjoyment of feudal privileges, including the administration of justice within their domains. They had annexed the territory of Coimbra between the Douro and Mondego, which had been in the hands of Christians who had long dwelt under Muslim rule, and had become used to the advantages of Muslim civilization, shown in their administration, their vocabulary and their customs. The union of the two regions was symbolized by the marriage of Sisnand Davidiz, the *alvazi* of Coimbra to the heiress of the former counts of Portucale. Under Afonso Henriques the capital was moved from Guimarães to Coimbra. The first king of Portugal had annexed the region from the Mondego to the Tagus, using the services of the international military orders and of Cistercian monks to hold and colonize this thinly populated area. The crown, not the early medieval landowners, governed this process, replacing the former magnates or *ricos-homens* by adherents of the monarch, whose rewards were great but whose dependence on the ruler was also greater. Under Sancho II, the king proved unable to control the unruly lords of the north, and was replaced by his brother Afonso, who had married the Countess of Boulogne, and grown to manhood at the French court. The deposition was effected by order of the papacy, and executed with the support of the urban middle classes of Lisbon and the military orders. Thus from 1248, when Afonso III was brought to Portugal and to power, the interests of the city and of the defenders of the frontier predominated.

The consequence was to enhance the power of the crown to produce new laws which overrode the local jurisdictions of the old aristocracy. The capital was now moved forward from Coimbra to Santarém on the Tagus and to Lisbon, whose commerce had become the chief source of wealth for the crown. Transactions were increasingly made in terms of money, and taxes and dues were paid in kind only where seignorial usages still prevailed. After the Castilian conquest of Seville in 1248, in which Galicians and Portuguese took part, the straits of Gibraltar were opened to commercial shipping, and Italian adventurers began a regular service between the ports of the Mediterranean and those of the north, especially of England and Flanders. Merchants from Oporto and Lisbon already frequented the ports of the English west country, carrying particularly cargoes of wine. The lack of precious metals in Portugal itself enhanced the importance of foreign trade in the eyes of the monarch.

The main source of geographical knowledge was still Ptolemy, who wrote in Alexandria in the second century A.D., with such derivative works as Solinus. The leaders in the construction and management of fleets were the Italians, and in 1317 the Portuguese crown engaged the services of a Genoese admiral, Emmanuele Pessagno, who as Manuel Pessanha denizened himself in Portugal. The royal fleet served for both naval and commercial purposes. With the completion of the reconquest of Portugal, the military orders ceased to perform the function of a supranational force, and when the western monarchies led by France decided to disband the Templars, D. Diniz seized the opportunity to convert it into the purely national Order of Christ which, in the hands of the royal family, was later to play a crucial part in the organization of the discoveries. The Order of Aviz, prominent in the Reconquest since 1180, played an even more conspicuous part in preserving Portuguese independence in 1386. Under royal control the military orders did not at once lose their religious purpose. But the church adapted itself to changed circumstances. No longer did families of rural magnates found their own monasteries, which in the south were few. The new mendicant orders served especially the growing urban populations, whilst the bishops who governed new parishes in the cities heeded the wishes of the monarch and the needs of his subjects. The king himself had rarely taken the field at the head of his armies: he was now increasingly the dispenser of justice who, with the aid of professional advisers, himself issued laws of general application and saw to their execution.

The elements of Portuguese society had therefore been brought together in the fifth to eighth centuries, and had after many difficulties attained independence from the Leonese empire in the twelfth. For the great historian of the nineteenth century, Alexandre Herculano, Afonso Henriques and his barons had created the Portuguese nation by their efforts and energies. They had required consent and collaboration of Rome, which then sought to restore its influence over all Europe in the name of the Christian church. By the fourteenth century, Portugal had acquired the more complicated institutions of a modern nation. It had also to form a policy of its own. Afonso Henriques was the son of a Burgundian father and he had obtained the collaboration of English, Flemish and German crusaders for the conquest of Lisbon, which had now become the undisputed seat of the royal house. As papal authority was divided between rival claimants, the Portuguese rulers were obliged to seek other allies to sustain their independence. Portuguese merchants had long frequented the ports of England, where they sold wine, skins and wax. Beekeeping had been a Muslim activity, and now Portuguese candles lit the altars of England. The English connection with south-west France, brought about by a marriage alliance, formed the basis for a permanent understanding between the countries of the Atlantic seaboard, presaging the gradual rise of the western periphery of Europe that occurred in modern times. The export of wine, which formed a staple of Anglo-Portuguese trade, was in competition with the main product of English Guyenne, the region of Bordeaux. But this competition obliged the English and Portuguese rulers to intervene to settle quarrels and establish regulations and laws, which had anticipated the formation of a political alliance. From the twelfth century monarchs issued safe-conducts to each others' merchants. In England Portuguese and others were permitted to trade anywhere, perhaps in response to the rival attractions offered by Flanders. In London brokers were designated to deal with Portuguese. By 1353 the merchants of Oporto and Lisbon were sufficiently well-organized to negotiate a treaty of friendship with the English king, and without the intervention of Afonso IV. The treaty made by Afonso Martim Alho covered merchants, mariners and communities of the two great ports. In Portugal itself Afonso's son, Pedro I, granted privileges to resident foreigners, naming those concerned in 1363.[7] The greatest Portuguese chronicler, Fernão Lopes, who had the royal documents in his hands, states that as many as 450 merchant ships were to be seen at anchor in the Tagus. He was looking back from less affluent times.

Political crisis

The crisis which divided the Iberian Peninsula in the last third of the fourteenth century and created the conditions which obliged

Portugal to seek its fortunes overseas, thus generating the epic cycle of the century of discovery, was touched off by the internal and dynastic problems of Castile.

In 1340 the rulers of Portugal and Castile had united to resist a last attempt by the sultan of Morocco to invade the Iberian Peninsula and recover control over the Straits of Gibraltar: they had defeated him on the Salado not far away. Ten years later the king of Castile, Alfonso XI, died of the Black Death whilst attempting to wrest Gibraltar from the kingdom of Granada. His legitimate heir, Pedro, soon found himself engaged in a war to the death with his illegitimate family by an Andalusian mistress. England, still holding Guyenne, was immersed in the long struggle with France known as the Hundred Years War. Both parties were prepared to look for effective allies in the Iberian Peninsula. France supplied the bastard Henry (II) with men and money, enabling him to seize the throne, forcing Pedro to take shelter with his namesake, Pedro of Portugal. This king wisely refused to be drawn into the conflict, but Galicia upheld the loyalist cause, and from there Pedro went to Bordeaux in English Guyenne to seek the aid of its governor, the Black Prince. Thus reinforced, Pedro returned to fight the battle of Nájera, in which Henry was defeated and fled to France to obtain more men and more money. This time, the English there were reluctant to repeat their involvement, and Henry brought Pedro to battle and captured and killed him with his own hand. So did the bastard house of Trastámara win possession of the throne. But his rival had left the legitimate heiress of Castile in Bordeaux, and the Black Prince's younger brother who succeeded him there, married her and so acquired her claim to the throne. Meanwhile, the Portuguese Pedro had died and had been succeeded by his son Fernando, who, misjudging the capacity of John of Gaunt by his brother's striking victory at Nájera, did not hesitate to conclude an alliance with the pretender. He had himself a claim to the Spanish succession through his mother and was easily convinced by Galician loyalists. This led to a first Castilian invasion, in which Braga was occupied. Fernando then accepted the disadvantageous treaty of Alcoutim of March 1371, by which he undertook to make a Castilian marriage, relinquishing his own claim. The Galician loyalists then set about a formal alliance with John of Gaunt, concluded at Braga in July 1372. This first Anglo-Portuguese alliance brought down another invasion by the Castilians, who reached Lisbon in September, forcing Fernando again to submit in the treaty of Santarém of March 1373, by which he was obliged to become the ally of his enemy. The English claimant was unable to offer more than promises.

Under this threat, Fernando resumed negotiations for a formal alliance with John of Gaunt, which was concluded at London in June 1373. The English pretender to Castile was influenced by commercial interests, since his claim had resulted in the closure of Castilian ports to English ships. But Fernando took steps to defend his cities whilst not denouncing the treaty of Santarém until his Castilian enemy died in 1379. The new king of Castile, Juan I, seemed a less formidable opponent. Still under the influence of Galician loyalists, Fernando renewed the treaty with John the Gaunt, who sent a small force under his brother to aid in the defence of Lisbon. But in England John of Gaunt's credit was low, and the Portuguese council hesitated to risk further depredations. In a secret agreement, Fernando undertook to evacuate the English, who had made a poor impression, and to marry his infant heiress to a Castilian prince. But the Castilian king then became a widower, and the arrangement was altered so that he himself should marry the infant heiress and assume the title of king of Portugal. When Fernando died in October 1383, the Castilian succession seemed almost assured.

Revolution and Avis

But as Juan I of Castile prepared to assume the government of Portugal in his own name, the Portuguese rebelled in favour of the leadership of an illegitimate son of Pedro, João, whom he had made master of the military Order of Avis. The minister who had negotiated the surrender to Castile was killed, and the Master of Avis was proclaimed Defender of the Realm. His support came especially from the military orders and from the citizens of Lisbon, which now possessed a strong guild organization. Only part of the old aristocracy and the ecclesiastical hierarchy – itself divided and weakened by the Great Schism – took the part of Castile. A first Castilian attempt at invasion reached Lisbon but was frustrated by the outbreak of plague. In 1385, the representatives of the cities were assembled at Coimbra, where they heard the legal argument in favour of the accession of the Master of Avis. It rested on the fact that the infant princess was disqualified by her marriage to a foreigner, as were Pedro's other illegitimate sons by the papacy's refusal to legitimize them. The Master of Avis thus became João I from April 1385. He had already sent to England to propose the restoration of the Alliance, but only a small contingent of English archers arrived to participate in the crucial battle fought at Aljubarrota on August 14, 1385. The king of Castile was there put to flight, and the independence of Portugal assured for two centuries. In May 1386, the permanent Treaty of Windsor placed the Anglo-Portuguese Alliance on a more stable and enduring basis, each party committing his heirs "forever." The treaty was followed by João's marriage to the daughter of John of Gaunt, Philippa of Lancaster, the mother of a new royal family which brought to Portugal the customs of the English Plantagenets. They were to become known as the "illustrious generation," "*a ínclita geração*," the third brother being Prince Henry, who as Master of the Order of Christ, devoted his efforts and resources to the enterprise of the discoveries.

Almost thirty years elapsed between the epic struggle of D. João and his men to maintain Portuguese independence and the conquest of Ceuta. His friends had acquired power and pelf, and occupied the posts in the royal household. A new generation heard tales of their feats, and aspired to match them. Portugal had remained on alert, since no peace had been concluded with Castile, only a series of truces. John of Gaunt had retired from the scene in 1387, after concluding a treaty with Castile, by which he would renounce his claims to the Castilian throne in return for an indemnity and the marriage of a daughter, Philippa's half-sister, to the heir to the Castilian throne. He had died without realizing his royal ambitions, but his son, Philippa's brother, later seized the English throne from his cousin Richard II and became Henry IV. Philippa herself imbued her sons with high ideals of morality and duty, adding Plantagenet tales of chivalry and knight-errantry to what they knew of their father, now a national hero and founder of a dynasty.

Ceuta

The chronicler Fernão Lopes stresses the desire of the Portuguese princes to show themselves worthy of their father in undertaking the conquest of Ceuta. There were certainly other motives. The cost of defence had been very high, and had led to inflation of unprecedented proportions. D. João I had recognized his debt to the urban population by granting the organized craftsmen a guildhall, with their own judge and access to himself. The development of overseas trade depicted by Fernão Lopes had taken a not altogether favourable turn. It was now easier for Portugal to trade with England than with Flanders, which took Castilian wool for its textile trade. The trade with England called for the exchange of wine against woollens and seemed incapable of the expansion which Portugal required. During the Castilian crisis the Muslim kingdom of Granada had enjoyed a period of unparalleled prosperity under Yusuf and Mohammed V, who had gained control of the Magrib during the dynastic disputes of its rulers. But after the death of Mohammed V in 1391, the power of Granada was eclipsed whilst the Magrib seemed about to fall into anarchy. It was assuredly to the advantage of D. João I to claim the leadership in the war against Islam, which would gain him the favour of Rome and demonstrate that he had resumed the policy of his forebears. The opportunity to occupy this position now presented itself.

Before the Portuguese decided on the conquest of Ceuta, the ships of that port had fled to take refuge at Málaga, and its defence depended on the help of the neighbouring *kabilas*, whose services it was in no position to reward for more than a short period. D. João I and his sons were undoubtedly aware of this situation when they grasped the unique opportunity that presented itself in 1415. What they could hardly have foreseen was that after the conquest, their garrison at Ceuta would not be able to control the valuable trade between Europe and the Magrib, but that it would have to be supplied from Portugal itself, thus stimulating commercial and military activity in the Algarve and obliging D. João's sons to place their first successful venture in and ever-expanding wider context, one which led to an empire of worldwide proportions.

Harold V. Livermore

Notes

[1] It is conveniently described in D. Stanislavsky, *The Individuality of Portugal* (Austin: U. of Texas Press, 1959).

[2] The origin of the name of Lisbon is uncertain. Olissippo may be of Phoenician origin, the ending -ippo being found in southern Spain and Portugal as far north as Leiria, Colippo. The form Ulyssippo seems to result from a conscious confusion with the hero of the Odyssey.

[3] W. Reinhart and others have stated them to be Quads, but C. Courtois, *Les Vandalls et l'Afrique*, finds no conclusive evidence. In Portugal, they are called Sueves and not Quads by Hydatius. Procopius uses only the word Sueves for both groups. Their passage through Gaul is not documented, it being assumed that they accompanied the Vandals and Alans. The possibility that they, or part of them, arrived by sea, has been put forward, but no evidence is available. Orosius, who fled from them by sea, perhaps from Oporto, gives no indication that they had arrived by sea.

[4] The mythical account of Charlemagne in the *Chanson of Roland* dates only from the First Crusade, c. 1120.

[5] His occupation of the territory is noted under 868 in the *Chronicle of the Goths*: the statue was erected in 1968.

[6] Guimarães or Vimaranes is named after a Wimara, but this was quite a common first name. It is traceable to about 926.

[7] The belief that they included the Scotch, mentioned by Shillington and Chapman, p. 49, arises from a confusion with the Cahorsins, read as *Escoceses*.

The planisphere of Angelino Dulcert, 1339

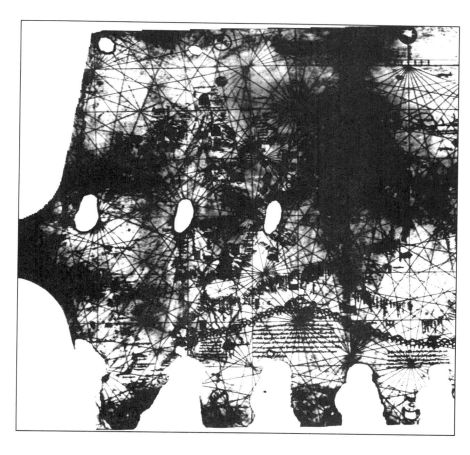

The portolan of Guillem Soler, 1385

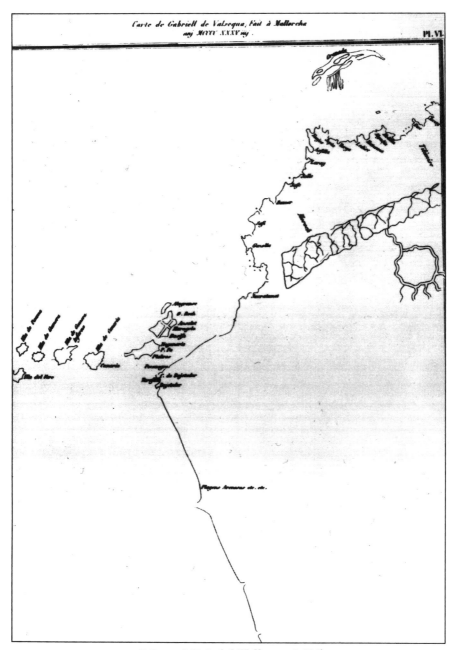

Map of Gabriel Vallseca, 1435

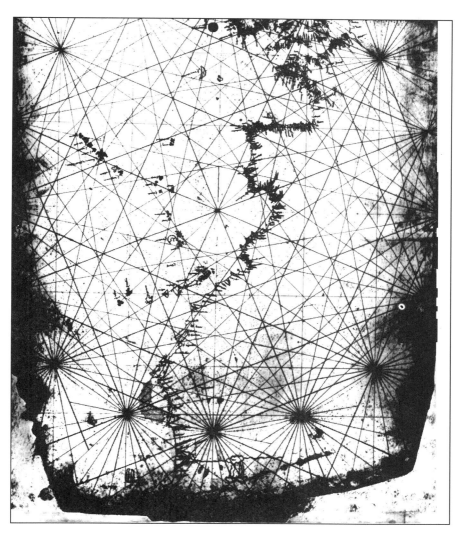

Map of Andrea Bianco, 1448

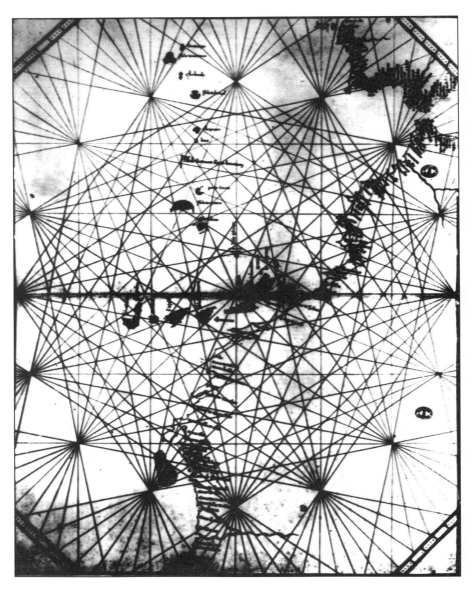

Chart of Grazioso Benincasa, 1467

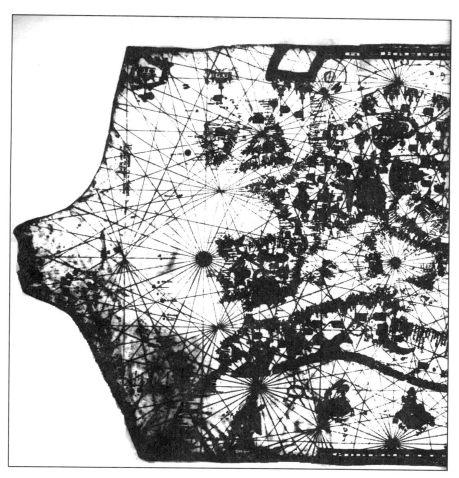

Map of Jaime Bertran, 1482

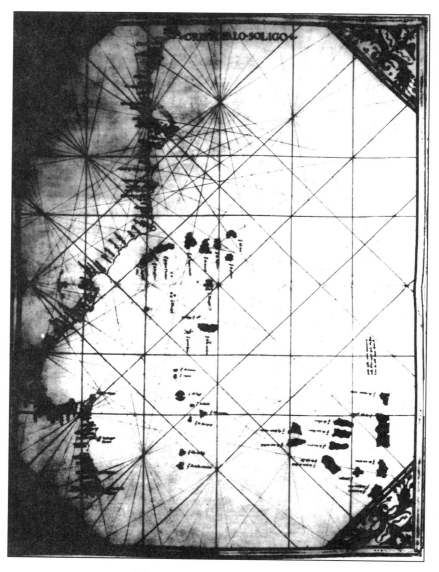

Map of Cristofal Soligo, 1489

Chapter II

Medieval Atlantic Exploration: The Evidence Of Maps

Anyone who has ever seen a late medieval mappamundi or portolan chart will be able to appreciate the sentiments of a Sicilian songster, captured in a mass-setting of the third quarter of the fifteenth century: enchanted by the beauty of the maps, he searched them for a lovelier isle than his own, albeit without success.[1] The finest surviving example of the cartography of the period, the "Catalan Atlas" of the Bibliothèque Nationale, Paris, generally attributed to Cresques Abraham of Majorca, is as rich and intricate as a spilled jewel casket, resplendent with powerful images of exotic beings and untold wealth.[2] Maps of even greater magnificence, larger and more densely illuminated, are recorded but lost.[3] These were royal gifts, intended for ostentation as well as use, but the more modest and practical portolan charts would be drawn with grace and adorned with illustrations or, at least, with fine calligraphy and a delicate web of rhumblines. It was a period in which maps could inspire more than music. It was almost certainly a map – perhaps even the Catalan Atlas itself – that in 1402 induced the Poitevin adventurer, Gadifer de la Salle, to embark on a quest for the mythical "river of gold" which led to his ruin. In the late fourteenth century, the anonymous author of the *Libro del conoscimiento de todos los reynos* constructed from the legends of maps a fantastic journey of the imagination which reached beyond the limits of the known, even of the accessible world.[4]

In the present century, some historians have been enthralled by these maps, overestimating their value as evidence; others, more prudent, have been reluctant to succumb to their siren-like allure. The maps give a true picture of their makers' mental images of the world: that is not in question. But whether they can be accepted as proof of a growth in real knowledge is a matter on which opinions are sharply divided. In 1969, Professor Charles Verlinden's contribution to the Colloque International d' Histoire Maritime was greeted with something very close to derision because of his ready acceptance of cartographical evidence of a fourteenth-century discovery of the Azores; towards the end of his life, the distinguished Portuguese historian, Armando Cortesão, jeopardized his considerable reputation by his dogged insistence on basing his theory of a pre-Columbian discovery of America on the evidence of maps; and the late Eva Taylor incurred accusations of excessive susceptibility as a result of her championship of the reliability of maps in this connection.[5] Credulous assessments of the value of map evidence, in default and even in defiance of other documents, have had redoubtable defenders; but some of their most zealous partisans have carried their interpretations to such extremes of excessive protestations that the maps have lost all credibility.[6] Today their spokesmen seem to work in isolation from other scholars, advancing theories, ignored elsewhere, in circles of their own.

In partial consequence, for instance, fourteenth-century exploration of the Azores (the particular point of dubious orthodoxy for which I wish to argue in these pages) is dismissed or ignored by textbooks in current use, because of, rather than despite, the cartographic evidence in its favor.[7] Respect for fifteenth-century traditions that the Azores, together with Madeira (to which many of the same arguments apply), were discovered by followers of the Infante Dom Henrique of Portugal has played a part in this. Henrique may have been the first to colonize and exploit these islands, but that does not preclude earlier discovery and exploration; it is possible, without contradiction, to admit both a fifteenth-century exploration which determined its exact whereabouts and configuration. The example of Madeira is, in a sense, decisive: as we shall see, all surviving Atlantic maps datable, without question, to the last quarter of the fourteenth century, show Madeira, Porto Santo and the Desert and Savage Islands with a verisimilitude that defies disbelief. Thus we cannot exclude the possibility of prior knowledge of the Azores, either, merely out of deference to traditions associated with Dom Henrique. In part, too, scruples concerning the evidence of fourteenth-century knowledge of the Azores may have derived from the widespread conviction that navigators were incapable – from timidity or technical insufficiency – of sailing so far out to sea: the Azores are over 700 miles from the nearest land. Yet this may be to underestimate the mariners' proficiency and daring. Equally prejudicial to the cool consideration of the evidence is the repugnance we may feel at unwarrantable inferences made from map evidence in favor of pre-Columbian theories of the discovery of America. The reputation of the maps should not be allowed to suffer, as it were, by contagion, but evaluated on its merits.

The purpose of these pages is to offer a tentative word in vindication of the maps. I hope to suggest that it is possible to reach different conclusions on the problems respectively of a fourteenth-century discovery of the Azores and a pre-Columbian discovery of America and to show the limits of the usefulness of cartographic evidence in determining the extent of Atlantic penetration by Columbus's day. My guiding principles will be that maps must be read with caution; that, without corroboration from other documents it would be rash to accept cartographers' evident growing interest in the Atlantic as proof of growing knowledge; and that the appearance of new lands on maps does not necessarily signify new discoveries. We should remember the warning, uttered by the Infante Dom Pedro of Portugal in 1443, that in the maps of his day unknown regions "were not drawn except according to the whim of the men who made them."[8] Though a considerable body of secondary literature is available, offering a variety of readings, I take it for granted that only the maps themselves or the best available facsimiles can yield reliable readings of place-names and legends and the versions I give are my own. Finally, I shall advocate a stricter discipline in the dating of surviving maps than has characterized previous discussion; this, I believe, tends to make the case for fourteenth-century knowledge of the Azores more cogent.

Discovery in phases

Atlantic exploration before Columbus can usefully be divided into three overlapping phases: first, the breaking out of Mediterranean vessels into Atlantic waters in the late thirteenth and early fourteenth centuries; second, from the early fourteenth to the early fifteenth centuries, the creation of a zone of navigation in previously unexplored waters, bounded by the Azores in the north, the Canaries in the south and the Iberian and African coasts in the east, and linked by the Atlantic wind-system; finally, a period of increased interest in and speculation about the remoter Atlantic, which stimulated further exploration and yielded new discoveries, but which cannot be shown to have led navigators to the New World before 1492. My concern is with the second of these phases, because its effect was broadly to fix the configurations of pre-Columbian knowledge of the Atlantic; but to be understood it must be set briefly in the context of the other two.

Portugal, the Pathfinder

In the first phase, some seafarers turned northwards when they reached the Atlantic, like the Zaccaria family of Genoa, who tried to monopolize the English alum market, or the Frescobaldi of Florence, who acquired a sizeable stake in English wool. They made something of an economic breakthrough, but added nothing to geographical knowledge or to the reach of exploration. Others, however, turned south into waters unsailed – as far as we know – for centuries, off the west coast of Africa. Record of only one such voyage has survived: that of the brothers Vivaldi, who from Genoa in 1291 departed *ad partes Indiae per Oceanum*, thus apparently anticipating the task Columbus was to set himself almost exactly two hundred years later. The Vivaldis presumably envisaged a circumnavigation of Africa rather than a transnavigation of the Atlantic, but the galleys they deployed were hardly suited to either purpose, too low and shallow for rough Atlantic waters, too dependent on inshore sailing for the inhospitable African coast. The Vivaldi were never heard of again, but it is likely that there were other journeys in the same direction, albeit with less ambitious aims. It was probably in the course of such expeditions that the Canary Islands were discovered according to Petrarch, writing in the 1340s, Genoese armed ships had sailed to the Canaries *memoria patrum*. In 1337, he had professed himself almost as well informed about the "Fortunate Isles" as about Italy or France.[9]

The third phase, beginning in the 1420s, was distinguished by what one might call the discovery of Atlantic "space": of navigable – and potentially exploitable – stretches of ocean beyond the zone of established navigation. The number of Atlantic charts or of charts which included the Atlantic multiplied. Mapmakers invested costly blank parchment in the depiction of the ocean, which was strewn – to a far greater extent than in the fourteenth century – with imagined or reputed islands. Known archipelagoes were charted with a new precision and in the second half of the century the islands of Cape Verde and of the Gulf of Guinea were added to them.

It was in the second phase, however, that the other archipelagoes of the eastern Atlantic, including the Azores, were first explored and mapped. This phase can be said to have begun in the 1330s. To summarize: in 1339, some of the Canary Islands, albeit misplaced slightly to the north, with three islands, in a position suggestive of those of the Madeira archipelago, appeared for the first time on a surviving map.[10] Thereafter, within the span of a couple of generations, there were so many voyages, accumulating so much knowledge, that an almost complete picture of the islands of the east-central Atlantic became available in Latin Christendom. The transformation of that picture by the time of maps reliably dated to the 1380s, in which, as we shall see, the Canaries are shown almost complete, with the Savage Islands, the Madeira archipelago and most of what I take to be the Azores, was a remarkable achievement: hazardous to the vessels, novel to the technology and unparalleled in the experience of sailors of the time. To understand why and how knowledge of the Atlantic was so thoroughly revolutionized in such a relatively short span, it is necessary to reconstruct the stages of the change in some detail. Because the winds of the Atlantic naturally constitute a system of ducts, which tend to take ships south-west from the pillars of Hercules and at most seasons force a wide northward sweep out to sea upon returning sail traffic, the exploration of the Canaries was necessarily the first stage.

The Canaries

Like patches of twilight in the Sea of Darkness, the Canary Islands in the Middle Ages lay, never utterly unknown, but long unvisited, except by susceptible imaginations. By the time of their rediscovery at the end of the thirteenth century or early in the fourteenth, knowledge of them transmitted from antiquity was encrusted with fables of St. Brendan and St. Ursula, Merlin and the Earthly Paradise. Indeed, the exact notions of the archipelago which early explorers took with them on their first forays into the Atlantic are hard to identify among the myths. Of the supposed references to the Canaries in ancient literature, only those of Pliny are convincing. Pliny's circumstantial details – concerning, for instance, the number of islands and their climatic heterogeneity – seem to correspond to the geographical realities of the Canaries. His "Nivaria" evokes Tenerife, with its snow-capped peak, and his "Pluvialia" may well refer to one of the relatively rainy westerly isles. His description, repeated by Solinus and Isidore (those great mediators of classical learning in late antiquity) was identified with the Canaries in the era of rediscovery: his collective name, "The Fortunate Islands" was appropriated by mapmakers. The rest of his nomenclature was borrowed in humanist circles. The terms "Canary Isles" or "Isles of Canary," current from the 1340s, also seem indebted to Pliny's name, "Canaria," for one island.[11]

Although some historians have "detected" real places and events in the undergrowth of any myth or legend, no other demonstrable references to the Canaries were inherited from ancient writers. Mentions of remote islands by Plutarch and Horace are too vague to inspire reliance and might refer to any or all of the great mass of islands known or thought, in antiquity and the Middle Ages, to lie in the western ocean. The same applies to the western isles, Hesperides and

Elysian Fields, which have sometimes been taken as allusions to the Canaries or even the Azores, but which might equally be wholly fabulous, without any basis in actual islands. Yet all this material helped, in the period of rediscovery, to shroud Pliny's relatively precise information in mystery, which was deepened by confusion with other island myths of late antique (Brendan and Ursula) or (in the case of the Merlin legend) even earlier origins.[12] It is hard to say whether the enchantment spun into this tissue of fable increased or diminished the lure of the Atlantic for late medieval explorers. If Arab navigators were deterred by the Sea of Darkness, the mariners of Latin Christendom seem to have evinced a more adventurous spirit. While Arab geographers recorded no advances in the field, in western Europe the corrupt traditions gradually changed, in the fourteenth century, in the light of observation and experience.[13]

The chronology of late medieval exploration of the Canaries cannot be reconstructed with any certainty. The first authenticated visit, at an unknown date probably prior to 1339, was attributed in most sources to the Genoese, Lanzarotto (or Lancelotto or Lanzarote) Malocello, who found the island which still bears a version of his name. The dating and authenticity of many of the earliest documents are so debated that the exact circumstances of Malocello's voyage – whether under Genoese or Portuguese auspices, whether of reconnaissance, conquest or trade – are matters for speculation. But his vagabond career (in Ceuta, Portugal and, perhaps, France as well as his native city) and attainment of fame are features of the tradition of explorers and early conquistadors as it was to be established over the next century or so.

It was perhaps diffusion of knowledge of Malocello's achievement by Genoese and Majorcan mapmakers that excited efforts to trade, evangelize, enslave and conquer in the islands, with great intensity in the 1340s and a modest regularity thereafter. Whoever commissioned Malocello's voyage, it is certain that the first expedition of which a detailed account survives (copied, apparently, by Boccaccio and dated 1341) was in part, at least, a Portuguese enterprise.[14] The point is worth emphasizing, as it contributes towards a growing picture of Lusitanian maritime activity in the fourteenth century.[15] This expedition, moreover, demonstrates cooperation between Portugal and Italian – specifically, in this case, Genoese and Florentine – experts, which characterizes the early history of Portuguese overseas expansion and establishes a *prima facie* case for continuity between the "medieval" colonial experience of western Mediterranean peoples in their home waters and the "modern" history of empire-building in the Atlantic.

Moreover, although it sailed from a Portuguese port under Italian command, the "1341" expedition included, at a lower level, Castilian personnel and mariners "from other parts of Spain." Thus almost at the very outset of the story, a modest Castilian presence can be detected which would eventually grow to preponderance. And it was via Italian merchants in Seville that the surviving account was transmitted to Florence and to Boccaccio's hand. Seville, therefore, appears already in its future role as the data bank – so to speak – the overseer and information exchange, of Atlantic navigation.

Because of changes in toponymy, the route of the voyage cannot be retraced accurately. But it is not hard to recognise the Canaries in the account. Depending on how one reads the text, the expedition can be seen to have visited at least thirteen islands (and perhaps as many as nineteen): if all the islets and great rocks are counted, the Canary archipelago can be said to contain thirteen islands (Lanzarote, Fuerteventura, Gran Canaria, Tenerife, La Palma, Gomera, Hierro Graciosa, Lobos, Alegranza, Santa Clara or Montaña Clara, Roque del Este Roquete). The possible references to more islands may be explained as the product of duplication or ambiguity. Six of the isles visited were inhabited: this fits the real situation in the Canaries closely enough, for, at the time, there were several inhabited islands, and visitors may not have had an opportunity to observe signs of life on all of them. The description of Tenerife – with its numinous combination of high mountains and low clouds, snow and fierce defenders – is unmistakable. While less obviously unequivocal, the descriptions of the other islands fit the real topography of the Canaries. To the author of this account, the Canaries were *insulas nuncupatas Repertas* – or perhaps the punctuation should be made to read *insulas nuncupatas "repertas."* The excitement of new discovery rapidly communicated itself to merchants, like the Florentines of Seville who reported it home; mapmakers like Angelino Dulcert, who (if a later interpolation is not responsible) recorded the discovery of Lanzarote on his map of 1339; and humanists, like Boccaccio, who had a particular interest in the anthropological implications of the news. Over the next few years, would-be missionaries and would-be conquerors formed an equally receptive public.

It was in Majorca that the news from the Canaries had the greatest impact. This is not surprising, although the Majorcans' role as early leaders in the late medieval "space-race" in the Atlantic is too often forgotten or ignored. Majorca was itself something of a "colonial society" and "frontier zone": reconquered from the Moors only a century previously in 1229, it was briefly, from 1276 to 1343, the center of an independent kingdom which lived by trade and, therefore, from the sea. It was a center, too, for the technical developments in shipping and cartography which helped to make Atlantic navigation practicable on a large scale. Majorca's mapmakers, the most renowned in Europe, were assiduous gatherers of geographical information, aided by the large Jewish community, from whom many of them were drawn. Exploration of the Canaries was, in a sense, a natural extension of existing Majorcan interests in Africa and the Atlantic: Majorcan shipping carried Catalan trade to northern Europe in the late thirteenth and early fourteenth centuries; and the dispensations Majorcans enjoyed to trade with infidels peculiarly fitted them to take part in navigation along the African coast. The island, moreover, had long been a Genoese staging-post for westward navigation; indeed, the Vivaldis themselves had called there. Finally, it was the home of a school of missionaries, chiefly Franciscans, inspired by Ramon Llull's methods of evangelization: peaceful persuasion, enhanced by charity and apostolic example, expressed in native tongues. Llullian missionaries were to be among the most frequent early travellers to the Canaries.

At least four voyages from Majorca to the Canaries were licensed in April 1342. Françesc Desvalers, Pere Margre and Bartolomeu Giges – we know nothing of them save their names, though the first has been linked with a certain En Valers, said to be lately returned from Tartary in a document of 1379 – were authorised to make two expeditions in the cogs, *Santa Creu, Santa Magdalena,* and *Santa Joan* to islands *vocatas perdudes vel de Canaria,* also referred to as *repertas.*[16] This nomenclature seems to establish a link in contemporary minds between these islands, the *insulae repertae* of the "1341" account, the Plinian "Canaria" and the islands of the Brendan myth, one of which was traditionally called "Perdita." That at least one of this pair of licenses bore fruit in an actual voyage is shown by the chance survival of a mariner's claim for wages. Other licenses were issued in the same month for voyages by Bernat Desvalls and Gillem Safont, *simile mandatum,* and to Guillem Pere, citizen of Majorca, "to equip and make a voyage to the isles newly found in the parts of the west," again expressly in a cog. A detailed account of what may be a fifth expedition of about this time survives in a corrupt version in a printed book of the next century, which describes a fortuitous landfall in the islands by pirates (probably, though not expressly, Majorcan) pursuing a galley or fleet of the King of Aragon: though dated 1370, the account can be shown from internal evidence more plausibly to relate to the early 1340s. These pirates seem to have regarded themselves as the first discoverers of the islands: this raises the possibility of a casual Majorcan discovery independently of the voyages of Malocello and of the Portuguese, but may be explained alternatively as the result of a corruption in our text:[17] or a claim advanced, like those of the Portuguese to the discovery of Madeira, in despite of earlier explorations.

A gap in the Majorcan archives conceals the next few years' activity, though it seems unlikely that the hectic pace of the early 1340s can have been long sustained. The wage claim of Guillem Joffre indicates the commercial failure of the voyage on which he shipped and the death of one of its leaders, Pere Margre. This may have been a disincentive to other potential explorers but continued activity during the sparsely documented years is indicated by the record in the Catalan Atlas of the voyage down the coast of Africa to the "river of gold" (perhaps the Wad Draa, alchemically transmuted, or arguably the Senegal) of Jaume Ferrer in 1346.[18] It was formerly thought that Atlantic exploration suffered a "check" in the mid-fourteenth century because of the effects of the Black Death and the technical insufficiency of ships and nautical aids.[19] When archival records become available again from 1351, there is little evidence to support this. It may be, however, that some of the commercial impetus of the earliest voyages was lost, as most of the expeditions of the next generation appear, from surviving records, to have been the work of missionaries.

The voyage of Joan Doria and Jaume Segarra of 1351 is exceptionally well documented. In May, they obtained a Bull from Clement VI for a mission to the Canaries: they were to be accompanied by twelve Catalan-speaking natives of the islands (evidence here of the influence of Llullian methods of evangelization) who had been captured by previous expeditions. The following month they obtained a royal licence to sail from Majorca. The completion of their journey is suggested by the fact that in November of the same year Clement VI founded the diocese of "Fortuna" or of the Fortunate Islands, which was established at Gran Canaria and lasted until 1393.[20] Records survive of five further missionary expeditions between 1352 and 1386, and it is not unreasonable to suppose that there were others of which no notice has come down to us. It may be that the apparent shift of emphasis in the Majorcan voyages from commerce and conquest to conversion and pastoral care is connected with the re-absorption of Majorca into the Crown of Aragon in 1343.[21] Thereafter, Majorca had no specific interest in making sovereign conquests. On the other hand, it is apparent that the Crown of Aragon inherited, at least for a time, Majorcan pretensions in the region, for a precious document of 1366 preserves royal instructions to the sea-captain Joan Mora, to patrol the archipelago and exclude interlopers from other states. This shows that shipping from outside the Crown of Aragon was active in these latitudes at the time, though, unfortunately, its provenance is not given.[22]

Slavers and perhaps fishermen might be presumed to have been frequenting the islands at the time, but no notice has survived of a renewed attempt at conquest from outside the Crown of Aragon until 1370, when the first partial or temporary success seems to have been achieved, though the disappearance of the original documents, which might constitute the evidence, has cast doubt on the whole episode. According to presumed copies of much debated authenticity, on 29 June 1370, the King of Portugal granted two islands, which he called "Nossa Señora a Franqua" and "Gumeyra," to Lansarote da Framqua, who is described as "admiral" and "our vassal" and who is said to have found and conquered the islands in question for the Portuguese king ("trobou e nos gannou"). An interpretation consistent with other known facts of the islands' history is that this conquest saw the erection of the tower on Lanzarote, attributed by later conquistadors to Lanzarote Malocello, who may have been the same "Lansarote da Framqua" to whom the grant of 1370 was addressed. The cognomen "da Framqua" could refer to the island seigneury, part of which the admiral may have wished to dedicate to Our Lady under that avocation for reasons of personal devotion or even possibly as a result of having been in French service, though there is no firm evidence to link Malocello, or any other "Lancelot" who may be in question here, with France. By this interpretation, the island of "Nossa Señora" would be Lanzarote, as a marginal note to the lost document is said to have claimed. As the toponymy of the Canaries was not yet definitively established, it is not necessary to suppose that "Gumeyra" was the island we now call "Gomera," but the balance of probabilities seems to incline that way, as the cartography of the time assigned more or less accurate positions and standard names to all major islands of the archipelago. Other copies of documents relating to this lordship, of 1376 and 1385, of the same provenance as that of 1370, purport to show that Lansarote da Framqua continued to hold or attempt to hold at least part of his island possessions and died in their defence on Lanzarote in or shortly before 1385. This recalls the tradition that Lanzarote Malocello spent about twenty years on his homonymous island.[23]

By the time of his death, he had been disputing possession with Castilian interlopers, as well as native Canarians, for at least ten years, in what the 1376 document called *"ficada guerra que ouve com os ditos gaanchos e castellaos."* It was natural that Castilian interest in the islands should have grown. The expedition ascribed to 1341 included Castilian

mariners and it was through Seville that news of it was brought to
Italy. In 1344, a prince of Castilian antecedents had been enfeoffed
with the islands by the Pope. Reacting to that event the following year,
the Castilian king had staked a claim of his own to the conquest of the
archipelago on the spurious grounds that the islands, with much of the
African mainland, had belonged to his remote Visigothic predecessors
and that "the kingdoms of Africa are of our conquest."[24] Frequently in
the third quarter of the century, Majorcan and Catalan missionaries
must have sailed through Castilian waters to reach the islands. And
Aragonese defense in the 1360s or – more doubtfully – Portuguese
conquest in the 1370s may have made the Canaries a theater of war
involving Castilian interlopers in a period when, according to tradition,
expeditions were being sent from Seville (though such traditions are not
confirmed by contemporary evidence until the 1390s). It is not necessary,
however, to admit such traditions, or make any assumptions about
presumed Castilian navigation to the Canaries, for purposes of the present
argument. Frequent communications with the islands, from the 1330s
onwards, are sufficiently attested by an impressive variety of sources.

This period of fairly intensive activity by navigators was
accompanied by a gradual increase in geographical precision
concerning the Canaries, reflected in contemporary maps. In
cartographic sources, the discoveries seem, as it were, to take shape.
Whereas, in the early fourteenth century, the Hereford Mappamundi
characteristically showed only a speculative mass of Atlantic islands, as
though torn from the ragged western hem of Africa, by the time of the
Dulcert map of 1339, at least three of the islands of the archipelago
were clearly distinguished. These two maps served different purposes:
the first was devotional, designed to adorn an altar as an image of the
perfection of God's creation (though the visitor to Hereford Cathedral
today will find it dismissed to an aisle), while the second was practical,
intended as an aid to navigation; but the differences between them also
reflect the achievements of Lanzarotto Malocello. Dulcert has "insula
capraria" and "Canaria" – both names associated with the Canaries – in
what are probably speculative positions, though suggestive of Madeira,
about the latitude of northern Morocco, with the legend, *Insulle
s[an]c[t]i brandani sive puellarum*, nicely blending the myths of Brendan
and Ursula. What could be "Pluvialia" (one of Pliny's names for the
Canaries) lies close by. But off what is perhaps the Wad Draa the map
shows *Insula de lanzarotus malocelus, vegimarin* (corresponding to the
present Isla de Lobos, a small islet between Lanzarote and
Fuerteventura) and *la forte ventura*. All are recognisably marked and
the first is emblazoned with a St. George's Cross, perhaps in honor of

Malocello's provenance. The somewhat later but evidently closely dependent British Library map, Add. MS. 25691, shows *[Ca]praria* just below the latitude of the westernmost extension of Africa, with a large *Insula de columbis* to the south (possibly alluding to the Brendan myth), then just to the south-east *Canaria*, below which comes the legend, *Insulle de sanbrandini*. But to the south-east again, in roughly correct position, come the identifiable Lanzarote, Fuerteventura and Lobos.[25]

The next relevant map of reliable date is the Pizigani portolan chart of 1367 in Parma (Kamal, IV, fasc. 1, no. 1289). Here place-names associated with the Canaries begin to coalesce into a recognizably single archipelago. Gomera and Hierro seem to be consciously depicted: certainly, there are eight distinct islands shown. The Catalan Atlas allows no room for doubt concerning the identities of the islands depicted in the position of the Canaries. Of the eleven largest islands, only La Palma is omitted. *Graciosa, laregranza, rocho, Insula de lanzaroto maloxelo, Insula de li vegi marin, forteventura, Insula de Canaria, Insula del infernio, Insula de gomera, Insula de lo fero* appear as we read in order. The corresponding modern names are: Graciosa, Alegranza, Roque, Lanzarote, Lobos, Fuerteventura, Canaria, Tenerife, Gomera, Hierro. Mount Teide, the great peak of Tenerife, is graphically depicted. The *Libro del conoscimiento*, compiled perhaps at about this time, names eleven islands of the Canaries and includes the name *tenerefiz*, as well as *Infierno* for the first time.[26] The roughly contemporary work of Guillem Soler (one version of which bears the date 1385) improves on the Catalan Atlas and excels some later maps in placing the archipelago in its true position relative to the trend of the African coast. The depiction of the Canaries is also remarkably complete: Santa Clara is added, so that eleven of the twelve largest islands are shown; Hierro has been thought to have been omitted but is in fact faintly visible in the Florentine version of the map, whereas in the other version (in Paris) the relevant section is torn.[27]

In view of the ample evidence of frequent sailings to the islands in the period concerned, there is no reason to question the substantial reliability of these maps. It is worth stressing that, even were corroborative documents not available, the evolution of the cartographic image of the islands, from the speculations of the Hereford Mappamundi to the information recorded in late fourteenth-century portolan charts, would raise a strong presumption in favor of a thorough exploration of the islands. This evolution can, as we have seen, be demonstrated from maps of unimpeachable authenticity, without calling any of questionable date into consideration. If it is admitted that the maps we have cited are evidence of knowledge of the

Canaries in the period, it must be admitted that they show knowledge of Madeira, too. In the Catalan Atlas and the work of Soler, Madeira, Porto Santo, the Desert Islands and the Savage Islands are all shown in creditably authentic positions, under recognizable versions of their modern names. Although unconfirmed by explicit references in any other contemporary documents, the proposition that they were genuinely known must benefit from the same presumption in its favor as we have claimed for the case of the Canaries. Finally, as we turn to consider the more problematical case of the Azores, the slow evolution of the cartographic tradition of the Canaries should also be kept in mind – an evolution occupying at least two generations'span in time. It would not be unreasonable to expect the accurate mapping of the Azores to take at least as long.

The Azores

To understand the early cartography of the Azores it is essential to set all prejudice aside and, in particular, to distinguish the case of the Azores from that of America. The presumed cartographic evidence for pre-Columbian navigation to the New World rests on three sources: the maps that depict an island under the name "Antilia" with other commonly associated islands;[28] the world maps of German provenance that show an antipodean land (insular or, in one case, apparently continental in character), usually called "Hesperides," in or beyond a narrow Atlantic;[29] and the Atlantic Chart of Andrea Bianco of 1448, which depicts an "authentic island" (*ixola otinticha*) at its extreme southern margin (but well short of the left-hand or "western" edge), south of the western part of the Gulf of Guinea: in a superimposed legend the island is said to be 1,500 miles *longa a ponente*.[30] These lands are not shown on any of the maps whose reliability we have so far established (although it must be said that the Bianco map is generally well informed). Nor, of course, have they the support of any non-cartographic evidence of the sort available for the Canaries. The Antilia group is anyway unlikely to be intended for America (even setting aside the perhaps deceptive argument that it is in quite the wrong place) because of its early first appearance (1424), its traditional character, its indebtedness to a well attested legend[31] and its confusion – as we shall see – in some mapmakers' minds with the Azores. None of these considerations is sufficient to refute the identification of Antilia with America, but, in default of other evidence, they justify our wariness. The maps which show the Hesperides are all *mappaemundi*, not portolan charts; they are classifiable as literary compilations to which practical navigation contributed little or nothing. Bianco's *ixola otinticha* is a unique case, inexplicable as it stands and unillumined by any other source; any interpretation of it is necessarily speculative; whatever the meaning of the phrase *1,500 mi[li]a longa a ponente*, the actual location of the island on the map, within the Gulf of Guinea and perhaps about a hundred miles from the African coast, suggests no part of the New World.

Nor should we allow the case of the Azores to be obscured by the insubstantial arguments which have characterized some discussion of the early cartography of the Cape Verde Islands. Though, from 1413 onwards, islands of apparently mythical origin appear in portolan charts south of the Canaries – a large island known as Ymadoro or Himadoro and two sausage-shaped ones under the names of "Illes de Gades" and "Dos ermanes" – the presumption that these are pre-figurations of the Cape Verde Islands can only be justified on the hypothesis that every rumored or fabled island must be a reflection of perceived reality. There is no evidence outside these apparent cartographical speculations of any reported discovery of the Cape Verde Islands in the first half of the fifteenth century.[32]

The presumed early cartography of the Azores, however, is of a much more impressive and substantial character. The archipelago does not appear fully and accurately mapped, on surviving charts, from before the 1480s. Yet, even at the most conservative estimate, most of the islands had by that time been thoroughly explored and much frequented for some fifty years. Their colonization is documented from 1439 onwards. We should not, therefore, expect too much of the earliest attempts at depiction. We should also make allowance for the technical problems faced by high-seas navigators of the late Middle Ages in recording their course in little-known waters.

Previous attempts to identify the Azores on portolan charts and to reconstruct the process of their mappings have foundered on the unreliable chronology of the maps. In the attempt which follows, I avoid arguments which rely on assigning dates to undated maps or on assuming a date equivalent, where an almanac is included, to the start of the almanac. The Medici Atlas of the Laurentian Library (Kamal, IV, fasc. 2, nos. 1246-1248), for instance, opens with an almanac beginning in 1351;[33] but the Atlas has every appearance of being a collection of folios by more than one hand, drawn at different times. The fifth folio, which shows the Atlantic, most closely resembles the versions of Guillem Soler, one of which is dated 1385, and other maps of similar date or in the same tradition. The Catalan Atlas is conventionally attributed to 1375, because that year is used as the starting-point for the computation of the Golden Number, but 1376 and 1377 are also mentioned in its accompanying texts; it conforms closely to the description of such an atlas in the French royal library catalogue, dated 1380, but possibly interpolated or revised later; and its date should also be considered in the light of the record of the imminent dispatch of a mappamundi by Cresques Abraham to the King of France by the Infante of Aragon in November, 1381.[34] In view of the fact that Guillem Soler's map of 1385 is almost identical in its representation of the Atlantic, save that it is slightly more complete, the Catalan Atlas can be assigned with some confidence to the late 1370s or early 1380s. For most undated maps, however, it is impossible to suggest anything like so narrow a range of possibilities.

Two Venetian maps, the "Pinelli-Walckenaer" of the British Library (sometimes said to be Genoese) and the dependent "Combitis" Atlas of the Biblioteca Marciana, are traditionally dated 1384 and *c.* 1400 respectively, the former because of the starting-point of its almanac.[35] But both have features which suggest a much later origin: the perfunctory treatment of a group of islands in the eastern Atlantic, probably derived from early attempts to represent the Azores, is a common feature of maps of the mid- and late fifteenth century and is not found on any known late fourteenth- or early fifteenth-century example. The Mediterranean toponymy of both maps includes features not found before the fifteenth century.[36] Unless and until reliable dates can be assigned, it is best to leave these maps out of account when trying to establish the chronology of the mapping of the Azores.

By using the handful of reliably dated maps as points of reference, three stages can be discerned in the depiction of islands which might be intended for the Azores. First, in maps of or about the 1380s, clusters of islands reminiscent of groupings of the Azores, or some of them, appear in the latitudes of the Azores but displaced well to the east of the archipelago's true position; these are the only possible attempts to represent the Azores until the 1420s;[37] secondly, from the 1420s onwards, in positions overlapping with the true position of the Azores, a tradition is established of placing a large, rectangular island or islands, usually bearing names associated with the myth of Antilia and the Isle of Seven Cities.[38] Only one map in this tradition attempts to give these islands, with other, smaller ones nearby, anything resembling the true relationship of the Azores to each other.[39] Mapmakers who knew the true position of the Azores, from 1439 onwards, either excluded this group altogether or retained it in a new, speculative position. Thirdly, a group of three maps of 1439-48 shows a string of islands which even the most sceptical scrutineer would willingly identify as the Azores, in roughly their correct position: the first two of these replace the old Azores-like clusters of fourteenth-century origin with these new depictions, suggesting that, in the minds of the cartographers, the traditional clusters were identified with what we think of as the Azores;[40] in the third map, by Andrea Bianco, the traditional clusters are reinstated, but the Azores are included in place of the Antilia group suggesting that in Bianco's mind the Antilia group, represented a prior attempt at depiction of the Azores.[41] Finally, it is common for fifteenth-century maps to retain schematic versions of the fourteenth-century clusters, or of the Antilia group, or both, long after the true position of the Azores had become known, presumably in deference to their cartographic sources; this shows what an important influence tradition had become in the mapping of the Atlantic. It should not be taken to mean that these islands must have been imaginary or fabulous at the time of their first inclusion.

What I have called the first phase can be discerned in the Guillem Soler maps and their contemporaries and derivatives: the fifth folio of the Medici Atlas, the Catalan Atlas, the Catalan portolan charts of Paris (Kamal, IV, fasc. 4, no. 1390) and Naples (Kamal, IV, fasc. 3, no. 1331) and the dated maps of Niccolò de Pasqualini (1408) and Mecia de Viladestes (1413). These all have features in common in their depiction of an Azorean group of islands. All, except the Catalan Atlas, show eight islands, which share a more or less common sequence of names; the Medici Atlas omits or conflates certain names: a central cluster of three islands, for instance, is called "Insule de ventura sive de columbis" while most of the maps show "Ventura" and "columbis" or "li columbi" as the names of two islands of the group. The Catalan Atlas omits the two most southerly islands – otherwise called "Capraria" and "Lovo" – altogether, perhaps by inadvertence. The *Libro del conoscimiento*, of the late fourteenth century, lists eight islands, with recognizably the same names (in a Castilian or Aragonese form) as are shown in the maps. All the maps show the Azorean group on more or less the same meridian as the westerly isles of the Canaries (well displaced to the east, of course, from the Azores' true position) and on a rhumb north by north-west from a center near Lanzarote or Fuerteventura, through the Madeira group: although one would actually have to steer a course to the north-west to reach the Azores from the Canaries, magnetic variation, variable winds, unfamiliar currents and cartographical error (assuming that all these maps belong to a single tradition) might account for the difference. The entire archipelago, in all these maps, is "stretched" over a far greater area of ocean than in reality and the size of the islands is much exaggerated: this is also a feature of the early cartography of the Canaries.

For the identification of the islands depicted, or rather for the solution of the problem of whether they are identifiable, the way they are clustered in definable groups is the most important common feature of maps of the first phase. To understand the significance of this, it is important to consider how the Azores appear as one approaches them under sail from the south-east. Santa María is encountered first, lying well to the south of the main archipelago. São Miguel appears as a relatively large island, "broadside on" to the north. To the north-west again, the central group of the archipelago is formed by two small clusters: Pico, Faial and São Jorge make up the more southerly cluster, Graciosa and Terceira lie slightly to the north-east in relation to it. Beyond the central group again, to the north-west, lie Flores and Corvo.

The Azorean identity on maps

How does the reality of the Azores, thus described, correspond to the clusterings on the early maps? Superficially, the resemblance seems clear: the substitution of an archipelago of eight islands for one of nine might be explained by the fusing of two outlines on the horizon, or the omission of a small island like Graciosa. The maps all show a central cluster of islands, with two isles well out to the north and others well removed to the east and south: to that extent, reality and cartographic image seem well matched. It is against the background of these general similarities that Armando Cortesão has tried to link particular islands found on the map with real ones.[42] His effort, however, has been unconvincing. In particular, the relationship between Santa María and São Miguel does not fit that of the two small southerly islands called Capraria and Lovo in the maps; nor can one feel satisfied with the displacement of Terceira from a position on the north-east flank of the central group to one south of it: how could a navigator approaching the islands from the south-east have made such an error of observation, or a cartographer, following his account, such an error of interpretation? The omission of Graciosa rather than, say, Faial, appears arbitrary, and is made largely in order to permit the identification of the two most northerly isles of the maps as Flores and Corvo. Yet that identification also seems unsatisfactory, since in every case the maps show these two islands slightly to the east of the meridian of the central group, whereas in fact they are well to the west.

We may do better by abandoning Cortesão's identifications and starting again from scratch. The central cluster of three islands shown in all the maps could represent more than three "real" islands, particularly observed when standing well out to windward. But it seems unlikely that vessels should normally have chosen to make such an approach and, as a matter of common sense, it is appropriate to try first the tentative hypothesis that the cluster of three represents São Jorge, Faial and Pico: indeed the relationship one to another of these islands on the map does closely resemble the real relationship of these islands, arranged like the apices of a triangle. From this central group, two islands stand out to the north and east on the maps, as in reality: Terceira and Graciosa; to be sure, the "Corvi Marini" and "Conigi" of the maps lie far to the north of the cluster of three, whereas Terceira and Graciosa are within sight of their neighbors; but this sort of elongation is not atypical of the early cartography of Atlantic archipelagoes generally. To the south-east of the central cluster, we find in the maps, as in reality, a relatively long island, looming broadside on as one approaches from the south-east. The "Brazil" of the maps thus corresponds to São Miguel. This leaves the problem of identifying the two small islands of Capraria and Lovo well to the south. When one recalls, however, that Santa María lies well to the south of the rest of the archipelago; that a little way off Santa María to the north we find the rocky Formigas, and that early cartography habitually exaggerated the size of islets and rocky outcrops, particularly, to take a pertinent example, in the case of the Canaries, the problem seems to dissolve. It does not appear to me that Flores and Corvo are represented on any map of the fourteenth or early fifteenth centuries, or that there is any reason to suppose that they must have been discovered along with most of the rest of the archipelago. They lie much further to the west than the other islands; there is no record from before 1452 that they were known to the Portuguese settlers who had begun to colonize Santa María and São Miguel from 1439; and though a freak wind or a deliberate attempt at exploration might have led seamen to them, there is neither point nor merit in such a speculation, whereas it is satisfactory and consistent with the evidence to suppose that fourteenth-century knowledge of the Azores was limited to the southern and central islands of the archipelago.

Maps of what I call the second stage – those which introduce islands whose nomenclature is connected with the legends of Antilia and the Seven Cities – belong to the history of the mapping of the Azores only in a modified sense. It is, on balance, marginally more likely that the appearance of Antilia, from 1424, reflects, if anything, a sighting of the Azores than of the New World: the position of Antilia, at its first appearance, on the Nautical Chart of 1424 in the James Ford Bell Collection, Minneapolis, does at least coincide with that of the Azores. But neither identification is satisfactory. The main islands of the Antilia group, in all cases of their inclusion in fifteenth-century maps, have conventional, rectangular shapes; and although, at the start of the tradition, Antilia is placed in a position suggestive of the Azores, other islands are dotted around at random. Only two mapmakers seem to have identified the Antilia group with the Azores: the Cristofal Soligo map, of uncertain date, groups eleven islands, including some bearing the traditional shapes (and in one case a traditional name) of islands in the Antilia group, in a fan-shaped archipelago covering much of the central north Atlantic; Soligo gives to this archipelago and its islands names associated with the Azores in the fifteenth century.[43] This looks like a late attempt at synthesis of two cartographic traditions. In the other case, that of Andrea Bianco, the identity of the Azores and the Antilia group does appear to be presumed; and it may be worth adding that in a chart of Battista Beccario of 1435, the Antilia group is labelled, *de novo reperte*, which could be interpreted as a reference to Portuguese voyage to the Azores of the early 1430s.[44] But these indications in favor of identifying the Antilia group with the Azores – while more impressive than those which link Antilia with America – amount to very little. Even if a real sighting of the Azores (or *a fortiori* of any other land) did lie behind the Antilia tradition or contribute to it, it would still be necessary to assert a literary or legendary origin for the tradition as well. As the necessary explanation is also sufficient, it is supererogatory to adduce others. Like Cipangu, whose traditional shape it resembles, Antilia was, as far as we know, an island reputed, not reported.

Within a few years of the first appearance of Antilia, however, the cartography of the Azores was genuinely transformed by what I have called the three maps of the third phase: the Gabriel Vallseca map, dated 1439, now in Barcelona;[45] an undated Catalan map in Florence (Kamal, IV, fasc. 4, no. 1463); and the Atlantic portolan of Andrea Bianco, dated in London in 1448, now in Milan.[46] All these maps show the Azores as a group of islands strung out serially or, in the case of Vallseca, almost serially, on a north-west to south-east axis, in a position corresponding very closely to that really occupied by the archipelago, except that it extends rather too far north. Both Catalan maps show nine islands, Bianco's seven. On the maps in Florence and Venice, each island bears a name of its own. One name which occurs in both, Isle of Hawks (*faucols* in the Catalan, *falconi* in the Venetian map) anticipates the toponymy of the Azores as it would come to be fixed: this was the Portuguese collective name for the archipelago from 1439. The remaining names are descriptive or traditional. The size and mutual relationships of the several islands are random; but their position and orientation make them clearly intended for the Azores. The makers of all three maps seem to identify the newly depicted archipelago with traditionally depicted islands: with it the two Catalan maps replace the traditional Azorean clusters – Vallseca omitting the latter altogether while the map now in Florence retains only *liconigi* and *Illa de corps marins*, which had always been shown as a pair remote from other islands, in their traditional position. This suggests that Vallseca identified the Azores with the traditional Azorean clusters as a whole, while the second author made broadly the same identification, excluding only the two most marginal of the traditional islands. Bianco evidently took a different view. His 1448 map retains the traditional clusters, while omitting the Antilia group, to which he had given some prominence in his maps of 1436.[47] Hence Bianco appears to have regarded the Antilia group as an attempted representation of the Azores: as we have seen, this was an unusual identification at the time, duplicated, as far as we know, only by Cristofal Soligo. Most mapmakers, on becoming aware of the real position of the Azores continued to represent the traditional islands as well, shifting the Antilia group westward.[48]

How can this new precision, at least in the position and orientation of the Azores, arising relatively suddenly in maps of the 1430s and 1440s, be explained? Vallseca offers some elucidation in a famous gloss, still legible beneath an equally famous ink-blot, made when George Sand was looking at the map. "These islands were found by Diego de Silves pilot of the King of Portugal in the year 1427."[49] This is broadly compatible with other traditions about the beginnings of Portuguese exploration of the Azores, which date it to the early 1430s, and with the almost continuous documentation of the Portuguese colonies in the islands from 1439.[50] It is thoroughly consistent with the character of late medieval mapmakers' techniques that Vallseca should have departed from cartographical tradition to include a reported new discovery in this way. A note on the "Yale Map of 1403" by Francesco Beccario expressly states that the author modified the map to take account of mariners' information.[51] Andrea Bianco's 1448 map is by universal assent an attempt to incorporate recent news about the African coast culled by Portuguese explorers. The world map of the Laurentian Medici Atlas was modified at least twice in the fifteenth century to accommodate new contributions.[52] It is therefore reasonable to accept Vallseca's adjustment of the position of the Azores as based on an authentic report.

This begs the question of how his informants fixed their position with an accuracy so superior to that of their fourteenth-century predecessors. Unless this question is satisfactorily answered, confidence in the validity of the evidence of fourteenth-century Azorean voyages is bound to be undermined. It is hard to discern any haven-finding technique that may have been new to the generation of "Diego de Silves." We know of no direct computations of longitude made by professional seamen until the 1480s at the earliest, and even then with indifferent accuracy. Navigational tables, trigonometrically based, which enabled pilots to correct their course when deflected by wind or current, were evidently in practical use in the 1430s, when Andrea Bianco, himself a ship's captain, included a set in his atlas of 1436. But they had been known since the late thirteenth century, at least, when they were described by Ramon Llull, and the history of their diffusion among practical navigators is obscure.[53] The problems of dating the emergence of the use of the astrolabe and quadrant for determining latitude are not relevant here. For purposes of navigation in the area of the Azores, latitude can be adequately determined by an experienced sailor with the naked eye, and even the earliest presumed cartographic records of the Azores were roughly right as far as latitude was concerned. In all probability, "Diego de Silves" and his contemporaries navigated by means of the same aids as their predecessors: compass, hourglass and a good eye for the speed of the ship, the drift off course and the height of the sun or the Pole Star. If they were able to judge their course on the high seas more accurately than their forebears, it can only have been because of the progressive effects of experience of the Atlantic, gradually but decisively accumulated over a long period. For the same reasons, similar "breakthroughs" appear in the cartographical evolution of the image of the Canary Islands: it is not surprising to find them also in the case of the Azores.

It is, of course, one thing to say that the islands depicted on the maps genuinely resemble the Azores and another to claim that these resemblances derived from real knowledge; one thing to aver that sailors of the time were capable of finding the islands, another to demonstrate that they actually did so. We may, however, advance the argument some way further, first by meeting the remaining objections to the cartographic evidence, then by adducing such corroborative material as we have.

The strongest reasons for doubting the maps lie in the difficulty of verifying their data. Many bear no reliable date; they are vulnerable to emendation by later hands; their treatment of the Azores, in particular, is open to charges of vagueness and, as we have seen, islands are often almost unrecognizably displaced from their true positions. Moreover, the toponymy of fourteenth-century cartographers is classical and mythological and they include many unquestionably speculative islands. None of these caveats, however, definitely invalidates the maps, nor is anything in the cartographers' depictions of the Azores demonstrably unauthentic. That the Azores appear only as a result of interpolation is possible but improbable: the Catalan Atlas and the Soler maps, which constitute the essential evidence, betray no hint of the intervention of later hands, and fourteenth-century mapmakers are unlikely to have wasted parchment in order to leave space for interpolators to work in; it gradually became normal to allow increased space to the Atlantic – and that in itself is a strong indication of the vibrancy of late medieval interest in exploration of the ocean – but, among surviving maps, it is only with the Nautical Chart of 1424 that space seems to be included speculatively, to be filled in later. The surviving maps represent only a small sample of those which must have been available in widely dispersed centers: interpolation would have had to be widespread and systematic to yield consistent results. Imprecision in the location of islands is only to be expected: if they were completely accurate, it would be a sure sign that they were forgeries, as no means of fixing one's position at sea with exactitude were available in the period. Navigators could take rough readings of latitude and, in our maps, latitudes are always roughly right or, at least, within the margin of error to be expected from cartographers who relied on readings obtained without instruments by direct observation of celestial bodies with the naked eye.[54] Longitudinal accuracy was unknown until the fifteenth century. As far as the classical and mythical toponymy of the maps is concerned, this is again just what one ought to expect of the period. The modern nomenclature was not fixed until well into the fifteenth century: a fourteenth-century map which appeared to anticipate it would be highly suspect. Learned cartographers who received mariners' reports of newly discovered islands naturally assigned them names which, if not purely descriptive (as, in some cases, they were) would be drawn from existing tradition. As for the inclusion of speculative islands, it was not only in the fourteenth century that such speculations were recorded as if they were facts. Notional islands continued to appear on nineteenth-century Admiralty charts. Genuine discoveries tend to breed speculation in their turn and Atlantic conditions are, as experienced sailors know, conducive to false sightings.[55] Inclusion of speculative islands might as well be read as evidence of the sailors' knowledge of the Atlantic, as of their ignorance. Finally, we must confront the most influential of all objections to the cartographical evidence: S. E. Morison's insistence (unquestioned even by advocates of the maps) that whereas the Azores are aligned from east to west the early alleged cartographic depictions show them running from north to south.[56] This is simply false on both counts. The Azores are grouped around a roughly north-west to south-east axis. They are encountered, as one approaches from the south, in the clusters defined above: Santa María and Formigas well to the south; to the north, São Miguel on its own; then the cluster of Pico, São Jorge and Faial, well to the north-west, with Terceira and Graciosa separated from them a little to the north-east. Flores and Corvo, lying well to the west, do not enter into the picture. It is in clusters of this sort, arranged in the same way, that the islands are depicted in late fourteenth-century maps: the admitted exaggerations of size and distances are characteristic, visible to a lesser extent in the early cartographic tradition of the Canaries. There are maps which show eastern Atlantic islands bearing names traditionally associated with the Azores, strung out from north to south, but those maps are not of the fourteenth century. The "Pinelli-Walckenaer" and the "Combitis" are, as we have seen, wrongly attributed to the fourteenth century. Others – such as the Benincasa and Bertran charts of the 1460s to 1480s – date indisputably from a period after the position of the Azores was accurately determined.[57] Their sketchy onion-strings of eastern Atlantic islands may ultimately have derived from early attempts to depict the Azores, but in the second half of the fifteenth century had become traditional.

One vital objection to the cartographic evidence remains: why, if the Azores were indeed explored in the fourteenth century, are there no documents of the time, apart from the maps, which explicitly refer to them? Clearly, spurious traditions of later invention, which would throng the North Atlantic in the Middle Ages with imaginary precursors of Columbus, must be discounted. But it is hardly surprising that uninhabited islands should be ignored by our surviving sources: they were understandably of little interest to slavers, conquistadors and missionaries, who, for instance, were responsible for the Canarian voyages documented above. It may be worth pointing out that the Majorcan sailing licenses which speak of "islands of the west" do not specifically exclude the Azores, but it is only common sense to take them as referring to the Canaries.

It is, however, possible to claim the discovery of the Azores as a by-product of the Canary run and to assign a corroborative value, for alleged voyages to the Azores, to the evidence of navigation to the Canaries; in other words, the documents which refer to the Canaries may be treated by implication as evidence of knowledge of the Azores. Two circumstances may be cited in favor of this proposition. First, there is the sheer scale of navigation to and from the Canaries in the fourteenth century; secondly, the influence of the Atlantic wind system. Since the discoveries, made by Rumeu de Armas, of a formidable body of documents on the activities of the missionary see of Telde, from the 1350s to the 1380s, and of the document on Joan de Mora's expedition of 1366, the Canary voyage can no longer be seen as an occasional or sporadic indulgence of the period. Whether or not one accepts Verlinden's contentious reconstruction of the career of Lanzarotto Malocello, the Canaries continue to appear as much frequented islands. Once that is admitted, a context in which to understand the discovery of the Azores begins to emerge. It will be remembered that most of the early sailing licenses for the Canaries refer to cogs, which were generally unsuitable for tacking against the wind. Though the name "cog" was relatively new, it does not seem to have denoted a different type of ship from a traditional Mediterranean *navis* (Catalan *nau*). There is no reason to suppose that it was other than square-sailed. Rigged to catch a following wind, such vessels could only return from the Canaries by either of two expedients: they could limit homeward navigation to the most favoured season of the winter, when south-westerlies are frequent enough to grant a safe passage. Indeed, from what we know of the timing of early voyages, that was understandably the most favored method and route. But given the frequency of sailings, the duration of the period over which they took place, and the unreliable nature of the winds, it is unreasonable to suppose that the alternative route, making use of the pattern of prevailing winds, was not also employed. This meant striking north in search of the westerlies that would take one home. Such a course would touch or skirt Madeira and it would be generally expedient, and sometimes necessary, to reach the latitude of the Azores before turning east. The same return route is well attested for some Guinea voyages of the fifteenth century.[58] Against the background of current knowledge of frequent sailings to the Canaries, the roughly contemporary discovery of the Azores seems natural, even inevitable. The process can be compared with the Portuguese discovery of Brazil in 1500 in the course of a wide sweep out into the south Atlantic in search of the westerlies that would carry the fleet round the Cape of Good Hope. This, on a larger scale and in reverse, was a reflection of the journey the Majorcan cogs might have made on their return from the Canaries in the north Atlantic in the fourteenth century, like an image in a shaving mirror.

Thus fourteenth-century maps of the Azores should be considered vindicated, while fifteenth-century maps of America should not. Yet it is possible to wrest evidence of another, hitherto largely unremarked discovery, from fifteenth-century Atlantic maps. In what I have labelled the third stage of Atlantic exploration, Columbus's was not the only practical attempt to exploit the alluring uncertainties of the Atlantic. Flores, Corvo, the Cape Verde Islands and the isles of the Gulf of Guínea were explored in the 1450s and 1460s. Cartography, lagging as usual behind discovery, did not incorporate them – or, indeed, delineate previously known islands with perfect accuracy – until the 1480s. Yet, while slow to reflect discovery, maps were quick to encourage it: Bristol voyages of the last years of the century in search of the Isle of Brasil, or those of the Portuguese of the Azores to find Antilia, or of Columbus himself, suggest this. Even in world maps – which gave their compilers a welcome chance to speculate about the Orient – the greatest concentration of novelties of the fifteenth century, after those drawn from the reception of Ptolemy, lay in the Atlantic. The extent of speculation about the Atlantic, in both world maps and sea charts, is the most remarkable feature of the cartography of the time. It shows what a stimulus to the imagination Atlantic exploration was, and how consciousness of an exploitable Atlantic grew in the century before Columbus's voyages. Maps helped to induce potential explorers to see the ocean in a new light. In that respect, whatever one thinks of the cartographic record of discoveries of new lands, they are evidence of at least one authentic discovery of transcendent importance: the discovery of Atlantic space.

In the following chapter, Charles Verlinden will suggest how many of the aforementioned Italian navigators were co-opted by the Portuguese monarchy to promote its growing interests in the Atlantic. Until near the end of the XV century, Portugal dominated all exploration there and (save for the Canary Islands) all settlement. These Italians in Portuguese service were joined by the Flemings, and their participation in the developing Portuguese empire was esteemed throughout the XVI century.

Felipe F. R. Fernández-Armesto

Notes

*This article previously appeared in *Renaissance and Modern Studies* vol. XXX (1986): 12-34 (here with kind permission).

[1] *Johannes Cornogo, Complete Works: Recent Researches in the Music of the Middle Ages, and Early Renaissance*, ed. R. L. Gerber, XV (Madison, 1984), viii-ix.

[2] The best reproduction is *Mapamundi: the Catalan Atlas of the Year 1375*, ed. G. Grosjean, (Zurich, 1978); where the map is cited hereafter, a reference to sheet III of this edition may be understood. On the problems of authorship, the correct form of the name of Cresques Abraham and general questions concerning the atlas, see *El Atlas Catalán*, (Barcelona, 1975).

[3] R. A. Skelton, "A Contract of World Maps at Barcelona, 1399-1400," *Imago Mundi, XXII*, (1968), 108-09.

[4] P. E. Russell, *El Infante Dom Henrique e as Ilhas Canárias* (Lisbon, 1979), p. 19; *Fontes Rerum Canariarum*, XI, 106; *Libro del conoscimiento de todos los reynos, tierras y señoríos que hay en el mundo*, ed. M. Jiménez de la Espada, (Madrid, 1877).

[5] IXe *Colloque International d' Histoire Maritime* (Seville, 1969), 276-79. Verlinden has replied in "La découverte des archipels de la 'Méditerrannée Atlantique' (Canaries, Madères, Açores) et la navigation astronomique primitive," *Revista portuguesa de história*, XVI (1978), 105-31; Armando Cortesão, "A Carta Náutica de 1424," *Esparsos* (3 vols., Coimbra, 1975), III, ix-211 [hereafter Cortesão, "Carta"]. I cite this edition because it includes the author's last revisions, but the maps and diagrams can be consulted in a larger and clearer format in *The Nautical Chart of 1424* (Coimbra, 1954); E. G. R. Taylor, "Imaginary Islands: a Problem Solved," *Geographical Journal*, CXXX (1964), 105-07.

[6] The credulous tradition has its origins in H. Yule Oldham, "The Importance of Mediaeval Manuscript Maps in the Study of the History of Geographical Discovery," *Report of the VIth International Geographical Congress* (London, 1895), 703-06, and its *reductio ad absurdum* in W. H. Babcock, *Legendary Islands of the Atlantic* (New York, 1922). For recent statements, see, for example, V. H. Cassidy, "New Worlds and Everyman: Some Thoughts on the Logic and Logistics of pre-Columbian Discovery," *Terrae Incognitae*, X (1978), 7-13, esp. p. 8 and Taylor, "Imaginary Islands," 105.

[7] George Winius and Bailey W. Diffie, *Foundations of the Portuguese Empire* (Minneapolis, 1977), 25, 61; G. V. Scammel, *The World Encompassed* (London, 1981), 245; S. E. Morrison, *The*

European Discovery of America: the Northern Voyages (New York, 1971), 95. Compare, however, the use of portolan charts by Mediterranean historians in M. Quaini, "Catalogna e Liguria nella cartografie nautica e nei portolani medievali," *Atti del I Congresso Storico Liguria-Catalogna* (Bordighera, 1974), 551.

⁸ "Nem direitamente nas cartas de marear nem mapamundo non estavan debuxados senão a prazer dos homens que as faziam." J. Martins da Silva Marques, *Descobrimentos portugueses*, 3 vols., (Lisbon, 1944-71), I, 435; *Monumenta henricina*, 15 vols., (Lisbon, 1960-74) VIII, 107.

⁹ *De Vita Solitaria*, ed. A. Altamura (Naples, 1943), II, vi, 3, p. 125; *Le familiari*, ed. V. Rossi, 4 vols., (Florence, 1933), I, 106: R. Caddeo, *Le navigazioni atlantiche di Alvise da Cà da Mosto, Antoniotto Usodirnare e Niccoloso da Recco* (Milan, 1928), p. 51.

¹⁰ Y. Kamal, *Monumenta Cartographica Africae et Aegypti*, 5 vols. in 16, (Cairo, 1926-51) [hereafter Kamal], IV, fasc. 2, no. 1222; K. Kretschmer, *Die Italianische Portolane* (Berlin, 1909), p. 118.

¹¹ *Naturalis Historia*, VI, 37; J. Alvarez Delgado, "Las Islas Canarias en Plinio," *Revista de historia* (La Laguna), Xl (1945), 26-51.

¹² Plutarch, *Vita Sertorii*, VII, IX; Horace, *Epod.*, XVI, 42; A. O. Lovejoy and G. Boas, *Primitivism and Related Ideas in Antiquity* (Baltimore, 1935), pp. 280-303; G. Boas, *Essays on Primitivism and Related Ideas in the Middle Ages* (Baltimore, 1948), pp. 168-69; E. Faral, *La légende arthurienne*, 3 vols., (Paris, 1929-34), III, 334; E. Benito Ruano, "Nuevas singladuras por las Canarias fabulosas," *Homenaje a E. Serra Ràfols* (3 vols., La Laguna, 1970), I, 203-21.

¹³ *La géographie d' Aboulféda*, ed. J. T. Reinaud. 2 vols., (Paris, 1848), II, 263-64; [Al-Idrisi], *Description de l' Afrique et de l' Espagne par Edrisi*, ed. R. Dozy and M. J. de Goeje (Paris, 1866); p. 197; R. Mauny, *Les navigations médiévales sur les côtes sahariennes* (Lisbon, 1960), pp. 81-88.

¹⁴ *Monumenta henricina*, I, 201-06 replaces earlier editions.

¹⁵ C. Verlinden, "Les génois dans la marine portugaise avant 1385," *Actas do Congresso de Portugal Medievo*, 3 vols. (Braga, 1966), III, 388-407.

¹⁶ F. Sevillano Colom, "Los viajes medievales desde Mallorca a Canarias," *Anuario de estudos atlánticos*, XXIII (1978), 27-57; A. Rumeu de Armas, "Mallorquines en el Atlántico," *Homenaje a E. Serra Ràfols*, III, 265-76.

Portugal, the Pathfinder

[17] A. Lutolf, "Zur Entdeckung und Christianisung der Westafrikanischen Inseln," *Theologische Quartalschrift*, XLVII (1877), 319-32; A. Rumeu de Armas, *El obispado de Telde* (Madrid, 1960), p. 31. I offer a new study of this text in chapter IX of *From the Mediterranean to the Atlantic* (in press).

[18] *Mappamundi*, ed. Grosjean, sheet III; Mauny, op. cit., pp. 96-97.

[19] P. Chaunu, *L' Expansion européenne du XIIIe au XVe siècle* (Paris, 1969), pp. 95-98.

[20] Rumeu, "Mallorquines," pp. 264-73.

[21] M. Mitjà, "Abandó des Illes Canaries per Joan d' Aragó," *Anuario de estudios atlánticos*, VIII (1962), 329.

[22] A. Rumeu de Armas, "La expedición mallorquina de 1366 a las Islas Canarias," ibid., XXVII (1981), 15-23.

[23] C. Verlinden, "Lanzarotto Malocello et la découverte portugaise des Canaries," *Revue belge de philologie et d' histoire*, XXVI (1958), 1173-1209; see his debate with E. Serra Ràfols in *Actas do Congresso de Portugal Medievo*, III, 388-407; *Revista de historia canaria*, XXVII (1961); and C. Verlinden, "La découverte" (cited in note 5 above), pp. 109-119. Verlinden has answered adequately the charge that the documents in question contain anachronisms; it remains true, however, that their provenance is tainted.

[24] *Clément VI: Lettres se rapportant à la France*, ed. J. Glénisson, E. Déprez and G. Mollat (1958), no. 1317.

[25] See n. 10 above; on whether Madeira is represented, I concur with the reservations of J. Mees, "Les Açores d' après des portolans," *Boletim da Sociedade de Geographia de Lisboa* (1900), 457, *Acta Cartographica*, III, 382.

[26] Ed. Jiménez, p. 50.

[27] Kamal, IV, fasc. 3, nos. 1320-1322; A. Cortesão, *História da cartografia portuguesa*, 2 vols., (Coimbra, 1969-70) [hereafter Cortesão, *História*], II, 49-50, 59.

[28] Cortesão, "Carta," pp. 146-202.

[29] D. Bennett Durand, *The Vienna-Klosterneuburg Map Corpus of the Fifteenth Century* (Leiden, 1952), plates XIII, XV, XVI reproduce some examples. See also, J. Parker, "A Fragment of a Fifteenth-century Planisphere in the James Ford Bell Collection," *Imago Mundi*, XIX (1965), 106-107 for the most remarkable example.

[30] Kamal, V, no. 1492; the reproductions in H. Yule Oldham, "A Pre-Columbian Discovery of America," *The Geographical Journal*, V (1895), 221-239, are more serviceable than the arguments.

[31] Cortesão, "Carta," pp. 146-202.

[32] A. Cortesão, "Descubrimento e representação das Ilhas de Cabo Verde na cartografia antiga," *Memórias da Academia das Ciências de Lisboa: Classe de Ciências*, XXI (1976-7), 229-50.

[33] On problems of dating see G. H. T. Kimble, "The Laurentian World Map with special reference to its Portrayal of Africa," *Imago Mundi*, I (1935), 29-33; Cortesão, História, II, 45.

[34] Kamal, IV, fasc. 3, nos. 1301-1307; see no. 1307 for the documents concerning the date; Cortesão, *História*, II, 48; see also n. 2 above.

[35] Kamal, IV, fasc. 3, nos. 1316-1319, 1333; Cortesão, *História*, II, 49-50.

[36] Information of Mr. Tony Campbell of the British Library Map Collection.

[37] Soler maps (Kamal, IV, fasc. 3, nos. 1320-1322); Catalan Atlas (n. 2 above).

[38] Cortesão, "Carta," pp. 146-63.

[39] Cristofalo Soligo: Kamal, V, no. 1510.

[40] Kamal, IV, fasc. 4, no. 1463; Cortesão, *História*, II, 150-52; *The Nautical Chart of 1424* (Coimbra, 1954), plate V.

[41] Kamal, V, no. 1492; cf. Bianco's 1436 version of the Atlantic in A. E. Nordenskold, *Periplus* (Stockholm, 1897), p. 19; R. A. Skelton, T. E. Marston and G. D. Painter, *The Vinland Map and the Tartar Relation* (New Haven, 1965), plate VI.

[42] Cortesão, *História*, II, 58-59, largely following Kretschmer, *Italianische Portolane*, pp. 686-87.

[43] Kamal, V, no. 1510. cf. Cortesão, "Carta," pp. 125, 152-53. For the contemporary use of Soligo's nomenclature see documents of 1460 in *Monumenta henricina*, XIII, 345-46, XIV, 20.

[44] Cortesão, "Carta," p. 147. The relevant section is reproduced in R. Hennig, *Terrae Incognitae*, 4 vols. (Leipzig, 1944-56), IV, plate III.

[45] Cortesão, *História*, II, 150-52.

[46] See n. 30 above.

[47] See n. 41 above.

[48] Cortesão, "Carta," p. 58, notes this westward shift but regards it as evidence that the Antilia group was meant to depict part of the New World.

[49] "Aquestes illes foram trobades per Diego de Silves pelot del rey de portogall." See Cortesão, *História*, II, 150-52. In the quotation, the reading "Silves" is conjectural, except for the initial "S."

[50] *Monumenta henricina*, II, 361; VI, 335; VIII, 43; IX, 235.

[51] For a description of this map, see H. Kraus, Catalogue no. 55 (New York, 1955), pp. 62-6.

[52] Kimble, "The Laurentian World Map" (cited n. 33), 33.

[53] E. G. R. Taylor, *The Haven-Finding Art* (London, 1956), pp. 117-21.

[54] P. Adam, "Navigation primitive et navigation astronomique," *VI* ᵉ *Colloque International d' Histoire Maritime* (Paris, 1966), pp. 91-110 (with discussion); C. Verlinden, "La découverte des archipels" (cited n. 5 above), 129-30.

[55] S. E. Morison, *The European Discovery of America: the Northern Voyages* (New York, 1971), p. 82.

[56] S. E. Morison, *Portuguese Voyages to America in the Fifteenth Century* (Harvard, 1940), p. 12.

[57] For a good reproduction of the relevant section of the Grazioso Benincasa map of 1467, see M. Mollat du Jourdin, C. M. de La Roncière et al., *Sea Charts of the Early Explorers* (London, 1984), plates 18-19, and of that of Bertran of 1482, Kamal, V, no. 1503. Cortesão, *História*, II, 184-96, provides a useful critical list of the Benincasa maps.

[58] Verlinden, "La découverte," 129; the evidence, though not the argument, of G. Coutinho, *A náutica dos descobrimentos*, 2 vols. (Lisbon, 1951), I, 165-95, suggests this, too. See the wind maps in Cortesão, "Carta," pp. 166-69.

Chapter III

European Participation in The Portuguese Discovery Era

Portuguese expansion was obviously European in itself, but but it is perhaps not generally recognized how many adventurers, cartographers and technicians of other European nations took part in it. The first foreigners to do so were the Italians, in fact as far back as the reign of King Dinis (r. 1279-1325), who opened Portugal to the world by creating on one hand the university and on the other, the fleet. On the first of February 1317 this enlightened monarch negotiated a contract with the great Genoese merchant, Manuele Pessagno.[1] He awarded to him the royal lands of Pedreira in Lisbon, together with an annual grant of 3,000 livres in exchange for his services as commander of the royal galleys – ones which the Genoese had brought with him to Portugal.

Pessagno – called Peçanha in Portugal – thus became a vassal to the king. His heirs were likewise to do homage to the Portuguese king and become his vassals. Until that time, Pessagno had been engaged in the sea trade with England and with Flanders; this is why his galleys had been engaged in Portuguese waters, often in association with another family of important Genoese merchants, the Marocello or Malocello. The contract of 1317 stipulates that Pessagno should always maintain at the disposition of the sovereign "Viinte homeens de Genua, sabedores de mar, taaes que seiam convenhaviis pera alcaydes de galees e pera arrayzes" – meaning that twenty Genoese officers should be ready to do service as captains and pilots of Portuguese ships whose crews were evidently to be Portuguese. These vessels were not only to be galleys, but also *navios*, that is, round ships such as cogs, better suited to navigation on the high seas.

All vessels with Portuguese officers were to be subject to the admiral, even corsairs.

The privileges granted to Pessagno and his heirs were confirmed by the king, D. Afonso IV in 1327. In 1340, Manuele Pessagno was still admiral and constructed ships for the crown. In 1342, his son, Carlo, succeeded him; then the office passed to Bartolomeo and thence to Lanzarote Pessagno. The line in fact was unbroken until the time of the Infante D. Henrique – Henry the Navigator – and always with the obligation to furnish Genoese officers. Among these was a member of the above mentioned Malocello family, who distinguished himself by discovering a part of the Canaries for Portugal prior to 1339, the date of the map by Angelino Dulcert, which informs us of the fact. Later, this Lanzarotto Malocello, as he was called, also occupied on Portugal's behalf the Canarian island called Lanzarote. (It was, of course, named for him.) This occurred in 1370, as a document of King D. Fernando informs us, dated 29 June of that year. In 1376, Lanzarotto was driven from the island by "the indigenes and others," the latter being the Castilians, who, as is well known, eventually became masters of the whole archipelago. Then in 1385, a patent of 8 November, issued by D. João I, of Aviz, founder of the new dynasty who was to preside over the beginnings of Portuguese expansion, informs us that Lanzarotto had recently been killed in attempting to reconquer his island[2], which he had apparently succeeded in (re)possessing for a time as a Portuguese vassal.

Thus it was that one of the Genoese officers of the Pessagno family gave to Portugal its first, though ephemeral, colony after having discovered it some thirty years earlier. Another, Nicoloso da Recco, provided in 1341 the first, and decidedly imperfect, description of the Canarian archipelago.[3]

In 1351 the Madeira archipelago appeared in the Medicean Atlas of the Laurentian Library in Florence. The discovery was made through the use of ships quite different from the galleys of the Mediterranean. Nicoloso da Recco had already possessed in 1341 two ships and a *"navicula minuta."* These vessels and others, close to the caravel which sailed the Atlantic in the next century, could return from the Canaries more quickly than before by setting their courses more to the west, in open ocean, where they could utilize the westerly trade winds – something which would lead almost automatically to discovery first of the Madeiras and then of the Azores. The Azores appeared in part – and under names different from the ones they bear today – in the *mappamundi* of Abraham Cresques of 1375. All the nomenclature of this archipelago is Italian on this Majorcan map, with certain typically Genoese distortions. Their discovery, then, was in all probability effected by fleets under the command of Genoese officers. For, until 1375, Lanzarote Pessagno was the Portuguese admiral, though in other respects lusitanized, must always have held the royal command of the Genoese officers, the *"sabedores de mar"*–the expert seamen. Italian nomenclature persists in Catalan and Majorcan maps from the end of the XIV century. On the Venetian map of Nicolo de Pasqualin from 1408, Madeira is no longer called "Legname" in Italian, but "Madeira" in Portuguese. This merely underscores Luso-Genoese collaboration to which I have already alluded many times. The official Portuguese act of possession dates from 1425, by João Gonçalves Zarco and Tristão Vaz Teixeira, gentlemen in the entourage of Prince Henry the Navigator. In the Azores, the taking of possession is later, for it was only in 1439, on the second of July that Prince Henry received from the young monarch, D. Afonso V, the authorization to populate it, that is, to colonize the archipelago. The discovery, or rather, the reconnaissance, then, was prior, not only for the Madeiras, but for the Azores, and is thanks to Genoese participation in the Portuguese discoveries.

After Portugal began its great, definitive expansion in the XV century, Italians continued to serve it, but under quite different conditions and in more subordinate roles. Antoniotto Uso di Mare, Alvise da Ca da Mosto, Bartolomeo Perestrello and Antonio da Noli, among others, make their appearances as commercial or administrative collaborators and no longer as initiators of navigations on the high seas and as fleet commanders. The Portuguese navy had arrived at maturity – as an autonomous force able to control the South Atlantic and the Indian Oceans for two centuries, to discover and to dominate worlds.

The Genoese Antoniotto Uso di Mare, or Usodimare, born in 1416, served Prince Henry in 1455-1456 and then became an agent of the Florentine firm of the Marchionni at Caffa in the Crimea in 1458. He died prior to 1462.[4] To believe his letter preserved in the library of the University of Genoa and addressed to his brothers on 12 December 1455, he sailed as far as the Gambia River on his own initiative. He had purchased some black slaves, some elephant tusks, some parrots and some civet cats and had sold the merchandise which he had brought back in a caravel. He does not reveal how he had acquired this ship; but given that exactly in the beginning of 1455, Prince Henry's monopoly on navigation in Guinea was confirmed by Pope Nicholas V, it is certain enough that Usodimare did not risk seeing his ship confiscated. He thus made his voyage on license of

Prince Henry and on a Portuguese vessel. Besides this, it is perfectly clear from his letter that this was the case for his second voyage, also treated in the letter. On top of this, he was then entrusted by the Portuguese king with an official mission, for he was to bring home to Africa the servant of a petty native king whom he had taken on board during his first voyage, doubtlessly on Portuguese instructions.

At the age of 22 years in 1454, after having made several voyages in the Mediterranean and after having been in Flanders, the Venetian, Alvise Ca da Mosto, or Cadamosto, wished to return to this land in the north of Europe "in order to earn some money." He thus embarked in the regular fleet of the Flanders Galleys on 8 August 1454, and "stopping at our customary ports of call," he arrived in Portugal, where contrary winds held the fleet back at Cape St. Vincent, close to the place where Prince Henry was often in residence. The Prince thereupon sent a secretary on a visit to the galleys, accompanied by one Patrizio di Conti, the Venetian consul, but at the same time an adviser to the Prince on commercial matters. These envoys bore samples of colonial products, notably the sugar of Madeira, of dragon's blood and of other products unspecified by the Venetian. It amounted to a veritable propaganda for recruitment, for the envoys of the Prince emphasized the benefits to be won and the conditions set forth by the Prince. Two possibilities were offered: either the merchant would outfit the caravel and furnish its cargo, or else the prince would outfit it and the merchant would undertake to provide the cargo. In any case, the ship would be a Portuguese one. Cadamosto purchased from the galleys merchandise suitable for Africa, while on his part Prince Henry agreed to equip a new caravel owned by one Vicente Dias of Lagos in the Algarve. Dias was one of the proprietors of ships destined for Guinea. At the Senegal River, Cadamosto came across Usodimare in a caravel belonging to another expedition; its cargo was his, but it was manned by squires of the Prince. This was Usodimare's first voyage; his second was in the company of Cadamosto, at least in part, namely at its departure from Lagos in the beginning of May, 1456.[5]

In the account of his second voyage, Cadamosto tells us of a sudden tempest which took him by surprise a little beyond Cape Blanco. He had then taken leave of the coast, and after three days and two nights, he had discovered two unknown islands. From one of these three others could be seen: they were parts of the Cape Verde archipelago. The ones sighted by Cadamosto were Santiago, Maio, Boa Vista and Sal, which are closest to the continent. This can be deduced by comparison of his account with the royal patents of 3 December 1460 and of 19 September 1462.[6] This latter one also reveals the part which the Genoese Antonio da Noli played in the discoveries. Noli employed his own vessels, a *barinel* and two *navios*, both types of round ships. This Genoese took possession of five islands of the group in the name of Prince Henry, in fact one more than those sighted by Cadamosto. Moreover, a document of 26 October 1462 shows that the discovery of seven other islands of the same archipelago was the work of Diogo.. Afonso, squire of D. Fernando, the adoptive son and successor of Prince Henry as lord of the islands.[7]

The discovery of the Cape Verde Islands is thus a striking example of Luso-Italian collaboration. Diogo Gomes, who claimed to have been sole discoverer of the islands, only visited them in 1463, as is shown by careful analysis of the manuscript by Valentim Fernandes, where the account of his voyage appears.[8] In 1462 Antonio da Noli became captain-donatary of Santiago and played an important role in the colonization of the archipelago until his death in 1496 or 1497.[9] Even earlier, a lusitanized Italian, Bartolomeo Perestrello, played an analogous role at Porto Santo in the Madeiras. He was captain-donatary there between 1446 and 1457 and his daughter, Filippa, married Christopher Columbus in 1479.[10]

The Flemings

In the Azores, it was the Flemish who participated in the Portuguese development. Colonization of the Azores began after Prince Henry received the proprietorship in 1439. In the beginning, it was the eastern part, the one closest to Europe, which received the greatest Portuguese attention. More towards the west, the first Fleming appeared on the island first named for Jesus Christ, but now called Terceira. On 2 March 1450, Jacome, or Jacques, de Bruges was named as its captain-donatary.[11] He had by then settled down in Portugal and had married there, but he had persuaded several companions from Flanders to join him. With these and with some Portuguese who joined them, he was responsible for the early development of the island until around 1474, the year in which his succession was decided upon.[12] He died at sea, as must have been the case with Ferdinand van Olmen (in Portuguese, Fernão d'Ulmo), the most famous of his successors. By then, the captaincy had been divided up and Van Olmen became captain of the part designated Quatro Ribeyras, of which a district is still called "Framengos."

In order to know more of Ferdinand van Olmen, it is necessary to analyze a document dated 24 July 1486, in which D. João II of

Portugal confirms a contract made on 12 June of the same year between the Fleming, and João Affonso do Estreito, rich sugar planter of Madeira, well-known through documentation concerning that island.[13] After some thirty years there, the Portuguese undertook a series of voyages in the open Atlantic to the west of the Azores archipelago. After 1475, there was considerable speculation over the island of the Seven Cities, which the document authorizes Van Olmen to search for. In the document, it is mentioned that Van Olmen had proposed to go in search of a large island, or islands, or else the coast of a continent. The Antilles and America were already being visualized in the mind of the Portuguese sovereign. This great monarch (r. 1481-1495) saw far in advance of all his predecessors. In 1487, he ordered exploration of the three routes which then seemed possible to reach India, that to the west, which Columbus had suggested, that to the southeast along the African coast, which the expert Portuguese navigator, Diogo Cão, undertook, and that by way of Egypt and the Red Sea, where he sent Pero da Covilhã. Covilhã reached Calicut in India ten years before Vasco da Gama, but on Arab vessels and over traditional routes of the Moslem navigators of the Indian Ocean.[14] The king, however, wished to develop a Portuguese route. To this end, there remained that around the coasts of Africa or that to the west, which Columbus envisioned. Of these, search for the first led Bartolomeu Dias around the Cape of Good Hope and into the Indian Ocean – which Vasco da Gama finally crossed a bit later. Ferdinand van Olmen was sent towards the west, for in the meantime, Columbus had passed into Spanish service. The voyage of the Fleming took place in 1487, but as we know from Las Casas,[15] he died at sea. If things had not developed in this way, it would have been he, in Portuguese service, and not Columbus, in that of Spain, who would have discovered America.

Some years before this, Prince D. Fernando, the heir of Prince Henry the Navigator, had called upon other Flemings to colonize the islands of the Azores group situated more to the west. The first of these Flemings was Joost de Hurtere, a nobleman from the present-day West Flanders. In 1468, on 21 February, when Jacques de Bruges was still captain of Terceira, De Hurtere was named captain-donatary of the island of Fayal by D. Fernando.[16] He had first arrived, accompanied by a little group of Flemish who initially caused him a great deal of trouble. Then he was named captain when he returned to Lisbon in search of some Portuguese as reinforcements. He married one Brites de Macedo, lady of honor at the court of the Prince, and this paved the way for his lusitanization and that of his descendants. Then, on

28 March 1481, Joost de Hurtere also became captain of the island of Pico.[17] Meanwhile, still other Flemings were arriving in the Azores, but these could never have been very numerous, if because we know from Valentim Fernandes that by the very first years of the XVI century, the Flemish language was already "lost"– even in Fayal, which was still being called the "*ilha dos framengos*", "the Flemish island." The number of well-to-do colonists who claimed to have been of Flemish origin could only increase in time, especially since doing so was a means whereby they could advertise their noble origin like the descendants of De Hurtere. Joost died in 1495; his son succeeded him and lived until 1549. His son, Manuel de Hutra Cortereal was named captain in 1550 by D. João III. The De Hurtere family was thereafter completely lusitanized.

Willem van der Haegen, in Portuguese Guilherme da Silveira, was for some time captain of the island of Flores and settled at São Jorge, but the chronology is extremely vague. We only know that he arrived in the Azores in two *urcas* from Flanders, round ships which surely brought with them other Flemish companions.[18]

The Italians again

In the XVI century, we return to the Italians. By that period almost all of them were associated with the great merchant houses so well known in the international economy of the time. Thus the Florentine, Bartolomeo Marchioni, was a partner of the original concessionaire, Fernão de Noronha, in the outfitting of the *Bretoa*, which was sent in 1511 to Brazil in a search for dyewood. He was also interested in the Rio dos Escravos trade in Africa between 1486 and 1495. In the Cabral expedition which touched in Brazil on the way to India, he was associated with the brother of the Duke of Bragança and with still another important Italian businessman and adventurer, Girolamo Sernigi. The ship they outfitted brought home a load of pepper and other spices. He was thus occupied until 1518. Sernigi visited India in 1514, together with his brother and two nephews. In 1510, he even commanded a ship in the fleet of Diogo Mendes de Vasconcellos which went to Malacca. All of this activity, of course, involved big business of the time, but had little in common with the discoveries and administration of the XIV and XV centuries in which Italians were involved. The Affaitati of Cremona and a number of others did much the same and realized large profits. These men, together with their factors, or business agents, who traveled to India with the Portuguese were greatly esteemed by Afonso de Albuquerque, who was both capitalist and conqueror. Still another Italian, Francesco Corbinelli was to die in India, seemingly in 1526. He had first served as merchant and as ship's captain, but finally became royal factor at Goa. A Florentine, in many ways he was a throwback to an earlier age in that like his countrymen of two centuries before, he was charged with an important official function.

The list is hardly exhausted by the above mentioned. For instance, Giovanni da Empoli was another Italian who participated in the establishment of Portuguese power in India; he provided the subject for a whole book by the Florentine historian, Marco Spallanzani.[19] He made three voyages to the Orient, in 1503-1504, in 1510-1514 and 1515-1517. The first of these voyages brought him to the Malabar Coast, the second to Malacca and the third to Canton in China, where he died. In the first and second of these voyages, Girolamo Sernigi played an important financial role. Then one Leonardo Nardi became the factor of the great merchant banker, Bartolomeo Marchioni. The collaborator of Marchioni in Lisbon, he departed for India in 1501 in the fleet of João da Nova. He was then factor for Marchioni, but not of the Portuguese king, as was Corbinelli. The captains of Italian ships in the Portuguese fleets bound for India were numerous enough; one could mention besides Sernigi and Corbinelli, Giovanni Buonagrazia, who participated in the second voyage of Vasco da Gama in 1502. Many of these men have left letters which augment surviving Portuguese documentation, such as those of Mateo da Bergamo, the factor of Gian Francesco Affaitati.

All the Italians mentioned until now have been Florentines with the exception of the Affaitati of Cremona. But a special place should be reserved for Lodovico de Varthema, of Bologna. He travelled from Italy in 1500 via the Red Sea route and returned with the Portuguese fleets in 1508 after having been created *cavaleiro* by D. Manuel I for his services rendered during the Portuguese campaigns in India. He published his *Itinerario* in 1510. The India Varthema knew was that of the late Middle Ages, prior to the changes about to be introduced by the Portuguese predominance – established during precisely the armed conflicts in which he took part. Together with the Portuguese, Duarte Barbosa and Tomé Pires, he is our best source on the commerce of the Indian Ocean up to that moment. He had even penetrated to the Moluccas before the Portuguese arrived there. He had also traded independently in Burma, where he sold textiles and coral. Throughout he describes the local products with precision, including spices and fruits. He passed by Malacca and Sumatra with a Persian merchant, and he seems indeed to have been to Ternate five years before the

Portuguese arrived there in 1512. From Java he returned to Calicut, but then passed to Cananore, where he entered Portuguese service. He was named factor at Cochin, where he remained a year-and-a-half before returning to Europe in a Portuguese fleet, sailing via Pemba, the Comoro Islands, the Madagascar channel and the Cape. His *Itinerario* of 1510 largely precedes Tomé Pires, whose *Suma Oriental*, written at Malacca between 1513 and 1515 did not reach Portugal until almost a decade later. Duarte Barbosa only finished his book in 1517.[20]

As to South Germans who were involved in India, there figured most significantly the Hirschvogels of Nuremberg. Their agent, Lazarus Nünberger, resided there after 1515, and he seems to have been preceded there by Ulrich Imhof, in the firm's service since 1505.[21] These seem to have been interested primarily in precious stones. The factor, Georg Pock, worked for them for nearly nine years in India before his death there in 1529. His letters illustrate graphically the political and economic difficulties experienced there by the Portuguese.[22] Towards the end of his stay, the era of the discoveries had nearly passed. It should be remarked that no German occupied such official functions in the fleet or in the administration as did the Italians and the Flemings.

From this brief survey, it can be observed that Portuguese expansion did not take place in a vacuum; while the Portuguese themselves were at all times fully in control of the process, they were significantly aided by other Europeans, both as individuals and as groups.

Charles Verlinden

Notes

[1] João Martins da Silva Marques, ed.& comp., *Descobrimentos Portugueses; Documentos para a sua história, publicados e prefaciados por João Martins da Silva Marques*, 3 vols. in 5 (Lisbon: Instituto da Alta Cultura, 1944-1971), I, 28.

[2] Silva Marques, *Descobrimentos*, 186.

[3] Silva Marques, *Descobrimentos*, 76.

[4] R. Caddeo, *Le navigazioni atlantiche di Alvise da Cá da Mosto, Antoniotto Uso di Mare e Nicoloso da Recco* (Milan, 1928), 68.

[5] Caddeo, *Le navigazioni*, 260.

⁶ José Ramos Coelho, ed., *Alguns documentos do Arquivo Nacional da Torre do Tombo acerca das navegações e conquistas portuguesas* (Lisbon, 1892), 27, 31.

⁷ Coelho, ed., *Alguns documentos*, 32.

⁸ António Baião, ed., "O manuscrito de Valentim Fernandes," (Lisbon: Academia Portuguesa de História, 1940), especially 120.

⁹ Charles Verlinden, "Antonio da Noli e a colonização das ilhas de Cabo Verde," in *Revista da Faculdade de Letras de Lisboa*, III série, no. 7 (1963), 28-45.

¹⁰ Prospero Peragallo, *I Pallastreli di Piacenza in Portogallo e la moglie de Cristoforo Colombo* (Genoa, 1898).

¹¹ Silva Marques, *Descobrimentos*, 470.

¹² *Annales da Ilha Terceira*, I, 493 and *Archivo dos Açores*, IV, 159.

¹³ Ramos Coelho, *Alguns documentos*, 58.

¹⁴ Conde de Ficalho, *A viagem de Pedro da Covilhã* (Lisbon, 1898).

¹⁵ Bartolomé de las Casas, *Historia de Indias*, Augustín Millares Carlo, ed., 2 vols. (Mexico City: Fondo Economico de Cultura, 1951), 69.

¹⁶ A. Ferreira de Serpa, *Os framengos na ilha do Faial. A família Utra (Hurtere)* (Lisbon, 1929), 31.

¹⁷ Serpa, *Os framengos*, 133.

¹⁸ J. Cunha da Silveira, "Willem van der Haegen, tronco dos Silveiras dos Açores," *Revista Insulana* (1949). Via royal patent of D. Sebastião, 1578.

¹⁹ Marco Spallanzani, *Giovanni da Empoli, mercante e navigatore fiorentino* (Florence: S. P. E. S., 1984).

²⁰ Charles Verlinden, "Lodovico de Varthema dans l'Ocean Indien," in *Atti del IV Convegno Internazionale di Studi Colombiani*, 2 vols. (Genoa: Istituto di Studi Colombiani, 1987), II, 425 ff.

²¹ C. von Imhoff, "Nürnberger Indienpioniere. Reiseberichte von der ersten oberdeutschen Handelsfahrt nach Indien," in *Pirckheimer Jahrbuch* (Nürnberg, 1987), 11 ff.

²² Hedwig Kömmerling-Fitzler, "Der Nürnberger Kaufmann Georg Pock in Portuguiesisch Indien und in Edelsteinland Vijayanagar," in *Mitteilungen des Vereins für Geschichte der Stadt Nürnberg* (Nuremberg, 1968), 137 ff.

Chapter IV

T he maritime expansion of Portugal was no sudden miracle that began with a wave of the wand of Henry the Navigator, born 1394, died 1460. Henry, who navigated so little, has been as often as not the subject of pseudo-scientific hagiography. The now-usual label "Navigator," seems to date only from 1868 when the English writer R. H. Major published his *Life of Prince Henry Surnamed the Navigator,* which was a remarkable and persistent best-seller because of its romantic interpretation of the *Cronica dos feitos notaveis que se passaram na conquista de Guiné por mandado do Infante D. Henrique.* This in turn was written by Gomes Eanes de Zurara during the lifetime of the prince with all the flattery that a courtier, who is at the same time a chronicler, is prone to manifest towards a prince who protects him. From Major this romantic biographical material passed to Raymond Beazley's *Prince Henry the Navigator,* which appeared in 1890 with the same appellation made popular more than 20 years earlier in Major's title and with the same use and interpretation of Zurara, who – surprisingly enough – never uses the now famous surname in his flattering *Cronica.* For Beazley, too, Henry was a saintly character who spent all his days in work and often passed the night without sleep building up his wonderful knowledge. I paraphrase Beazley who quotes almost literally from Zurara.

This was in 1890. Our subject requires that we should try to find out in which perspective Henry appears at the end of the 20th century as a result of protracted and still more penetrating investigation.

Prince Henry in Modern Perspective

En route to success

Born 4 March 1394 in Porto, D. Henrique, the third son of the founder of the new dynasty of Aviz, D. João I, actually became a prince of some importance when his father in 1408 asked the Cortes, or estates, to grant him five *contos* a year to keep up his household. The eldest of the three brothers, Duarte, the future king, received eight *contos*, while Pedro, the future regent, was given five as was Henry. This allowed the princes to maintain their royal status, *"as suas honras e estados."* With what was added to buy "lands and properties," Henry disposed by the age of 14 of 10 *contos* a year.[1] At 17 he had concentrated his possessions around Viseu, Lamego and Guarda in the Beira.[2] When he was 20 he gave great feasts at Viseu, demonstrating his passion for luxury and showing off, about which Zurara, in his *Cronica de Ceuta*, said it was "such that his entourage appeared to some foreigners as the court of the king himself." That he intended to play a role that placed him at the same height as his brothers was from now evident. He already knew how to promote his image.

At the assault of Ceuta in Morocco, just opposite Gibraltar, in 1415 he behaved as a knight – indeed he was dubbed there by his father – but he held no important command. This did not prevent him from obtaining in 1416 the title of duke of Viseu, a town he already possessed.[3] He was twenty-two.

In 1420 he became *"regedor e governador do Mestrado da Ordem de Cristo,"* regent and governador of the Order of Christ. This gave him means that he would use as we shall see. He now controlled Tomar, the capital city of the order, which he called *"minha vila,"* showing how much he considered as his own the possessions of the Order of Christ. He organized the fairs that were held there and let houses and shops to merchants. Seeing how much this yielded he did the same at his ducal town of Viseu and later at two other places of his estates in Beira, namely Pombal and Tarouca. He followed this policy with remarkable continuity, which shows that he saw far when his economic advantages were concerned. He was really a successful economic entrepreneur.

In 1421, he acquired rights on a fishery in the Tagus River and – even better – in 1433 the monopoly of tuna fishing along the coast of the Algarve, which allowed him either to operate with his own ships or to license others to do so. Later when the Atlantic coast of north-western Africa was visited by his ships, he instructed his crews to hunt seals, since their oil could be utilized in his soap-works, of which he enjoyed the monopoly not only in Portugal itself but in his island of Madeira. Coral, too, interested him and he acquired its monopoly in

1450 after termination of the contract of the Italian Bartolomeo Florentin and the Frenchman Jean Forbin of Marseilles. The saintly knight of the chronicle appears here as a successful capitalist and, like a capitalist of his and other times, he invested what came from business in real estate and in new industrial activities as dyeing and producing textiles at Batalha and Lagos.[4]

A hand in oversea development

Zurara in his *Cronica dos feitos notaveis que se passaram na conquista de Guiné*, slants the biography of Henry as if the exploration of the northern parts of the Atlantic coast of Africa were by far the most spectacular aspect of the activity of the Infante, but it was worthwhile briefly to examine whether the achievements by the Infante in the islands on the one hand and along the African coast on the other justify what traditional historiography represents when under the influence of the magnificently written chronicle of Henry's panegyrist.

The Madeiras and the Azores had already been reconnoitered in the XIVth century, but their actual possession and the beginning of their colonization were the accomplishments of Prince Henry.

The uninhabited archipelago of the Madeiras was occupied in 1425 by the Portuguese João Gonçalves Zarco and Tristão Vaz Teixeira, two noblemen of the retinue of the prince. As a consequence, King D. Duarte gave the island in fee to Henry. He did so immediately after his accession to the throne by a royal deed of 26 September 1433. The real colonization and settlement could now start. A document of the same date for the Order of Christ says that the settlement was "*novamente,*" i.e. newly, undertaken, which shows that it is really the prince who made it possible and that the first occupation of 1425 was of little consequence. He now used his own financial and economic means for that purpose, as well as those of the Order of Christ. The infante had realized that more naval and human resources were needed than merely two noblemen with their crews, as in 1425.

On 8 May 1440 Tristão, "*cavaleiro da minha casa,*" was granted part of Madeira through a deed of the Infante as lord of the islands. Tristão Vaz Teixeira was the same man as one of those who took possession in 1425. He had now to administer his hereditary fief "*em justiça e em direito,*" "in justice and law." He received the monopoly of the grain mills, as feudal lords generally enjoyed, and this shows, by the way, that the population had already increased. Estates were granted to newcomers who were obliged to till their land and make it productive within five years, which presupposed first the heavy work of deforestation, and afterwards the introduction of new plants, among which sugarcane became rapidly the most important. There was obviously a flow of people that came in the ships of the Infante, lord of the island. Livestock also had to be imported and, as deforestation made headway, more of it was needed. It had, after a while, to be fenced or tied in order that the new fields should not be damaged, which shows both the development of agriculture and of population. All this implies active navigation for the ships of the Infante, all the more so that meanwhile the second largest island of the archipelago, namely Porto Santo, had been granted in 1446 to Bartolomeo Perestrello, a second generation Italian immigrant, who was already "*cavaleiro da casa*" of the prince and was granted by him the whole island, "*minha ilha*," as he says in the document of appointment. We know through the Venetian Ca da Mosto or Cadamosto, that in 1455, some nine years later, Porto Santo was highly productive and that the population enjoyed an excellent living standard since the island had much grain and was "*abbondante di carne di bovi*." The oxen and cows were of course imported by sea and in 1458 we learn that there were herds of them, another proof of intense navigation by agents of the prince.

The beginning of the production of sugar of Madeira was equally an achievement of D. Henrique. In 1452 he concluded an agreement with his *escudeiro* Diogo de Teive, who is granted the right to have a machine (*engenho*) constructed to produce sugar. This is the beginning of an industry that would make Madeira, for a series of decades, the greatest producer of sugar in the world. The agreement says that one third of the production must be delivered to the Infante who completed the outfitting by supplying a sugar press. This was a real business association and all the details of the production were regulated in the deed of agreement. Other producers of sugar were soon to arrive, among them foreigners, as for example, the German nobleman who was allowed by the prince to come with eight compatriots and was granted permission in 1457 to plant vines and canes.

To the Madeiras the Azores were soon added. On July 2, 1439, Henry was permitted by the regent of King D. Afonso V, then seven years old, to populate and colonize seven islands of this second Portuguese archipelago. A short time before, the Infante had sent ships with livestock in order to supply the colonists that he would send to the uninhabited islands. Also the regent D. Pedro, Henrique's elder brother, had interests in the Azores, but his death at the battle of Alfarrobeira in 1449, left the whole archipelago to D. Henrique. This too, of course, implied intense activity by the ships of the Infante. In this sense he deserves the label of navigator, even though he had others to do the navigating for him.

The same happened along the Atlantic coast of north-west Africa, but with many fewer ships and men than in the navigation to the islands, of which he dreamed for a while to create a kingdom for himself, as shown for instance in a document of 1450 in which he speaks of "*minha* real *autoridade como senhor das ilhas.* (My *royal* authority as lord of the islands.)"[5]

African interests

The African coast is what Zurara's chronicle concentrates upon, and there he shows Henrique not as an economic entrepreneur, but as an heroic knight who conquered Guinea. Of the 97 chapters of his *Chronicle* only seven treat, and then very superficially, the islands. The others describe with infinite detail the individual voyages of men of the Navigator along the coast, and even more the capture of Moorish and Negro slaves, who amounted to 927 between 1441 and 1448, as stated in the last chapter but one.

The outlines are nearly as follows. In 1434 Gil Eanes went beyond the insignificant Cape of Bojador, where Portuguese navigation along the African coast had stopped up to then, although we know that some Genoese and some Catalans had been further considerably earlier. In 1435 another ship of the prince went 200 miles more to the south. Each time there was only one ship and not even a caravel: the first time a *barca*, the second a *barinel*, both smaller than the caravel. In 1436 the desert-belt was passed and Cape Blanco, another 200 miles southward, was reached. Then, until 1441 there were no other voyages, but that year Antão Gonçalves and Nuno Tristão went to Rio de Oro, where they captured a few Moorish villagers who were thereupon enslaved. This episode and a series of others of the same kind are presented by Zurara in his most brilliant, heroic and chivalrous style. What he calls the conquest of Guinea is made up of a series of similar stories. In 1448 the bay of Arguim was reached and a fort was built on a small island which became a base for the slave trade. A year later began the Portuguese civil war between the followers of the regent D. Pedro and part of the nobility ranged around the bastard line of Bragança. The result was the death of D. Pedro at Alfarrobeira and the triumph of the Braganças. These now dominated the young king Afonso V who at 15 had become of age. In this conflict D. Henrique had not supported his brother, but nevertheless he was more or less suspect to the victorious party. The king therefore suggested that Zurara, who was the official chronicler, should write the biography of the prince and we know that he did so in a manner as to show Henry as a young hero of the struggle against heathens and Moslems in Africa, a hero who was dreaming chivalrous, and not ambitious, political dreams. Zurara successfully achieved this purpose, and the image of Henry that he drew with such accomplished literary talent obviously impressed most of his contemporaries, exactly as it has impressed so many ill-documented historians in later days.

Surprisingly enough, although he outlived the Infante, Zurara did not bring his biography up to his hero's death in 1460. That year, Pedro de Sintra had reached present-day Sierra Leone and Liberia, but it was too late for Henry to hear of this.[6] He had remained interested in Africa's coast, for it had allowed slave-trade and had produced still more trading advantages, sometimes even gold-dust. But even so, the prospecting had involved only one or two ships at a time. This, together with the preceding long interruptions, as from 1436 to 1441 and from 1447 to 1455, proves that the great majority of the crews and ships of the prince were bound for the Madeiras and the Azores, where Portuguese colonization was progressing so well under his direction. The real image is exactly opposite to what Zurara makes his readers think.

Concerning the African coast, a problem is raised by the famous bull of Pope Nicolas V dated January 8, 1455. The last sentences of this bull show clearly its real purpose, namely the papal confirmation of the monopoly of granting licences for navigation to the islands and to the African coast that Henry had secured in 1443 from the then 11-year-old king D. Afonso V. During the years preceding 1455, non-Portuguese vessels, mostly Spanish, had been appearing in African waters.[7] These were now to be repelled not only by Portuguese force, but by papal excommunication against intruders as well. The long and rhetorical *arenga* or introduction of the bull was obviously inspired by the envoys of Henry and stated that, over a period of 25 years, a Portuguese army had conquered Africa as far as Guinea. But there had been no such army in evidence any further south than Ceuta and northern Morocco: There is also a mention of the "southern shores" and even of the "*polum antarticum*" and of the Indians (*Indos*) who are Christians. That was enough for the Portuguese historian, or more exactly essayist, Joaquim Bensaúde to write in 1942 a very superficial, excited and chauvinist book *A cruzada do Infante D. Henrique*, where he sees Henry as a crusader against the Turks through an alliance with the supposedly Christian people of India. This was of course as silly as if one were to insinuate that Henry intended to explore the Antarctic because of the phrase "*polum antarticum*" in the *arenga* of the bull. We have seen that in Henry's lifetime the Gulf of Guinea was not properly reached, so that it was impossible by then to imagine the real southward extent of Africa. Nevertheless some people persist in seeing Henry as thinking of circumnavigation and crusades although even Zurara's panegyric scarcely goes that far.

In conclusion, we can discern what has been the real significance of Henry in the history of Portuguese navigation and expansion.

Henry was not the romantic knight and hero that appears in Zurara's chronicle. He was a realistic entrepreneur, though one who nevertheless did not forget that he was a royal prince surrounded by noblemen, and who respected knights far more than he did successful merchants. He therefore certainly enjoyed the manner in which Zurara had painted his portrait. But he utilized the noblemen of his own retinue in his island-world of the Atlantic and along the African coast, whence came slaves, seal-oil and possibly gold-dust. Most of his endeavour was towards the islands: the Madeiras, the Azores and even the Canaries, where he was outstripped by the Castilians. Before his time, Portuguese navigation was coastal even towards northwestern Europe, i.e. England and Flanders. Only the men of the Peçanhas, the Genoese admirals of Portugal, reconnoitered the archipelagoes in the XIVth century, which later would so greatly interest the Infante. What really was the most important aspect of his achievement was that, as a consequence of this enterprise in the archipelagoes, the Portuguese became used to sailing the high Atlantic. Following the African coast *per se* was not at that time the real problem. In that regard the great difficulties would start only after his time and mainly under the great king D. João II (1481-1495), who would make possible for his country the rounding of the Cape of Good Hope, the finding of the sea route to India and even the later possession of Brazil. He was the man who laid the foundation of what has been called the Portuguese Empire. What Henry had done was to initiate ocean-going navigation, although he himself never crossed more than the Strait of Gibraltar. He had also undertaken Portuguese colonization on the islands. Uncritical and ill-documented historians have therefore credited him with what came after him, as if he had consciously foreseen and prepared it, but such feedbacks belong to the realm of imagination, not of scientific historical investigation.

Charles Verlinden

Notes

¹ A. J. Dias Dinis, *Estudos Henriquinos*, (Coimbra, Comemoração do V Centenário da Morte do Infante D. Henrique, 1960), I, document of 7 April 1408, no. 9, 381-84.

² Dinis, *Estudos Henriquinos*, I, royal document of 27 April 1411, no. 11, 386-90.

³ Dinis, *Estudos Henriquinos, I*, no. 12, 392-93.

⁴ For all this see the very accurate study in Dinis, *Estudos Henriquinos, I*, no. 12, 11-107.

⁵About Henry's activity in the islands see Charles Verlinden, "Formes féodales et domaniles de la colonisation portuguaise spécialment sous Henri le Navigateur" (*Revista Portuguesa de História*, IX, 1960): 1-44. See also C. Verlinden, "Henri le Navigateur songea-t-il 'a créer un 'Etat' insulaire?" (*Revista Portuguesa de História*, XII, 1969): 281-92.

⁶ Dinis, *Estudos Henriquinos, I*, no. 12, 317-69.

⁷ J. W. Blake, *Europeans in West Africa (1450-1560)* 2 vols. (London, 1942).

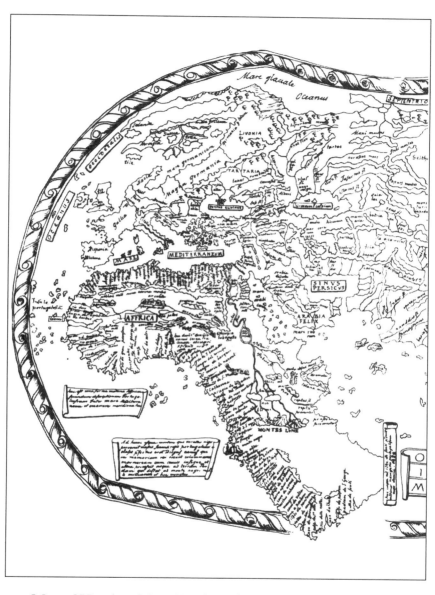

Map of Henricus Martellus (1489), first to reflect the voyages of Cāo and Dias

Africa and the Atlantic Islands

Chapter V

The Work
of
D. João II

The fourteen-year reign of D.João II set events in motion which determined the course of Portuguese history for almost five centuries. His father, D. Afonso V, was uninterested in the African initiatives of their uncle, the Infante D. Henriques, alias Prince Henry the Navigator, and had farmed the Guinea trade and new explorations out to the businessman, Fernão Gomes. But in 1474, seven years before D. João's own reign had begun, he asked and obtained the African proprietorship from his father. Then, after only one additional year of the Gomes concession, he stepped in to manage the Guinea trade personally.

Had this not occurred, Portuguese and European expansion as a whole might have taken a far different course. Certainly, Gomes would soon have received unwanted company in Guinea, in the form of foreign interlopers, and he would not have had the strength to repel them. Columbus may never have found a patron for his enterprise because Queen Isabella's espousal of his project no doubt proceeded rather from a rival's jealousy of the Portuguese crown's expansionism than from any eager geographical interest. Columbus or, rather, his brother, was turned down flatly by Henry VII of England and the French court provided him with some wine and entertainment, but nothing else. Help might conceivably have come through the private merchants of Bristol, though it would not seem the Columbuses had thought of them. Howevermuch one might eschew the great-man theories, one is forced to admit that the career of D. João II made a decisive difference, not only to Portuguese history, but to the whole sequence of overseas discovery and development.

As ruler, D. João II's father, D. Afonso V, shares the distinction with his first cousin, Charles the Bold of Burgundy, of epitomizing the disintegrative tendencies in late medieval polity. Though very different in personality, they were alike in that both embodied a style and a way of life without future in a more modern society – by them government was conceived as no more than an extended family affair, with themselves as *pater familias*. War was made as chivalric amusement, preferably with profit, rather than as part of any coherent national policy. Impulse or caprice determined the course of their diplomacy. In short, that they possessed any sense at all of government as an abstraction is dubious, while they certainly lacked all notion of what Jacob Burkhardt called "the state as a work of art" – that is, as a means of shaping their rule to achieve deliberate ends. By contrast, D. João seemed to grasp it all through instinct.

Few of his actions are frivolous or impulsive. Perhaps even more than his cousins and neighbors, Fernando of Aragon and Isabella of Castile, he was the ordering principle in a nation tainted by late feudal disarray and he ranks among the greatest "new monarchists" of the Renaissance, though he is seldom mentioned by authors of Western Civilization survey texts – no doubt because their own specialties are located in northern Europe and they are little conscious of Iberia as a whole.

It is known that his tutors espoused the ideas of statecraft which had guided his grandfather, the late regent and Infante D. Pedro, ideas which exalted the idea of kingship as responsible to the nation and which viewed the aristocracy as merely part of this whole – rather than as privileged intimates virtually on a par with royalty itself. From the very beginning, D. João acted to divest the court nobility of what he considered their excessive lands and prerogatives (especially those of administering justice on behalf of the crown), and this involved him in a dangerous struggle with those his father had grossly overendowed. Recent writers have been at pains to show how filled with other activities besides navigation and expansion his famous grand-uncle's career was, but D. João's life as king was filled with a diversity of affairs far greater – not to speak of weightier and deadlier. Hence it is all the more remarkable that his actions in what would later have been called "the colonial sphere" were so single-minded and consistent.

Asia as a conscious goal

There are evidences that soon after Prince Henry's death, the idea of reaching Asia and its spices by sea had begun to dawn on the Portuguese. The terminology is of course confusing, if because "the Indies" was a broad and elastic concept and Europeans of the time could not possibly have had a clear idea of how Asia related to the bottom of Africa. In spite of the almost unquestioned sway which classical Alexandrian schools of geography held among late medieval and early renaissance scholars, such antique sources portrayed Asia so inconsistently that someone who studied certain atlases drawn according to the ideas of Strabo would have conceived Africa as a mere continuation of Asia poking into the Atlantic Ocean under Iberia, while another scholar who had consulted, for instance a Ptolemaic mappamundi like that of the Wilton Codex in the Huntington Library, might have seen Africa as joined at bottom to a great southern land mass also undergirding the Indian Ocean and walling it off from the Atlantic.[1] Other Ptolemaic maps then current showed Africa as mostly bulge, with a knob called the Promontorium Prassum at its base, after which it fell away and ran smoothly toward the Red Sea. Fortunately, as Professor Almeida has suggested in another essay of this volume, the early Portuguese navigators were not overly impressed by the erudite geographers with their classical atlases. To them and to D. João, finding a sea route to Calicut and the sources of the valuable pepper and cinnamon trade appeared more a matter for practical exploration than for theorizing in libraries.

Around the idea of creating and monopolizing this sea route and its rich trade all the other overseas initiatives of D. João can be neatly ordered. If maritime objectives during Prince Henry's lifetime did not fall so neatly into place, it need be recalled that the Infante commissioned only about a quarter of the southward voyages during his period of activity.[2] Moreover, until very near the end of his life, probably not enough information had been available in Portugal to allow him to contemplate anything so precise. One of the Infante's greatest contributions to Portugal's future empire was to gain in 1455 from Pope Nicholas V the exclusive concession for navigation south – and eastwards to the Indies.[3] This all came about through a curious intermingling of the medieval crusading impulse with the national interest.

In the mid-1440s, Prince Henry became enthralled with the vision that he was about to locate the lands of the immortal and pious bishop-emperor, Prester John. Thereupon he wrote to the rulers of Christendom and extended a remarkable invitation, redolent of the crusading spirit. Subordinating all private advantages of his own, he called upon his coreligionists to join him, first in seeking out the legendary Christian champion and then in combining with him to descend on Jerusalem and deal the paynim sultans of Asia a mighty coup-de-grâce. The monarchs of course politely begged off, giving

Prince Henry their blessings. Meanwhile, the new Castilian king, Enrique IV, showed not the least interest in pressing his claims to the Canaries nearby.

Their reactions proved fatal for Prince Henry's medieval vision, but they virtually awarded Portugal the exclusive rights to expand down the African coast and towards Asia. Prince Henry had thereupon dispatched an ambassador, one Fernão Lopes de Azevedo, to Pope Eugenius IV with the petition that Portugal be granted the ecclesiastical perquisites pertaining to Ceuta and exclusive rights to its African discoveries in light of the heavy expenses it was incurring. The Holy Father responded gratefully by granting these requests and entrusting to Prince Henry and his Order of Christ the task of doing battle with the Islamic heathen in Africa.[4] The following pope, Nicholas V, went even further. In his bull, *Romanus Pontifex*, of January 8, 1455 (new style), he proclaimed that "the Conquests extending from Capes Nun and Bojador, plus all the coast of Guinea to and including the Indies, [are] perpetually...the sovereign property of King Afonso."[5] This bull and the subsequent one, *Inter caetera*, of 1456, promulgated by his successor, Calixtus III, sweepingly awarded to Portugal an African and Asian monopoly, temporal as well as spiritual. At the very time of D. João II's birth, Portugal had thereby gained exclusive rights to navigate to the Orient. All subsequent bulls of Pope Alexander VI after the discovery of America incorporated this provision.

Abandoning the Canaries and protecting the sea route

Just prior to his accession to the throne in 1481, D. João had been deeply involved in limiting the damage caused by his father's succession war. In 1475, Afonso, a fortyish widower, had decided to marry the teenage Infanta Juana, putative daughter of the Castilian king, Enrique IV. He had done so in order that he might claim Enrique's throne, thereby uniting Castile with Portugal. But Enrique's half-sister, the Infanta Isabella, and her new husband, Fernando of Aragon, had other ideas, and their cause was strengthened by widespread doubts over Juana's legitimacy. Afonso's opportunism was a perfectly normal move on the dynastic chessboard, and the prospects would have sorely tempted any Portuguese ruler (even D. João, as Infante, seems to have underwritten the marriage). But the scheme had one grave defect: Spaniards felt the same xenophobia toward Portuguese rulers that the Portuguese had felt toward Spaniards in the 1380s when Juan I of Castile had tried to claim their throne and failed at Aljubarrota. As Afonso advanced into Castile, his support crumbled among all but die-hard factionalists opposed to Isabella; his forces, or half of them, were routed in December, 1476 near the northern Castilian town of Toro. Afonso lacked enough money and troops to risk further campaigning and he withdrew. By then, the king had had enough of ruling and did not stop retreating until he had reached monastic life and become an honorary Franciscan. This left his son, as regent, to come to terms with Isabella, whose position as queen of Castile was now unassailable.

In the negotiations following the abortive Portuguese campaign, D. João moved to gain from the inevitable sacrifice of Juana's claims one concession from the Spanish rulers which he perceived as essential to the future of Portuguese overseas expansion. It was obvious to him that further interference in Castilian dynastic politics was impossible; he was himself already wed to the Portuguese princess, Leonor, while his father, newly married to the Castilian claimant, was in the process of abdication. He must thus have reasoned that if Juana still worried Isabella and Fernando, renunciation of her titles might be used to gain explicit Spanish recognition of the papal bulls regarding Africa; this was bitter enough for Juana and for her husband, King D. Afonso V, but expediently necessary. At the same time, Portuguese claims on the Canary Islands ultimately seemed expendable, too, if because D. João knew the Spanish would not give them up without a fight. Some time around 1482 he also sacrificed them to gain a free hand in Africa.

The treaty of Alcáçovas, named for the Alentejan town where it was negotiated, embodied these provisions along with recognition that Granada would henceforth be regarded purely as a Spanish concern. It was signed in September 1479. The following spring, upon ratification of the treaty by the Catholic Kings, D. João (worried over constant interloping by Spanish and Hispano-Flemish vessels) obtained an amplification from them that they would "neither of themselves send ships to Africa, nor would they consent that any of their subjects...without permission...should go to trade in the islands or lands of Guinea..."[6] In August 1481, D. Afonso died of a fever and D. João became king in his own right.

Mina: the evolution of an African strategy

His claims thus secured *vis-à-vis* his rivals, one of D. João's earliest acts as ruler was to have a fort and trading post constructed in Guinea. Not only did he realize that the older one at Arguim Island faced desert wastelands too far up the coast for direct access to the gold and Guinea pepper Europeans wanted, but he knew that an actual Portuguese presence on the Gold Coast itself would better solidify his claims and provide a safe haven for explorations still further down the African shoreline. Moreover, it was not to be supposed that foreign privateers would actually keep clear of the gold coasts no matter what kind of diplomatic agreements he made; detecting and catching them would be so much the easier with a base of operations on the spot.

Until 1482 when his fort was constructed, no similar operation had been undertaken where an expeditionary force freighted down a prefabricated castle from Portugal in its own ships and then sought an appropriate site for its construction. Fortunately, D. João had able commanders and mariners at his disposal. He chose as the expedition's commander one Diogo de Azambuja, an old and experienced servant of the regent, D. Pedro. Then no sooner had Azambuja arrived on the Gold Coast with his load of numbered stones than he met one of D. João's ship captains currently trading in the region and well acquainted with it. Together, the pair negotiated with the Bantu chief, Caramansa, for a suitably defensible spot, watered and with a safe harbor. It was located on the coast of present-day Ghana at 5.09 N. latitude and 1.19 W. longitude. In enlarged form (by the Dutch, who captured it in 1637 and held it until 1849) the fort with many of its original stones still exists today. It acted as a *feitoria*, or warehouse and trading post, for alluvial gold from the Niger basin and other rivers, for slaves and for other products, both African and Portuguese. At the same time, D. João moved the Portuguese base of operations, established by Prince Henry at Lagos, to Lisbon, where it both outfitted fleets and received goods from the authorized Guinea expeditions. It also welcomed investments in the African trade from foreign businessmen, though by royal decree, interlopers and pirates were to suffer death and confiscation of goods.[7]

Enter Diogo Cão

D. João seems to have set new explorations in motion even before the Castle of S. Jorge da Mina was completed. As captain of these undertakings, he had another experienced mariner in mind, Diogo Cão. Cão was of an old Trasmontane family and is first recorded as having returned from Africa in 1480 with some Spanish vessels caught interloping in the Guinea trade. Over the next fifteen years, he was not only to make important maritime discoveries smoothing the way to the Cape of Good Hope itself, but he created useful contacts with native rulers which D. João seized upon to strengthen his ties with the papacy and thus further his spiritual claims as exclusive lord of all navigation in African waters.

In contrast to the unusually full chronicling of other facets in D. João's reign, the sources regarding Cão's activities and those of his fellow navigator, Bartolomeu Dias, are fragmentary and vague, no doubt because in the prevailing vision of chroniclers like Ruy de Pina and Garcia de Resende, pens and learning should properly be devoted to higher matters, namely, the doings of monarchs, diplomatists and courtiers; those of navigators belonging to the *escudeiro*, or petty noble, class were perceived as of little more consequence than the activities of service personnel. Lacking the perspective of later generations, they blandly ignored Cão's and Dias's activities, leaving modern researchers to reconstitute their achievements through patents, chancery documents and later writers to whom their activities held more meaning. Aside from what the navigators actually discovered, very little else is known about them. In dealing with Cão, I regard as by far the most enlightening the synthesis of the Romanian-Italian historian, Professor Carmen Radulet, who believes that Cão made not two voyages of discovery, as researchers from A. Fontoura da Costa to Damião Peres have supposed, but three. Of Dias I will speak later.

As Radulet sees matters, historians of the recent past have mistakenly postulated only two voyages because they assume that their sequences necessarily must jibe with dates incised into surviving stone pillars, or *padrões*, which Cão left at intervals along the African coast. Having made this basic assumption, they were then confronted with other facts, as found, for instance, in globes or charts made by contemporary foreign geographers, such as Behaim and Soligo. To square their assumptions, they had either to declare these in error, or else they had somehow to twist or rearrange sequences of events to explain them. Their end results Radulet found so unsatisfactory that instead of accepting the literal truth of the *padrões*, Radulet has set out to reexamine all the data, including the previously accepted ideas about them.

She now believes that Cão's first voyage took place in 1482, or just before that year, and struck into the unknown at Cape Ste. Catherine, 2° S. latitude, the point at which Fernão Gomes's navigators had stopped exploring. Cão soon entered a region where his Bantu-speaking interpreters were unable to understand the local languages. He therefore captured some negroes to train as linguists on future excursions before going on to discover the great river he called the *Rio do Padrão*, presently known as the Kongo or Zaire. The *padrão* was a memorial pillar of wood or stone, erected on the site of a discovery to record and claim it for the king, and it bore the appropriate data carved or chiselled into its surface; in this case Radulet believes the original was of wood, erected on a promontory at the river's estuary. This much is shown on the Pedro Reinel map discovered in the regional archives of Bordeaux and made known only in 1960.[8] Cão then may have returned to Portugal at the end of 1482 or the beginning of 1483, or he may have gone on a bit farther to plant a second wooden *padrão* at Cape Lobo, as the Cristofal Soligo map and an inscription on the surviving stone *padrão* known as Santo Agostinho would suggest. Upon his return to Portugal, he received as a reward the title *cavaleiro*, or knight, from D. João, while his pilot, Pedro de Alenquer, was made *escudeiro*, or squire. Almost immediately, preparations began for a second voyage.

It must, Radulet continues, have taken place in the spring of 1483. By then, she thinks D. João had decided wooden pillars were too impermanent and had ordered ones fashioned of stone to replace them. Accordingly, Cão bore these in the hold of his ships and began this voyage much as he had the previous one, though now of course he had a convenient stopping place in Mina. His first move beyond it would have been to replace the wooden *padrão* at the River Zaire with the more permanent stone version found there in the XIX century, the one named for S. Jorge. By that time the Kongolese captured on his first expedition could presumably be of service as interpreters and Cão then must have sent an embassy to the Manicongo in order to establish relations and obtain information about the area.[9]

She believes the fleet then continued on to Cape Lobo, where it located the S. Agostinho pillar. This may have replaced a wooden one placed there at the end of the first voyage, or it is also possible in her opinion that it was simply dated as of 1482 in order to establish the priority of discovery in the region as a whole – not necessarily as the date of that Cape's specific discovery.[10] The fleet afterwards should have proceeded as far south as the Bay of João de Lisboa, or as known today, Lucira (13.51 S. latitude). At this point, Cão doubled back to the mouth of the Congo to make contact with the ambassadors left behind. When he did not encounter these, he took some natives as hostages and let it be known that he would return with them for exchange after fifteen moons had passed. On the voyage home to Portugal, he discovered an island on New Year's day, 1484 which he named for it the Ilha do Ano Bom (Annobón Island at 1.24° S. latitude; 5.37° W. longitude). The date of his arrival in Lisbon must have been prior to April 8, for on that date and on the 14th, D. João officially rewarded him with various monies and titles – the whole occasion apparently being utilized to call attention to Portugal's achievements and claims. Radulet does not believe that the date of the awards necessarily indicates that the actual discoveries were made just prior to these announcements – but only that the crown wished to call public attention to them at that moment.

Diogo Cão's third and last voyage Radulet believes to have begun in the autumn of 1485, just as most other historians do. On this one, he indeed exchanged the hostages for the Portuguese emissaries, sent an official embassy to establish relations with the Manicongo, and then continued his coastal explorations southwards, planting two more *padrões* in its course, the first at Monte Negro and the second at Cape Cross (21.45° S. latitude) before going on to Cape Farilhões (22.10° S. latitude), the journey's deepest penetration before returning to the Congo and retrieving the Portuguese ambassadors, together with ones sent to Portugal by the Manicongo. Both of the positions Cão attained on this last voyage are indicated on contemporary maps and globes, those of Martin Behaim, who dates the last *padrão* at Cape Cross as from 18 January 1486 and the *Insulario* of Henricus Martellus, who records the farthest point.

Besides the epigraphs found on the *padrões* themselves, the Cão expeditions have left one other evidence of their presence, on cliffs above the rapids of Ielala, 170 kilometres up the Zaire. The site is so inaccessible that few people have visited it, and writers have used one or both of two photographs to decipher the words chiselled there. To the left of the main inscriptions are images of the *quinas*, or royal coat of arms, and a cross, whose proportions are reminiscent of that atop the *padrões*. To their right, in spiny late gothic letters, an inscription in archaic Portuguese spelling reads: "Here arrived the ships of the illustrious monarch, Dom João the Second of Portugal: Diogo Cão, Pedro Anes, Pedro da Costa/Alvaro Pyris (Pires), Pero Escolar A..." After this break, at a distance to the lower right and obviously carved by a different hand are other names: "João de Samtyago (Santiago), Diogo Pinheiro, Gonçalo Álvares + of sickness João Álvares /" and on a different rock, the name "Antam."[11]

There seems no doubt whatsoever over the inscriptions' authenticity, but under exactly what circumstances and on which of Cão's voyages the inscriptions were made is anything but clear. It seems highly unlikely that all the expedition's ships sailed up the river that far, and while in the first cluster of names, the captains of ships are cited, the other names are not familiar. Probably these are of some of the crew members ordered to sail up the river as far as they could go, likely in ships' boats rather than in the expedition's own caravels, and because it would have been impractical for them to carry a heavy *padrão* along, they were instructed to record their presence in some similar fashion instead. The little cross and the words *"de doença"* – "of sickness" – might indicate that much of the group by that time was sick and that one member, João Álvares, had already died. It might be that the second cluster of names was not meant to form part of the would-be padrão, but merely represented graffiti bearing the names of the actual explorers. It is possible that they gave up their chiseling when they felt too ill to continue – or else were menaced by somebody or something. Probably both persons doing the incising were working simultaneously and both broke off at the same moment. Why no date is recorded can likewise only be conjectured; it could be one was intended but never completed, as with the name "Antam," whose patronymic is conspicuously absent.

Death – or disgrace?

Following Cão's last voyage, his name disappears entirely from contemporary records, and this has led to much speculation over what fate might have befallen him. It is not surprising that in the case of such a national hero as Cão, Portuguese scholars would spare no effort in combining all surviving contemporary information into some reasonable explanation. The most popular of these, however, that of Abel Fontoura da Costa and Damião Peres, Carmen Radulet finds more amusing and ingenious than warranted by any actual documentation.

Fontoura da Costa had drawn attention in the 1930s to the oration of the Portuguese papal ambassador, Vasco Fernandes de Lucena, delivered in 1484 at the coronation of the new pope, Innocent III. In it, Lucena had proclaimed in flowery Latin that as a result of Portuguese explorations, "we have now effectively discovered an enormous part of the African coast, arriving last year almost at the extreme limit of Africa, the Promontorium Prassum, the promontory where the Sinus Arabicus begins..."[12] To Fontoura da Costa, the words could only mean that upon return from Africa the year preceding, Cão had told his king he had found the classically postulated termination of Africa at the point where it joined the Arabian Sea – and that the ambassador had been instructed to brag of this achievement before the great assembly of Christendom.[13] Whereupon, taking his cue from Fontoura da Costa's idea and improving on its implications, a younger contemporary, Damião Peres, in his *História dos Descobrimentos*, speculates that Cão had mistaken an insignificant bay on the Angolan coast, today called Lucira Grande, as the traditional cape at the end of Africa – and then boasted to his ruler about finding the long-sought promontory. Peres speculated that when Cão discovered his error and reported it to João II, the monarch never forgave him: "D. João II was not a man to pardon mistakes like that of Diogo Cão – a navigator on whose abilities so many hopes were justifiably placed and who ultimately came to fall into such a lamentable confusion that he mistook for the termination of Africa one of its landlocked capes."[14] The result, Peres believed, is that D. João, feeling himself deceived, had simply washed his hands of Cão and the great navigator thereafter disappeared from the scene.

Radulet points out that Cão was in all likelihood too experienced a navigator to hang such a sweeping assertion on such an insignificant cape, whose nature could easily be verified through a minimum of effort.[15] Rather, she believes that a humanist ambassador like Lucena had probably fallen into the error after conversing with some erudite geographer who had assumed that Cão had as good as found the Promontorium Prassum anyway, or would have by the time he uttered his words.[16] She feels a much more logical explanation for Cão's disappearance was that he expired during his third expedition. For although expressed oddly, a legend in Latin on Behaim's globe at about the right latitude proclaims "hic moritur" – "here he dies"! At least this idea of Cão's death seems the more reasonable – and simplest – explanation.[17] It has occurred to me that if Cão had indeed been taking solar readings from his various explorations down the coast and from them calculating his latitude, then geographers in Lisbon might have applied his southernmost reading to their favorite Ptolemaic map – and so decided the mythical promontory had about been reached.

The emissaries Cão sent to and received from the Manicongo as a byproduct of his explorations resulted in cordial relations and the conversions to Christianity of the chieftain, his son, and his court. These diplomatic exchanges between Europeans and native peoples beyond the pale of previous European contacts may be regarded as the first of their sort in the expansion of Europe. Among their many aspects portentous for the future, one of the most striking is that while the two kings treated with one another as equals; in other aspects the relationship foreshadowed technical aid from the developed to the developing world, for along with the clerics and ecclesiastical paraphernalia, D. João sent Portuguese craftsmen and their tools in order to help the Congolese achieve a higher technical and material plane. Modern cynics have seen in all this no more than the king's desire to strengthen his cause with the papacy, but it seems to me he was fully capable of acting from more than one motive.

Dias in the harness meant for Diogo Cão

Diogo Cão had been D. João's chosen instrument to find the way to the Arabian Sea and the wealth of India, and upon Cão's death, he selected another experienced seaman of the same background and class to continue the exploration. It can thus be no surprise we know about as little of Dias personally as of Cão himself. In fact, even less, because at least Cão was said to be from the Tras-os-Montes and there is even a house in Vila Real which tradition holds to be his birthplace. Not even that much can be said of Bartolomeu Dias; aside from his status, like Cão, as an *escudeiro* of the Casa Real, it is only absolutely certain he commanded the fleet of three caravels in 1487-1488 which finally discovered the Cape of Good Hope and that twelve years later he perished in a storm en route with Cabral's fleet to India – rather fittingly near the great headland he had discovered. It also seems convincing from known archival documentation that he headed the *Armazém de Guiné* in 1497-1498, the royal storehouse at São Jorge da Mina. The problem is that there are other mentions of navigators also named "Bartolomeu Dias" to be found in the archives of Portugal and also Italy – both before and after the date of his death (a familiar problem in a country where many patronymics are as common as the British "Smith," "Brown" and "Jones")! These mostly serve to confuse matters, though if one is to assume he was born around 1450, some Italian mentions of a Portuguese merchant captain-royal privateer named Bartolomeu Dias operating in Genoese and Pisan waters during the 1470s could indicate where he obtained his navigational expertise.[18]

No real reports of his voyage exist from close to the time it was made; there are only some legends on the Henricus Martellus map of 1479 indicating calling points en route, plus a scanty note of Christopher (or Bartholomew?) Columbus penned in a margin of the famous Columbian copy of the *Imago Mundi*. To gain a better idea, one must depend on the scanty reporting in the *Asia*, of João de Barros, written sixty years afterwards. From these few sources, plus a passing mention in the *Esmeraldo de Situ Orbis*, of Duarte Pacheco Pereira, it is possible to obtain an approximate idea of one of the world's most epochal discoveries.

Barros reports that, having been sent southwards to pick up and continue Cão's explorations, Dias sailed beyond the last *padrão* erected by that explorer on December 4, 1487, and continued into unknown waters. On the 23rd, he passed the present Hottentot Bay. Then, one gathers that the weather became stormy and that contrary winds made forward progress extremely tedious. At any rate, he put out to sea and finally could run for thirteen days with sails at half-mast. The air becoming much cooler, he decided to seek the coast again and headed northwards, eventually making a landfall at the "Bahia dos Vaqueiros," seemingly today's Mossel Bay,[19] at 23 East latitude and 35 South longitude. He then followed the coast far enough eastwards to make sure this was its true trending prior to turning homewards for Portugal, stopping at S. Tomé (where he picked up Duarte Pacheco Pereira) and at S. Jorge da Mina.

The Henricus Martellus map of 1489 confirms Dias's progress down the coast, if not his swing out to sea, while the Columbus notation seems to confirm Barros in this, since it indicates Dias's southernmost point to be at 45 degrees south and not 35. Aside from the possibility that Columbus may have been in error, one of the many explanations offered for this is that his extra ten degrees beyond the actual latitude of the Cape signifies the total extent of the southward swing prior to its discovery. It is quite understandable, incidentally, that Columbus should have been mindful of Dias's accomplishments: he was present in Lisbon at the time and witnessed the navigator's return.

The overland attempts to contact Prester John and India

Dias's great voyage to the Cape has far eclipsed other reconnaissance operations launched by D. João at almost the same moment. One of these, or rather, group of them, involved the penetration of Africa from west to east. It was prompted by a report of 1485 or 1486 made by one João Afonso Aveiro, who had visited Benin. While there, Aveiro had heard of a great ruler of rulers many moons to the east, who he believed might fit the image of the Christian emperor, Prester John. D. João thereupon dispatched a number of emissaries to him by various routes – via Timbuctu, Takrur and the Mossi peoples. Apparently, none arrived, or at least nothing for sure is known about the results. The exalted person sought, however, is now known not to have been the emperor of Ethiopia at all, but the Oni of Ife, to whom the rulers of Benin accorded a certain suzerainty.[20]

Then, almost at this same time, D. João was approached by a Wolof king of the Senegal region, named Bemoi, who had fled his kingdom and sought Portuguese help in gaining his reinstatement. Probably as an added inducement, he converted to Christianity. D. João seems to have conceived the episode as an opportunity to establish a *feitoria*-fort complex at the mouth of the Senegal and in so doing to establish a base of operations for penetration into the interior; accordingly he outfitted a large expedition and returned Bemoi, now Christened and given the king's own baptismal name. Unfortunately, a fatal altercation developed soon after arrival between Bemoi and the Portuguese fleet commander, Pedro Vaz da Cunha. Accusing Bemoi of treachery and betrayal, Cunha had him killed and sailed home.[21]

The final attempt involved sending two Arabic-speaking messengers disguised as merchants to Abyssinia and India via the Red Sea. The search was both to find Prester John and to report on conditions in India. While the combination may seem purely medieval, one gathers the king to have been less interested than Prince Henry in crusading opportunities; rather, he probably thought it a good idea when launching eastwards into unknown and largely hostile territory to have a powerful coreligionist ally at hand. For the messengers, disguise was possible because by the end of the XV century, the Moroccan wars of Portugal had produced a number of Arabic-speakers. Of the two, a minor courtier named Pero de Covilhã elected to visit India, while the other one, Afonso Paiva, chose to proceed alone towards Ethiopia. Covilhã actually seems to have visited Cannanore and Calicut before hearing of Paiva's death in Cairo. He then trekked into Ethiopia, whence he was hospitably received, but forbidden by the negus, or Emperor, to return home to Portugal. All this would never have been known had not the embassy of D. Rodrigo de Lima been sent from Goa in 1520. Covilhã was still alive and told his story to Frei Francisco Álvares, a priest of the Lima mission. Álvares further reported that before continuing his journey to the mountain fastnesses of Abyssinia, Covilhã said he had managed to meet a Portuguese representative of D. João in Cairo and had transmitted a report to him on what he had encountered in India.[22] If he had, no trace of it has survived. From the confusion registered by Vasco da Gama and his men during their initial contacts in Calicut, Covilhã's intelligence would not seem to have been very informative, if indeed it ever really did reach Lisbon at all.

The visit by Christopher Columbus

Not all of D. João's activities involved Africa and the East, for around 1484, he was approached by Christopher Columbus, who with his brother had been residing in Portugal. Columbus, of course, came with his famous proposal, in hopes of gaining Portuguese sponsorship. No mention of the meeting has ever been found in the Portuguese archives, and had the chronicler, João de Barros, not mentioned it around sixty years later, we might never have known that it occurred. Even Barros is unsure why the king refused Columbus's project, but he thinks that a royal commission, presumably consisting of D. João's chief navigational experts, considered it naive and ill-conceived. It must have pronounced that Columbus had grossly underestimated the length of a degree and hence the size of the globe – and that he would not reach Cipango half as easily as he imagined. Barros also implies D. João, for all his courtesy toward the Genoese, thought him vain and given to fantasy.[23] It is interesting, though, that D. João was apparently willing to reconsider Columbus's proposal after the Dias expedition had not been heard from after so many months. The Columbusses in fact had returned to Lisbon for their second interview when Dias sailed back in triumph from the Cape. That homecoming seems to have ended Columbus's chances in Portugal.

After Columbus had found Spanish patronage and returned from his epochal first voyage, it is clear enough that João believed he had encroached upon Portuguese rights to navigate to Africa and the south. Once he had become embroiled in actual negotiations with the Castilians on the basis of bulls issued by Pope Alexander VI, however, he appears to have known what he wanted. Before accepting the papal proposals, he succeeded in getting the longitudinal meridian of demarcation moved far enough west to include within Portuguese territory the bulge of Brazil. Two years later, before he could activate his cherished project of sending an embassy to India via the Cape, he died at age 43, probably of Bright's Disease.

So much is reasonably certain about maritime activities during the reign of D. João II, but what has caused the real squabble among historians are the discoveries which might, or might not, have occurred. To wit, could the New World possibly have been found during this period by the Portuguese and not by Columbus?

The great *sigilo* controversy

This question has prompted the longest-running controversy in Portuguese historiography, and it began over the *sigilo* – or secrecy – interpretation of the late Jaime Cortesão. To say the very least, it has rumbled through the historiography of the discovery period for seven decades and has pitted not only Portuguese scholars like the late Luís de Albuquerque, Avelino Teixeira da Mota, and Duarte Leite against it, but even more vociferously, the Brazilian, Tomás Oscar Marcondes de Sousa. Nor did the controversy end with the Lusophone world: the American historians, Samuel Eliot Morison and Bailey W. Diffie also disparaged the thesis and went to lengths to demonstrate its falsity.[24] Only Cortesão's brother, Armando, the famous historian of cartography who outlived him by more than a decade, defended his ideas, but did so in a book that drew little critical attention.[25] It was studiously avoided by the historical fraternity, and no one was prepared to reopen the controversy after it seemed so definitively laid to rest. In spite of all this, I am now inclined to believe there may have been a good deal of truth, if not in the *sigilo* thesis itself, then in what it really attempts to prove, namely that there had been extensive Portuguese explorations in the western Atlantic and even Indian Oceans before Columbus.

My aim here is not so much to describe all the attacks on the thesis – I will rather sum them up – but to argue that Cortesão's fundamental mistake was that he put his arguments on the wrong basis, namely he tried to prove a consistent policy of official secrecy as the reason that a number of Portuguese explorations in the Atlantic before Columbus have never become known. So preoccupied did his opponents become with pronouncing his *sigilo* thesis as pure hokum that they virtually failed to examine the possibility that there had indeed been some prediscoveries in the Atlantic, either before or after the voyages of Columbus. This I now propose to do.

But even before doing so, perhaps it is best for me to make my own position clear. I do not consider *any* prediscoveries very important. Only if a voyage was followed by a chain of circumstances – settlements, commercial exchanges, territorial conquest or other occupation – does it seem to me of much consequence. At best, a lone voyage along a deserted coast before it was supposed to have been discovered might be worth a sentence or two in a general history, or perhaps an entry in the *Guinness Book of World Records*. But unlike some historians, I can't really say that I care very much about such speculation and will only indulge in it on rare occasions – of which I admit this is one.

The *sigilo* thesis was first put forward by Cortesão in the year 1921 in an address, seemingly at the Sociedade de Geografia, and it was printed the following year in an article called "A expedição de Pedro Álvares Cabral e o descobrimento de Brasil."[26] Its substance, developed in a series of articles and a book that followed, is that both Prince Henry, who died in 1460 and the Portuguese king, D. João II, who reigned from 1481 to 1495, made extensive explorations in the Atlantic Ocean during their periods of authority, but deliberately and effectively hushed all word of them, even from their own archivists. This was ostensibly out of fear that interlopers, or in the case of D. João II, fear that the more powerful Catholic Kings, Isabella and Ferdinand, might preempt the lands and the trade that they gave access to. In proof of this, Cortesão adduced a number of royal decrees promulgated in the reign of D. João II forbidding participation of foreigners in voyages to those newly discovered lands of coastal Africa guaranteed by papal bulls issued to his great uncle, Prince Henry, or, otherwise prohibiting the transmission or possession of charts and maps pertaining to the region. Then Cortesão proceeded to suggest that the Portuguese had not only discovered America before Columbus, but very probably had turned the Cape of Good Hope and sailed into the Arabian Sea soon after Dias's voyage of 1488. But everything, he maintained, had been kept in such deep secrecy that even the Portuguese archives held no record of them.[27] I believe it was Morison who snorted that this was the first case on record where lack of evidence became the proof that something had taken place!

Of all the assaults on the thesis, perhaps that of my late collaborator, Bailey Diffie, was the most systematic. It appeared in *Terrae Incognitae* and was called "Foreigners in Portugal."[28] Diffie demonstrated that D. João II's decrees were in fact as porous as a colander. Not only did D. João himself employ foreigners, or allow them to be employed, on voyages of discovery, but up-to-date cartographical information gained from them promptly appeared both on maps circulating within Portugal and those made by foreigners. For example, less than a year after Bartolomeu Dias had returned from the Cape of Good Hope in 1488, the German cartographer, Heinrich Hammer, alias Henricus Martellus, had published in his mappamundi of 1489 a near-perfect charting of all the voyages of Diogo Cão and that of Dias, in a rendition which afforded the first accurate picture of the West African coast. If D. João indeed wished to keep foreigners away from information concerning his discoveries, as indeed he might have, it seemed that almost everything worth knowing became known, anyway, and very quickly.

The result of all this has been that for much of my lifetime, no respectable historian has dared argue for any voyages outside the universally accepted canon. This is namely that after the discovery of the Cape of Good Hope by Bartolomeu Dias in 1488, no further Portuguese passages in the Atlantic seem to have taken place until Vasco da Gama's first voyage to India in 1497-1499 and Pedro Álvares Cabral's discovery of Brazil in 1500. To explain the long hiatus, historians have speculated on the illness of D. João II as among the probable causes, on the high costs of outfitting expeditions, of other demands of D. João's time and similar reasons for delay. Of these, I must admit that none seemed particularly convincing, since the monarch had previously acted with such decisiveness in sending out Diogo Cão, Dias and others, and even seems to have had a team of navigators in reserve who operated out of São Jorge da Mina in Guiné. Nor did he have the sort of personality that was easily derailed from its purpose.

So eager was he to find a route to India in the wake of Diogo Cão's discoveries that he sent not only Dias in search of the southern cape, the way around Africa, but three additional expeditions – two to attempt the crossing of Africa from west to east by land, and one via

Egypt down the Red Sea – all at about the same time. Why, then, would he have waited seven years, or for the rest of his life, to send out even one additional explorer? Something which seems highly improbable. Nonetheless, since the historical field of combat over the issue had been left looking like the Meuse-Argonne in 1917, no one was eager or willing to go over the top to reopen what seemed like a decisive win for reason against nationalistic wishful thinking.

A new approach

As a matter of fact, neither I, nor my Portuguese colleague, Professor Luís Adão da Fonseca, of the University of Porto, are inclined to reopen the controversy along the lines that official secrecy prevented anything from being known. I think *sigilo* has been around long enough and is indefensible, anyway. It stands in the way of serious inquiry – granted that governments both then and now do not divulge everything they know. (In fact, governments nowadays seem to protect their secrets even when there is little to be gained and I do not begrudge D. João and his court a few of them.) But that is not the point. Rather than hiding behind theories of official secrecy, it is time to reexamine the issues on other grounds. For what has been passed off as secrecy may not have been secrecy *per se*, but lack of documentation due to a number of other factors, at least one of them bordering on the sinister.

Professor Fonseca recently wrote a little book on Bartolomeu Dias to commemorate the fifth centenary of his discovery of the Cape, and in it he takes a much more reasoned line in favor of some exploration in the Atlantic immediately following the return of Dias. For one thing, he points out that in his discovery of the Cape, Dias used caravels as his vessels, but that caravels were too small to support any mission to the Indian west coast, which would necessarily take on a diplomatic and trading character (as well as an armed character).[29] Anyone familiar with the lateen sail used by caravels and with the circumstances of Dias's expedition will remember that he had enormous trouble as he sailed southwards along the coast in making headway against the Benguela current and its accompanying winds which directly countered his progress. Caravels with aerodynamically efficient lateen primary sails can move slowly forward to within 10 degrees of the wind, but the handling of the lateen sail is labor-intensive and clumsy and severely limits the size of the vessels on which it can successfully be employed. Larger vessels must use square sails lacking the aerodynamic qualities of the triangular sail and cannot navigate anywhere as close to the wind, above all when driven by the unfragmented square sails of the late XV century. Hence a larger *nao* or carrack could never have followed Dias's course taken to discover the Cape. Even Dias and his lateen-rigged caravels encountered such difficulty as he neared it that he was forced out to sea, where he made a long detour, sailing too far south before doubling back to reach the long-sought promontory. Obviously, on its own voyage to South Asia, a future full-scale expedition could not follow anything like the routing Dias used to round the Cape.

The Portuguese archives are sparse for this period, but if one is content with bits and pieces of evidence, it would seem that Dias remained stationed in São Jorge da Mina after his great voyage and remained assigned to caravel duty, as were his friends and associates Duarte Pacheco Pereira and the famous pilot who had served Diogo Cão, Pero de Alenquer. There are also lists detailing the provisioning of caravels operating out of São Jorge da Mina, or Elmina, as it is called, in the years following 1488, outfitted with enough ship's biscuit and other provisions for long sea voyages.[30] What was going on?

Professor Fonseca thinks it is most likely that D. João had sent Dias and Alenquer out once again and very soon after their return in 1488 to search for alternative ways to reach the Cape which would better serve as a routing for larger ships. For, he reasons, to assume that Vasco da Gama was dispatched in 1497 simultaneously to find a new Atlantic route around the Cape and to visit India on a diplomatic and trading mission is highly unlikely.[31] Rather, it would appear far more sensible that Dias and Alenquer had again been at work in the meantime to find a feasible route for large, square-rigged vessels to employ. It is also interesting that on the great voyage to India of Da Gama in 1497, Alenquer was his pilot and Dias accompanied the expedition from Lisbon as far as São Jorge da Mina, where he had long been stationed. It would therefore be most logical to assume that Da Gama was being guided. One will recall that the ships did not follow the coast at all, as Dias had done, but launched out into the Atlantic, where they did not sight land again for 93 days. What taught them to do that?

Meanwhile, there is another mysterious circumstance for which historians really have no explanation. It is that after the return of Columbus from his first voyage had involved D. João in protracted negotiations both with the papacy and with Castile, the monarch even implied that he would go to war unless the line of demarcation as proposed by the pope were moved 270 leagues farther to the west; you may remember that Alexander VI had proposed a line fixed only 100 leagues west of the Cape Verde Islands. Even though no one then knew how to reckon longitude with any precision, Columbus had been at pains to show that he had been much farther to the west; so, the distance as demanded by D. João II must have seemed concessible.[32] But why did the Portuguese king demand it in the first place? (Of course the bulge of Brazil turned up on the Portuguese side.)

Brazil as a by-product?

There seem two possibilities. The first is that Dias, or possibly his colleague, Duarte Pacheco Pereira, had sighted land while seeking an alternative way towards the Cape from far to the west – the only possible route for large sailing ships – or else suspected it was nearby. Land alone should not have surprised contemporaries if one bears in mind that on Ptolemaic and other maps, the Atlantic was full of islands, most of which do not actually exist, including one called Antilia and others named for St. Brendan and still others called the Satanazes. The second possibility, though it would not imply prediscovery of Brazil, would also indicate that D. João's ships had been far out into the Atlantic, for then he would have asked the additional space to guarantee sailing room for the big, westward detour his Cape-bound ships would necessarily have to make if they were to reach the Indian Ocean.[33] Either way, the indication is that after the discovery of the Cape by Dias, there had been other trips into the Atlantic to prepare the way for what became Vasco da Gama's voyage to Calicut. Incidentally, in later years Portuguese ships frequently came in sight of Brazil en route to India if winds did not allow an earlier turn to the southeast.

If Dias or Pereira indeed sighted Brazil during one or more of these preparatory voyages, there was certainly nothing in contemporary Brazil as seen from the deck of a vessel that would convince either the navigators or the king that what the Portuguese already had found in Africa was less attractive. Nothing to suggest that this was indeed Cipango or Cathay or even worth wasting time on when India was in sight. One must consider that work done in determining latitude for positions along the African coast, effected on D. João's orders from the early 1480s, must have resulted in a fair idea of the length of a degree of either latitude or longitude, and hence the true size of the earth. So the Portuguese must have calculated that they were not dealing with Asia – and it is logical to assume D. João was so keen on finding it in the opposite direction that, had Dias told him about palm trees and naked savages, he would have calculated that this was precisely what he did not wish to waste his time upon.

However, if his explorers had indeed sensed or sighted land to the west, one can imagine that in any negotiations with the Spanish, he simply did not wish to be robbed of more territory – he had already lost the Canary Islands to the Spanish by the treaty of Alcáçovas after the fiasco at Toro. One will recall that he accused Columbus of having trespassed on Portuguese domains after his return in 1493, and even though he might have not been very excited by any lands possibly viewed by Dias, or whomever, I suspect he drew the line – literally – over the prospect of losing them. That was quite another matter from having any particular plans for their use, as he certainly did for Asia.

In this, I think we are misled by Columbus. After all, he had promised enormous things to the Catholic kings in return for his voyage, namely the riches of Cathay and at least Cipango. But all he had found were naked savages and a smidgen of gold. Nonetheless, hardly the person to stop at this disappointment, he rather did his best to play up what he had found. Please remember that until Cortés and Pizarro came along, the Spanish discovery in America was not even known to be worth what the Portuguese had already found in Africa. But thereafter – something Columbus could hardly have known – his discovery kept getting better and better until it became the mineral and industrial giant – or giants – we all know today.

Hence his own representations, then false, have become a thousandfold truer than he could have dared hope. So why should we assume that, had the Portuguese indeed sighted the bulge of Brazil at any time after 1488, they should have conceived of its import as in our eyes? They were even then trying to sail around Africa for the real payoff. So neither the proponents nor the opponents of prediscovery should try to read the impact of any Brazilian find through our own magnifying spectacles. To D. João and his advisers, it likely would have appeared an unpromising place to spend their limited money – when on the trail of something vastly more worthwhile.

Incidentally, another Portuguese colleague, Alfredo Pinheiro Marques, has pointed out in the epilogue to this volume something not noticed before by historians – namely that when Columbus was seized in the Antilles by the crown's representative, Bobadilla, in 1500, during his third voyage, the news of Vasco da Gama's finding of Calicut had only very recently been learned by the Catholic Kings. He reasons that Queen Isabella's fuse was then very short because she realized that Columbus had been deceiving her (though possibly unwittingly) about finding the Indies. If true, this would tend to indicate that the Spanish monarchs did not consider the real estate so far discovered by the Genoese to be of great value.

But we must return to the *sigilo*, the secrecy thesis. Don't we still need Jaime Cortesão to explain to us why there are no documents concerning the Atlantic discoveries of this period? I think not. In the first place. please remember that the court chroniclers of D. João II's reign, Garcia de Resende and Rui de Pina, were gentlemen interested in court politics and in the people who mattered, namely the nobility and the courtly, and that the doings of the petty *fidalguia*, the service personnel, sailing around in distant places, were not deemed worthy of much attention. Second, aside from any destructive occurrence, like the great earthquake of 1755, which damaged the royal archives, we must remember that not every document made has been preserved unto our own day; one should rather say that most were not. Besides which, not every chancery document or corroborating letter we might desire was made in the first place. Searching in the Renaissance past hardly yields the sure results one can expect from perusing back copies of the *New York Times* for a city ordinance passed during Mayor Jimmy Walker's time.

But there appears a better reason than these. I believe that a more logical choice than any *sigilo* explanation would be to assume that all the pertinent chancery documents from the reign of D. João II were simply stolen, and probably shortly after his death.

A different kind of conspiracy

Any such theft would have resulted from no more than a family cabal, but it would easily have set Jaime Cortesão on the false trail of his *sigilo* thesis. Starting with the missing documentation around the Columbian years, he increasingly widened this lacuna into his sweeping theory that many important, but unknown, discoveries took place over the better part of a hundred years, ones which remain hidden because of an official secrecy extending even to the monarchy's own record-keeping. He and his brother after him insinuated each gap in the Torre do Tombo archives into vital information deliberately suppressed – a cover-up, they had it, dating back to the beginning of the XV century.

Whoever the culprit or culprits involved in the missing documentation, it is most unlikely that D. João II himself was among them. After all, the purpose of any secrecy would have been served merely by keeping foreign crewmembers and observers from sailing on Portuguese exploring missions and from obtaining charts and maps which might tell them where to go. Even though the measures were not very effective, the last thing one might want to do is to conceal one's accomplishments from one's self – and ultimately from posterity.

As I hinted earlier, there may have been something more sinister at work which had little or nothing to do with any passion of D. João's for state secrecy. It was even touched upon by Jaime Cortesão's brother,

Armando, in a book called *The Mystery of Vasco da Gama*, which appeared as late as 1973. In it, he attempts to strengthen the secrecy thesis put forth by Jaime, but in trying to defend the all-but-discredited notion, he adds some new elements which have rather the opposite effect.[34] One of these is to include material which suggests why in fact the chancery papers are all missing – then fail to take the hint himself. And the reason has less to do with any *sigilo* than it does with the bad blood between D. João and the most powerful noble clan in Portugal, the Braganças.

It seems all to have begun with D. João's father, D. Afonso V, wearing his heart too much on his sleeve, so to speak, and lavishly endowing his nobility with, at least in D. João's opinion, far too much of the royal patrimony. At the very beginning in his own reign, D. João sought to regain some of the royal lands and incomes which he considered that his father had only given away because they had been wheedled from him by those who knew best how to exploit his almost pathological generosity. In D. João's mind, by far the worst offenders were the Braganças.

As a Renaissance monarch, there were no flies on D. João when it came to keeping tabs on his subjects via informants, and in 1483, soon after he had come to the throne, he was able to intercept correspondence indicating that D. Fernando, scion of the Braganças, was attempting to depose him and had even brought the Catholic Kings into knowledge of his intent. D. João arrested him in Évora, and after a trial in which the Duke acknowledged his wrongdoing, had his head chopped off. He was mistaken if he believed this would put an end to the matter. Only a year later, he got wind through another informant of a second plot against him, this time one to assassinate him during an outing. He learned that the chief culprit was no less than his own brother-in-law, D. Diogo, the Duke of Viseu – and another Bragança. Instead of going on the outing, D. João remained in his castle at Palmela, between Lisbon and Setubal, and summoned the Duke to his quarters. When the culprit appeared, alone, D. João stabbed him to death with his own hand.

But there was one young Bragança who had joined his court as a page and had always behaved himself; he was a polite lad of some fourteen at the time and D. João did not proscribe him because he had obviously played no part in the conspiracy. As it turned out, D. João's own son, the Infante D. Afonso, died as the result of a fall from a horse while clowning with some of his companions. Thus did the legitimate line of Avis end with D. João's own death in 1495. He was succeeded by none other than the well-mannered young lad whose meekness had saved him, as D. Manuel I. D. João's own axe and dagger, incidentally had put the lad in direct line to the throne.

Sigilo as an instrument of revenge

I am not suggesting that D. Manuel in person necessarily conceived of destroying D. João's archives. But one must remember that no monarch then or now is devoid of his attendant relatives and retainers, and in this case, the parties surrounding D. Manuel must have literally burned for revenge, if not on D. João, who was now out of their reach, then upon his memory.[35] D. João had virtually set D. Manuel up in his imperial future: all D. Manuel had to do to initiate a rich empire was to send out Vasco da Gama and Pedro Álvares Cabral. He was indeed the Fortunate King.

But the Braganças were not about to acknowledge D. Manuel I's debt to his predecessor; no doubt but what the angry new dynasty and their allies were anything but ready to give credit where credit was due, especially when they now happened to be in control of Portugal's informational services. D. João II's state papers must have thereupon gone up in smoke or otherwise disappeared without a trace. It is interesting that the chronicler, João de Barros, when writing during the 1550s, in contrast to his very detailed reporting on earlier dealings with the Manicongo, on the baptism, training and murder of Bemoi, and on the voyages of Diogo Cão, could report little about the navigations of Dias to the Cape and next to nothing about the all-important negotiations at Tordesillas.[36] At first glance, one would be inclined to presume that by such uneven reportage, the famous chronicler displayed no proper sense of what was relatively more or less important. But this is probably not true at all: in 1904, the historian, Anselmo Braamcamp Freire, inventoried the surviving materials from D. João's reign and discovered that all chancery documents from the years 1489 and 1493 through 1495 were missing, the critical years in question, from which most reportage of three generations later would naturally have come! The combination of such glaring omissions in the chronicles and the documentation missing in exactly the same areas of D. João's chancery papers would rather induce one to conclude that the earthquake of 1755, which destroyed parts of the Torre do Tombo, the royal archives (on which such lacunae are usually blamed), had nothing to do with the lack of documentation here: the papers were no doubt long gone when the tremor occurred.

By contrast the state papers of D. Manuel I are in far better shape; many, to be sure, are missing, as one might expect over more than 400 years, but there is nowhere in them such a glaring gap.

Coincidence, perhaps, but it could better be that documents establishing D. João II's activities had been spirited away by the hangers-on of the Braganças, indeed for a kind of state secrecy, but one motivated purely out of court hatred and jealousy. The net effect, as in the theory of the Cortesãos, is a masking of our knowledge – though from quite other concerns than a desire to avoid Spanish competition! In short, I believe in a *sigilo* – a conspiracy of silence – but one aimed at the reputation of D. João II! One can believe that the Cortesão brothers were correct when they asserted that D. João II *tried* to keep his navigators' activities secret from the public – but of course it is silly to assert that such secrecy could have been extended to his own internal records. Whereas no secrecy *vis-à-vis* future generations could be more mightily effective than someone else's chucking out D. João's chancery papers. Thereafter, the Braganças could bask in his credit due for the India enterprise.

Upon D. Manuel's accession, all D. João's old navigators were pressed into his service, and he thereupon directed the passage to Calicut – and the discovery of Brazil. There is no reason to believe the seamen were at all politicized or were not as willing to serve D. Manuel as they were D. João II; he was simply everyone's new master. Even Vasco da Gama, whose name was not generally associated with D. João II, may in fact have been one of the late king's navigators, for an early chronicler of India, Fernão Lopes de Castanheda, remarked of him that "he was experienced in the things of the sea, in which he rendered much service to D. João II."[37] It is usual enough in a new reign that the favorites of the old king tend to be ignored, especially if the succession is not from father to son. In the case of D. João's navigators, the generalization might hardly apply, any more than it would to the royal equerries or to his stewards. For men like Dias, Pereira and Cão might be national heroes today, but then they were merely squires i.e., of the *escudeiro* class, and had little in common with the higher nobility. D. Manuel I simply took over the whole team – and it would have been ungrateful and unwise for any of them to have sung too many praises of their old boss thereafter. Especially Da Gama, for while he may previously have served D. João II, least of all was he about to bite the hand that made him the Count of Vidigueira.

In fact the only one of the navigators with literary inclinations was Duarte Pacheco Pereira, author of the *Esmeraldo do Situ Orbis*, a work which did not appear in print until the XIX century and is so cryptic and disjointed that it has not attracted widespread attention despite the fact that it even received an English translation in the 1930s from the

Hakluyt Society. Pereira, however, was highly respected in his day and anything he says is likely to be true enough, providing one can place it in its proper context. In the work's first book, he writes (to D. Manuel): "In the third year of your reign, in the year of Our Lord 1498...your Highness ordered us to discover the Western region, a very large landmass with many large islands adjacent, extending 70° North of the Equator and...28° on the other side of the Equator, towards the Antarctic pole. Such it its greatness and length that on either side its end has not been seen or known."[38] Vasco da Gama had just sailed to India, and I would guess that the trip mentioned by Pereira was conceived as a mere adjunct, in case his colleague should fail. No doubt D. Manuel had learned that he might have some lands coming to him under the Tordesillas treaty of 1494 and wanted at least to have a peek at them.

Brazil, of course, was only discovered, officially at least, two years later, and while it would seem Pereira or someone else in royal service had thus navigated past it, his trip would seem to have been impressionistic and hurried; possibly the islands here referred to were Trinidad and Curaçao, for it is more than likely that he trespassed on Spanish territories as defined by Tordesillas, either because longitude was still a mystery or else because D. Manuel's advisers wished to have no more than a look at that stage. It is also likely that when Cabral's squadron called two years later, no one was sure what part of the reconnaissance mentioned by Pereira had actually been touched; hence the later confusion over whether what had just been found was an island or the mainland. (Professor Francis Dutra, also calls attention to the fact that Pereira does not say "ordered *me*," but "ordered *us*" – and suggests that Pereira may not have made the voyage personally.) Cabral could well have stopped off in Brazil because it was becoming apparent that Spanish navigators sailing from the Caribbean Islands were coming too close for comfort – though no doubt the voyage of Pinzón (which actually sailed along part of present-day Brazilian northwest) could not yet have been known. But that of Alonso de Ojeda (who carried Amerigo Vespucci on board, incidentally) could have been, and in that event, it would have been reasoned that it was high time to put in a formal appearance to reinforce Portugal's rights in the region.

To emphasize what I said earlier about Brazil's lack of allure for India-smitten Portuguese at the turn of the XV century, all but one account (that of Vaz Caminha) emanating directly or indirectly from Cabral's voyage in 1500 give that great country but a few lines centering mostly on parrots; then the expedition happily sailed on to

Asia. It is interesting, incidentally, that on this very trip, Bartolomeu Dias was along, perhaps because, this time, the king and the navigators wished him to show them where he or Pereira (or one of their colleagues) may have previously made a landfall. Only one unimportant supply ship was dispatched to Portugal with the news of discovery.

Far more interesting to me is the question of whether expeditions had been sent beyond the Cape of Good Hope between its discovery by Dias and the death of D. João II. There is some indication of this in both the humanist chronicler, Damião de Góis, and in an Arabic writing which turned up in the 1950s in a Russian library and which was written by none other than Ibn Majid, traditionally, but probably erroneously, supposed to have been the Da Gama expedition's pilot from Malindi to Calicut. Ibn Majid indicates that the "Ferenghi" ("Franks" – viz., the Portuguese) had been in Mozambique and (perhaps) Sofala earlier – and lost ships in a storm or tidal wave or otherwise through unfamiliarity with coastal conditions.[39] One has only to pair this with Góis' statement in chapter XXIV of his chronicle of D. Manuel, that there was not one, but several voyages East of the Cape prior to Da Gama's famous voyage: "*correndo os nossos muito mais allem do Cabo de Boa Esperança atte chegarem a hos limites e termos de çofala e Moçambique*" – "Our people were cruising far beyond the Cape of Good Hope until they arrived at the limits and the lands of Sofala and Mozambique."[40] If this indeed were so, it is easy to see why the news would have been suppressed by the Braganças, since if the event had occurred under D. João II, it would show that he was the real author of the India enterprise, while if any such disaster had occurred in the reign of D. Manuel, it would smack of failure.

Beyond this, if the Portuguese were indeed active in the Indian Ocean prior to Da Gama's great voyage of 1498, it would indicate that India was receiving the real attention and that the "Western region" was conceived as of little or no account. All of what I have said in fact adds up to this: we are prone to assume that any discovery of Brazil would have, so to speak, "made waves" in Portugal – if because it is so important to us. But in the years 1488 to 1500 and beyond, the Atlantic was seen only as a means to reach Asia. I maintain that neither a *sigilo*, a conspiracy of silence, nor even the machinations of the Braganças, are necessary to explain that if the Portuguese had indeed been first in Brazil or even first in the New World itself, their minds were riveted elsewhere. (Just as, one might add, was that of Christopher Columbus.)

Notes

By far the best and most recent treatment of D. João II and especially his administrative methods is: Manuela Mendonça, *D. João II. Um percurso humano e político nas origens da modernidade em Portugal* (Lisbon: Editorial Estampa; Imprensa Universitária no. 57, 1991).

[1] I have used Leo Bagrow, *History of Cartography*, as revised and enlarged by R. A. Skelton and translated from the German by D. L. Paisey (Cambridge, Mass.: Harvard U. Press, 1964). The best general set of maps to illustrate these variants are to be found in: *Claudius Ptolomaus; Cosmografia Weltkarten* (Würzburg: Edition Georg Popp, 1977).

[2] See Bailey W. Diffie and George D. Winius, *Foundations of the Portuguese Empire, 1415-1580* (Minneapolis: U. of Minnesota Press, 1977), 465-471.

[3] See Charles Martial de Witte, "Les bulles pontificales et l'expansion portugaise au XV siècle," *Revue d' histoire ecclésiastique*, 48 (1953), 49 (1954), 51 (1956) and 53 (1958).

[4] See Gomes Eanes de Zurara, *Cronica de Guiné*, Chapter XV. I have used the Livraria Civilização edition of 1937, as edited by José de Bragança.

[5] Texts in *Descobrimentos Portugueses; Documentos para a sua historia, publicados e prefaciados por João Martins de Silva Marques*, 3 vols. in 5 (Lisbon, Instituto da Alta Cultura, 1944- 1971, I (1944), 503-513; 535.

[6] See "Contrato de paz feito entre D. Afonso V de Portugal e os reis de Espanha," Toledo, 1480, Marco 6, as reprinted in: *As Gavetas da Torre do Tombo*, 11 vols. – date (Lisbon: Centro de Estudos Históricos Ultramarinos, 1960-date) VII (1968), Doc. 4185, 314-15.

[7] See Maria Emilia Cordeiro Ferreira, "Casa da Mina," in Joel Serrão (ed.), *Dicionário de história de Portugal*, 4 vols. (Lisbon: Iniciativas Editorias, n.d.), III, 64-66.

[8] This Pedro Reinel map was discovered in the Departmental Archives of the Gironde, Bordeaux, by the French scholar Jacques Bernard in 1960. It seems to have come to the attention of the editors of the *Portugaliae Monumenta Cartographica* too late for inclusion in the first volume, but was included in the fifth and final one, on pp. 182-183. Dr. Armando Cortesão dated it as between 1482 and 1487, most probably 1485.

[9] See Carmen M. Radulet, "As viagens de descobrimento de Diogo Cão; Nova proposta de interpretação," in *Mare Liberum*, No. 1, (1990), 189-190.

[10] Ibid.

[11] The photographs are reproduced in *Mare Liberum*, 203, but are clearer in Damião Peres, *Descobrimentos Portugueses*, 2nd edition (Coimbra: author's edition, 1960), plate XXXIV, opposite p. 283.

[12] An English version of the Latin text is to be found in a small book on the subject, as translated and annotated, with introduction by Francis M. Rogers: *Obedience of a King of Portugal* (Minneapolis: The U. of Minnesota Press, 1958).

[13]See Abel Fontoura da Costa, "As portas da India em 1484," in *Anais do Clube Militar Naval*, Nos. 3 & 4 (1935), 374.

[14] See Peres, *Descobrimentos*, 277.

[15] Radulet, "Viagens de Cão," 193.

[16] Ibid, 194.

[17] Ibid, 195-198.

[18] Luís Adão da Fonseca, *O essencial sobre Bartolomeu Dias* (Lisbon: Imprensa Nacional-Casa de Moeda, 1987), 32-35.

[19] João de Barros, *Da Asia*, decade I, book III, chapter IV. In the 1778 edition, this is on p. 187 of I parte I.

[20] C. F. Beckingham and G. W. B. Huntingford (jt. eds.), *The Prester John of the Indies*, 2 vols. (London: The Hakluyt Society, 1961), I, 1.

[21] Barros, *Da Asia*, decade I, book III, chapters VI-VIII. In the 1778 edition, this tale is on pp. 200-223.

[22] Beckingham and Huntingford, *Prester John*, as described by Frei Francisco Álvares, in his chapter CIV, II, 369-379.

[23] Barros, *Da Asia*, decade I, book III, chapter XI, 245-246.

[24] I will list here only a few of the representative works rejecting the *sigilo* thesis. In order of mention by author, there are: Luís de Albuquerque, *Dúvidas e certezas na história dos descobrimentos portugueses*, 2nd edition, 2 vols. (Lisbon, Vega, 1990-1991); Avelino Teixeira da Mota, *Mar, Além-Mar: estudos e ensaios e ensaios de história e geografia*, 2 vols. (Lisbon: Junta de Investigações do Ultramar – *Agrupamento de Estudos de Cartografia Antiga*, 1972), I; *Os falsos precursores de Pedro Álvares Cabral* (Lisbon: Portugália, 1950); Tomás Oscar Marcondes de Souza, *O descobrimento da America* (São Paulo: Brazilense, 1944); Duarte Leite, *Descobrimentos Portugueses*, 2 vols. (Lisbon: Cosmos, 1958-1960), I; Samuel Eliot Morison, *Portuguese Voyages to America in the FifteenthCentury* (Cambridge, Mass.: Harvard U. Press, 1940); Bailey W. Diffie, "Foreigners in Portugal and the Policy of Silence," *Terrae Incognitae*, I (1969).

[25] Armando Cortesão, *The Mystery of Vasco da Gama* (Coimbra and Lisbon: Junta de Investigações do Ultramar-Lisboa, 1973).

Published in English, as was the author's *History of Portuguese Cartography*. He explains that much of the *Mystery* was to have been included in that work's first chapter.

[26] See Jaime Cortesão, *A expedição de Pedro Álvares Cabral e o Descobrimento do Brasil* (Lisbon: Aillaud e Bertrand, 1922).

[27] For his full-blown thesis, see his *A política do sigilo nos descobrimentos; nos tempos do Infante D. Henrique e de D. João II* (Lisbon: Comissão Executiva das Comemorações do Quinto Centenário da Morte do Infante D. Henrique, 1960).

[28] Diffie, "Foreigners," 23-34.

[29] Luís Adão da Fonseca, *O essencial sobre Bartolomeu Dias* (Lisbon: Imprensa Nacional-Casa de Moeda, 1987), 32-35.

[30] All these documents are conveniently reprinted in: *Bartolomeu Dias. Corpo Documental-Bibliografia* (Lisbon: Comissão Nacional para as Comemorações dos Descobrimentos Portugueses, 1987).

[31] Fonseca, *O essencial*, 34.

[32] Max Justo Guedes, in *O descobrimento do Brasil* (Lisbon: Editorial Vega, 1989) provides a useful discussion of the negotiations preceding the Tordesillas treaty. See 36ff.

[33] Alfredo Pinheiro Marques made this suggestion.

[34] A. Cortesão, *Mystery*, 174-175. Cortesão, perhaps a little like Columbus, seems so absorbed in his theory, in this case that of the *sigilo*, that he fails to perceive what Braamcamp Freire suggested when he wrote of the missing documentation: "*Seria propositada a destruição? é bem possível se attendermos aos misteriosos casos que então se deram, e a propósito de nos negócios, já não digo propriamente do Estado, mas da Corte, se adoptar política muito diversa da do finado Rei.*" See Anselmo Braamcamp Freire, "A chancellaria de D. João II," in *Archivo Historico Portuguez*, II (1894), 338. He inventoried the chancery papers of the reign and obviously associated with their lacunae the rivalry between the dynasties. It seems that natural causes, chiefly the Terremoto of 1755, have little or nothing to do with their absence from the archives, since the excisions are too precise.

[35] One can recall what happened to the memory of Richard III of England and of Enrique IV of Castile when their rivals and enemies came to power. That the Braganças should have done the same would hardly be surprising.

[36] The disproportion is enormous: Barros, for example, takes 10 folio pages to tell of Bemoi's conversion, his life in Lisbon, his return to the Congo and his death, while Dias' journey to the Cape is reported in two folio pages and the negotiations at Tordesillas,

which in effect gained Brazil for Portugal, only a half page. It is inconceivable that if the documentation were then to be found, he would not have written far more.

[37] Fernão Lopes de Castanheda, *História do descobrimento e conquista da India pelos Portugueses*, 4 vols. (Coimbra: U. Press, 1924-1927), I, 9 (Livro I, Capitolo II).

[38] Duarte Pacheco Pereira, *Esmeraldo do Situ Orbis*, tr. & ed. George H. T. Kimble (London: Hakluyt Society, 1936), 10-13. One of the curious echoes of this statement is to be found in the letter written from Lisbon by an Italian merchant, Giovanni Matteo Cretico, dated 27 June 1501 and after the news of Cabral's visit to Brazil had been circulated there. While other witnesses and apparently Cabral himself thought his new "Santa Cruz," as he called Brazil, to be an island, Cretico wrote: "...They judged that this was mainland because they ran along the coast more than two thousand miles, but did not find the end." This is printed in William B. Greenlee (ed. & comp.), *The Voyage of Pedro Álvares Cabral to Brazil and India. From Contemporary Documents and Narratives.* (London: The Hakluyt Society, 1938), 120. Cretico clearly confuses the limited and brief stopover in Brazil by Cabral with the trip made or reported by Pereira. Oddly, Greenlee did not associate the two statements and assumes that Cretico was merely confused! See footnote 4, same page.

[39] See T. A. Chumovsky, *Três roteiros desconhecidos de Ahmad Ibn-Madjid, o piloto àrabe de Vasco da Gama* (Moscow & Leningrad: Academy of Sciences of the U.S.S.R., 1957), 42-43. It seems to me not enough attention has been paid to this important document, perhaps because of differences of opinion over the identity of the author as Vasco da Gama's pilot and because when the Portuguese version appeared in 1957, it was felt that the translation from Arabic to Russian to Portuguese was perhaps too inexact to be trustworthy. But more basically, I suspect, scholars were reluctant to reopen the question of prediscovery. The objections raised then, including those of Damião Peres, now seem rather more like quibbles. Among the ideas rightly rejected, however, was that Ahmad Ibn-Majid, the author, had been the pilot of Vasco da Gama in 1498. Contemporary accounts state that the pilot was a Gujarati, while Ahmad Ibn Majid was an Arab, but of course he might easily have borne the same name as the author. See G. R. Tibbetts, *Arab Navigation in the Indian Ocean before the Coming of the Portuguese* (London: Royal Asiatic Society, 1971), 9-11. Another later Arab writer, Qutb-al-Din al-Nahrawali, the

one on whose writings the identification rests, commented on the early presence of the Portuguese, saying: "At the beginning of the 10th century of the Hegira [1495-1591], among the horrifying and extraordinary events of the era was the arrival in the Indies of the accursed Portuguese, one of the nations of the accursed Franks. One of their bands had departed from the Strait of Ceuta, had penetrated the Sea of Darkness (the Atlantic) and had passed behind the mountains of Al-Komr in the region where the Nile has its source. They proceeded eastwards and passed a place close to where the sea is narrow; on one side there is a mountain, while the other side is toward the Sea of Darkness. There their ships ran aground and were wrecked. No one escaped. For some time, the Portuguese thus continued [to send vessels that way], but none succeeded until one of their caravels finally made its way into the Indian Ocean. [Having arrived on the western coast of the Indian Ocean and the east coast of Africa], then they continued to search the sea until the moment when a capable pilot appeared to serve them called Ahmad ibn Majid." Gabriel Ferrand, *Instructions nautiques et routiers arabes et portugais*, 3 vols. (Paris: 1921-1928), III, 184.

[40] Damião de Góis, *Chronica do felicissimo Rei D. Manoel*, 4 vols. (Lisbon, 1566-1567), I, Chap. XXIV, fol. 17v. In the most recent edition (4 vols., Coimbra: U. Press, 1949-1955), the text is to be found in I, 47-48. I owe this quote to my colleague, Professor Charles Verlinden, who cited it in a lecture at Brown University in the summer of 1992. The text continues: "*...terras habitadas de gente com quem tinhão tratto pelo mar & negocio hos da costa de Melinde & Mobasa & da Ilha de S. Lourenço. Has quais viages todas se fezerão por mandado deste inuencavel Rei D. Ioam, com muito trabalho seu, & despesa da sua fazenda, nauegação já esquecida de todo o genero humano, por tanto spaço de tempo, quanto se pode ver em hum discurso que disso fiz na mesma chronica do Principe D. João, que compuz de novo em lingoagem portuguesa & assi em hum livro que fiz em lingoa latina. Assi que falecido el Rei D. João, socedeu no Regno el Rei D. Emanuel, ho qual como herdeiro universal de toda ha machina & peso destas nauuegações, não contente do que já era descuberto, mas antes muito desejoso de passar adiante...*" The known part of his chronicle of D. João II ends with that monarch's accession and the part of which Góis speaks has never been found. It may be irrelevant to this discussion, but it is known that he made many enemies and died while in the prison of the Inquisition.

Chapter VI

Early Portuguese Expansion in West Africa

The activities of the Portuguese in Africa form a distinctly different pattern within the realm of European expansion from that of the Spanish in America. The most notable feature of the Portuguese expansion is the absence of any significant conquests, and with it all the emotional issues that surround the meaning of the American expansion. True, Africa was eventually conquered by Europeans, but for the most part this conquest took place after 1850 in the aftermath of the Industrial Revolution and as a part of what is often called "The Second Imperialism." Portugal's most significant conquests in Africa, the occupation of a stretch of the Angolan coast and expansion inland some 100 kilometers can scarcely compare with the Spanish efforts. The colony of Angola never overthrew a significant African state, for though it did deprive Ndongo of considerable land, the ruling elites continued in Matamba in the dynasty founded by Queen Njinga (1624-63).[1]

The lack of colonization in Africa was not a result of any distinctive nature of Portuguese policy; the Portuguese would have been perfectly happy to make major conquests, and they certainly put as much effort as that of their Spanish brethren into their African colonies in Morocco and Angola. In fact, they simply fell far short.

Some historians have explained this shortfall of Portuguese ambitions in Africa in terms of the African climate which inhibited military operations through increased mortality to Europeans.[2] But the point is only partially true. The highlands of Angola were quite healthy even if the coast was not, and a significant Portuguese-descended population did develop in Angola without its leading to any great increase in Portuguese territory.[3]

Rather, it is obvious that it was successful African resistance rather than climate that led to the thwarting of Portuguese expansionism.[4]

The Africans fight back

In west Africa, African resistance began just off the coast. When the earliest Portuguese ships began appearing in Sub-Saharan waters in the 1450s, they continued a long-standing tradition of raiding coastal peoples for slaves or whatever merchandise was deemed valuable. It was a policy that had begun in the Mediterranean and continued in the Canaries and along the Saharan coast from the end of the fourteenth century. These first raids along the coast of modern Senegambia were successful in that they caught the African population of the area completely off guard. But it was not a very long time before African resistance began to respond to this new threat. Because the sea-going vessels of Portugal were incapable of navigating successfully in the coastal and estuarial waters of west Africa, military success was only possible if the Portuguese could land soldiers in smaller, oar-powered craft to launch raids. But once they left their ships the Portuguese were faced with African soldiers in craft that were both larger and designed for the specific environment of the coast. It was a one-sided affair, and a number of Portuguese were killed in the following years attempting to continue what was ultimately a disastrous policy of raiding.[5]

In the light of this experience, acquired at the very start of their relations with sub-Saharan Africans, the Portuguese crown recognized that promoting peaceful commerce was more likely to increase its revenues than a policy of raiding. To this end, therefore, King Afonso V dispatched Diogo Gomes on a series of diplomatic missions to the states of western Africa that stretched from 1456 to 1462.[6] Although Gomes met with considerable distrust and sometimes open hostility stemming from the policy of raiding, he eventually made peace with the significant powers of the area.

Having established this new policy, the Portuguese expeditions after 1460 which visited the area from Sierra Leone to that of South Africa proceeded entirely differently from the earlier Portuguese tactics. They sought to develop friendly relations with African rulers first, and to develop peaceful commercial relations, administered if possible though state control. To this end, they cultivated exchanges at the elite level, and sought to promote Christianity not only to save souls, but as a means of developing a sense of commonality with African rulers and political authorities.

By the end of the fifteenth century this policy was in full force. According to Hieronymus Münzer, there were many African princes

residing in Portugal, studying and perhaps becoming inclined towards
a pro-Portuguese policy upon their return home.[7] Study of Portuguese
administrative records reveals much the same thing – gifts of clothing
and money to students in Lisbon from African states are documented,
as are the maintenance costs of keeping up student hostels, along with
a few precious documented statements of these students or their royal
sponsors about their problems or aspirations.[8]

The actual effectiveness of the policy varied. The Portuguese
government had supported D. João Bemoim (usually called "Bemoi" by
moderns) as a candidate to the throne of Great Jolof through the same
policies that brought so many princes to Portugal, and when he had the
opportunity to return home in 1488, a promising opening (from the
Portuguese point of view) was lost when the captain of the ship bearing
him to the Senegal murdered him in an argument.[9] On the other hand,
Portuguese trade and influence was probably well represented in the
conversion of the Kingdom of Kongo after 1491. Despite its being a
stormy relationship, the correspondence between King Afonso I of
Kongo (1509-43) and Lisbon reveals a ruler willing to tolerate the
misconduct of local Portuguese merchants and their royal supervisors
to continue a commercial and diplomatic relationship with Portugal.[10]

Of course, without a genuine military presence or the means to
force policy, Portugal's program to increase its influence in Africa
through offering education and Christianity to African states was
limited. When Portuguese interests and those of Kongo clashed, there
was no question whose policies would win out, as for instance in
1526 when Afonso decided to institute strict controls of the activities
of Portuguese merchants in his state.[11] Or when the king of Benin,
after a promising opening, received Dominican missionaries coldly in
1531, making it clear that he would control the fate of the Portuguese
in his kingdom.[12]

The Portuguese leave their mark

However, these dramatic confrontations did not undermine the
overall results of the peaceful and generally cooperative relations
between African states and Portugal in the XVI century. The process
of cultural exchange began with formal Christianization, as in the case
of Kongo,[13] and a few other states in the years that followed (Warri, the
Temne states of Sierra Leone),[14] and with other items of culture. By
the end of the XVI century most of the elite of African societies on the
coast could speak Portuguese, which remained the language of
international commerce until late in the XVII century, even in areas
where Portugal was driven from the coast by the Dutch in the early

XVII century. African clothing styles incorporated not only cloth from Europe, but even hats and other made-up clothing elements.

Although Africans all along the coast began to adopt elements of European culture, the process of cultural acceptance was entirely under the control of the Africans themselves. Unlike in the Americas, where everything from religious conversion to new city plans can be explained as the socio-cultural aftermath of conquest, Africans took what pleased them and adopted it to their own use. This borrowing is most obvious in regard to clothing, where Africans adopted elements of European clothing, but combined them with African clothing to create a new mixture of styles.[15]

The development of African Christianity represents another example of African acceptance of European ideas but adopting them as well. The Kongolese were converted, according both to European accounts and those of their own authorship, such as the letter of Kongolese King Afonso I, and through miracles and visions in which the Virgin Mary, Saint James Major and Jesus were revealed to Africans. But if accepting the existence of these Christian figures allowed the Kongolese to be Christians, they continued to believe in the immortality and imminence of their ancestors, rather than in a strictly Christian Heaven and Hell. They managed to transform the concept of charms (*nkisi* in Kikongo) by using their names to mean "holy" when employed in an abstract or an adjectival form.[16]

These transformations of European culture were possible, of course because Europeans were present in Africa as invited guests rather than as conquerors. Europeans were compelled to accept, and accept they did, the new and novel transformations of their own culture in the hands of Africans. Indeed, it is fairly clear that Europeans themselves, who resided for long periods in Africa, soon became more or less culturally Africanized, even if they held proudly to a few symbols of their European origin or ancestry through language, naming patterns or formal religious membership.

Slaving

At first glance, given this background of Portuguese policy and its results, it seems surprising that from a very early date, this relationship should have involved the trade in slaves. Already in 1500 more than 5,000 slaves were leaving African ports each year, bound for Europe, and the islands of the Atlantic. This number had nearly doubled, to 9,500 per year by the end of the XVI century, while the XVII century witnessed a further fourfold increase to nearly 36,000 per year by 1700.[17] Although the great increase in the slave trade lay more in the late XVII century than with the earlier periods, the export of slaves was still very significant for many of the African states engaged in the Atlantic trade.

Much of the increase in the volume of the trade came from new areas and states entering the trade as much as from an increase in exports from some regions. The Gold Coast went from being a slave importer to being a major exporter during the later XVII century, while the ports on the coast of modern Togo, Bénin and Nigeria did not begin their export pattern until the late XVI century, and it was not until the second half of the XVII century that they became major exports. Senegambia, Sierra Leone and central Africa, however, those areas where Europeans did a great deal of their business in the earlier periods, were long term exporters of slaves, and slaves were always very prominent among their exports.[18]

Historians with a demographic bent have shown in recent years that the annual export of so many thousands of people had a negative effect on the African economy. Even if whole populations were not swept away into the holds of slave ships, as an earlier generation may have believed, serious demographic consequences still followed long term participation in the trade. Age structures became distorted as productive adults were lost to African states and regions, while the propensity of African merchants to sell and European merchants to buy males had potentially disruptive impacts on the sex ratio and sexual division of labor of the remaining population.[19]

Attaching the responsibility

Given this background, historians have found themselves compelled to argue that somehow Africans had been forced to participate in the slave trade. Unlike some other trade, the slave trade would seem to have negative consequences for those who engaged in it, and it is difficult to see that participation as a willing one.

It is easy, perhaps, to see some connection between the diplomatic connections pioneered by Portugal, the continued Portuguese presence in Africa and the offshore islands, such as São Tomé and the Cape Verdes and the apparent willingness of Africans to yield up their lifeblood in such numbers. Alternatively, historians have sought to explain the paradox of the peaceful exchange of people for European goods through the vehicle of differential development. Sixteenth century relations might prefigure those of the post-industrial era, in which economic power evidenced by a highly productive manufacturing sector was manifested in the ability to force less developed countries to engage in suicidal policies of underdevelopment.[20] If African underdevelopment was not manifested in all branches of production, then perhaps it was critically absent in the question of weapons production, where superior instruments of war emerged from European workshops and factories and could be selectively presented to Africans in exchange for slaves.[21]

These explanations have not worn well, however. It is hard to see pre-industrial Europe as the economic powerhouse of the post-industrial epoch. Even if one admits that the European economies employed more power-driven tools and machinery or better accounting devices than those of Africa, the last two decades of research in European economic history have certainly gone a long way to dispel any notions that Europe was capable of purveying economic dependency to the rest of the world. It is sobering to consider, in this regard, that Africans imported virtually nothing from Europe that they did not already produce themselves. It is virtually impossible to argue that the trade of Europe with Africa, conducted on the small scale that it was, made much difference in the competitive position of African industry, even the textile or metal industries, which would have been most affected by European competition.[22]

Slaves for guns?

Even the celebrated gun-slave cycle theory of African participation in the slave trade, whereby Africans were forced to sell slaves to buy guns in order to defend themselves against other Africans who had been supplied guns and needed to obtain slaves to pay for them, is hard to argue for the period before the advent of the flintlock musket after 1680. Weapons were only a small part of the imports into Africa before that period, and European weapons were not the most important part of the "art of war" as practiced in Africa before the 1680s. While the gun-slave theory may help to explain the post-1680 expansion of slave exports (though that also remains to be proven), it will hardly serve for the earlier periods.[23]

Unfortunately, so often the common explanations of the development of the slave trade are grounded on a fairly superficial understanding of African politics and social structure. It has never been appropriate, for example, to speak of the slave trade in any given instance as involving "the Africans" trading with "the Europeans." Neither the possession of slaves nor the means to make policy on trade was vested in such a collective group. African societies were not democratic, and the decision to participate in foreign trade and choose which commodities were appropriate to trade was not made collectively. Thus, historians have not spent nearly as much time as they should in studying the motivations of those people who did make decisions to engage in the trade.

African societies were not only not democratic, they were also not egalitarian. The division of wealth between rich and poor might have been less in Africa than in Europe or in Asia, but there was a division nevertheless. In these circumstances, it might not be too surprising that the people who made decisions to go to war, capture slaves, sell these slaves to overseas dealers were only considering their own interests and that of their immediate supporters, and not the overall good of their country, much less their region, continent or even race.

Consider, for example, a celebrated and well documented military operation from the period of early Afro-European contact, Afonso I's attack on Munza around 1513. The event, which is described in Afonso's own letter to D. Manuel I of Portugal of 15 October 1514, began when Munza, apparently a ruler of a small state in the mountainous region that separated Kongo from Ndongo, attacked the province of Mbamba, then governed by Afonso's son. A large army was dispatched from Kongo with Afonso at its head to punish Munza, and perhaps to extend the Kongolese authority further, since we know that Kongo was engaged in territorial expansion in the area at the time. In course of time, Afonso sent 410 slaves that his forces had captured back to his capital to be exported on the *Gaio*, a ship that would soon leave for Portugal. Other participants in the war sent back others, for one of Afonso's Portuguese assistants sent a further 190 back, and perhaps the total number captured exceeded 1,000 people. Many of these slaves were exported, although others were retained in Kongo.[24]

Although this letter is full of denunciation for the Portuguese in his kingdom, who Afonso argued, had cheated him, were lazy, told lies about him and failed in their Christian duties, he makes it perfectly clear that the causes of the war lay in the politics of his expansion, that he captured many slaves personally, that he intended to export them and that he did none of these things under any sort of external pressure. No one has "stirred him up" against Munza, and he makes no claim that some Portuguese had stirred Munza up against him. He mentions other wars in his correspondence, and although he and his successors occasionally complained that renegade Portuguese illegally aided his opponents, he never implies that he would have lived in peace without the Portuguese.

Obviously, Afonso's interests were not damaged by the loss of the people involved in this war, or the others he waged during his over 35-year reign. The thousand slaves or more were lost to Munza, not to him. Like other conquerors, he no doubt felt that the lives of the soldiers lost in the action were worth the glory of conquest or the profit of the spoils. Many of the slaves that were captured and returned to his royal city were employed there. We know that one of the principal causes of Kongo's centralization was the great concentration of people, many of them slaves, in the royal city and its immediate environs, so that this war benefited Afonso doubly by adding to that process as well as increasing his wealth and securing or extending his borders.

This small incident can serve as a microcosm of the mechanisms whereby Africans, through peaceful interactions with Portugal, became involved in the slave trade. Many African political and economic elites employed slaves in their service to increase their wealth and personal following. The ethos of warfare and the capture of people as spoils were well built into their world view. While the slaves were valuable to them at home, there was a point, as there always is in economic choices, where exporting some exceeded the utility of keeping them. Clearly this was the logic that drove them to decide to sell their slaves, probably not from estates or household service, but newly acquired from war or purchase.

One may, of course, argue that Afonso, and many other African rulers were somehow cynically exploiting their own people, distorting the regional demography, robbing future generations of development potential all to benefit short-term selfish considerations of greed and power. Naturally, such an indictment is possible, but it must be made with some caution. The idea that the state exists to serve the greater good of all the people in an area is a modern concept, born, along with that of mass democracy and government responsibility, in the post-Industrial era, and not always faring so well there. European and Asian rulers were equally cavalier about their subordinate and subject populations, rarely considered long term economic consequences of their actions for their region, much less the development potential of their states. Afonso and his cohorts were simply at home in a world that viewed such matters as typical and commonplace.

Thus it came to be that in West Africa Portuguese settlements were confined mostly to coastal enclaves, and when compared to Brazil, their development began late. Only in 1571 was a *doação*, a patent of donation, accorded to a Portuguese *donatário*, or proprietor, one Paulo Dias de Novais, granting him the 35 leagues to the south of the Kwanza River and stretching an unspecified distance into the interior. While (to judge from the provisions of his charter) the purpose of the colony was to be agricultural, in actuality, the dry coastal weather conditions were unsuitable for traditional European crops and fevers lay in wait for newcomers unaccustomed to the climate.

Dias did not succeed in organizing and landing a party of colonists on Luanda Island until 1575, where the settling parties soon discovered that they were not without the company of others of their countrymen: other Portuguese – slavers – had preceded them there, and their activities proved to be the determining ones. Nor were matters helped by the welcoming gift sent by the Ndongo, as the region's ruler was called – 100 slaves.

A few years later, most of the settlers moved over to the mainland, when in 1579, war broke out between Ndongo and the colonists, perhaps because Dias had let it be known that he intended to monopolize the export of slaves from the entire region.[25] Dias de Novais, acting in concert with King António I of Kongo sought to conquer Ndongo in a series of wars between 1579 and 1590. Kongo dropped out after suffering an early defeat, but Dias de Novais managed to hold on to a section of the coast and a few forts along the rivers, especially a town called Massangano, near the confluence of the Kwanza and Lukala Rivers.

Paulo Dias de Novais died in 1589, while in 1590, a serious Portuguese defeat in the upriver region led to virtual military stagnation. The fabled silver mines of Cambambe whose existence had fired up Portuguese plans of conquest were never found, and thereafter, until well into the XVII century, all the sporadic wars between the Ndongo and the Portuguese could produce were more slaves, alternately traded for cloth in more peaceful moments or else captured directly in times of shooting. This was not for lack of ambitious plans, but despite talk of crossing Africa and exploiting the gold mines of the Zambezi valley from the west, nothing was done to achieve such an unlikely project. No other Portuguese colony was founded in West Africa until Benguela, down the coast many leagues to the south, in 1615.[26]

From all of the above, it should be concluded that throughout what historians of Europe call early modern times, Portuguese discoveries and coastal settlements in Western Africa did not lead to European domination over any appreciable numbers of African peoples, nor did it much interfere with the body politic. Instead, the indigenes, no doubt helped by the climate, successfully contained and constrained Portuguese expansionism at their expense.

John K. Thornton

Notes

[1] The best survey remains David Birmingham, *Trade and Conflict in Angola. The Mbundu and their Neighbors under the Influence of the Portuguese 1483-1790* (Oxford: Clarendon, 1966).

[2] This was the explanation of Birmingham, *Trade and Conflict.* The widespread idea that African diseases were responsible for the absence of early European conquest is best represented by Kwame Nkrumah's decision to build a statue to the Anopheles mosquito in Ghana after that country attained its independence in 1957.

[3] A good description of XVII century Angola from the perspective of the Portuguese colonist is found in António de Oliveira de Cadornega's chronicle and description, composed in 1680-81, *História das guerras angolanas (1680-81)* (mod. ed. Mattias Delgado and Manuel Alves de Cunha, 3 vols., Lisbon, 1940-42, reprinted 1972). See also n. 25.

[4] This was already obvious by 1594, when Pero Rodrigues, a Jesuit chronicler, summed up the first two decades of Portuguese expansion in Angola, in "História da residéncia dos Padres Jesuitas em Angola," in António Brásio, ed., *Monumenta Missionaria Africana* 1st series, Angola (15 vols., Lisbon, 1952-88), 4: 456-81. The later chronicles of Cadornega, *História* and the *Catálogo dos governadores de Angola* (originally composed in the late XVIII century and updated by various hands after that). There are several recensions of the *Catálogo* published in modern times, see the version in Elias Alexandre da Silva Corrêa, *História de Angola* (Lisbon, 1937).

[5] This period is covered in detail, with full references to the primary sources in John Thornton, *Africa and Africans in the Making of the Atlantic World 1400-1680* (Cambridge: Cambridge U. Press, 1992).

[6] Gomes's own account, "De Prima Inuentione Guine" written about 1490 in Latin, can be found in the manuscript of the Lisbon-based Bohemian printer Valentim Fernandes (mod. ed. António Baião, *O manuscrito 'Valentim Fernandes'*, Lisbon, 1940).
A French translation, *De la Première découverte de la Guinée* with the Latin original on facing pages was published in Dakar in 1959.

[7] Münzer's account, "De Inventione Africae maritimae," is published in Brásio, ed. *Monumenta* second series, Guiné (5 vols., Lisbon: Agência Geral do Ultramar, 1958-80) 1: 214-53.

[8] Some of the records are printed in Brásio, *Monumenta* 1st series, 2: 66-9 and 15: 46.

[9] A fully documented study, Avelino Teixeira da Mota,"D. João Bemoim e a expedição portuguesa ao Senegal em 1489", *Agrupamento de cartografia antiga*, series seperata, no. 63, (Lisbon, 1971).

[10] This correspondence is fully published in Brásio, *Monumenta* 1st series, vols. 1, 2, 4 and 15, *passim*. A French translation of a major portion was published by Louis Jadin and Mirelle Dicorati, *La correspondance de D. Afonso, roi de Congo* (Brussels: Academie Royale de Sciences d'Outre-Mer, 1980).

[11] On the early relations between Kongo and Portugal, see John Thornton, "Early Kongo-Portuguese Relations, 1483-1575: A New Interpretation," *History in Africa* 8 (1981): 183-204.

[12] For a modern discussion, see Alan F. C. Ryder, *Benin and the Europeans 1472-1897* (London: Longmans, 1969), 70-75.

[13] John Thornton, "The Development of an African Catholic Church in the Kingdom of Kongo, 1483-1750," *Journal of African History* 25 (1984): 147-67.

[14] For an overview, see Lamin Sanneh, *West African Christianity* (Maryknoll: Orbis, 1982).

[15] Thornton, *Africa and Africans*, chapter 8.

[16] The theological elements of this conversion are discussed in John Thornton, "Christianity in Africa," a paper presented at the conference "Race: Discourse and the Origins of the Americas" Washington, DC (Smithsonian Institution), 30 Oct.-1 Nov., 1991.

[17] The figures derive from Thornton, *Africa and Africans*, chap. 5.

[18] Thornton, *Africa and Africans*, chapter 4.

[19] Patrick Manning, *Slavery and African Life: Occidental Oriental, and African Slave Trades* (Cambridge: Cambridge U. Press, 1990), using a simulation model that he has been developing since 1979, see also John Thornton, "The Demographic Impact of the Slave Trade on Western Africa," in Christopher Fyfe and David McMaster, eds. *African Historical Demography*, vol. 2 (Edinburgh, 1981), 691-720.

[20] See, for example, the work of Walter Rodney, *The History of the Upper Guinea Coast 1545-1800* (Oxford: Clarendon, 1970) and *How Europe Underdeveloped Africa* (London: Bogle Louvertone, 1972, and Washington, DC: Howard U. Press, 1974, with different pagination).

[21] An old concept, the "gun-slave cycle"dates back to abolition debates of the XVIII century, see the most recent formulation in the work of Joseph E. Inikori, for example "Introduction" *Forced Migration: The Impact of the Export Slave Trade on the African Societies* (London: Hutchinson, 1981), 13-60.

[22] See the recent debate published in the journal *African Economic History* 19 (1990), lead article, presenting this position, by John Thornton, "Pre-Colonial African Economy and the Atlantic Trade," comments by Ralph Austen, Patrick Manning, Ann McDougall, and Jan Hogendorn, and a reply by Thornton.

[23] See the discussion in Thornton, *Africa and Africans*.

[24] The letter is published in Brásio, *Monumenta* 1st series, 1: 294-323. An English translation appears in William McNeil and Mitsuko Iriye, eds. *Modern Asia and Africa* (Oxford: Oxford U. Press, 1971), 44-74.

[25] For a basic treatment and analysis of the Angolan wars, see David Birmingham, *Trade and Conflict in Angola. The Mbundu and their Neighbors under the Influence of the Portuguese 1483-1790* (Oxford: the Clarendon Press, 1966). The classic contemporary source in António de Oliveira de Cadornega, *História Geral das Guerras Angolanas*, 3 vols., 1680, as reprinted in 1940 and 1972, the latter edition being the only one generally available, as edited and annotated by José Matias Delgado and published by the Agência Geral do Ultramar.

[26] For Benguela, see Delgado's edition of Cadornega, III, 168-185.

A̲t the coronation of Pope Innocent VII in 1485, the Portuguese ambassador, Vasco Fernandes de Lucena, delivered his celebrated *Oratio de Obedientia* in which he communicated the following prospects:

Vasco da Gama and His Successors

> Lastly, to all these things may be added the by no means uncertain hope of exploring the Barbarian Gulf, where kingdoms and nations of Asiatics, barely known to us and then only by the most meager of information, practice very devoutly the most holy faith of the Savior. The farthest limit of Lusitanian maritime exploration is at present only a few days distant from them, if the most competent geographers are but telling the truth. As a matter of fact, by far the greatest part of the circuit of Africa being by then already completed, our men last year reached almost to the Prassum Promontorium, where the Barbarian Gulf begins, having explored all the rivers, shores and ports over a distance that is reckoned at more than forty-five hundred miles from Lisbon, according to very accurate observation of the sea, lands and stars. Now that that region is explored, I seem to be able to perceive how many and how large accumulations of fortunes and honors and glory will befall not only all of Christendom but also, and chiefly, you, Most Blessed Father, and your successors, and this most sacred See of Peter. [1]

From an objective standpoint, the claims of Vasco Fernandes de Lucena appear erroneous, or perhaps based upon an excessively optimistic evaluation of the explorations of Diogo Cão. Or still more probably, taking full account of this international gathering, the Portuguese crown viewed the circumstances as propitious for obtaining further recognition on the part of the Holy See for its enterprise then in progress.[2] Thus, despite any "errors," the outcome was more than satisfactory. On 18 February 1486, in his bull, *Ortodoxae fidei*, the pope conceded to D. João II concrete economic privileges and the assistance of the religious orders for a future crusade against the infidels of the Orient.

The strategy of D. João II does not represent so much an innovation in Portuguese political behavior as it witnesses to the king's preoccupation with a legal matrix capable of guaranteeing the exclusivity of his navigation, commerce, evangelization, and in a broader sense, sole presence, in a certain overseas area. Surveying the whole series of the so-called "expansion bulls," beginning soon after the conquest of Ceuta, the Lusitanian sovereigns attempted to formalize from a juridical viewpoint *vis-à-vis* other European powers all territories deriving from their discoveries and expansion. D. João II, especially after the struggles with Castile concluded by the treaty of Alcáçovas, showed himself to be particularly insistent on international recognition of Portuguese rights theretofore acquired and on the definition of those which could guarantee future developments of Portuguese expansion. In 1479, through the treaty of Alcáçovas, Portugal renounced its pretenses to the Canaries and to the conquest of the Kingdom of Granada, but which reserved for itself the exclusivity of navigation, of commerce and of exploration, not only in the "seas of Guinea," but also in a region not well defined, situated generally in the South Atlantic.[3]

After the return in 1493 of Christopher Columbus from his celebrated first voyage into the western Atlantic, the politic of the Portuguese crown received a counterblow when, based upon the traditional interpretation of what had been ratified at Alcáçovas – and subsequently by the Holy See – whatever discovery the Genoese navigator might have made, it was located in an area tacitly assigned to future Portuguese expansion. Nevertheless, preempting the principle of the value of an actual discovery and the rights deriving from it, the Castilian crown successfully claimed the possession and usufruct of the lands discovered by Columbus. The election to the pontifical throne of Pope Alexander VI offered Castile its real chance to resist Portuguese presence on an international plane, since the bulls all favor the Spanish arguments (*Inter caetera, Inter caetera II, Eximiae devotionis, Piis fidelium, Dudum siquidem*). All these documents emanating from this pope during 1493 induced D. João II to accept the idea of direct consultations with the Catholic Kings. It is on this basis that D. João II and the Catholic Kings, after complex negotiations, succeeded in arriving at a new juridical definition of the zone for future expansion of the two Iberian countries. The concrete result of which was the promulgation on 7 June 1494 of a new treaty between the two crowns, the Treaty of Tordesillas.[4] In it D. João II renounced all pretenses to the lands discovered by Columbus and to a region not specifically defined situated in the western Atlantic Ocean, to the west of a line traced from pole to pole at 370 leagues from the Cape Verde Islands, while Portugal retained not only the exclusivity of its presence not only in the seas of Guinea and consequently the possibility of circumnavigating Africa. It also reserved for Lusitanian expansion an area situated in the southern part of the Atlantic, one which turned out to coincide at least in part with Brazil.[5]

Following the death of D. João II, his successor, D. Manuel, at last possessed sufficient juridical guarantees *vis-à-vis* Spain and the rest of Europe to allow him to set in motion the project for the circumnavigation of Africa – into which so much time and effort had been invested by his predecessor.[6] As a consequence and as a formalization of the rights which he now potentially enjoyed, on the occasion of Vasco da Gama's return in 1499 with news of the real possibility of reaching India by sea, D. Manuel added to the royal title used by D. João II that of *Senhor da Conquista, Navegação e Comércio da Etiópia, Arábia, Pérsia e da Índia*.[7] This title, too often seen only as an expression of dreams of grandeur, actually expresses a juridical unity as a first step in pursuing a politic of expansion.[8] And in this sense it is no coincidence that D. Manuel employed it in writing to the Holy See on 25 August 1499, immediately after the feasibility of his projects became a certainty.[9] Of course neither the juridical principles nor the consequent titles of legitimation might serve as justifications for non-European nations and peoples – even though they did sanction the potential right of expansion, dominion and "*conquista*" of those two European countries which through bilateral treaties and bulls had managed to arrogate these prerogatives to themselves.

This long prologue has been necessary to explain and to understand in its correct dimensions the philosophical basis upon which the expansion of Portugal developed, not only on the western coasts of Africa and in Brazil, but also in the Orient, in the construction of the entity which we might give the title of "Portuguese Asian empire."

Portugal, the Pathfinder

Vasco da Gama and the first sea voyage to India

After having resolved the principal questions of a juridical nature
which defined its bounds from those of Spain, the Portuguese crown,
following the decisions of D. Manuel, could put the circumnavigation
of Africa to the great test. In this sense, the expedition led by Vasco da
Gama in 1497 still displayed all the characteristics of an exploration,
while everyone supposed that its success, at least from a theoretical
standpoint, was debatable.[10] In one of its dimensions, the voyage is well
enough known, thanks to the diary of an unknown passenger usually
(though he probably not correctly) identified as Álvaro Velho. It
provides much information as to personnel and events of the passage.[11]
But in regard to another, extremely important aspect, the question
concerning exactly where Da Gama sailed in the Atlantic prior to
reaching the Cape of Good Hope and what kind of navigational
conditions and problems he might have encountered, the diary is vague
and clearly written by a landlubber; all we know for certain is that it
departed from Lisbon on 8 July 1497 and that after leaving the Cape
Verde Islands, the four ships sailed for three months beyond sight of
land, indicating that they did not seek to follow the route used by Dias
in his discovery of the Cape of Good Hope. Since the outward voyage
to the Cape occupied much more time than what became normal for
subsequent voyages, four-and-a-half months against a more usual
three, one would like to know what route he took. The one thing
certain is that the voyage was far longer and more arduous than that of
Columbus five years before, equal to halfway around the earth at the
equator, and it was surely of equal significance because it created
permanent links between Europe and the Orient, just as Columbus did
between Europe and the two hitherto unknown continents.

Whichever routing Da Gama successfully, if tortuously, used to
navigate the South Atlantic, by 22 November he had successfully
reached the Cape of Good Hope. Near there, at the Angra de São
Braz, the supply vessel was abandoned, its cargoes and crews integrated
with those of the ships remaining.

Starting up the African coast, his crews ill with scurvy, on
Christmas day, Da Gama first stopped for refreshment on the east
African coast at a port which the diarist inevitably calls "Natal" – a
name it still bears. Pausing again for water in southern Mozambique,
he learned that it might be possible to obtain pilots at a port farther up
the coast, Malindi, for the crossing of the Arabian Sea to India. The
reports indeed proved true: after one other sojourn at Mozambique
Island, the ships continued on to Malindi, arriving at the end of

136

March. There they not only found a suitable pilot, one Ahmad Ibn Majid, but received a warm welcome.[12] They were now within easy reach of their goal.

For Ibn Majid navigated Da Gama and his ships directly eastwards across the Indian Ocean to a landfall near Calicut, where they arrived on 20 May 1498. Of Da Gama's meeting with its ruler, the Samorin, only a few things need be said here: the Portuguese were eager to establish trading relationships and the Samorin willing, but, naturally enough, the Arab traders whose commerce ultimately reached Europe through the Red Sea were less than enthusiastic at prospects of competition. Moreover, the Portuguese, who were used to trading with Africans, appear to have brought the wrong merchandise with them for exchange: fortunately, they were able to obtain a moderate cargo of pepper, anyway, if because the Samorin wished to encourage future, more lucrative, relations.

Da Gama's initiative established a totally different relationship with Asia than Columbus's voyage did to what turned out to be a new and unfamiliar world. For the Portuguese commander encountered not Stone Age peoples, as did the Genoese, but Moslems and Hindus whose prosperity, armament, and numbers precluded any large-scale conquest such as that conquest undertaken by the Spaniards in Columbus's wake. The best the Portuguese could do was to accommodate themselves to the situation, first seeking trade only, but when they encountered opposition from their Moslem rivals, applying their naval power to specific and small areas on land, and for the rest, seeking to dominate the water of the Arabian Sea with their navies.

When after some two years, the expedition returned to Portugal, confirming positively that it was possible to undertake maritime voyages between Lisbon and India, King D. Manuel, by calling himself "Lord of the Conquest, Navigation, and Commerce of Ethiopia, Arabia, Persia and of India", set the machinery in motion for the succeeding political and military actions.

During the expedition of Vasco da Gama it was confirmed that at least a part of the Indian potentates were strongly conditioned to the presence of their Islamic merchants – and that as a consequence, it was necessary in India to attempt the imposition of a Portuguese supremacy, a supremacy which, in that decisive moment, could hardly be economic or religious – only military. In that sense one must assess the *regimento* (standing orders) of the second expedition to India, that led by Pedro Álvares Cabral.

The Second Expedition: enter Pedro Álvares Cabral

Pedro Álvares Cabral was named captain general on 15 February 1500 of a substantial fleet, consisting of 13 vessels both *naus* and caravels, outfitted both by the crown and by Portuguese and foreign merchants. It departed for India on 9 March 1500 from Lisbon with some of the most famous captains and pilots of the last years of the XV century and transported some 1,200 to 1,500 men, including sailors, soldiers and merchants.

This time, it was less a matter of an expedition to carry out reconnaissance so much as a diplomatic, military and mercantile one. His experience had shown Vasco da Gama that relations with the Indian potentates were not comparable to those with whom the Portuguese were used to dealing on the west coast of Africa – and that as a consequence, the regiment which was given to the new commander is far more complex and its execution far more difficult and unforeseeable than was imagined at his moment of departure.[11]

In this initial phase, that of the passage through the Atlantic, according to the route indicated by Vasco da Gama, on 22 April 1500, Brazil was "officially" discovered.[12] Of it, Cabral sent news to the king and proceeded on the *volta do largo* – as the sweeping passage was called – en route to the Cape of Good Hope. In spite of considerable navigational problems and the loss of four ships during a great storm at the latitude of the Cape, the fleet, reduced to six vessels, arrived at Calicut on 13 September of the same year. After a first contact, in which relations with the Samorin appeared to be developing favorably, despite the somewhat negative experience of Vasco da Gama, the atmosphere was poisoned through the opposition of the Arab merchants, obliging Cabral to resort to force – relying on that naval supremacy of which the Portuguese were fully aware. After the encounter at Calicut, the captain-general set sail for Cochin, whose ruler, an enemy of the Samorin, had indicated his interest in establishing friendly relations with the Portuguese. Subsequently, the rajas of both Cannanore and Coylan followed the example of their colleague in Cochin; and in this way Cabral succeeded not only in buying a satisfactory quantity of spices, but also in preparing the groundwork at Cochin for a future *feitoria*, or factory. The fleet departed from Cannanore on 31 January 1501 and, despite the loss of another ship and difficulties in negotiating the passage around the Cape, returned to Lisbon at the end of July of that year.

The name of Pedro Álvares Cabral remains primarily associated with the discovery of Brazil, even though the expedition he led resulted in some decisive steps in maritime, military and especially diplomatic history. In the maritime theatre, he established the most rapid route between Lisbon and India, as determined by the monsoon system, so that the two years needed by Vasco da Gama was accomplished in only 17 months. In the military one, he demonstrated to the Indian potentates the clear Portuguese naval superiority which also served to translate itself into a practical military advantage. In respect to diplomacy, he inaugurated the practices, fully to be exercised in the future, of closing alliances with Indian princes, alliances which assured Portugal not only real territorial conquests, but, through agreements or treaties with a number of rulers, often at odds with one another, the possibility of using their ports, in which to establish *feitorias* and concentrate commercial activities.

On the third expedition, dispatched to India in 1501, sources are very meagre. A few Italian ones primarily of a mercantile nature have been found, and these do succeed in providing indications – hitherto unpublished – of what transpired. Through a careful study of these testimonies, Mme Geneviève Bouchon has succeeded in establishing its route and reconstructing in broad outline the regiment of the voyage which took place between 1501 and 1502 of the four caravels commanded by João da Nova.[13] On this voyage, until recently considered purely commercial in nature, there were two caravels outfitted by the king and two more outfitted by Bartolomeu Marchioni and his associate, D. Álvaro, son of the Duke of Bragança.[14] The little fleet left Lisbon on 9 March 1501 – hence prior to the return of Pedro Álvares Cabral, on 12 September 1502. During these 18 months, João da Nova, according to these Italian sources, passed through Kilwa, Mozambique, Mombasa, Malindi, Cannanore (where he laid the foundations for a new factory), and Cochin. But the fleet, not provided with gold, had difficulty in obtaining pepper and spices, and in order not to miss the monsoon, its departure from the Malabar coast appears to have been precipitous. On the basis of these data, together with an analysis of the political shifts in India, Mme Bouchon has concluded that the expedition was not simply commercial in nature so much as one primarily for exploration – even though it was financed in large part by merchants. This thesis can be well documented in spite of the paucity of Portuguese source material, and it could also explain the carving found on a rock in Colombo in which there is inscribed the Portuguese coat of arms and the date 1501. According to the distinguished French researcher, João da Nova could therefore very well have been the first European to discover Ceylon, a

good five years before the "official" disembarcation on that island of
D. Lourenço de Almeida.[15]

Vasco da Gama asserts his prerogatives

Upon his return from his first voyage to India, Vasco da Gama
received from the King, D. Manuel, a number of rewards, both
honorific and material, and was also nominated Admiral of India. The
concession of this title, although it recalls in certain ways the special
favor granted Christopher Columbus by the Catholic Kings, seems
rather different, if not in substance, then in philosophy, seeing that D.
Manuel, possessed of all the traditional juridical trappings of the
epoch, at the moment in which he assumed the title of *Senhor da
Conquista, Navegação e Comércio da Etiópia, Arábia Pérsia e da Índia*, might
also create the title of *Almirante da Índia* quite naturally, as an extension
of the existing one of *Almirante de Portugal*. The concession to Vasco da
Gama of this revivified office, the historian of jurisprudence, António
Vasconcelos de Saldanha, has demonstrated to be from December of
1500, even though the chroniclers are at odds on its exact date, and
even though the sole transcription of the *Regimento* according it might
be dated only from 23 November of 1521.[17]

When in 1502, there was readied for sailing to India a great fleet,
whose command was supposed to devolve on Captain-General Pedro
Álvares Cabral, Vasco da Gama invoked the rights which he possessed
deriving from his title as Admiral of India and practically constrained
the king to nullify the initial nomination and to concede to him the
command of the expedition. Thus in the fleet which departed from
Lisbon between February and the beginning of April of 1502, there
sailed besides the Admiral of India in their roles as captains three of his
close relatives (Estevão da Gama, Vicente Sodré and Brás Sodré). The
regimento of Vasco da Gama envisaged two distinct but complementary
objectives: to impose Portuguese supremacy upon the Malabar Coast,
above all in those port cities where the trade in spices was concentrated
and to stabilize the treaties and agreements of a diplomatic and
mercantile nature with those sovereigns who, in opposition to the
Samorin of Calicut, had shown themselves inclined to recognize
Portugal. In this light should be viewed some of the most important
undertakings of the mission, such as the contacts with Cochin and
above all the heightened encounters with the Samorin and the reprisals
which are connected with them.[18]

Along these same lines the activities of the successive fleets can be
grouped, such as that of 1503 as led by the future governor of India,
Afonso de Albuquerque (three ships charged with constructing a

fortress in Cochin in order to defend the city, the local ruler and the interests of the Portuguese crown) and that of Francisco de Albuquerque (another three vessels on trading and military errands). More or less the very same political directives are encountered in the *regimento* prepared for the expedition commanded by Lopo Soares de Albergaria which departed from Lisbon for the Malabar Coast on 22 April 1504.

From this moment on, there exists not only a growing Portuguese engagement in the Indian Ocean, but also a diversification of the expeditions dispatched to the Orient: there followed the discovery of new emporia, the preservation of those already discussed, or else their military or diplomatic *conquista* and their consequent involvement with the Portuguese crown in the complex machinery which regulated the relationships not only between the Indian kingdoms but also those of the Far East.

Thus bulwarked by juridical rights guaranteed by the papal bulls and accurately defined in international treaties, and in possession of juridical and formal prerogatives (which underlay the new royal designation of "Lord of the Conquest, Navigation and Commerce of Ethiopia, Arabia Persia and of India"), D. Manuel, through his regular launching of expeditions, passed progressively through the phase of "discovery-recognition" to that of economic and political dominion.

In 1505, D. Francisco de Almeida was nominated not simply as captain-general of a great fleet, but as governor-general for three years, with the possibility, after having constructed Portuguese fortresses at Cannanore, Cochin and Coylan, of assuming the title and powers of viceroy. As will be shown in Chapter X by George Winius, "The Estado da India on the Subcontinent; the Portuguese as Players on a South Asian Stage", from this moment on the concrete foundations were laid for the creation of the Portuguese Estado da India – or according to a different formula – of the Portuguese Asian empire, which with it ups and downs would enjoy a lifespan of more than four centuries. It would leave a deep impression both on the course of history for many European countries as well as on those of Asia itself.

Carmen M. Radulet

Notes

[1] In *The Obedience of a King of Portugal*, tr. with commentary by Francis M. Rogers (Minneapolis: U. of Minnesota Press, 1958, 47-48. See also the more recent edition of the *Oration de Obedientia*, in *Orações de Obediência. Séculos XV-XVII*. Introduction and bibliographical notes by Prof. Dr. Martim de Albuquerque (Lisboa: Edições Inapa, 1988).

[2] On this question, see in particular, Giuliano Macchi, "L'avventura definita. Un secolo di viaggi e scoperti portoghesi," in *Quaderni Portoghesi*, 4 (1978): 21-48, and Carmen M. Radulet, "As viagens de descobrimento de Diogo Cão. Nova proposta de interpretação," in *Mare Liberum*, 1 (1990): 192-94.

[3] Cf. Carmen M. Radulet, "Os descobrimentos portugueses e o Tratado de Alcáçovas," in *Portugal no Mundo*, ed. Luís de Albquerque (Lisboa: Publicações Alfa, 1989), II, 13-26.

[4] Between the treaty of Alcáçovas and that of Tordesillas a profound difference exists, since, while at Alcáçovas the questions regarding regions beyond Europe constitute only a part of a traditional peace treaty, at Tordesillas, the questions of extra-European expansion are negotiated explicitly.

[5] See Francisco Contente Domingues, "A disputa pela posse do Atlântico e a política de D. João II," in *Portugal no Mundo*, ed. Luís de Albuquerque (Lisbon: Publicações Alfa, 1989), II, 51-67. See also, Winius, "Enterprise Focussed on India," this volume.

[6] Luís Felipe Thomaz, in an original study entitled "L'idée imperiale manueline," in *La Découverte, le Portugal et l'Europe. Actes du Colloque* (Paris: Fondation Calouste Gulbenkian, Centre Culturel Portugais [1988] 1990), 35-103. He demonstrates the existence of an overseas politic of D. Manuel, one not only coherent, but aiming rather than at an economic empire, at one based on ideas of religion and ecumenism.

[7] See the analyses of the progressive expansion of the titles of the Portuguese kings, in António Vasconcelos de Saldanha, "Conceitos de espaço e poder e seus reflexos na titulação régia portuguesa na época da expansão," in *La Découverte, Le Portugal et L'Europe. Actes du Colloque* (Paris: Fondation Calouste Gulbenkian, Centre Culturel Portugais [1988] 1990), 105-29.

[8] Vasconcelos de Saldanha distinguishes in the Portuguese juridical and political literature of the XVI century four basic tendencies: a) the preference accorded the pontifical bulls as basic title deeds for territorial acquisition and political dominion; b) the admissibility of the "*descoberta*," accompanied by acts of the taking of

possession, as the concretization of the same territorial acquisition, including political and economic dominion; c) in matters of discovery and expansion, due consideration to be given to the community of interests existing between Portugal and Castile; d) the definition and usage of the royal titles as a form at once magniloquent, public and concise in the constitution and affirmation of indisputable rights over an area (*espaço*) and toward the exercise of a power."Vasconcelos de Saldanha, "Conceitos de espaço e poder," in *La Découverte*, 109.

[9] Document published in António da Silva Rego, *Documentação para a História das Missões do Padroado Português do Oriente – Índia* (Lisboa: Agência Geral do Ultramar, 1947-1958), I (1947), 6.

[10] For that concerning the voyage of Vasco da Gama, cf. Winius, "The Estado da India," in this volume.

[11] See William B. Greenlee, *The Voyage of Pedro Álvares Cabral to Brazil and India* (London: The Hakluyt Society, second series, 1937) and Abel Fontoura da Costa and António Baião, *Os sete únicos documentos de 1500, conservados em Lisboa, referentes a` viagem de Pedro Álvares Cabral* (Lisbon: Agência Geral das Colónias, 1940).

[12] See in this volume the considerations of George Winius in his article, "The Enterprise," and Bailey W. Diffie and George Winius, *Foundations of the Portuguese Empire, 1415-1580* (Minneapolis: U. of Minnesota Press, 1977), esp. chap. 13, "Cabral the Captain Who Touched Four Continents," 187-94.

[13] Geneviève Bouchon, *A propos de l'inscription de Colombo (1501); quelques observations sur le premier voyage de João da Nova dans l'Océan Indien* (Coimbra: Junta de Investigações Científicas do Ultramar/Centro de Estudos de Cartografia Antiga 1980) Série separatas, no. CXXXIX.

[14] Bouchon, *A propos de l'inscription*, 21-22 et passim.

[15] See Bouchon, *A propos de l'inscription*, also the analyses of the cartographical relating to the island and the notices transmitted to Italy on the research regarding Taprobana/Ceilão, passim.

[16] Cf. Radulet, *Introdução*, in Carmen M. Radulet and António Vasconcelos de Saldanha, jt. eds., *O Regimento do Almirantado da Índia. A questão da concessão do cargo*. Introdução e notas de Carmen M. Radulet e António Vasconcelos de Saldanha (Lisbon: Edições Inapa) 1989), 8.

[17] On this complex question see António Vasconcelos de Saldanha, in *O Regimento do Almirantado*, 9-12.

[18] In this regard, see the synthesis proposed in B. W. Diffie and G. D. Winius, in *Foundations*, chap. 15, "From Discovery to Conquest," 222-226.

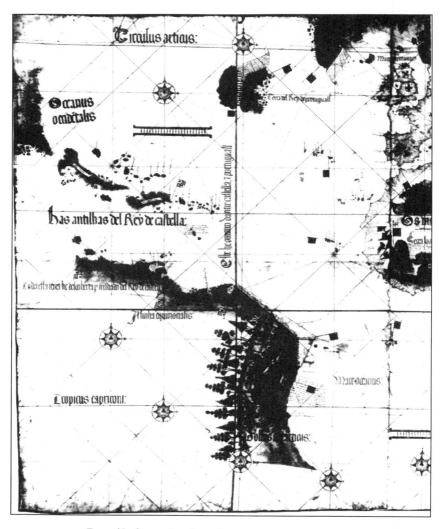

Brazil, from the Cantino mappemonde, 1502

Chapter VIII

Brazil: Discovery and Immediate Aftermath

The first recorded sighting of Brazil by the Portuguese took place on 22 April 1500. During the late afternoon of that day, "a very high rounded mountain and other lower ranges of hills to the south of it, and a plain covered with large trees" were seen by the men of a Portuguese expedition led by Pedro Álvares Cabral. The name Monte Pascoal was given to the 1758-foot-high mountain, located 18 miles inland at 16° 53'.[1] The expedition, consisting of 13 ships, had sailed from Belem on the outskirts of Lisbon on 9 March 1500. Pedro Álvares Cabral (also known as Pedro Álvares de Gouveia) had been appointed leader or *capitão-mor* of the expedition on 15 February 1500. A native of Belmonte (born in 1467 or 1468), a knight in the Order of Christ, and a *fidalgo da casa real*, Cabral was chosen by King Manuel I (r. 1495-1521) as the person best qualified to follow up Vasco da Gama's epoch-making voyage to India of 1497-1499.[2]

Cabral's armada passed through the Canary islands on 14 March and on 22 March it sighted the island of São Nicolau in the Cape Verde archipelago. The following night, in clear weather, one of the armada's ships was lost. A month later, Monte Pascoal was sighted. In the days following the sighting of land, Cabral thought he had discovered an island, which he named Ilha da Vera Cruz. Sailing northward, he found a harbor which he called Porto Seguro (now Baía Cabrália).[3] He remained there eight days. Edzer Roukema estimates that Cabral discovered fifty-three-and-a-half nautical miles of coastline during the time he was in Brazil.[4] On 2 May, Cabral continued on his voyage to India.

To announce the news of the discovery of Brazil to King Manuel I, Cabral sent one of his remaining twelve vessels – the former supply ship – back to Portugal with reports of what had transpired since his departure. Exactly when this news reached Lisbon is not certain. To the dismay of historians, very little information regarding Brazil during these early years seems to have been officially divulged. In his letter dated 29 July 1501 to the Catholic monarchs Ferdinand and Isabel, his father- and mother-in-law, King Manuel explained that he delayed the announcement until all the surviving ships of the Cabral expedition to India had arrived back in Portugal.[5]

A paucity of information

Despite the importance of Cabral's visit to Brazil, relatively little is known about the man, the expedition, and the motives behind the sighting and his brief stay in Brazil.[6] Even less is known regarding the voyages to Brazil the following decade. Writers on Brazil's discovery and the early years of its history bemoan the loss of many of the documents belonging to this period. Correspondence, maps, and reports housed in Lisbon's Casa da India were destroyed by the terrible earthquake and tidal wave of 1755. Other documents have been lost by fire, theft, pillage, and the ravages of time. However, it also may be that documents concerning the discovery of Brazil did not survive past the early decades of the sixteenth century. All the major chroniclers of the period – Damião de Góis, Jerónimo Osório, João de Barros, Gaspar Correia, Fernão Lopes de Castanheda, and António Galvão – first published or, in the case of Correia, completed their major works between 1551 and 1571.[7] Yet, without exception, they omit much that is of importance and are frequently in disagreement about the dates of an armada's departure from Lisbon and its return, its route, the number and size of the ships, and the names of the captains, pilots, and the vessels themselves.[8] Even the best of chroniclers not infrequently garbled earlier details and sometimes telescoped several events into one. The situation worsened as time passed and chroniclers born in Brazil, like Frei Vicente do Salvador, and chroniclers resident there, like Gabriel Soares de Sousa, tried their hands at sketching the colony's early history[9]

Cabral, his captains, pilots, and other members of the fleet that landed in Brazil wrote letters that were sent back to Portugal on the former supply ship. Yet only two pieces of all that correspondence have survived: the reports by Pero Vaz de Caminha and Master John. Both are the original manuscripts.[10] The valuable letter of Pero Vaz de Caminha does not seem to have been known by any of the chroniclers mentioned above. The recent history of the manuscript dates from the late eighteenth century when it was found in what is now the Arquivo Nacional da Torre do Tombo in Lisbon probably during the reign of King José I (r. 1750-1777).[11] A faulty copy of that document was first published in 1817 and soon was used by Robert Southey in the second edition of the first volume of his three-volume *History of Brazil*.[12]

Vespucci

This scarcity of documentation from Portuguese sources has forced historians to turn to the correspondence of foreigners living in Portugal and of foreigners who were in contact with such writers. The most famous – or infamous – of these foreigners was the Florentine Amerigo Vespucci. Vespucci, who was in the employ of Lorenzo di Pier Francesco de' Medici since 1483, was in Seville by the late 1480s or early 1490s.[13] In this Spanish port city he worked with such countrymen as Donato Nicolini and Gianotto Berardi in the capacity of ship provisioner and merchant banker. On 18 May 1499, Vespucci sailed to the New World with Alonso de Ojeda and returned in 1500. Sometime after his return, he travelled to Portugal and was there by the latter part of 1500 or early 1501. Vespucci was a member of the 1501-1502 Portuguese expedition sent to explore the coast of Brazil in the aftermath of Cabral's discovery in 1500. By early 1505 (if not sooner), he was back in Spain and in April of that year he became a naturalized citizen of Castile and Leon. In 1508 he was appointed chief pilot of Castile. He died in Seville four years later in 1512.

Vespucci's reputation as a mariner, navigator, and cosmographer has suffered as time has passed. During the last years of his life, he was lionized for his discoveries and his abilities as a navigator and cosmographer. But only a few years after his death, the printed accounts of his discoveries began to be called into question. During the past century-and-a-half, there has been bitter and heated debate over Vespucci.[14] Today, thanks to studies by Alberto Magnaghi[15] and Giuseppe Caraci,[16] almost all historians are in agreement that the Latin translation of a letter containing an account of his 1501-1502 voyage to Brazil, supposedly written to Lorenzo di Pier Francesco de' Medici, and entitled *Mundus Novus Albericus Vespucius Laurentio Petri de Medicis salutem plurimam dicit* (first published sometime between 1503 and 1504), is a forgery and was not written by Vespucci. The same verdict is passed on the letter, describing four voyages to the New World and addressed to Pier Soderini, a former schoolmate and, at that time, Gonfaloniere of the Florentine Republic. Supposedly written on 4 September 1504 from Lisbon, it was first printed in Florence in 1505 or 1506 with the title *Lettera di Amerigo Vespucci delle Isole Novamente*

Trovate in Quattro Suoi Viaggi. This letter to Soderini was later revised, translated into Latin as *Quatuor Navigationes*, dedicated "to the most illustrious René, King of Jerusalem and Sicily, Duke of Lorraine and Bar," and appended to Martin Waldseemüller's *Cosmographiae Introductio*. The *Cosmographiae* also included Waldseemüller's map of the world with the name "America" on the newly discovered "fourth part" of the world: South America. Careful study makes it clear that the *Mundus Novus* and the *Lettera* were compiled by careless forgers who may have used some of Vespucci's correspondence.[17] These forgers not only garbled these letters but added fabrications and exaggerations. As a result, what had been considered important sources for the study of the early voyages to Brazil have lost most, if not all, of their value.[18] However, these forged Vespucci accounts were widely disseminated. Samuel Eliot Morison points to fifteen editions of the *Mundus Novus* published in Florence, Venice, Paris, Augsburg, Antwerp and Nuremberg in the five years, 1503 to 1507. In addition, Vespucci's account was incorporated into collections of voyages like that of Fracanziano da Montalboddo's *Paesi Novamente Retrovati*, beginning in 1507.[19] The translation of the *Lettera* into Latin and its inclusion in Waldseemüller's *Cosmographiae Introductio* greatly facilitated the dispersion of the *Quatuor Navigationes* attributed to Vespucci. When these printed Vespucci forgeries first arrived in Portugal is not known. But the account of the 1501 voyage to Brazil by the chronicler António Galvão in his posthumously published (1563) *Tratado...de Todos os Descobrimentos* is an unacknowledged summary of Vespucci's *Mundus Novus*.[20]

This leaves three letters written by Vespucci to his patron Lorenzo di Pier Francesco de' Medici between 1500 and 1502. The first of these was written from Seville on 8 July 1500 and recounts Vespucci's voyage with Alonso de Ojeda. The second, penned in Bezeguiche (now Dakar) in Cape Verde on 4 June 1501 while Vespucci was en route to Brazil, gives a report of Cabral's voyage to India, probably obtained from Italians aboard two ships returning from the expedition and anchored in the harbor of Bezeguiche while Vespucci was there. The third, written sometime in the second half of 1502, recounts the Florentine's 1501-1502 Brazilian voyage. The originals of the second and third of these letters have disappeared. However, an early sixteenth-century manuscript copy of the "Cape Verde Letter" has survived, as has a late sixteenth- or early seventeenth-century copy of the letter from Lisbon, called the "Bartolozzi Letter." It was not until 1745, 1827, and 1789 respectively that the three letters were first published.[21] Though some nineteenth-century writers, like Francisco

Adolfo de Varnhagen and Clements R. Markham, challenged the authenticity of these three letters, most scholars today accept them as authentic.[22] Based on what has been discussed above, more and more historians are coming to the conclusion that Vespucci made only two voyages to the New World.

Verdicts on Vespucci by some historians trained in navigation and cartography are harsh. The Portuguese scholar Duarte Leite wrote: "The portrait of Vespucci, a renowned astronomer, acute cosmographer, skilled navigator and audacious discoverer, is purely imaginary and was made up by his compatriots, whom other admirers followed, thanks to the printing press. In truth, Vespucci was a cunning Florentine, vain, ambitious and with a superficial knowledge of exact sciences, who as a merchant made two voyages with Spaniards and Portuguese, whom he assisted in their discoveries."[23] Samuel Eliot Morison and Francis M. Rogers concluded: "We regard all the pretentious apparatus of celestial navigation in Vespucci's writings as so much dust thrown in the eyes of important Spaniards and leading Florentines."[24] Morison continues his evaluation of Vespucci: "His distances are palpably wrong.... His claim to have used lunar distances to find longitude is fantastic.... So, too, with Vespucci's calculations of latitude. Most of them were a long way off; some were fairly accurate."[25]

But these comments are based to a great extent on information found in Vespucci's *Mundus Novus* and the *Lettera*. Some have argued that since Vespucci had no direct responsibility for the publication of the *Mundus Novus* and the *Lettera*, he should not be blamed for their faults and his reputation besmirched.[26] In fairness to Vespucci, it should be pointed out that, to date, there is no evidence that the *Mundus Novus* or the *Lettera* were known in the Iberian peninsula during the Florentine's lifetime.[27] Therefore, it is argued that his place in the history of discoveries should be based on his authentic correspondence (the three letters mentioned above and dated from 1500-1502) and the navigational skills that were rewarded with the post of pilot-major of Castile, 1508-1512.

On the other hand, given the lack of source material for the early Brazilian voyages, many historians have felt compelled to use the information in the *Mundus Novus* and the *Lettera* as well as that in the three authentic letters written by Vespucci to his patron from 1500 to 1502. Such historians have tried to explain away the frequent contradictions and exaggerations and use only the information that seems to fit in with other already known facts. When attempting to reconstruct the events which Vespucci has described, they are often forced to provide the reader with a caveat similar to that of Samuel

Eliot Morison, who wrote: "From now on I am telling the story of the two voyages to Brazil very much as Vespucci does, warning the reader that many items have been challenged as false or exaggerated."[28] Though historians like Morison believe that the *Mundus Novus* may have been based on a careless compilation of several letters written to Lorenzo di Pier Francesco de' Medici and other Florentines and thus be of value, Vespucci scholars like Giuseppe Caraci earlier had criticized this use of information from the *Mundus Novus* and the *Lettera*. Caraci argued that since these two publications were the work of forgers, they were tainted from their source and hence of little or no use to historians.[29] If Caraci's argument is valid – and a growing number of scholars are leaning toward his point of view – then those interested in the early discoveries along Brazil's eastern coastline during the first four years after Cabral's visit in 1500 and using Vespucci as a source are limited to the Florentine's "Cape Verde" and "Bartolozzi" letters.

Other Italians

Besides Vespucci, there were other Italians in the Iberian peninsula who provided information about the early Portuguese voyages of discovery to India and, to a much lesser extent, Brazil. A number of these Italians – especially those from Florence – sailed on these early voyages to India and Brazil and supplied ships and merchandise and reported on their experiences. According to Greenlee, of the Italians residing in Lisbon in 1500, the largest number were from Florence. Many of them were engaged in banking and commerce.[30] One of the most important of these Florentines was the merchant-banker Bartolomeo Marchioni who "financed, in part, one small ship, the *Anunciada*, on Cabral's voyage."[31] He continued to do the same for subsequent Portuguese voyages. Another Florentine merchant was Girolamo Sernigi, who wrote concerning the Vasco da Gama voyage of 1497-1499. Still another important Florentine source was Giovanni da Empoli, who travelled to India in 1503 as a member of Afonso de Albuquerque's fleet.[32]

In addition, other Italians garnered information from Lisbon's waterfront neighborhoods. Though some of this information was hearsay or garbled and thus not always reliable, much was correct and frequently unavailable from surviving Portuguese sources. Fortunately for historians, some of the data sent home by Venetians ended in the diaries of Marino Sanuto and Girolamo Priuli. Giovanni Matteo Cretico (called "Il Cretico" because of an earlier seven-year stay on the island of Crete), was secretary to Domenico Pisani, Venetian ambassador to Spain. Both were in Lisbon in 1501. So was Piero

Contarini, Venetian ambassador to Portugal, and his successor Pietro Pasqualigo, Ambassador Extraordinary.[33] Another secretary to Pisani was Angelo Trevisan di Bernardino. Earlier in his career, Trevisan had been the secretary of the famed Venetian diarist, Domenico Malipiero. Still another Venetian, Leonardo Massari, arrived in Lisbon on 3 October 1504 and remained there until 1506, secretly gathering information regarding Portuguese overseas commerce. On his return to Venice, he compiled an account regarding the first nine Portuguese voyages to India with mentions about Brazil.[34]

In addition to Florentines and Venetians, there were Genoese in the Iberian peninsula who were interested in the Portuguese voyages. Useful to historians is Piero di Nofri di Giovanni Rondinelli, who resided in Seville but had close ties with Lisbon. Also present in Lisbon was the Cremonese merchant-banker, Giovanni Francesco de Affaitati, who represented his family in the Portuguese capital until his death in 1528.

Important to scholars, especially when combined with the small pieces of information available from Portuguese archives and foreign sources, are a handful of maps, especially those drawn during the first decade of the sixteenth century.[35] However, these maps are not without problems. Sir Robert Southwell, one of England's envoys to Lisbon in the 1660s, remarked that the Jesuit António Vieira, the great seventeenth-century Luso-Brazilian figure, "has the art of making the scriptures say what he pleases."[36] A similar comment can be made about the interpretation of early sixteenth-century maps. None of these extant charts were personally drawn during the voyages being mapped. Caraci, comparing the three authentic letters of Vespucci with the maps of the early sixteenth century, observed: "These letters [of Vespucci] give us direct, personal and unequivocal evidence, while the contemporaneous nautical maps, whatever they may be, represent on the whole nothing but some collective and indirect documents, nearly always discordant."[37] Furthermore, though it was common for explorers and navigators in the sixteenth century to name newly discovered capes, rivers, islands, etc. after the saint on whose feast day the discovery was made, the cartographical sources using place names to determine dates of discovery are far from infallible.[38] However, in the absence of other documentation, place names provide grounds for some useful conjectures.

Cartographers and historians list nine maps which were prepared during the first decade of the sixteenth century and which show the newly discovered Brazil. However, only five can be dated with any precision as to year: The Cantino mappemonde of late 1502; that of Vesconte Maggiolo (Maiollo), dated, Genoa, 8 June 1504; that of

Giovanni Matteo Contarini, author of the first printed world map of 1506; the planisphere attributed to Martin Waldseemüller of 1507; and the mappemonde of Johannes Ruysch of 1508. Only two seem to have been drawn by Portuguese: The Cantino mappemonde and the so-called Kunstmann III, the latter frequently dated c. 1506 but probably prepared several years later.[39] Other maps of importance include an anonymous one usually dated c. 1503 but probably later, called Kunstmann II and which depicts a Brazilian Indian being roasted on a spit; the planisphere of Nicoli di Caveri (c. 1503-1504); and the Pesaro or Oliveriana mappemonde of c. 1506-1508. Also valuable are several maps which date from the second decade of the sixteenth century: The 1511 mappemonde of Vesconte Maggiolo; the fragment from the world map of the Turkish admiral and cartographer, Piri Re'is (c. 1513), a map known to be based on an earlier Portuguese one; and the nautical chart of Francisco Rodrigues (c. 1513). In addition, because there was so much controversy at the time over the measurement of latitude, the work of Duarte Pacheco Pereira, *Esmeraldo de Situ Orbis*, probably written between 1505 and 1508, is essential for determining the accepted figures of his contemporaries for the latitudes of the South Atlantic.[40]

Of prime importance for understanding early Portuguese discoveries along the Brazilian coastline is the so-called Cantino mappemonde of 1502 named after Alberto Cantino, agent for the Ercole d'Este, Duke of Ferrara. Considered one of the most beautiful examples of Renaissance map-making art, the chart was prepared by an unknown Portuguese cartographer who was paid "twelve golden ducats" by Cantino for his work. Information for it may have been obtained surreptitiously from the Portuguese crown's master map or *padrão real*. The so-called Cantino Map was completed in Lisbon sometime between mid-September and the end of October of 1502 when Cantino left Portugal for Italy and took the map with him. On 19 November of that year, Cantino, writing from Rome, informed the Duke of Ferrara that the map had been sent from Genoa.[41] The map reveals Portuguese activity in North America by Gaspar Corte-Real and in Brazil by Cabral, Gonçalo Coelho, and possibly others. It includes the newly discovered island of Ascensão in the Atlantic. For Brazil there are seven place names denoting Portuguese discoveries.

Five mysterious years

The Portuguese activity that took place in Brazil during the years 1500 to 1505 is largely wrapped in mystery. The little that is known of these six years of discovery is often greatly disputed and it is difficult, if not impossible, to reach a consensus. Even the best historians studying the Portuguese in Brazil are in disagreement about dates and places of new discoveries and the identities of the discoverers themselves. Yet within four years after Cabral's arrival, more than two thousand miles of Brazilian coastline had been explored and included on Portuguese maps. As John L. Vogt pointed out: "Over half a century and a score of voyages had been necessary during the fifteenth century before the West African coast was thoroughly explored as far as the Cape of Good Hope. In sharp contrast to this, only five [sic] expeditions in the course of four years were required to explore Brazil's eastern coastal regions."[42]

A major effort to clarify what happened during the initial exploration of the coast of Brazil was made by Portuguese and Brazilian scholars with the appearance of the three-volume *História da colonização portuguesa do brasil*, edited by Carlos Malheiro Dias. This monumental work was published in Porto from 1921 to 1924 to commemorate the 100th anniversary of Brazil's independence and contains reproductions and paleographic transcriptions of many of the important documents dealing with the period. Since its publication, a growing number of scholars have applied their archival, cartographic, and navigational skills to make clearer the faint details of the Portuguese presence along coastal Brazil. These latter scholars have been aided by several documents and maps that have come to light since the *História's* publication as well as by the above-mentioned studies on Vespucci.

What then can be said with any degree of certitude about Portuguese activity along the coast of Brazil from 1500 to 1505, especially when few, if any, modern accounts are in complete agreement? As Cabral and eleven ships of his fleet continued their voyage to India on 2 May 1500, leaving behind two *degredados* and two sailors who jumped ship the previous day, the former supply ship, following Cabral's instructions, sailed for Portugal.[43] From this time onward, the mystery begins. Most of the sixteenth-century chroniclers identify the supply ship's captain as Gaspar de Lemos, though the chronicler Gaspar Correia named André Gonçalves as the captain. A few others think André was a slip of the pen for the pilot Afonso Gonçalves, who had been on Vasco da Gama's first voyage to India.[44] The best evidence seems to be that it was Lemos who returned to Portugal but almost nothing is known about him. There is a debate among historians whether Gaspar de Lemos returned directly to Lisbon or whether he sailed northward to determine whether this newly discovered coast was part of an island or a land mass. How many, if any, of the seven Brazilian place names on the Cantino Map is

Lemos responsible for? Those who believe he sailed northward argue that the Cabo São Jorge, which most scholars have identified with today's Cabo de Santo Agostinho (south of Recife, Pernambuco), found on the Cantino map of 1502, was discovered by Lemos before returning to Portugal and named after one of his favorite patron saints. Others argue that there is no firm evidence from the Cantino or other contemporary maps that Gaspar de Lemos discovered the future Cabo de Santo Agostinho and that he did little or no exploring because he had orders to return directly to Portugal. Exactly when Lemos arrived in Portugal and whether he brought back brazilwood, parrots, and Amerindians is not certain.

In the summer of 1501, when King Manuel informed Ferdinand and Isabel about Brazil, which he called "Santa Cruz," he stated that "it seemed that Our Lord miraculously wished it to be found, because it is very convenient and necessary for the voyage to India, because he [Cabral] repaired his ships and took water there."[45] Given King Manuel's remarks, a number of historians argue that João da Nova, leader of the third of Portugal's armadas sent to India, stopped briefly in Brazil on the way to his destination. The Galician-born João da Nova was *alcaide pequeno* of Lisbon and led a fleet of four ships, part of which had been supplied by private merchants. There is dispute about the exact date when the armada left Lisbon, with Damião de Góis and João de Barros giving the date of 5 March 1501. When, where, and if he touched Brazil is not known.[46] If he did not discover Cabo São Jorge, he may have made his landfall there. João da Nova is credited with discovering Ascension Island on this voyage though it is not certain on what leg. He successfully returned to Portugal with all four ships on 11 September 1502 and his discoveries in the South Atlantic and in Asia were recorded on the Cantino map completed before the end of October of that year.

Though some have questioned whether João da Nova touched Brazil on his voyage, there can be no doubt that a three-ship expedition was prepared by King Manuel in 1501 to carefully explore the Brazilian coast.[47] Furthermore, Amerigo Vespucci has provided an account of the voyage in two of his authentic letters.[48] From Cape Verde Vespucci wrote to his patron: "You have learned, Lorenzo, as well by my letter as through the letters of our Florentines of Lisbon, how I was called while I was in Seville by the King of Portugal; and he begged me that I should dispose myself to serve him for this voyage."[49] Why Vespucci was invited to sail on this 1501 voyage to Brazil is something of a mystery. One suggestion is that Vespucci may have wanted to help finance the expedition since Vicente Yáñez Pinzón had returned to Spain in September of the previous year with a cargo of brazilwood. Others think that Vespucci sailed on this voyage as a commercial representative for Florentine interests.[50] Still others claim that he was invited because of his experience as a navigator and cosmographer.[51] In a letter of 16 September 1504, the Florentine merchant Giovanni da Empoli described Amerigo Vespucci as the discoverer of Brazil.[52] Several eighteenth-century authors credited Vespucci with the command of the 1501-1502 expedition. In 1730, when the Brazilian-born Sebastião da Rocha Pita published *Historia da America portugueza*, he stated that King Manuel had sent to Brazil "Amerigo Vespucci, the Tuscan-born and illustrious cosmographer of those times to reconnoiter and examine the seas and lands of that region [Brazil]." According to Rocha Pita, the monarch then sent Captain Gonçalo Coelho to follow up Vespucci's voyage in greater detail.[53] In 1747, when Diogo Barbosa Machado published the second volume of his *Bibliotheca Lusitana*, he described Gonçalo Coelho as one "very skilled in the science of cosmography" who, at the order of King Manuel, sailed from Lisbon with six ships to explore "the lands and ports of America newly discovered by Amerigo Vespucci."[54] Robert Southey, in his *History of Brazil*, states that King Manuel "gave the command to Amerigo Vespucci, whom he invited from Seville for that purpose."[55]

Vespucci failed to give the reason for his participation or to identify the leader of this 1501-1502 expedition to Brazil. Several modern writers have tried to make a case for Fernão de Loronha or André or Afonso Gonçalves as leader of the 1501-1502 expedition.[56] However, new evidence makes it clear that it was Gonçalo Coelho, the same man who was to lead the 1503-1504 expedition. A map drawn by the Genoese cartographer, Vesconte Maggiolo and dated Genoa, 8 June 1504, has the legend written across the territory of Brazil: "Tera de Gonsalvo Coigo vocatur Santa Croxe" ("Land of Gonçalo Coelho called Santa Cruz"). As the late Avelino Teixeira da Mota pointed out, since the 1503-1504 expedition of those years was still in Brazil at the time the Maggiolo map was dated, the legend had to refer to an earlier voyage of Gonçalo Coelho, i.e., 1501-1502.[57] Little is known about Gonçalo Coelho although, as mentioned above, Barbosa Machado described him as one "very skilled in the science of cosmography" and credited him with the authorship of a manuscript entitled "Descripção do Brasil," written "in a clear and sincere style," and later presented to King João III.[58] Coelho is not listed in Sousa Viterbo's *Trabalhos náuticos dos Portuguezes nos séculos XVI e XVII*.[59] This work was based heavily on the crown's registry books housed in the Arquivo Nacional da Torre do Tombo. Though there were at least six fairly well-known Gonçalo Coelhos mentioned in archival sources in that time period, 1475-1525, there is no conclusive evidence that any of them was the Gonçalo Coelho in question here.[60]

Furthermore, little is known about the 1501-1502 voyage itself. Vespucci wrote to his patron: "But the most notable of all the things which occurred to me in this voyage I collocated in a small work, to the end that when I reside at leisure I may apply myself to it, to win renown after my death. I was intending to send you an epitome, but His Serene Highness [King Manuel] retains my work. When he returns it to me I will send a summary."[61] Unfortunately, this "small work," like many of the other documents of this time period, has not come to light and does not seem to have survived. As Vespucci tells it, the expedition left Lisbon on 13 May 1501. It first sailed down the coast of North Africa and in the harbor of Bezeguiche encountered two ships from Cabral's expedition – *the Anunciada* and that of Diogo Dias – returning from India, probably in early June. Vespucci wrote that he and his companions spent eleven days at Bezeguiche taking on wood and water. They then sailed southwest by south in the direction of Brazil. Vespucci wrote: "We sailed on the wind within half a point of southwest, so that in sixty-four days, we arrived at a new land which, for many reasons that are enumerated in what follows, we observed to be a continent."[62] Where in Brazil Gonçalo Coelho's expedition first made landfall and when is not known. Some authors think it was south of Cape São Roque at latitude 5° 29' S. Vespucci continued: "We ran the course of the land for about eight hundred leagues, always in the direction of southwest one-quarter west." How far south along the Brazilian coastline did the expedition travel? According to Vespucci: "We coursed so far in those seas that we entered the torrid zone and passed south of the equinoctial line and the Tropic of Capricorn, until the South Pole stood above my horizon at fifty degrees, which was my latitude from the equator. We navigated in the Southern Hemisphere for nine months and twenty-seven days."[63] The Argentine historian Roberto Levillier took Vespucci literally (and also accepted as authentic the *Mundus Novus* and the *Lettera*) and, using a wide variety of maps from the sixteenth and seventeenth centuries, concluded that Vespucci was "the first navigator to survey the River Plate and travel as far south as Patagonia."[64] But Brazilian scholars like Max Justo Guedes, though accepting the 50° S latitude of Vespucci (which clearly coincides with the notarial information of Valentim Fernandes which reported a voyage of 760 leagues along the

coast of Brazil before turning southward to a latitude of 53° S)[65], argue
that the 1501-1502 expedition never went that far south while in view
of the coast. By carefully comparing the above-mentioned maps,
Guedes argues that the 1501-1502 voyage only followed the Brazilian
coast past Rio de Janeiro at 23° S as far as Cananeia at 25° S.[66] On the
Cantino map of 1502 there are seven place names connected to Brazil.
From north to south they are: 1) Cabo de São Jorge; 2) the island of
Quaresma; 3) São Miguel; 4) Rio de São Francisco; 5) Bahia de Todos
os Santos; 6) Porto Seguro; 7) Cabo de Santa Marta. As mentioned
earlier, Cabo de São Jorge has been identified as Cabo de Santo
Agostinho. The island of Quaresma was also called island of São João,
the island of São Lourenço, and ultimately the island of Fernão de
Noronha. The Cabo de Santa Marta matches the island of Santo
Amaro of Duarte Pacheco Pereira.

The Portuguese then sailed southward, arriving at and naming Cabo
[de] Santo Agostinho (8° S). By October 4, the expedition seems to
have reached the mouth of the Rio São Francisco and, in early
November, Bahia's Bay of All Saints. They continued further
southward reaching Porto Seguro, the landing place of Cabral, and
retrieved the two *degredados* that Cabral's expedition had left behind.[67]
The expedition continued to sail southward. On 1 January 1502, they
reached Guanabara Bay (23° S) and named it Rio de Janeiro in honor
of the date of discovery. They returned to Portugal, arriving in Lisbon
on 22 July 1502.

The Lisbon-based Cremonese merchant, Giovanni Francesco de
Affaitati, reported to Pasqualigo, the Venetian ambassador in Spain,
who, in turn, passed the information along to Venice from Saragossa
on 12 October 1502: "The caravels, ordered last year to discover
the land of the Parrots or of Santa Cruz, were back on July 22; and
the captain related having discovered more than 2500 miles of
new coast, and not having reached the end of said coast, the said
caravels came laden with dye-wood and cassia, and they did not bring
other things."[68]

After his return from the Gonçalo Coelho expedition, Vespucci
seems to have planned to return to Seville. On 3 October 1502, the
Genoese Pietro Rondinelli, writing from Seville, remarked: "Amerigo
Vespucci will be here in a few days; he has had to put up with a tiring
voyage and little reward, although he deserves more praise than the
average man."[69] It is not known whether Vespucci returned to Seville
"in a few days." If he did, did he remain in Spain the remainder of his
life? There is no evidence (other than the apocryphal *Lettera*) that

Vespucci ever made a second Portuguese voyage to Brazil. Instead, he may have decided to return to Seville, given the Portuguese experience where he had had to endure "a tiring voyage and little reward."

Sometime during the second half of 1502, Vespucci wrote an important letter (the "Bartolozzi" missive) to Lorenzo di Pier Francesco de Medici about what he had seen on his voyage to Brazil. Vespucci found Portuguese America to be "very delightful" and thought it "near the terrestrial paradise." He was impressed with the large number of "green trees" with their "aromatic perfumes" and their "infinite variety of fruit." The Florentine wrote of "the quantity of birds and their plumage and colors, and their songs." He saw an "infinite variety of wild animals," so many in fact, that "it would have been hard for them to have entered Noah's ark." However, the inhabitants of Brazil had no domesticated animals. Like Pero Vaz de Caminha, Vespucci was impressed that the new found land was "inhabited by people completely nude, men as well as women, without covering their shame." He observed that their "bodies [were] well proportioned, white in color with black hair, and little or no beard."[70]

Dyewood

The commercial possibilities for brazilwood and other American products soon became apparent. Within several months of the return of Gonçalo Coelho's 1501-1502 expedition, Brazil had been rented out. As Rondinelli wrote from Seville on 3 October 1502: "The King of Portugal leased the lands which were discovered for him [in Brazil] to certain New Christians and they are obliged each year to send six small ships and to discover each year three hundred leagues farther and to build a fortress in the land discovered and to remain there three years, and the first year they are to pay nothing and the second one-sixth and the third one-fourth, and they agree to carry enough brazil-wood and slaves, and perhaps they will find other profitable things."[71] The Venetian Leonardo Massari reported (in late 1506 or early 1507) that "the trade in brazilwood was granted to Fernão de Loronha, New Christian, for ten years by His Majesty the King, for four thousand ducats per year; and Fernão de Loronha has sent, at his own expense, ships and men to the New World."[72] However, John L. Vogt has clearly shown that Massari erred when he stated that the lease was for ten years instead of the three years mentioned by Rondinelli.[73]

Jaime Cortesão has made a good case for a 1502-1503 voyage to Brazil.[74] There is evidence that this expedition may have been led by the New Christian merchant Fernão de Loronha, head of the consortium that had acquired the Brazil lease, and that it rediscovered the island (variously named Quaresma, São João, São Lourenço) which now bears a version of his name, Fernão de Noronha.[75] On 16 January 1504, King Manuel awarded Fernão de Loronha the "island of São João which he has now newly found and discovered fifty leagues at sea from our land of Santa Cruz."[76] The purpose of this voyage was to gather brazilwood and was part of Loronha's three-year contract. It left Portugal sometime after the return on 22 July 1502 of the 1501-1502 Coelho expedition. By July of 1503, it was reported in Seville that four ships had returned to Portugal with a cargo of Amerindians and brazilwood.[77] Relatively little is known of this voyage. But a plausible conjecture is that it followed earlier Portuguese routes to the Cape Verde islands and across the Atlantic and made landfall near Cabo São Roque. From there it sailed southward, eventually reaching Porto Seguro, today's Baía Cabrália. Guedes argues that a number of place names on the Caveri map date from this voyage.[78]

In 1503, still another expedition sailed to Brazil. This time, there were six ships. According to Damião de Góis, the expedition left Lisbon on 10 June 1503 and four ships were lost "because they still had little information about the land." The two that returned carried brazilwood, monkeys, and parrots.[79] While there is no doubt that Coelho made this voyage, Góis's brief account seems suspiciously similar to that given in the *Lettera* and *Quatuor Navigationes*.[80] Whether this 1503 expedition was the second of the three required in Fernão de Loronha's contract is not certain. Nor is it clear when Coelho returned to Portugal. There is also a possibility that Fernão de Loronha sent an expedition separate from that of Gonçalo Coelho.

John Vogt has made a good argument that a voyage to Brazil sponsored by Fernão de Loronha took place in late 1504 or early 1505. He points to a letter of 1506 which "states that in the previous two years 32,306 brazilwood logs had been received from Santa Cruz [Brazil] by the factor of the Portuguese feitoria at Antwerp." Vogt adds: "This represents shipments totalling almost eight hundred and fifty tons of brazilwood.... The conclusion to be drawn is that the dyewood represented the cargo of a second [sic] expedition dispatched by Loronha."[81] Leonardo Massari wrote: "In the three years since the New World was discovered [sic], each year they have brought from it twenty thousand quintals [hundred-weights] of brazilwood, which is obtained from a large, heavy tree; but it does not tint with the same perfection as that [dyewood] which we bring from the Levant;

nevertheless, much of it is shipped to Flanders, and from there to Castile and Italy and many other places; it is valued at two and a half ducats per quintal, and the trade in brazilwood was granted to Fernão de Loronha."[82] Massari's figures may have referred to the three years Fernão de Loronha had the contract which ended in 1505. It is uncertain whether the Venetian's estimates are too high, though generally he was well-informed. Twenty thousand quintals roughly equalled one thousand tons (of brazilwood) and would have required at least five or six ships to transport. Massari added: "All the expense required in shipping this brazilwood to Lisbon is only one half ducat per quintal; in this land [Brazil] there are entire forests of these trees."[83]

From the evidence discussed above, it is clear that a new chronology is required for the Portuguese expeditions sent to explore and exploit Brazil in the aftermath of Cabral's landing in 1500. In the five years following the return of the supply ship from Cabral's fleet, there were at least four expeditions to Brazil: 1) 1501-1502 led by Gonçalo Coelho; 2) 1502-1503, the first of the three sponsored by Fernão de Loronha as part of his contract with the crown; 3) 1503-1504 or 1505, also led by Gonçalo Coelho; 4) late 1504 or early 1505, the third and last sent by Fernão de Loronha under the terms of his three-year lease of Brazil.[84]

With the expiration of Loronha's contract at the end of 1505, the dyewood trade was opened to all Portuguese traders. It especially flourished during the following decade. In the meantime, there were challenges to Portugal's monopoly in Brazil. In 1504, the 120-tun French vessel *L'Espoir* from Honfleur, captained by Paulmier de Gonneville, visited Brazil and eventually left loaded with brazilwood.[85] Soon other French vessels would sail to Brazil and return to Europe with cargoes of dyewood. The stage was now set for a bitter rivalry between Portugal and France for control of what would eventually be half of South America. Before the struggle would end, a hereditary captaincy system would be inaugurated in the 1530s to promote Portuguese settlement in Brazil, followed by the arrival in 1549 of a governor-general for all of Portuguese America. A major blow to French designs was the loss of "La France Antarctique" in what is now Rio de Janeiro and the destruction of the French colony there. A little more than six decades after the arrival of *L'Espoir* in Brazil, the French were definitively ousted from the region around Rio de Janeiro.

For the Portuguese, however, the glamour lay in Asia during the XVI century and not in their South American acquisition. But around 1530, a new agricultural export product appeared there for which

European consumers displayed a seemingly bottomless appetite: sugar. Hitherto grown and processed with great success on a smaller scale in the Madeiras, it was to give Brazil its identity – and indeed its supremacy – in the XVII century, when Portuguese Asia came under attack from the northern European East India companies.

Francis A. Dutra

Notes

¹ The quotation is from Pero Vaz de Caminha. The English translation is by Charles David Ley, ed., *Portuguese Voyages, 1498-1663* (London: E. P. Dutton, 1947), 42. A slightly different translation is found in William Brooks Greenlee, ed., *The Voyage of Pedro Álvares Cabral to Brazil and India from Contemporary Documents and Narratives.* (London: Hakluyt Society, 1938), 6-7. For the information on Monte Pascoal, see Samuel Eliot Morison, *The European Discovery of America. The Southern Voyages. A. D. 1492-1616.* (New York: Oxford U. Press, 1974), 223.

² The best biography of Cabral in English is by James Roxburgh McClymont, *Pedralvarez Cabral (Pedro Alluarez de Gouuea). His Progenitors, His Life and His Voyage to America and India* (London: Bernard Quaritch, 1914).

³ Several recent and helpful discussions of the Cabral voyage and Brazil include Max Justo Guedes, "O Descobrimento do Brasil" in *História Naval Brasileira* (Rio de Janeiro: Serviço de Documentação Geral da Marinha, 1975), Vol. I, Tomo I, 139-175 and Luís de Albuquerque, *Os Descobrimentos Portugueses* (Lisbon: Publicações Alfa, 1983), 149-174. See also, Damião Peres, *História dos Descobrimentos Portugueses* (3rd ed.; Porto: Vertente, 1983), 327-349.

⁴ Edzer Roukema, "Brazil in the Cantino Map," *Imago Mundi* XVII (1963): 10.

⁵ Greenlee, *Cabral*, 41.

⁶ Cabral, as a reward for his safe return with four of his ships, was granted the post of *capitão-mor* of the 1502 expedition to India. However, at the last minute, the commission was given to Vasco da Gama. Cabral spent the remainder of his life in relative obscurity. He married the niece of the great Afonso de Albuquerque and died about 1520.

⁷ Damião de Góis, *Chronica do felicissimo Rei Dom Emmanuel* (Lisbon, 1566-1567); the best modern edition is *Cronica do*

Felicíssimo, Rei D. Manuel. 4 vols. (Coimbra: Universidade de Coimbra, 1949-1955). Jerónimo Osório, *De rebus Emmanuelis gestis Lusitaniae invictissimi virtvte et avspicio gestis libri dvodecim* (Lisbon, 1571). There is a Portuguese translation, *Da Vida e Feitos del Rei D. Manuel.* 2 vols. (Porto: Livraria Civilização, 1944). João de Barros, *Décadas da Ásia* (Lisbon, 1552-1615). A modern edition, entitled *Ásia*, was edited by Hernani Cidade and Manuel Múrias. 4 vols. (Lisbon: Agência Geral das Colónias, 1945-1946). Gaspar Correia, *Lendas da India.* The first published edition, edited by Rodrigo José de Lima Felner, dates from 1858-1866. A more recent edition of four volumes was reprinted in 1969. Fernão Lopes de Castanheda, *História do Descobrimento e Conquista da India pelos Portugueses* (Coimbra, 1551-1561). There is a modern edition edited by Pedro de Azevedo. 4 vols. (Coimbra: Universidade de Coimbra,1924-1933). António Galvão's *Tratado* was posthumously published in Lisbon 1563. It was translated into English and published by Richard Hakluyt in 1601. A Portuguese-English edition was reprinted with the title *The Discoveries of the World, From Their First Original unto the Year of Our Lord 1555* (London: Hakluyt Society, 1862).

 [8] To date, at least three "Relações das Armadas" – lists of the expeditions to India and their sailing dates with the number of ships, their names and captains and, at times, their fate – have been published. The earliest of these lists was compiled by the crown secretary Luís de Figueiredo Falcão and included the Portuguese voyages to India beginning with that of Vasco da Gama in 1497 and ending with that of Dom Jerónimo de Almeida in 1612. Luís de Figueiredo Falcão, *Livro em que se contém toda a Fazenda e Real Patrimonio dos Reinos de Portugal, India e Ilhas Adjacentes e outras Particularidades* (Lisbon: Imprensa Nacional, 1859), 137-190. The list composed by Simão Ferreira Paes begins with the voyage of Bartolomeu Dias and ends with that of the Viceroy João da Silva Telo de Meneses, 1st Count of Aveiras, in 1650. Simão Ferreira Paes, *As Famozas Armadas Portuguesas, 1496-1650* (Rio de Janeiro: Ministerio da Marinha, 1937). The title of the manuscript is "Recopilação das famosas Armadas Portuguezas que para a India foram desde o anno em que se principiou sua gloriosa Conquista (1496-1650)." The "ano 1496" refers to the earlier voyage of Bartolomeu Dias, 1487-1488, which discovered the Cape of Good Hope. *The Relação das Náos e Armadas* starts with the voyage of Vasco da Gama and ends with that of Luís de Mendonça Furtado in 1653. *Relação das Náos e Armadas da India com os successos dellas que se*

puderam saber, para Noticia e instrucção dos curiozos, e amantes da História da India (Coimbra: Biblioteca Geral da Universidade de Coimbra, 1985). The original is in the British Library, Codice Add. 20902. Yet these lists also differ on important points. In addition, there are two known "Livros das Armadas," dating from the 1560s, with pictorial representations of the ships, the names of their captains, and what happened to them on the voyages to India from 1497 to the 1560s. One of these manuscripts, "Memoria das Armadas," is preserved in the Academia das Ciências in Lisbon and covers the years to 1566; the other, "O Sucesso dos Visoreis," compiled by Lizuarte de Abreu, is in the Pierpont Morgan Library in New York and covers the period to 1563. Though these two works agree on the number of vessels in Cabral's expedition, they differ as to the names of the captains of several of the ships. Furthermore, there is no guarantee that the pictorial depiction of the vessels matched the reality.

⁹ Gabriel Soares de Sousa, *Tratado Descritivo do Brasil em 1587*. 4th ed. (São Paulo: Companhia Editora Nacional, 1971), Capítulo I (41-42) and Frei Vicente do Salvador, *História do Brasil, 1500-1627*. 5th ed. (São Paulo: Edições Malhoramentos, 1965), Livro I, Capítulos I, II (56-59); Livro II, Capítulo I (111.)

¹⁰ *Os Sete Únicos Documentos de 1500 Conservados em Lisboa Referentes à Viagem de Pedro Álvares Cabral* (Lisbon: Agência-Geral do Ultrmar, 1968). This is a corrected reprint of the 1940 edition. See also Jaime Cortesão, ed., *A Carta de Pero Vaz de Caminha* (Rio de Janeiro: Livros de Portugal, 1943). It was reprinted in *Obras Completas*, XIII (Lisbon: Portugalia Editora, 1967).

¹¹ Pero Vaz de Caminha's letter does not seem to have been known by Diogo Barbosa Machado, *Bibliotheca Lusitana Historica, Critica, e Cronologica*. 4 vols. (3rd ed.: Lisbon: Atlântica Editora, 1965-1967), first published in 1741-1759.

¹² Greenlee, *Cabral*, 4-5. The first edition of Robert Southey, *History of Brazil*, was published in London, 1810-1819. A revised edition of Volume I was published in 1822.

¹³ For the most recent biographical sketch of Vespucci, see that of Ilaria Luzzana Caraci in *The Christopher Columbus Encyclopedia* (New York: Simon and Schuster, 1992), II, 686-688.

¹⁴ Two brief well-informed summaries of the Vespucci controversy in English are found in Morison, *European Discovery*, 304-312 and Bailey W. Diffie and George D. Winius, *Foundations of the Portuguese Empire, 1415-1580* (Minneapolis, 1977), 456-462.

[15] Alberto Magnaghi, *Amerigo Vespucci*. 2 vols. (Rome, 1924). There is also a one-volume revised edition (Rome, 1926).

[16] Giuseppe Caraci, "The Vespucian Problems – What Point Have They Reached?" in *Imago Mundi* XVIII (1964), 12-23, summarizes a lifetime of research on Vespucci.

[17] Also considered fraudulent is the fragmentary letter of September-December of 1502, the so-called "Frammento Ridolfi." See Caraci, "Vespucian Problems," 14.

[18] Borba de Morães argues that although the *Mundus Novus* has lost "much of its documental value" for historians, the work "is in reality the first printing extant about Brazil." See Rubens Borba de Morães, *Bibliographia Brasiliana*. 2 vols. (Amsterdam/Rio de Janeiro: Colibris Editora Ltda., 1958), II, 349.

[19] Morison, *European Discovery*, 304.

[20] See Galvão's *Discoveries of the World*, 98-99.

[21] See Luís de Matos, "Un Aspect de la Question Vespuccienne: L'Auteur du *Mundus Novus*" in *Charles Quint et son temps* (Paris: Centre National de la Recherche Scientifique, 1959), 158n.

[22] Francisco Adolfo de Varnhagen, *Vespuce et son premier voyage* (Paris, 1858); and Clements R. Markham, ed., *The Letters of Amerigo Vespucci* (London: Hakluyt Society, 1894), iii.

[23] Duarte Leite, História dos Descobrimentos. 2 vols. (Lisbon: Edições Cosmos, 1959-1960), I, 650. The English translation is that of Morison, *European Discovery*, 294.

[24] Morison, *European Discovery*, 294.

[25] Morison, *European Discovery*, 294-296.

[26] Frederick J. Pohl, *Amerigo Vespucci. Pilot Major* (New York, 1944). A reprint edition was published in 1966 (Octagon Books).

[27] Caraci, "Vespucian Problems," 21.

[28] Morison, *European Discovery*, 280.

[29] Caraci, "Vespucian Problems," 12-23.

[30] Greenlee, *Cabral*, 145.

[31] Greenlee, *Cabral*, 146.

[32] See Bailey W. Diffie, "The Legal 'Privileges' of the Foreigners in Portugal and Sixteenth-Century Brazil," in Henry H. Keith and S. F. Edwards, eds., *Conflict and Continuity in Brazilian Society* (Columbia, South Carolina: U. of South Carolina Press, 1969), 9-10.

[33] Donald Weinstein, ed., *Ambassador from Venice. Pietro Pasqualigo in Lisbon, 1501* (Minneapolis: U. of Minnesota Press, 1960).

[34] "Relazione de Lunardo da Chá Masser," 67-98. The "Relazione" is appended to Prospero Peragallo, "Carta de El-Rei

D. Manuel ao Rei Catholico" in *Centenário do Descobrimento da América* (Lisbon: Academia Real das Sciencias, 1892).

[35] See the list given by Max Justo Guedes, "As Expedições Portuguesas e o Reconhecimento do Litoral Brasileiro" in *História Naval Brasileira* (Rio de Janeiro: Serviço de Documentação Geral da Marinha, 1975), Volume I, Tomo I, 224.

[36] Quoted by C. R. Boxer, *Salvador de Sá and the Struggle for Brazil and Angola, 1602-1686* (London: The Athlone Press, 1952), 166n.

[37] Caraci, "The Vespucian Problems," 13.

[38] Roberto Levillier, *America. La Bien Llamada.* 2 vols. (Buenos Aires: Editorial Guillermo Kraft Ltda., 1948), II, 13; Jaime Cortesão, *Os Descobrimentos Portugueses-IV* in *Obras Completas*, vol. 24 (Lisbon: Livros Horizonte, 1975), 1065.

[39] See Armando Cortesão and Avelino Teixeira da Mota, eds., *Portugaliae Monumenta Cartographica.* 6 vols. (Lisbon, 1960-1962), I, 15-16.

[40] For a recent biographical sketch, see that by Francis A. Dutra in *The Christopher Columbus Encyclopedia*, II, 531-532. There have been three Portuguese editions of *Esmeraldo de Situ Orbis*, the latest edited by Damião Peres (Lisbon: Academia Portuguesa da História, 1954). There is an English translation by G. H. T. Kimble (London: Hakluyt Society, 1937).

[41] *Portugaliae Monumenta Cartographica*, I, 7-8.

[42] John L. Vogt, "Portuguese Exploration in Brazil and the Feitoria System, 1500-1530: The First Economic Cycle of Brazilian History." PhD dissertation, U. of Virginia, 1967, 6-7. Vogt lists five voyages: Cabral, Lemos, João da Nova, and those of 1501-1502 and 1503-1504. I would add a sixth, 1502-1503.

[43] See letter of Pero Vaz de Caminha in Greenlee, *Cabral*, 32.

[44] One of the strongest proponents arguing that Gonçalves was captain of the supply ship is Roukema, "Brazil," 19-23.

[45] Greenlee, *Cabral*, 43.

[46] The apocryphal 1505 letter of King Manuel suggests that he did. This letter was actually a news tract published in Italian by Master Johannes Besicken. For the Italian with a Portuguese translation, see Peragallo, ed., "Carta de El-Rei D. Manuel," 8-35. The reference to João da Nova and Brazil is on 21. There is an English translation. See *Copy of a Letter of the King of Portugal Sent to the King of Castile Concerning the Voyage and Success of India* (Minneapolis: U. of Minnesota Press, 1955). For a brief discussion of the "letter," see Greenlee, *Cabral*, 42n.

[47] The author of the anonymous narrative of the expedition to India wrote that on Cabral's return voyage, at Beseguiche, "we found ourselves with three small ships which our King of Portugal sent to discover the new land." Greenlee, *Cabral*, 90.

[48] Pohl, in chapter eight of his *Amerigo Vespucci* provides English translations of the Florentine's "Cape Verde" and "Bartolozzi" letters regarding the 1501-1502 voyage on 126-136. A slip of the pen dates the former letter as July 4, 1501 (p. 126). His "Vespuccian Texts" (p. 234) gives the correct date of June 4. Morison argues that in 1789 Bartolozzi "printed a very inaccurate text which appears in all collections of Vespucci's letters," (p. 305). With the help of Dr. Gino Corti, Morison made a fresh translation of much of Vespucci's letter (the part describing Brazil) written from Lisbon in 1502, using the original manuscript. See *European Discovery*, 284-286.

[49] Pohl, *Vespucci*, 126

[50] Greenlee, *Cabral*, 151-152.

[51] Caraci, "Vespucian Problems," 16n.

[52] Quoted by Rolando A. Laguarda Trias, "Christóvão Jaques e as Armadas Guarda-Costa," *História Naval Brasileira* (Rio de Janeiro: Serviço de Documentação Geral da Marinha, 1975), Volume I, Tomo I, 249.

[53] Rocha Pita, *Historia da America Portugueza desde o anno de mil e quinhentos do seu descobrimento até o de mil e setecentos e vinte e quatro.* (2nd ed.; Lisbon, 1880), Livro I, Capitulo 90 (p. 28).

[54] Barbosa Machado, *Bibliotheca Lusitana*, II, 391.

[55] Southey, *History*, I, pp. 14 and 24 of the first and second editions respectively.

[56] See, e.g., William B. Greenlee, "The Captaincy of the Second Portuguese Voyage to Brazil, 1501-1502," *The Americas* 2:1 (July, 1945): 3-12 for Loronha; and Roukema, "Brazil," 19-23 for Gonçalves.

[57] Avelino Teixeira da Mota, *Novos Documentos sobre uma Expedição de Gonçalo Coelho ao Brasil, entre 1503 e 1505* (Lisbon: Junta de Investigações do Ultramar, 1969), 6. See also Jaime Cortesão, *Descobrimentos*, 1082-1085.

[58] Barbosa Machado, *Bibliotheca Lusitana*, II, 391.

[59] Francisco Marques de Sousa Viterbo, *Trabalhos Náuticos dos Portuguezes nos Seculos XVI e XVII.* 2 vols. (Lisbon: Academia Real das Sciencias, 1898). There is a one-volume facsimile edition with a new introduction by José Manuel Garcia and a slightly different

title: *Trabalhos Náuticos dos Portugueses. Séculos XVI e XVII* (Lisbon: Imprensa Nacional – Casa da Moeda, 1988).

[60] Furthermore, there is no evidence that the Gonçalo Coelho who explored Brazil was the father of Duarte Coelho, first lord-proprietor of Pernambuco, as Morison asserts in *European Discovery*, 280. See Francis A. Dutra, "Duarte Coelho Pereira, First Lord-Proprietor of Pernambuco: The Beginning of a Dynasty," *The Americas* 29:4 (April, 1973): 416-418.

[61] Pohl, *Vespucci*, 131

[62] Pohl, *Vespucci*, 140

[63] Pohl, *Vespucci*, 131.

[64] Roberto Levillier, "New Light on Vespucci's Third Voyage. Evidence of his Route and Landfalls," *Imago Mundi* XI (1954), 37. This article summarizes part of Levillier's earlier *America. La Bien Llamada*.

[65] See Roukema, "Brazil," 17.

[66] Guedes, "Expedições Portuguesas," 228-239.

[67] See deposition of Valentim Fernandes 20 May 1503, quoted in Roukema, "Brazil," 20.

[68] The English translation is from Roukema, "Brazil," 19.

[69] John L. Vogt, "Fernão de Loronha and the Rental of Brazil in 1502: A New Chronology," *The Americas* 24:2 (October, 1967): 155.

[70] The translation is by Morison, *European Discovery*, 284.

[71] Greenlee, *Cabral*, lxvii n. For a slightly different translation, see Vogt, "Fernão de Loronha," 155.

[72] See "Relazione de Lunardo da Chá Masser," 83-84.

[73] Vogt, "Fernão de Loronha," 155-159.

[74] Cortesão, *Descobrimentos*, 1070-1079.

[75] A good biographical sketch of Loronha is found in Vogt, "Portuguese Exploration," 10-13; 70-112.

[76] The English translation is by Greenlee, "Captaincy," 10n. The 1504 grant is included in the 1522 confirmation by João III. *Alguns Documentos de Archivo Nacional da Torre do Tombo* (Lisbon: Imprensa Nacional, 1892), 459-460.

[77] Cortesão, *Descobrimentos*, 1071-1072.

[78] Guedes, "Expedições Portuguesas," 241.

[79] Góis, *Crónica*, Parte I, Capítulo LXV (p. 160 of the 1949 edition).

[80] The apocryphal *Lettera* dates the departure as 10 May 1503.

[81] Vogt, "Portuguese Exploration," 110. The letter mentioned by Vogt is from Arquivo Nacional da Torre do Tombo, Cartas de quitação de D. Manuel, número 15. The reason for the discrepancy regarding the number of expeditions sent by Loronha is that Vogt

does not count the 1502-1503 voyage suggested by Cortesão and accepted by Guedes. Guedes, on the other hand, counts the 1502-1503 voyage but not the 1505 voyage (mentioned by Vogt). Guedes, "Expedições Portuguesas," 224.

[82] "Relazione de Lunardo da Chá Masser," 83. The English translation is from Vogt, "Fernão de Loronha," 155.

[83] "Relazione de Lunardo da Chá Masser," 84.

[84] As mentioned earlier, this list differs from that of Guedes, who does not seem to have been aware of Vogt's doctoral dissertation. See Guedes, "Expedições Portuguesas," 224.

[85] Regina Johnson Tomlinson, *The Struggle for Brazil. Portugal and "The French Interlopers" 1500-1550* (New York: Las Americas Publishing Co., 1970). There is a good brief summary in Morison, *European Discovery*, 585-587.

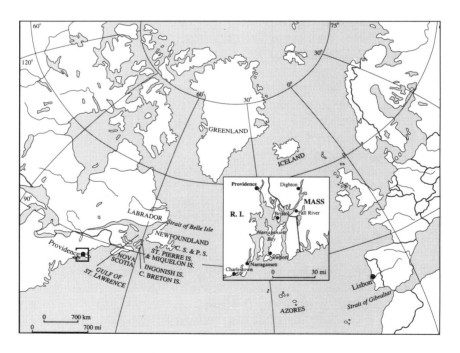

The North Atlantic Ocean

Chapter IX

In Northern Mists: the Boreal Atlantic

The title of this essay has been borrowed in part from a book written in 1911 by the Scandinavian historian, Fridtjof Nansen, because it summarizes the topic so admirably: what can be known with certainty about the earliest explorations of seas and lands above the 36th North parallel is pale and indistinct. With only one or two exceptions, *Portugal, the Pathfinder* concerns itself rather with discoveries which inaugurated the Westernization process than with geographical "whofoundits" *per se*; in the North Atlantic only a single Portuguese settlement was attempted, a private one at that, and the region has been included mostly for the sake of comprehensiveness. It follows, then, that this essay is not primarily concerned with prior discoveries and exact routes, but rather with what Portugal's contribution was to a chain of explorations in the region, inevitably followed by penetration and change – most of which took place only after the Portuguese had ceased to operate in the area except as fishermen. And in a broader context, it becomes evident that Columbus, married to a daughter of the captain of Porto Santo, fits into the pattern of westward sailings from the Portuguese Atlantic archipelagoes.

Save for a few new documents of secondary importance printed in the *Descobrimentos Portugueses*, assembled under the direction of João Martins de Silva Marques between 1944 and 1971[1], nearly all the ones elucidating the topic were assembled by the Canadian archivist, H. P. Biggar, in 1911 (with accompanying English translations for the Portuguese texts)[2] and by J. A. Williamson, in *The Cabot Voyages and Bristol Discovery under Henry VII*.[3] It is here that working as archivist or compiler rather than historiographer becomes attractive, for collecting and presenting surviving texts presents an easier job than saying what they mean. The interpreter, on the contrary, is presented with textual fragments plus a series of assertions at second and third hand, often dating from long after the fact. Depending on his skepticism or disposition to believe, as well as on his ability to project ship movements on crudely drawn maps and prevailing winds and currents, he can do no more than create new hypotheses, which then are added to the all-too-hypothetical literature. Since I am neither saltwater sailor, library sailor, nor cartographer, I can at least spare the reader a new round of supposititious routings and guesses of my own. I will rather sort through what has previously been investigated by others.

Dubious pre-Columbian voyages

It should be said from the outset that the urges of XV century mariners to explore the Atlantic and those of modern historians to write about the ensuing results have little in common. The ocean's extent and contents beyond its waters surrounding Europe were little known to sailors of the late Middle Ages, and when it yielded up the Madeiras, the Azores and the Cape Verde Islands on the Old World side, there remained every reason for contemporaries to dream, search for and "map" the existence of many similar and even more exciting ones just beyond the horizon. Their quest was engendered by "evidence" in the form of legend – like that of St. Brendan's islands and the Seven Cities of the mythical Antilia. This was the relevant stimulus for their exploration.

Modern historians, however, have mostly forgotten about the imaginary. Instead, they are conscious, as contemporaries were not, of the huge American continents and of the importance they came to assume in world history – and they are mindful of the more famous voyages of Columbus, Cabot, Verrazzano and others. "Were these really the first?" they speculate. There is just enough documental "detritus" around to fuel such speculation in form of second- and third-hand rumor or else of too-fragmentary documentation. Hence pre-Columbian voyaging in the Atlantic in late medieval times has been the subject of intense research.

But perhaps I have understated the case: probably nowhere in the whole realm of seaborne European expansion have modern researchers created more erudite analyses of trips that may never really have occurred than in just this theatre. Especially among Dr. Jaime Cortesão and some other Portuguese scholars, the notion that their navigators operating under direction or license of Prince Henry or D. João II must have discovered the Western Hemisphere before Christopher Columbus's famous voyage has fathered a line of reasoning that the Portuguese crown knew much more about the Americas than it cared to reveal; it deliberately kept silence lest other nations trespass before Portugal was able to take rightful possession.

As stated in my article on D. João II, I do suspect that Portuguese navigators discovered part of Brazil before Columbus sailed in 1492, but do not take the Cortesãovian *sigilo*, or secrecy thesis seriously, least of all when used as a blanket permission to suggest that almost everything discovered in the Atlantic had been previously found by the Portuguese.

A bouquet of indistinct voyages

One of the most farfetched of such speculations regarding northern Atlantic exploration is that of Cortesão himself over the westward sailing of Diogo de Teive and his Spanish collaborator, Pedro de Velasco. Teive has rightly been credited on his voyage with the discovery of Flores and Corvo as the most westwards of the Azores in 1452. On the same voyage, however, the pair continued out to sea beyond these islands and detected signs of land before returning to the Azores. But which direction is unclear; accounts indicate the northeast – toward the west of Ireland. Cortesão thereupon modifies this capriciously, interpreting the direction meant as northwest instead, and concludes the pair had approached Newfoundland![5] Even should he have been correct, the non-landfall of course could have had no consequences whatsoever. Leaving one to wonder what good did it for Cortesão to go to all the intellectual trouble. His learned colleagues, Damião Peres and Duarte Leite, both rejected his Newfoundland idea in their subsequent writings. Cortesão is still justly famous as an author and personality in Portugal; unfortunately, his pre-discovery ideas continue to inspire speculation among others who regard him as the ultimate authority.

To give another example, one which illustrates that discovery syndrome is not exclusively Portuguese. The Dane, Sofus Larsen, did his best in the 1920s to establish a link between two Danish voyagers, Pothorst and Pining, who supposedly made a trip to Greenland in the 1470s and the Portuguese, João Vaz Corte Real, governor at that time of Angra and Terceira. He even threw in a fourth party for good measure, a Dane – or perhaps a Pole – named Skolp or Scolvus. But his evidence hangs on gossamer threads. Aside from genuine doubts that the Pothorst-Pining voyage ever took place, Larsen tried to connect

João Vaz Corte Real to it by calling attention to the existence of: 1) a general letter expressing geographical curiosity by D. Afonso V of Portugal to his cousin, Christian I of Denmark: 2) a caption on the north Atlantic portion of a globe (1537) by the German cartographer, Gemma Frisius, "Strait of the Three Brothers, through which the Portuguese attempted to sail to the Orient and the Indies and the Moluccas"; 3) some captions on the far northern sections of the Vaz Dourado atlases, reading "Terra de João Vaz," presumed to refer to João Vaz Corte Real, captain of Terceira and Angra and father of the explorers, Gaspar and Miguel Corte Real. Samuel Eliot Morison has convincingly sprinkled cold water upon all of these "evidences"[6], leaving the late Boies Penrose only to remark, I think generously: "The fact that the younger Corte Reais a generation later sailed in these waters is certainly suggestive that their father may have blazed the trail, but at the present time the safest conclusion about this and the other fifteenth century Portuguese ventures across the Atlantic is: not proven."[7]

The "voyage" of João Vaz Corte Real has considerably less substance than the next one attributed to the Portuguese, that of Fernão Dulmo (or Van Olmen) and João Afonso do Estreito, both settlers in the Portuguese Atlantic Islands. Dulmo, also captain of the island of Terceira, petitioned D. João II in 1483 or 1484 to make a westward voyage in hopes of finding "a large island or islands or mainland, especially the Island of the Seven Cities, all at his own cost and expense," as the crown noted. Probably the ideas expressed to D. Afonso V a few years earlier by the Florentine geographer, Toscanelli, concerning the existence of Asian spice lands not far across the western ocean had circulated about Portugal and increased such interest and awareness, particularly of the Portuguese islanders who were by location that much the closer; through marriage, Columbus was one of these, himself. Moreover, as many historians have remarked, the contract awarded Dulmo by D. João II foreshadows the one granted Columbus by Queen Isabella: Dulmo was promised hereditary captaincy of all the lands he might discover, with all income and rights, including that of high justice. It is even possible that one of the reasons D. João turned Columbus's proposal down was that Dulmo had offered to accomplish about the same thing and that he inspired more confidence. If the Dulmian voyage indeed ever took place, however, it yielded no practical results; the Spanish cleric and chronicler, Bartolomé de las Casas, believed that Dulmo had perished at sea.[8] Morison calls attention to the fact that while the Azores may appear close to Newfoundland, (only 1054 nautical miles), the winds do not favor sailing in that direction from the Portuguese islands. He speculates that Dulmo and Estreito may have attempted to sail northwestwards, into the teeth of prevailing winds – and been forced to return home without sighting land. Hence the vagueness surrounding their results.[9]

Still vaguer and probably nonexistent in terms of their identification with existing islands were the "Satanazes" on an Italian chart of 1424, called the Zuane Pizzigano map, one of the chief XV century sources of imaginary insular geography. Yet Dr. Armando Cortesão, the younger brother of the more famous Jaime and an historical geographer of considerable merit, argued that the name "Satanazes" was Portuguese and that the allusion to devils as their inhabitants in one of its labels suggests a New World encounter between Europeans and eskimos.[10] Hence Cortesão was tempted to believe that explorers (though he was unwilling to guess who they might have been) could already have visited the Western Hemisphere prior the first quarter of the XV century! Although cautious in most other respects, he could not bring himself to believe that any of the islands on the Zuane Pizzigano map were wholly mythical. Nor was he alone in these speculations: Professor E. G. R. Taylor was inclined to believe that another of the imaginary islands, Antília, could be Newfoundland[11], an idea disparaged by Morison but recently revived by a Rhode Island physician who dabbles in historical research, of whom more later.

If modern supporters of pre-discovery theories such as those just mentioned have reasoned that the "Satanazes" refer to Eskimos, on grounds that the Vikings frequently clashed with these peoples and attributed evil motives to their behavior, Professor Onésimo T. Almeida, of Brown University (and the contributor of an essay to this volume), has adduced a more likely answer in his article, "Plutarch as a Possible Source for the Name of the 'Satanazes' on the Zuane Pizzigano Map of 1424." He suggests that the famous classical author is much more likely as the true source of the name. For, as Almeida demonstrates, the ancient Greek wrote in his *De Defectu Miraculorum* that west of Britain were various desert islands inhabited by demons. Almeida then in effect uses the "Ockham's Razor" of a simpler line of reasoning: the term "Satanazes" would therefore not need eskimos at all to explain their presence on a map of the early renaissance created in the Italian home of classical literary revival. Most of the other islands on the Zuane Pizzigano map are legendary, anyway, so why should one pick the "Satanazes" as having any greater claim to reality?[12]

The End of the XV century and the brothers Corte Real

Following the Columbian explorations and their aftermath, that is, in the period between 1492 and around 1500 or so, a significant change took place in the objectives of explorers. In the first nine decades of the XV century, they had searched either for the legendary islands and their fictive wealth, or else, as in the case of Toscanelli and Columbus, they had sought Marco Polo's Cathay as being located directly across the Atlantic from Europe. But whether or not one accepts Vespucci's "Mundus Novus" letter as genuine and undoctored, it was not long before explorers had ceased to regard the newly-discovered western lands in themselves as Asian Cathay and had instead begun to seek a way through them or around them to the real spicelands and/or lands of the Great Khan. That the new Columbian finds may have demonstrated some value (as in the case of the Caribbean islands) merely delayed the continuing search for Asia. If one considers what the coeval reconnoiterers had in their minds, namely civilized countries abounding in gold and spices, the northern territories when found were seen as mere incidents on the way to something else more exciting. We must not forget their intrinsic lack of appeal when reading of further northern explorations in this period. For if in the XVI century increasing numbers of fishermen flocked from Europe to the newly-discovered Grand Banks, this was merely a kind of collateral benefit in which the geographers and kings were barely interested – only enough so to levy harbor taxes on catches of cod as these arrived home.

But this is to get far ahead of the story. Following the initial two voyages of Columbus, the hopes of finding Cathay somewhere just across the Atlantic were still not dead (and it must not forgotten that Italy had been the original seedbed of such speculation). So it was perhaps only natural that another Italian, Giovanni Caboto (seemingly also of a Genoese family, though naturalized in Venice), should wish to try his own hand at locating Cathay through a westward voyage. While Columbus had been able to enlist the Castilian crown as his host after failing in Portugal, Caboto, who had been residing in Spain, had to wander farther afield before he reached the court of Henry VII in London and could arrange a similar contract. His own view was that Columbus had sailed too far south; he reckoned that the Khan should be located farther northwards. Of course this would easily appeal to the English; hence his contracts and voyages.[13]

Please note in this connection that Caboto (or as he became known in England, Cabot) chose as his home port the western city of Bristol, an enterprising hub of maritime activity, even then in trade with Iceland, Iberia, and with the Azores, and that its mariners had already launched speculative journeys in quest of the legendary Atlantic islands. Hence it should be no surprise to read later on in this essay that Azoreans were to cooperate with Bristol speculators in continuing the search for Cathay via northern waters even after both the English and Portuguese governments had become absorbed in other pursuits.

All writers from Harisse in the late XIX century to Morison in the mid-XX agree that Cabot's two voyages resulted in the discovery of Newfoundland, even though details are sketchy and Cabot kept no (surviving) journal like that of Columbus. Morison suggests that ice in the straits of Belle Isle to the island's north prevented Cabot from discovering the St. Lawrence; at least on his first voyage of 1497 – for had he done so, one would surely expect his successors to have been quick to follow up his lead and investigate the estuary in search of a passage westwards, just as Jacques Cartier did almost forty years later.[14] Anyway, it was obvious enough that his coastal exploration did not result in the location of a passage through to Asia; thus contemporaries, both in Bristol and in Portugal continued to search further.

Time had now come for Portuguese navigators to make their appearance as known (rather than as putative) explorers of North American shores. On October 28, 1499, D. Manuel I of Portugal, issued a permit to one João Fernandes, of Terceira, to "seek out and discover at his own expense some islands lying in our sphere of influence…"[15] It is possible, as Morison believes, that he thereupon made his first voyage to Greenland, probably in the company of a fellow Azorean, a nobleman called Pedro Maria de Barcelos. Fernandes, who was a small middle-class landowner, seems to have been the first to sight land, actually Greenland, and had it called by his shipmates for his bucolic nickname, "O Lavrador" – "The Farmer." Or this could have occurred on a subsequent voyage, made under English royal license dated March 19, 1501, which will be discussed below.

At any rate, conditions were next ripe for the two younger sons of João Vaz, who in their turn became explorers of northern waters – but hardly very fortunate ones. I am not prepared to speculate on their choice of latitude for their explorations beyond the suggestion by the late Boies Penrose, already quoted, that they may have chosen the region because their father had a special, but probably only passive, interest in it through his previous grant. Gaspar first set out, armed with a patent from D. Manuel dated May 12, 1500, in which he was granted extensive privileges. The document, incidentally, mentions that Gaspar had made a previous voyage to "search out and find some islands and a mainland"[16], but of this nothing is known. On the voyage, at about 50° N. Lat., he found a land with large trees which he called *Terra Verde*. On a follow-up voyage the next summer, Gaspar set out with three ships, sailed far into the north and encountered pack ice before turning south back to Newfoundland, where the expedition "persuaded" fifty-seven Indians to accompany them home. Then Gaspar apparently sent the other vessels back to Europe, while he continued on southwards. He never returned. The Cantino mappemonde of 1502 in the Biblioteca Estense, at Modena, contains evidence of his first voyage as a section of jagged coastline far to the north of the Caribbean and too far east (no doubt to place it on the Portuguese side of the Demarcation Line) and labelled "*Terra del Rey de Portuguall*," complete with Portuguese banners. In other respects it is unmistakably Newfoundland.

After Gaspar's disappearance, the youngest Corte Real brother, Miguel, set off in May of 1502 to find him – but disappeared in his turn. Other Portuguese led by João Fernandes, *O Lavrador*, thereupon picked up the traces of North Atlantic exploration from Bristol. All that remains of Miguel Corte Real is some wishful thinking and a wisp or two of "evidence" which have "traced" him and his shipmates to Narragansett Bay – to be discussed at the end of this essay.

The Anglo-Azoreans

At any rate, the future of Portuguese exploration in the North Atlantic belonged to the translocated João Fernandes and not to the Corte Reais. If indeed João Fernandes had visited Greenland in 1500, as noted above, he and Pedro de Barcelos seem never to have gone ashore; next, Morison speculates that Fernandes must have become nettled that a Portuguese royal grant containing more and better privileges than his and concerning the same regions was suddenly bestowed upon Gaspar Corte Real, a favored courtier.[17] So he hied himself to Bristol where he apparently had done business previously and was joined by two other Azoreans, plus two local merchants, Thomas Ashhurst and John Thomas. These then obtained a new royal patent from King Henry VII, whom one might expect to be eager to follow up the unfinished but possibly promising voyages of Cabot.

The patent, dated March 19, 1501, is a long-winded one; it occupies in its original Latin nine solid quarto pages of text in its reprint by Biggar – or about 3,300 words – and it goes into such detail that it specifies the amount of tax-free import subsidies each member of a vessel would be entitled to, as well as the question of citizenship for individuals born in the territories – and it even takes into account the problem of rape of native women by Europeans! One is slightly bemused by the fact that the petition by the Anglo-Portuguese partners and the very grant itself are both dated as of March 19, leading one to speculate on the lightning speed with which King Henry's lawyers would have to have spun off such legal terminology – and in a literary tongue like Latin – in days long before word processors existed! It may indeed reveal of the lawyers that like Father William in *Through the Looking-Glass*, they possessed remarkable jaws! More likely the patent had already been drafted and the written application was requested as a mere formality for the royal files.[18]

As matters developed, the lawyers might as well have spared their labors and those of their scribes, for no permanent settlements resulted. Moreover, one can only conjecture the results of the voyage, or seemingly, voyages. *O Lavrador* himself must have perished on the first, to judge from the fact that a new patent, similar to the one of March 19, 1501 was issued on December 9, 1502, omitting the name of João Fernandes, but carrying all the others.[19] Moreover, on 26 September of that same year, pensions of *£10* each per annum were bestowed on Francisco Fernandes, João Gonçalves and on their Bristol partners; no mention is made of João Fernandes. Besides the death of *O Lavrador* himself, these documents would suggest that one or more voyages had indeed been made. And the likelihood is strengthened by the miscellaneous entries which Professor Williamson has gleaned from the household registers of the monarch: on January 2, 1502, a reward of *£5* was given to "men of Bristol that found the isle;" "*£20* to merchants of Bristol who have been in the new found land...", *£5* "to men of Portugal who brought poppinjays and cats and other stuff..." Moreover, three indigenes "taken in the new found land" were mentioned by an English witness.[20] On December 6, 1503, pensions of *£10* per annum were appropriated to Francisco Fernandes and João Gonçalves "in consideration of their true service... as captains in the new found land.[21] But no accounts of the voyage(s) themselves have ever surfaced.

Morison, because of his extensive experience in practical navigation, was in my opinion by far the most trustworthy and accomplished reader of antique cartography from the North Atlantic theatre. He was not deceived by every imaginary curlicue recorded by contemporary mapmakers, but he was sensitive to data which appeared as a logical outcome of recently completed voyages. He calls attention to a map, now in the Oliveriana Library at Pesaro, Italy, which affords an insight into what the Anglo-Azorean expeditions must have accomplished. He places it as dating between 1504 and 1510 and probably made for one of the Medici; it is a mappemonde, but in its northwest corner, in a state of detachment from what is meant to be the North American continent are three bits of coastline, unjoined to one another, but which are palpably the adjacent coasts of Labrador and Greenland, and in the westernmost instance, possibly a part of the North American mainland visited by the combine. The Greenland portion bears the legend "Cavo Larbradore," while the Newfoundland section contains the names "bacalaos," "del Marco," "de la spera," and "Terra de Corte [Real]."[22]. As Morison points out, all these names appear for the first time, and they have since become part of the modern nomenclature, though in slightly altered form: "bacalaos" has become "Bacalieu," for example, and the "Cavo de la spera," Cape Spear. Please note in this respect one of the not uncommon geographical confusions which has become permanent: João Fernandes's nickname of "*lavrador*" has become assigned, not to Greenland, where it really belongs, but to the adjacent coast, now known as Labrador.[23]

It was most of a century before the English or any other government showed signs of settling the regions thus discovered by Cabot and the Anglo-Portuguese, but, as already noted, the fishermen were not slow to recognize the value that the Grand Banks, as they came to be called, were brimming with codfish must have been bruited throughout the Azores and the West Country alike as soon as Cabot, Miguel Corte Real and *O Lavrador* returned, for already on 14 October, 1506, D. Manuel of Portugal was busy regulating permits and taxes on imports from there.[24] And it is easy enough to imagine that fishermen from Portugal and England were almost immediately joined by others from the Basque country and Galicia, not to speak of the French ports, though no one is certain in exactly which years who of them appeared.[25]

João Álvares Fagundes and the lost colony of Ingonish

A generation went by before new letters patent were forthcoming from either the Portuguese or the English chanceries. But interest in the region was increasing, if because of the rich fisheries and because it was still believed that a sinus leading to Asia would presently be found in the region – a conviction that outlasted the XVI century. But governments were not interested enough to involve themselves directly; as always in the Americas, they waited for private initiative to take the lead.

Although one respected writer, Jean Denucé, has disputed the consensus that the shipowner and entrepreneur, João Álvares Fagundes, of Viana do Castelo, actually discovered the Gulf of St. Lawrence, the preponderance of scholars, including Morison, believe that he completed a voyage in or before 1520 to Newfoundland, and that he subsequently visited and gave names to a number of new places in the environs.[26] Biggar believes that he had explored the coast from Nova Scotia to Placentia Bay in Newfoundland, though perhaps as Cabot may have before him, mistaking the entrance to the Gulf of St. Lawrence for a large bay. Then, in 1521, he petitioned the crown and on March 13 and May 22, 1521, was awarded the proprietorship of the islands he had found, "in the style and form we have granted...Madeira," providing they did not appertain to the claims of the Corte Reais (those of the lost brothers, Gaspar and Miguel having been reserved for a survivor, Vasco). Morison has untangled the place names in the donation (São João, São Pedro, Sta. Anna and Sto. Antonio, Pitigoen, and the Onze Mil Vergines) as the present-day Penguin Island and the St. Pierre, Miquelon and their numerous islets.

Fagundes actually followed up on this letter-patent and became the only Portuguese to effectuate a settlement in the northern waters, even though a temporary one. For sometime between the date of D. Manuel's donation and 1525, Fagundes rounded up some volunteers from Minho and from the Azores and brought them to a "beautiful harbor" on Cape Breton Island, the one he had called São João. This harbor Morrison believes to have been Ingonish because it is easily the best and most protected on the island. But the little settlement soon faced hostility from the surrounding Indian peoples and from the Breton fishermen alike who cut the nets of the settlers and destroyed their houses. By 1525, the Portuguese had given up and returned home to Europe; the little settlement ceased to exist. Less than a decade later of course, Jacques Cartier appeared, and he heralded a French hegemony for the region which lasted into the XVIII century though Cartier himself did not succeed any more than Fagundes had in founding a permanent colony.[27]

If one is to assess the significance of the Portuguese in the northern mists, it must be admitted that from a standpoint, it was a dead-end. Only some antique maps bearing facsimiles of the *quinas*, or royal arms, remain in testimony of what was at best a sporadic, private enterprise of mostly Azoreans backed by a few papers which cost the crown only the time of its lawyers and its scribes. But it is a complete story which represents all the stages of European expansion, if only in miniature. For as in the rest of the two Americas, it began as a quest for the civilized riches of Cathay and the spice islands, it progressed through a period of reconnaissance and ended in economic exploitation (the cod fisheries and soon a fur trade) and in at least an honest attempt at settlement. Hence in a purely European context, the Portuguese pioneers were among the very first to penetrate the region and to inaugurate the inexorable process of its integration into the world economy.

An amusing and confusing sequel

There is a formidable *Wirrwarr* of will-to-believe, gullibility, amateurism, and some real, but uninvestigated evidence in Rhode Island, that early explorers, possibly Portuguese, visited there sometime early in the XVI century and I will end this article by describing it. There is of course no evidence to indicate where the Corte Real brothers actually disappeared, and one or both could actually have ended up hundreds of miles or even a thousand from where they were last seen.

In the last century Azorean whalers were recruited by operators in Rhode Island and nearby Massachusetts, and since then, their American descendants with Portuguese surnames have been augmented though immigration. As in the case of Italian-Americans, these descendants are eager to establish their footprints on the American historical landscape, and it is only natural that they are prone to investigate leads and some are over-willing to accept as valid evidence not all professional historians find convincing. And it must be remembered that a great many of the assertions in this essay are informed guesswork; hence its title. The following paragraphs will serve to remind readers that even false history can become history of a sort, and that it might well behoove responsible historians to make a fresh and concerted attempt to evaluate the evidence, if only to lay pseudo-history to rest.

The professionals of many communities throughout the world - chiefly lawyers, teachers, engineers and physicians – are often historical hobbyists whose chief intellectual pursuit involves the local scene. I have encountered them from Mexico to India, and I even commend their interest and zeal; some are very good and, of course, the past is no one's exclusive property. Almost every field would be the poorer were it not for them. But occasionally, they (as well as some others within the professional fold) go about their work in such a way that they leap to conclusions, combine fragmentary evidence in deceptive ways and mislead those without the time, interest or training to get to the bottom of what is being asserted.

Dr. Manuel Luciano da Silva is a Rhode Island physician who has devoted over thirty years to his attempt to prove that the Corte Reais, or at least Miguel, landed in the area between Mount Hope and Narragansett Bays, just between Rhode Island and Massachusetts and spent several years in the area, presumably as a maroon. To establish this, he adduces various arguments and bits of evidence: a strange stone tower built on a hill, a tidal rock with indistinct markings, allegedly

Portuguese words in local Amerindian languages, the outlines of a ruined fort, in or near which were found an early breech-loading swivel cannon, a sword of XVI century type and some skeletons. He has combined all this into a frothy pudding of pseudo-certainty, parts of which have been exposed as consisting in little but air, while other parts may still merit serious excavation and sifting.[28]

The *schlagober* topping of his concoction is the Round Tower in Newport, Rhode Island, a curious and useless flagstone edifice, consisting of a masonry cylinder a full storey high, standing on massive pillars and rounded arches. There is still a modicum of uncertainty over its origin. Dr. da Silva asserts it to have been built by the Portuguese – while others with equally little regard for reality have as steadfastly assigned it to the Vikings. There is no reason in either case why desperate little bands of maroons from either group should have spent their energy creating such a folly: the real challenge consists in explaining why anyone should have done so. The first documentary evidence of its existence indicates that it was on the land of a rich colonist towards the end of the XVII century; no early navigators mention it, in spite of its obvious visibility from the sea. Since it could have served no function – either as a place of worship, a shelter or a defence – but instead resembles in grosser form the kind of pergola wealthy English gentry of the XVIII century constructed about their landscaped estates, it can best be attributed to a wealthy landowner who wished to create something between a landmark and a gazebo – the same impulse recognizable on a humbler scale in those who place miniature windmills or large porcelain dwarves in their gardens. Some have suggested that it was a flour mill, but if so, it must be the only one in history with its ground floor open to the winds. Excavations have not revealed any of the evidences of habitation in or around it that one might expect of a refugee site, nor has recent carbon dating suggested that it precedes English settlement.

Dighton Rock deserves to be taken slightly more seriously, but perhaps not much more. It is – or was – a flat sandstone boulder at the mouth of the Taunton River which bears graffiti of both Indian and European origin. In 1917, one Professor Edmund Delabarre, a psychologist, late of Brown University, puzzled out (or imagined that he did) the name "Gaspar Corte Real" and the date "1511" on it.[29] Then others, including Dr. da Silva, purported to discern three Portuguese crosses and two crude Portuguese *quinas*, or royal arms on it (though other students of the stone made their own drawings and saw only childish stick figures with the "*quinas*" as two eyes, a dot for a nose and perhaps a slit for a mouth!).

Since then, Dr. da Silva's efforts have turned the rock into a state monument and a coffer-dam has prevented its daily inundations.

The late Professor Luís de Albuquerque, emeritus of Coimbra University, visited the United States not long ago to see for himself, and like Morison many years earlier, could make out nothing of the supposed inscriptions. Moreover, he wondered why XVI century Portuguese would have written "1511" in Arabic numerals, rather than the far more usual "MDXI" – especially when ingenious combinations of the many lines on the rock's surface might also have permitted this interpretation. His conclusion: the matter would have died a natural death decades ago, had it not been for Dr. da Silva's indefatigable efforts.[30]

If one wished to demonstrate with finality that Delabarre and Dr. da Silva created out of whole cloth the legend of a shipwrecked Corte Real in Narragansett Bay, then two other evidences adduced by the physician must be reckoned with. Neither ought to be too difficult to investigate, and I fully intend to do so in future. The first involves philology, and concerns the question whether a putative residence of the Corte Real brother, Miguel, and his crew would have left some evidence in the local Indian language(s). Since real Portuguese settlements in Africa, India and Japan have left words behind in the local dialects, it could be argued that the same should hold for any Portuguese residence among the Narragansett Indians (though rather short by the other standards). Da Silva maintains that this is indeed the case, and he offers some eighteen words with Portuguese meanings which he claims to have gleaned from Indian languages, though he is not overly specific as to which tongues these were and how, why and by whom the vocables were collected. A few, on the surface are ridiculous (viz. that the last syllables, "kinas" or *quinas*, in the name of an Indian chief are derived from the *Quinas*, or Portuguese royal arms, or that a word sounding like "Sagres" and meaning "wet by overflow" was derived from Prince Henry's home cape, which sometimes received doses of ocean spray!). But others should at least be traced out and explained – like *catana (cutlass)*, *machias, machial* (uncultivated land) *osso* (bone), *chapada* (a blow), *cochicho* (a lark or black bird). I was amused that many of the more plausible words could have come into Indian languages through unfamiliar terms and even epithets – XVI century Indians would not have been familiar with a big knife such as a cutlass, for example, and if the Portuguese displayed these, or called Indians "rascals" or "black birds" or threatened them with blows, such words might have been picked up. A philologist ought to make a

methodical study of the subject and pronounce, since the allegations of
Portuguese words in local Amerindian tongues will no doubt persist
until an expert convincingly explains them as distorted and wishful or
else shows that their origins were from other sources. For example, just
how careful was Dr. da Silva in taking his words from nearby
Algonquian languages, or could some of them have come from more
distant – and/or unrelated tongues used by other Indians in touch with
French or Spanish settlers, as in Florida, Paris Island, or in Québec?

Finally, there is a ruined fortification near Ninigret Pond,
Charleston, Rhode Island, to the west of Narragansett Bay. Called
"Fort Ninigret," it was long known, and the site is supposed to have
been occupied during the Revolutionary War and possibly that of 1812
possibly because it was close to the old Boston Post Road. A historian
writing just before the Civil War speculated that its origins must have
been Dutch.

If the present outlines are correct, the fort had three pentagonal
bastions reminiscent of Iberian fortifications found in colonial
Portuguese Africa and India – but it is not completely certain whether
these bastions represent the original, archaeological contours of the
fortification or whether the fencebuilder tracing the ditches
surrounding the fort merely fancied their existence. (Bastions,
incidentally, enable defenders to catch attackers attempting to mount
the walls in an enfilading fire.) Their outlines in any case are clearly
indicated in rounded beach stones averaging approximately 15 cm. in
diameter, suggesting that all or part of the defensive wall was built of
them, although palisades were far more common in hastily-built
structures. It could be, of course, that the stones were so collocated in
the XIX century, if merely to suggest an outline, but it is more likely
that the original structure represented a combination of stakes, with
stones at their base, since throughout the area, rocky outcroppings are
close to the surface and it may have otherwise been impractical to
anchor the butt ends of the timbers in a trench, as was usually the
practice.

But I suspect that there is no good reason that the bastions should
have been invented by anyone in the 1880s when the iron fence was
erected, especially since one is lacking on the side near Ninigret Pond,
a coastal inlet with two channels navigable only by very small ships.
Probably had the XIX century fencebuilder (even if he knew about
bastions and their use in early modern colonial military architecture)
simply conjured up the protruding pentagonal structures, he would
have made four of them – one for each corner (if only out of a whim

for symmetry) – and not simply placed them on the three angles facing the land. Moreover, it is clear enough from the contemporary inscription on a boulder within the fort that the three commissioners whose names appear after the text had little or no idea that the fort might have had European origins, let alone knowledge of XVI and XVII century defensive construction: they appeared to believe that the fort had been constructed by the indigenes![31] If the bastions are indeed of the XVI century, as I believe they are, then their architects certainly would not have considered attack from the sea as a real possibility and would have located them only on the corners facing the land. Hence I am inclined to believe that they belong to the original design.

If such be true, the fort is undoubtedly of Renaissance origin because military architects after the XVI century no longer employed structures like these. Corner bastions were no longer favored in Europe because enemy artillery by then had become too powerful and such corner projections presented juicy targets to knock apart. Rather, the star-shape came into vogue there, even though the obsolete construction with bastions might conceivably have been employed in colonial settings where defense was contemplated solely against indigenes, who lacked ordnance. Early colonial Rhode Island, however, would hardly have required a largish, bastioned fort in exactly that location: the area seems instead to have been variously occupied by Narragansett and Niantic Indians while the settlers lived elsewhere.

That the fort is of very early date is also indicated by its placement: Ninigret Pond has no strategic value and could have only appealed to the builders as a sheltered spot into which a small vessel might enter and moor for protection against storms. Had the architects instead desired to protect the land behind them from attack or invasion by sea, as possibly in the later Seven Years or Revolutionary wars, they not only would have not constructed bastions and so placed them, but would also have selected a completely different site, since it is most unlikely that defending a small inlet would have made sense. Nor could the fort have been designed to protect the post road, some 150 yards before it on the land side, as some locals appear to believe, simply because Fort Ninigret occupies lower ground than the road itself, while there are enough more suitable locations available nearby to rule out its construction for that purpose. But there is another consideration more certainly suggestive of its antiquity.

In an Indian burial mound some hundred yards away several items were found among the skeletons when the site was partially excavated in 1926: a sword, an early ring, a comb, buttons, and a very small breechloading cannon (43 inches long) of the type known as SW-2. Such guns were commonly mounted on swivels fired from the railings of vessels between about 1490 and 1530, but thereafter universally discarded in favor of the heavier and more reliable muzzle loading types; among other reasons were their propensity either to explode or for the breech plug so to expand from the heat of repeated firings that gunners could not remove it. Dr. da Silva found almost exact duplicates of both sword and and gun at the Museu Militar in Lisbon, as dating from the late XV or early XVI centuries.

The fact that the gun and the other objects were found in an Indian cemetery might suggest that the fort had been abandoned when the occupiers gave up and sailed off; they might have been buried with a sachem as his personal souvenirs. Or it could also be that some of the bones were of the Europeans themselves and that, as maroons, they were obliged to go native; moreover, nobody seems to know whether the excavations included the whole burial area or only part of it, in which case a good deal might remain uninvestigated.

If the fort and the artefacts are baffling, the investigations concerning it have all been uninformed. The "Dutch theory," can be discarded both on grounds of the antiquity of the gun and sword and the lack of any Manhattan or Dutch West India Company presence in the area; the W.I.C. would not have employed such outmoded weapons in any case, since it was founded in 1621, about a century after they went out of use. The "experts" who so believed were anything but students of ordnance or of European expansion. Score one for Dr.da Silva who knew the Dutch were not involved. But then he abruptly concluded that the Portuguese had been the mysterious visitors – probably, he supposes, Miguel Corte Real and his crew. He might be right, of course, but the remains could just as well have been left by others within the forty or so year period dated by the gun. So one would have to include Giovanni Caboto and his English, or even the murky activities of the slightly later Anglo-Portuguese of Bristol, for if one accepts the idea that Corte Real could have deviated so far to the south as Narragansett Bay from his last reported latitudes, then one might as well accord the privilege to everyone else who sailed around Newfoundland in the era! It is barely possible that the fort was built by some unknown French or Spanish expedition which took place just after the visits of Verazzano or Gomez in the 1520's. Portuguese, Basque and French fishermen could also have visited the area, but I would doubt that they were military enough to have built forts with bastions.

Though persuasive of an early European visit, the fort – nearly half an acre – seems far too large to have been constructed by castaways from such tiny expeditons if solely for themselves. The thirty or forty crewmembers of the small ships employed could scarcely have hoped to man its long walls or palisades and would surely have devised something to their own dimensions. But if they were allied with one group of Indians against common enemies, it is likely they would have required a larger enceinte. It was common in the expansion of Europe for reconnoitering expeditions to be welcomed by the weaker of two adversaries who sought to involve them in their quarrels; hence Cabral, Cortés and Champlain in other parts of the world.

Whatever the fort's origins, it seems to have been inhabited by Indians long after its builders disappeared. Apart from those in the burial mounds, no XVI century artefacts have survived within the enceinte since bedrock is so close to the surface that discarded objects of interest could not have become covered with earth, but would have been carried off as souvenirs and disassociated from the site.

Professor Almeida and I plan to investigate further, if not in time for this volume's deadline. We think the whole matter should be resolved, if possible once and for all; false history creates an intellectual clutter, but if there is something to all the allegations, that would constitute an interesting footnote in the European history of North America. He has been in contact with a researcher presently collecting material for a dissertation on the fort. But to our surprise, she divulged that she has not so far displayed interest or otherwise investigated the presence of the gun and sword; it seems she has been interested only in the American national history of the site. Nor does the Rhode Island Historical Society know the present whereabouts of an archaeologist who conducted diggings of some sort on the premises!

Perhaps some day an enterprising team of salvors and scuba divers will find the submerged remains of the Cabot or Corte Real or Fernandes vessels and a new chapter in exploration will be brought to the ocean's surface. But the sole conclusion to be drawn so far is that in the North Atlantic theatre, the mists have still not lifted sufficiently to permit historians a clearer view of its earliest contacts with European expansion.

George D. Winius

George D. Winius

Notes

¹ In the *Descobrimentos Portugueses; Documentos para a sua história, publicados e prefaciados por João Martins de Silva Marques,* 3 vols. in 5 (Lisbon: Instituto da Alta Cultura, 1944-1971). All currently reprinted under the auspices of the Comissão para a Comemoração da História dos Descobrimentos Portugueses. The years covered are 1147-1500.

² H. P. Biggar (ed.& comp.), *The Precursors of Jacques Cartier, 1497-1534; a Collection of Documents Relating to the Early History of the Dominion of Canada* (Ottawa: Government Printing Bureau, 1911).

³ J. A. Williamson (ed.& comp., with preface), *The Cabot Voyages and Bristol Discovery under Henry VII,* (Cambridge: Cambridge U. Press, for the Hakluyt Society, 1961).

⁴ Bailey W. Diffie, "Foreigners in Portugal and the 'Policy of Silence,'" *Terrae Incognitae,* I (1969): 23-34.

⁵ Jaime Cortesão, "The Pre-Columbian Discovery of America," *The Geographical Journal,* LXXIX (1937): 30-42.

⁶ Sofus Larsen, *The Discovery of America Twenty Years before Columbus* (Copenhagen: Levin and Munksgaard, 1925), with evaluation by Samuel Eliot Morison, in *Portuguese Voyages to America in the Fifteenth Century* (Cambridge, Mass.: Harvard U. Press, 1940), 36-41.

⁷ Boies Penrose, *Travel and Discovery in the Renaissance, 1420-1620* (Cambridge, Mass.: Harvard U. Press, 1955), 143.

⁸ See João de Barros, *Da Asia,* 9 vols., Lisbon, 1778, Livro I, parte I, 250; Bartolomé de las Casas, *Historia de Indias* (ed. Augustín Millares Carlo), 3 vols. (Mexico, D. F.: Fondo Económico de Cultura, 1951), I, 69.

⁹ Samuel Eliot Morison, *Portuguese Voyages to America in the Fifteenth Century* (Cambridge, Mass.: Harvard U. Press, 1940), 44-47.

¹⁰ Armando Cortesão, *The Nautical Chart of 1424 and the Early Discovery and Cartographical Representation of America,* (Coimbra: U. Press, 1954), 74-77.

¹¹ Eva G. R. Taylor, "Imaginary Islands: a Problem Solved," in *The Geographical Journal,* CXXX (1964): 109. Information supplied by Professor Onésimo T. Almeida.

¹² Professor Almeida was kind enough to supply me with a copy of his article, still in draft form.

¹³ Reproduced both in Williamson, *Cabot Voyages,* 204-05 and 226-27; and in Biggar, *Precursors,* 7-10 and 22-24, Biggar with both Latin and English texts.

¹⁴ Samuel Eliot Morison, *The European Discovery of America; the Northern Voyages, A. D. 500-1600*, 174. Of course Cabot may have found it on his second voyage, from which he never returned.

¹⁵ Biggar, *Precursors*, 31-32.

¹⁶ Biggar, *Precursors*, 32-37.

¹⁷ Biggar, *Precursors*, and Morison, *European Discovery*, 212-13.

¹⁸ Biggar, *Precursors*, 41-59

¹⁹ Williamson, *Cabot Voyages*, 250-61; Biggar, *Precursors*, 70-91.

²⁰ Williamson, *Cabot Voyages*, 214-16.

²¹ Biggar, *Precursors*, 91-92.

²² Morison, *European Discovery*, 242-44.

²³ See also Nansen, *Northern Mists*, II, 364.

²⁴ Biggar, *Precursors*, 96-98.

²⁵ Biggar, *Precursors*, 116-27.

²⁶ Morison, *European Discovery*, 228-29; Biggar, *Precursors*, xxii-xv, and 127-31.

²⁷ After this there may or may not have occurred one, two, or no last voyages, together with a possible attempt to colonize the island of "Barcellosa de Sam Bordão" by two sons of Pedro de Barcelos between 1525 and 1531 – this based on a previous reconnaissance by a third brother at some antecedent time. But documentation is so ambiguous that it is hard to establish whether any of this really amounted to more than intent. "Sam Bordão" was St. Brendan, and the mythical islands identified with his VI century voyage(s) were sprinkled variously around the Atlantic by subsequent cartographers. The Portuguese scholar, Manuel Baptista de Lima, attempted thirty years ago to identify "Barcellosa" with Prince Edward Island, but after re-reading his paper on the subject, I relegated the whole matter to this note. See Manuel C. Baptista de Lima, "Uma tentativa Açoriana de colonização da ilha demoniada 'Barcellosa' no século XVI," in the *Actas do congresso internacional da história dos descobrimentos*, V, parte I, Lisbon, 1961, 161-167. Cf., Biggar, *Precursors*, 100-01.

²⁸ Dr. Manuel Luciano da Silva's articles have been mostly printed in newspapers, but his ideas, save his ones on the mythical Antilia are to be found in three articles of the *Medical Opinion and Review*, "The Meaning of Dighton Rock," (February, 1966): 82-86; "Words from the Portuguese," (June, 1966): 108-13 and "Finding for the Portuguese," (March, 1967): 42-51. So persistent has been his campaign that on a recent visit to Rhode Island, da Silva

persuaded Portuguese President Mário Soares to accompany him on an official visit to Dighton Rock.

[29] See Edmond B. Delabarre, *Dighton Rock, a Story of the Written Rocks of New England* (New York: W. Neale, 1928).

[30] See Luís de Albuquerque, *Dúvidas e certezas na história dos descobrimentos portugueses*, 2nd ed. (Lisbon: Vega, 1990), 67-74.

[31] The inscription on a boulder at the center of the enclosure reads: "Fort Ninigret, memorial of the Narragansett and Niantic Indians. The unwavering friends and allies of our fathers. Erected by the State of Rhode Island, Wight R. Adams, M. P. Sheffield, Jr., D. Carmichael, Jr., Comrs, 1883."

[32] Nobody seems to know what became of the human remains, and it would be asking too much of local archaeologists of the 1920s that they should have made systematic grids and took stage-by-stage photos of the excavations. The "hardware" – the gun and the hilt – are beyond doubt genuine, but little more can be told from them.

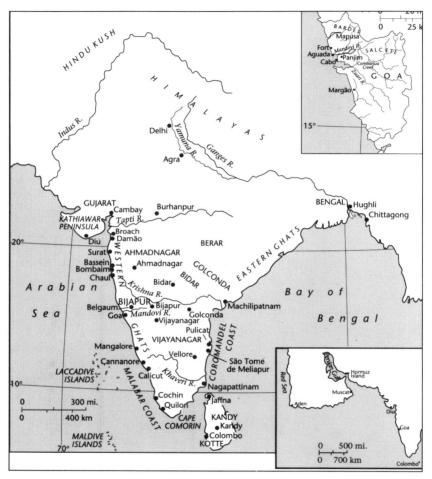

The Indian Subcontinent

Chapter X

Portuguese as Players on a South Asian Stage

The concept of discovery in the Atlantic sense hardly applies to early maritime contacts with the Eurasian land mass by the Portuguese: it was part of the same Old World as they themselves inhabited. Professor J. C. Heesterman, of Leiden, has observed that this vast, single continental area was indeed part of a disjointed cultural continuum: India was linked with Europe through remote common origins in language and through direct contacts in classical times, India with China via common roots in religion – but the whole through a remarkable similarity of feudal institutions. Europeans had made direct contact with China in the XIII and XIV centuries at the time of the Polos, Pegolotti and the monkish travelers, and of course the Islamic Middle East, though it blocked the way for Europeans, had constant intercourse with both Europe and India throughout the medieval period.[1]

Although not common, Europeans prior to Vasco da Gama's circumnavigation of Africa had made their way through this Middle Eastern politico-cultural barrier to India, like the Genoese, Adorno and Santo Stefano, the Venetian, Conti, or the Portuguese, Covilhã – all of whom arrived there before the sea route around Africa had been discovered. Da Gama did indeed explore his way around the Cape of Good Hope to Swahili Africa, but once he had done that, discovery in any Atlantic sense ended – he acquired an Arab pilot to take him across the Arabian Sea to Calicut, a route known and used for centuries by Omani Arab and Gujarati traders. The real significance of his expedition lay in finding a direct connection to the already visited and partially known, but made unfamiliar through the

AFOSO·DALBOQVERQVE

intermediacy of the Islamic world. Da Gama and his crews, though, found themselves in a surrounding far from unintelligible – in no ways as strange as the civilizations of Mexico, Yucatan and South America had been to the Spaniards.[2]

This essay has a dual concern: to describe how relations developed in India during the XVI century between Portugal and the nations of the subcontinent – and then to assess what difference to the process of European expansion the Portuguese presence might have made. Obviously, it can hardly hope to be more than suggestive.

In our book, *Foundations of the Portuguese Empire*, the late Bailey Diffie has pointed out that one of the very first persons with whom the Portuguese made contact upon landing in Calicut was a Spanish-speaking Moslem trader who had been born in the Mahgreb, not far from Portugal itself.[3] It can be gathered from the bluntness of his greeting to them in Castilian: "What the Devil brought you here?" – that he instinctively understood rivals from one theatre of operations had now arrived in another. But it would also seem that he and his cohorts who depended upon the Red Sea route to the European markets did not at first take the Portuguese challenge so seriously as they might have. Da Gama's weathered fleet and his paltry presents for the Samorin, however, were deceiving. By the time Pedro Álvares Cabral had sailed in two years later with a large fleet and lavish gifts for that ruler and obtained permission from him to establish a *feitoria*, or trading post, the Arabs and the Gujarati merchants who served the Red Sea route to the Mediterranean began to feel genuinely threatened.

The "Vasco da Gama Era"

There was enormous excitement back in Lisbon at Da Gama's homecoming, first in July, 1499, when Nicolau Coelho, commander of the faster *Berrio*, probably a caravel, arrived ahead of his commander, and then in August or the beginning of September, when Da Gama himself sailed in. The king, D. Manuel I, had already been preparing new voyages, and he lost little time in following up the promising contact. The Iberians, now that they had made direct connections with the Orient, did not intend to delay or to neglect their opportunity. From India's standpoint, the late K. M. Panikkar did not understate developments (if he did vastly oversimplify them) when, perhaps inspired by Toynbee, he proclaimed that the "Vasco da Gama era" of Indian history had begun.[4]

If the initial Indian response to the Da Gama visit had been friendly and mercantile, the promise of easy profit for the European newcomers quickly soured, following an act of aggression by the threatened Arab community in Calicut and a hostile overreaction to it by the Portuguese. In 1501, not long after the Samorin had permitted the Portuguese to found their *feitoria*, the established and now suddenly-threatened Moslem pepper traders incited a riot from the streets and destroyed the building just acquired by the Portuguese, killing the *feitor* and forty of his associates. To this the Portuguese response was fierce, but hardly informed or reflective: Cabral, the commander of the Portuguese fleet, instead of realizing that the attack was not the doing of the Samorin, but rather of the Moslem traders acting in their own interests, (an insight no doubt beyond his grasp at the time), bombarded the city with his naval guns. The reasons for Cabral's action were understandable enough: wherever Moslems were present, the Portuguese expected and even relished trouble. Moreover, they felt ill-at-ease in the strange surroundings and manifested the same insecurity that travelers are wont to when faced with the unknown. But, of course, they played directly into the traders' hands. The Samorin thereafter became one of Portugal's most implacable enemies, almost as a by-product of the Luso-Islamic rivalry born in the *Reconquista*.[5]

The native helping hand

If these, then, represent a preliminary stage – contact; the beginning of trade and a collision with rivals – the second, much more permanent stage in the long run, was that collaboration, based as it was on rivalries within subcontinent. Students of Spanish conquistador history in the Americas will immediately recognize the theme, for this is what gained Cortés and Pizzarro their successful entries into Mexico and Peru despite their grossly inferior numbers, and I should wonder if exactly that kind of welcome might not also have occurred in Europe if the Chinese Admiral Cheng-Ho, had circumnavigated Africa in 1409 (instead of turning back, as he did) and arrived in England or France with his fleet, as he could have, during the Hundred Years War. No doubt one or the other of the embattled monarchs would have tried to enlist the Chinese in their cause and acted as their sponsors!

In India, this collaboration with the newcomer was initiated by the royal Kolathiri house of Cochin, unwilling vassals of the Samorin down the Malabar Coast from Calicut, who saw in the Portuguese potential customers and their protectors against the Samorin. The raja of Cochin possessed a far better harbor than the Samorin (who in fact possessed no harbor at all, but simply roads), and in return for Portuguese protection, he provided access to an entire region laden with just the pepper Portugal fancied would make its crown and land rich.

Such collaboration afforded the Portuguese a first footing on the Indian subcontinent, and as a continuation of their crusade against Islamic competition, they next boldly attacked the whole Moslem maritime supply chain joining the pepper fields of South India with Egypt and the Mediterranean. Within a few years of Cabral's bombardment, the Mameluke rulers of Egypt, middlemen between the Indian sources and the distribution of spices to Europe and the Middle East were sorely afflicted by this blockage of their life-giving trade. They hurriedly constructed an armada at Suez and dispatched it to India, determined to drive the Portuguese from the Arabian Sea. The European and Levantine fleets then met in a great battle at Diu Island in 1509, indeed among the most decisive of world history. In it, the Egyptian task force was smashed and Egypt's fearful allies, the Gujarati, were cowed into passivity. No one of course knew it at the time, but thereafter, the Mediterranean as a whole and the Mediterranean Moslem world in particular was never to recover its original position as middleman of European trade with the East, even though Portuguese inability to monitor mass ship movements between India and the Red Sea did lead to a certain revival of the Moslem trade after 1550.[6]

The collaboration between the Portuguese and elements in India which had first occurred in Cochin increased a few years later when an Indian pirate captain named Timoja suggested to the Portuguese governor, then Afonso de Albuquerque, that another good harbor, at Goa Island between the confluences of the Mandovi and Zuari Rivers, could be had with a minimum of force. He pointed out that the area was Hindu, but that its ruler, the Sultan of Bijapur, Yusuf Adil Shah, had only recently acquired it and was highly unpopular; its inhabitants, he assured the Portuguese, would be happy at the change in their fortunes.[7]

To Albuquerque this appeared a sound proposition, for more than any leader the Portuguese afterwards produced, he understood the geopolitical implications of the Portuguese position: their existence in India depended upon seapower for the control of shipping; and this could only be secured by combined naval-trading bases at nodal points throughout the Indian Ocean. He therefore stormed and captured Goa in 1510, as part of a series of naval military operations which also carried Ormuz and Malacca. Though less obviously strategic than those two cities, Goa may have seemed the most important to him because it elevated the Portuguese presence in India to a status beyond mere guesthood in the lands of the Raja of Cochin. And it afforded a better point than did Malabar from which to sweep the entire west coast. After Albuquerque's death (1515), the Portuguese strengthened their position by obtaining new footholds along the Indian west coast and obtaining the right to fortify Colombo in Ceylon. They were then ready for business, entrenched (more or less) firmly to weather the rest of the XVI century. European influence was in India to stay.

During their long history, not one of the Portuguese enclaves was inhabited by anything like a majority of Europeans. Save perhaps for Bassein, acquired in 1534, none were agriculturally important or could even feed themselves; they were little more than trading and naval stations. The Portuguese were never more than an organizing minority and their continuing existence depended on the willing collaboration of Indic peoples within the Portuguese enclaves themselves.[8] If they displayed insensitivities and intolerances which made the lives of these native subjects less than pleasant, it must also be remembered that the lives of their fellow Indians, living under Moslem dynasties – as in Bijapur or in Mughal lands, were hardly rosy. The Portuguese were no saints, but were scarcely more cruel or greedy than those rulers – something critics of colonialism often conveniently forget.

Indian historians who criticize the Portuguese are curiously prone to consider the Mughals as a native dynasty, while they look upon the Portuguese as foreign, forgetting that the whole Islamic presence in northern India was intrusive and foreign, and that even though Islamic invaders arrived five hundred years before the Christian Portuguese, the Mughals themselves actually entered India a whole generation after Da Gama and Cabral! Moreover, Asian critics of Portuguese expansion overlook that, except in a very few instances, as in Goa itself, the Portuguese in India and Ceylon acquired their forts and territories by cession and by treaty; it was the Mughals who were the real (and forgiven) conquerors, as if they were less foreign, or less grasping. Most of the wars the Portuguese fought in the subcontinent were in fact defensive, even if brought on by misbehavior or the dominant maritime position they had engineered for themselves.

Professor Heesterman, the famous Indologist cited at the beginning of this article, views the Portuguese as no more than a minor power recently arrived on the Indian scene for whom there would have been no room had they not brought with them a novel means of making a living – and by that he meant control of the sea. He remarked that the great principalities of India, such as Bijapur and Gujarat, but especially the Mughals (who were more or less coeval with the Portuguese qua their arrival in India), were terrestrial expansionists who raised their revenues in the subcontinent principally by controlling and skimming off the internal tolls and duties on traded goods and foodstuffs. The Portuguese, he said, merely made a place for themselves by innovating the same thing on the water – something no Asian power had thought to do since navies were all but unknown in South Asia and the Arabian Seas.[9] About all the Portuguese did in India to ensure their existence, he suggested, was to create a specialized "beat" for themselves in this way. Students of Portuguese expansion have long speculated on the origins of the *cartaz*, or pass system, for maritime shipping, but in reality it is little more than a marine adaptation of what prevailed on land.

No European power of the XVI century remotely resembled a "modern" politico-economic organism (except in the technical sense that it was not strictly medieval), and the Portuguese did not create in India an operation which would fulfill any of the criteria today's analysts or propagandists could identify with later "Imperialism." Rather, the *Estado da India Oriental* was merely a limited maritime-commercial (and slightly coercive) organism – an estate rather than a modern state (in our monolithic definition of one) – which reflected circumstances and the wishes and needs of various groups: the crown, the Portuguese patronage system, the Church, and those of free-lance individuals who exercised private trade more or less within the auspices of the royal and viceregal aegis. It is often difficult to assess where the influence of one grouping ended and that of the other began – for instance, when the Danish historian, Niels Steensgaard, characterized the Portuguese system as "parasitic and derivative," meaning that it derived its income by skimming off the profits of trade generated by others, the late Dutch historian, Marie Antoinette Meilink-Roelofsz, denied this categorically.[10] On closer examination, it developed that Steensgaard based his ideas on the viceregal convoy and toll system of the Arabian sea, whereas Mevr. Meilink was thinking of the private traders who operated in the Bay of Bengal and around Malacca. Both were correct enough, but limited in their vision to one aspect of an archaic, in no way unitary, empire.

To begin with, there were the interests of the king in Lisbon, who of course never visited the East. It had been that monarch's intent from the beginning to control the spice trade, and he lost no time in creating of pepper and other valuable stuffs a personal, royal monopoly with his very own collection system, contracts, warehouses and personnel. Then to administer and protect this and the widely-spaced Portuguese enclaves in Asia, the crown established a military-style bureaucracy based in Goa, headed by a viceroy and organized around royal patronage (mostly involving the second and third sons of noble families who served the crown as their sole means of livelihood). The revenue to support this operation and its many fortresses was ingeniously provided by naval patrols and convoys which herded together the unorganized Indian sea commercial traffic and conducted it up and down the Indian west coast – something which, as Heesterman remarked, the (mostly Moslem) land powers had never thought of; the herded vessels were obliged to pay *alfândega* (customs) duties at all Portuguese-held ports they passed on their routes to other destinations. Of course the patrolling vessels suppressed, or attempted to, any shipping which ignored or defied the system, and Portugal carried on a running guerrilla warfare with the Samorin of Calicut, who sheltered hostile "pirates" in his stretch of the Malabar coast.[11]

Then finally, quite apart from royal or viceregal initiative, private Portuguese traders, in the form of *casados* (mustered-out soldiers who had formed households) quietly entered the "country" or intra-Asian trade – dealing in products which did not interfere with or were out of reach of the crown monopoly. These they traded back and forth for their private gain; in time, they built large and profitable networks, often interconnecting regions previously not in commercial intercourse with one another. This, in fact, may have been their most original contribution, for the Indo-Portuguese *casados* showed great imagination in finding new markets, and since they could draw on capital in form of (usually illegal) investments from the Portuguese bureaucracy from viceroys downward, they could probably develop new markets to better advantage than could their native competitors. One aspect of their activities which remains to be examined it that of profiting from connections with native rulers, whose henchmen some of them became.

Initial Portuguese relations in India

In order to make further generalizations, it might be a good idea at this point to take a general look at how the Portuguese interacted with their neighboring Indian powers. This will permit a further assessment of what impact their discovery of an European sea route to Asia had on India during the XVI century. Nearest to their point of entry in India, the Portuguese arrangement in Cochin provided a stable pepper supply and hence a favorable economic base. Relations with the native rulers were for the most part mutually advantageous. Save for the Samorin of Calicut, the Cochinese Mutta clan, or *tavazhi*, as the ruling family of the Kolathiri in Cochin, was the only other house on the Malabar coast with royal status, and they exercised a kind of feudal primacy over the numerous petty rulers to the south. The prestige of the Mutta sovereignty was extremely useful to the Portuguese in establishing their desired monopoly on the pepper trade, for by guaranteeing the house's independence from the Samorin, they exercised in effect the first European protectorate in Asia. With the Mutta blessing, the Portuguese then were able to create a monopolistic trading system along the southern segment of the coast. Initially, the royal factors employed Indian middlemen to procure Malabari pepper and ginger for the European market, but soon their employer in Lisbon opted instead for a series of fixed-price contracts negotiated with landowning Brahmins for annual quotas of pepper to be exported to Europe.[12]

A good deal has been written about the wisdom of this tactic, among other reasons because the Brahmins required payment in silver specie almost entirely, while on the crown's part, it could exercise very little control over quality, which was often inferior and virtually invited breaches of the monopoly through smuggling of the better sorts via alternative routes – which of course ended up in Venice via the Red Sea and Egypt.

If smuggling was a silent threat to Portuguese profitability on the southern Malabar coast, its northern portion required continued policing. Neither Calicut nor its neighbor, Cannanore, accepted the Portuguese presence willingly and both awaited their chances to combine against their common European enemy. Fortunately for Portugal, Governor Afonso de Albuquerque in 1513 succeeded in having the Samorin poisoned and in inducing his successor to allow construction of a Portuguese fort on his doorstep. But the rulers of Calicut were not permanently pacified by this imposition and in future were always ready to make trouble whenever the opportunity presented.

Similarly, difficulties developed at initially friendly Cannanore, for though its Hindu Kolathiri ruler remained passive, the port had a large Moslem trading community, whose activities were all but devastated by the Portuguese aim at monopoly. Accordingly, the head of this community, the Ali Raja, who also claimed sovereignty of his own over the Maldive and Laccadive Islands off the coast, virtually took over rule in Cannanore and left the Portuguese to hold down the lid on his smuggling and occasional insurrection. Fortunately for the Lusitanians, Viceroy D. Francisco de Almeida had had the foresight in 1510 to construct a fortress on a promontory before the entrance to the rajdom's principal harbor. Wars finally broke out between Cannanore and Portugal in 1542 and 1559, but the Portuguese clung to their fortress and, as happened so many times in India, they were able to obtain help from other strongholds when they needed it.[13]

By capturing Goa from the Adil Shah of Bijapur, the Portuguese deprived him of his only good outlet to the sea and of India's best import station for the horses of Arabia, much in demand not only by

Bijapur, but also in the other Islamic states of central India, and in the Hindu kingdom of Vijayanagar, the mightiest state to their south. Since all these powers used cavalry as their prime striking forces, the horse trade of those days resembled the arms trade in ours; for sixty years after Albuquerque's seizure of Goa, the rulers of Bijapur remained friendly enemies; not only did they require the horses the Portuguese now monopolized to protect them from their more dangerous inland enemies, but by and large, Bijapur was too laden with other rivalries and intrigues for the Adil Shahi to think seriously of recapturing the place – and often they even solicited Portuguese help; in this way, Governor Martim Afonso de Sousa was able to obtain the districts of Bardes and Salcete on either side of the island of Goa in 1545 in return for neutralizing a rival, Meale Khan. Relations, though, were always those of expediency with an occasional incursion and/or double-cross until in 1570, the Adil Shah entered into an alliance with three other Moslem states and the Samorin, all aiming to rid themselves of the Portuguese once and for all.

If the Portuguese ever had a real ally on the mainland, it was in the abovementioned Rajdom of Vijayanagar (or as the Portuguese called it, Narsinga). Not only did the two become trading partners (the Vijayanagari purchased the bulk the Arabian steeds imported by the Portuguese), but their partnership was based on having the same Moslem enemies. Vijayanagar, though of relatively recent origin, was the largest Hindu state of the whole subcontinent, and it acted as suzerain over all others of its coreligionists in south India. In 1565, however, after almost half a century of collaboration between it and Goa, the five most proximate sultanates, ones which had been formed at the breakup of the Bahmani Kingdom some seventy-five years earlier, entered into a combine against Vijayanagar and then defeated it unexpectedly in the great battle of Talikota. Directly they laid it waste. Not only was this a severe economic blow against Goa, but it encouraged the principal victors to try their luck against that viceroyalty seven years later, as shall be noted below.

The two greatest trading states in India of the XVI century, Calicut and Gujarat, were both on the western side of the subcontinent – and of course it was at Calicut that the Portuguese first attempted to establish themselves. The west coast was where the most important commercial action of the subcontinent took place up throughout the XVI century, and it need hardly be said that these states had built themselves up through greater proximity to the Mediterranean, Swahili African and Persian Gulf states. While Calicut with its pepper has already figured in this essay, I have not yet said much about Gujarat, aside from mentioning Diu as the location of the decisive naval battle of 1509. Curiously enough, though Gujarat was by far the larger and more diversified state than Calicut, its rulers made much the least trouble for the Portuguese in relation to their greater military and economic power. Often referred to as Cambay, its ports of Surat, Cambay, Broach, Bassein and Diu (the last two later ceded to the Portuguese) were not only exporters of such products as saltpetre, indigo, and an astonishing range of textiles, but also provided trading and shipping services throughout the whole Indian ocean from Aden on the northwestern side of the Arabian Sea all the way to Malacca and even the Moluccas.

Its greatest weakness *vis-à-vis* Portugal was that it did not possess a navy. Nor, perhaps because of its peculiar governmental structure, was it in a position to create one. According to the Indologist, Professor M. N. Pearson, of the University of New South Wales, the Moslem rulers of the essentially Hindu states of northern India all betrayed their origins by remaining in vision and tradition landlubbers from Afghanistan and central Asia whose vision and energies were concentrated on internal levies and on tolls from internal commerce (not to speak of rivalries with their similarly-minded inland neighbors); as a consequence, he says, they left their maritime port cities more or less to their own institutions and devices and only "creamed off" some of their profits in form of tributes – whose proportional value he believes was far below that of the ports' rich maritime trade. He thinks, in fact, that the traditional contributions thus levied represented a meager 6 percent of the total income of the state! As a result, the great port cities of Surat and Broach and Cambay were not taken seriously enough by their ultimate overlords nor given real support against the Portuguese convoy and levy systems. Instead, the maritime cities, despite their great economic power, were obliged to bow to the conditions and levies which the Portuguese imposed on their navigation.[14]

Only twice did the Gujarati attempt to challenge Portuguese dominance, in 1538 and 1545. In 1535, Governor Nuno da Cunha had acquired Diu Island, at the tip of the Kathiawar Peninsula, a strategic location the Portuguese had long coveted as a naval base from which both to monitor Gujarat and to anchor their convoys and trade to and from the Persian Gulf. Sultan Bahadur Shah, who had ceded the island to them in return for help against his own enemies inland, quickly received an education in geopolitics when he realized what use the Portuguese were making of the location. He thereupon hired Turkish mercenaries to help him rid himself of them, but he died in the attempt.

For the Portuguese had immediately constructed a powerful fortress there, and it withstood that fierce siege in which its walls were reduced almost to rubble (the Turks possessed artillery as good as that of the Portuguese defenders). This and the second Gujarati siege, undertaken eight years later, both failed, if only because the Portuguese seldom fought better than when defending their installations, and because they always built their fortifications at water's edge, where they could easily be reinforced and provisioned by relief convoys. Thereafter, in 1572-1573, the Great Mughal, Akbar, swallowed up Gujarat itself. Despite emitting some menacing noises, neither he nor his successors found it expedient to challenge the Portuguese system again. To do this, they would have had to construct and train their own navies.

Rather than from the Mughals, the *Estado da India's* greatest peril of the XVI century was to come from a combination comprising Bijapur, Ahmadnagar, the Samorin and the Sultan of Atjeh. Encouraged by their victory over Vijayanagar in 1565, the Adil Shah and the Nizam Shah enlisted the two other archenemies of the Portuguese and in 1570 went to war. That year, the Adil Shah invaded Goa itself and the Nizam Shah marched on Chaul; meanwhile, the Samorin was supposed to attack Portuguese Malabar installations and the Sultan of Atjeh, Malacca. But the Samorin's help was ineffectual, while Atjeh's fleet was defeated. The situation was worse in India, where Portuguese soldiers were grossly outnumbered and lacked enough artillery. Yet under the unyielding leadership of Viceroy D. Luís de Ataíde, the defenders gradually prevailed and the besiegers withdrew. Thereafter, until assaults by the Dutch and English in the next century, the Portuguese strongholds in India were never again seriously threatened.

Ceylon might hardly be called a Portuguese "discovery" – the island was known to the ancients as Taprobana. It is traditionally supposed to have been found by D. Lourenço de Almeida in 1505, son of the viceroy D. Francisco de Almeida, while in search of the Laccadive or Maldive Islands. Recent research by Mme. Geneviève Bouchon, however, has revealed the presence of a stone in Colombo with a Portuguese inscription dated 1502. But it even seems likely that the Genoese, Ieronimo de Stefano and Ieronimo Adorno, had visited it in 1493, if not Marco Polo two centuries earlier. In any case, nothing was done by the Portuguese to secure themselves a supply of Ceylon's famous and profitable cinnamon until 1518, no doubt because they had their hands full building the foundations to their empire in Asia. In that year, Lopo Soares de Albergaria, Albuquerque's successor, constructed a fortress at Colombo and made a treaty with the doddering "Empire" of Kotte – another example of willing collaboration, for Kotte needed the Portuguese to prop it up.

Quite naturally, the Lusitanians thereupon exercised a protectorate over Kotte; in 1557, they even succeeded in converting to Christianity its ruler, Dharmapala Suriya, who reigned as D. João Dharmapala, "by Grace of God, Perea Pandar" and as a vassal of the Portuguese king. His conversion did little to endear him to his Buddhist subjects, however, and he depended increasingly on his European coreligionists. When he died without male issue in 1597, he bequeathed his kingdom to Philip II and I, of Spain and Portugal, the only European monarch to become an oriental one in exactly this legal fashion. Upon the Iberian succession, according usual European practice, a good many of the feudal lands and offices within the kingdom were distributed among Portuguese, who thus served as its *aratchis* and *mudaliyars* along with a number of the more loyal and subservient native nobility.[15]

The Mughals, as noted, were latecomers in India, as compared with the Portuguese, for while the Europeans arrived in 1498, the founder of the Mughal empire, Babur, did not descend from the Khyber and begin his conquests until 1526. Once again, to compare the Mughals with the Portuguese is to compare a horse with a boat, for like all Moslem invaders of India by land, they were at home with cavalry, with systems of land revenues and tolls, and they did not even possess an outlet to the sea until Akbar (r.1542-1605) snatched Gujarat from its sultans in 1573. As conqueror not only of their lands bordering the Arabian Sea, but of maritime Bengal as well, he was wiser than his antecedents in understanding not only the benefits maritime commerce could bring but also his own limitations as a creature of the plains and hills. After briefly entertaining the idea of driving the Portuguese from India, he thought better of it (no doubt remembering his predecessor's two failed sieges of Diu). Thereafter, he concentrated upon developing the traffic around his maritime regions, calculating shrewdly that commerce created revenue and that regulating access to ports from their hinterlands afforded enough control for practical purposes. In the end, he was content to restrict his maritime activity to customs collection at his ports and he even saw fit to apply for Portuguese passes on the sea.

Where maritime trade did not yet exist in great enough volume, as in his recently-acquired province of Bengal, in 1579 or 1580, he even invited the Portuguese freelance trader, Pedro Tavares, to found a settlement there. (See chapter XIII, "Portugal's Shadow Empire in the Bay of Bengal.") I might also mention in connection with the Mughals that Portuguese *soldados*, or soldiers, who escaped from Goa were always welcome in Agra and Delhi as mercenaries, and thanks to the tolerance extended by Akbar to carry on their own religion (and even proselytize to it), there was a sizeable resident community of Portuguese and southern Europeans in Agra at the heart of the Mughal empire. It even appears to have been divided into parishes, two of which were Jesuit.

Akbar's most interesting dealings with the Portuguese in fact took place via the Company of Jesus. Akbar was not only a despot in the best Asian style, but he was unique in his time as a religious free-thinker. No Christian monarch would ever have dreamt about combining his revealed faith with other, essentially different creeds; it would not even have crossed the minds of the Mennonites or the Anabaptists, let alone of those monarchs who acknowledged Rome. Akbar, however, consulted sadhus and yogis, as well as the sufis, and then he wrote to the viceroy in Goa, soliciting visits from the Christian clergy to instruct him in the faith. One can imagine how this was misinterpreted as evidence that he was about to convert; the Jesuits hastened to his court and literally spent years demonstrating their truths – all to no avail. The one upshot was his own, new religion, the *Din-i-Ilahi*, which he proclaimed to be the "true light" – a synthesis of all the eternal verities. The difficulty with it was that its beauty was clear only to himself; even the most loyal of his courtiers could never quite grasp it. Despite the universal illumination it purportedly embodied, he never tried to impose it on his subjects and it failed to outlive him. Perhaps one might say of the affair that at least it indicates that the Portuguese had become part intellectually of the Mughal scene, if only in passing.[17]

The question now returns of what permanent importance all these developments held for India, for Europe, and for European expansion. Panikkar, as already remarked, proclaimed over forty years ago that the Portuguese had inaugurated the epoch of European colonial domination and named it the "Vasco da Gama Era" of Indian, and even Asian, history. While such dominion from Europe might have become true at the end of the XVIII century, it is absurdly premature to apply it to the XVI or to award the whole process of colonial usurpation a Portuguese label; the Portuguese merely maintained their system, one among several in India, which was by comparison with the Mughals small and self-delimiting insofar as its activities on land were concerned; it did not aim at (or even dream of becoming) a dominant power there, but was content to derive its income from dominion – though even that had its limits – over the sea lanes. Panikkar might better have counted the Portuguese as merely one among several tenants of India with foreign origins. Since he was really preoccupied with colonialism in a more modern form, he could better have labelled what he was talking about as the "Robert Clive Era." No doubt European presence had begun with the Portuguese, but foreign rule *per se* in India was much older, while domination by Europeans, in this case the English, did not begin until after the battle of Plassey, in 1757. If Panikkar did wish to employ his term "The Vasco da Gama Era," he should have applied it to the collaborative period between first European arrival and European seizure of Asian power by the Honourable East India Company's servants in Bengal.[16]

These sketches, brief as they are, should indicate that the Portuguese soon became actors in the Indian stock company of *dramatis personae*, and perhaps this was their greatest contribution; if one thinks of it as no foregone conclusion, but as the result of determination and luck, then one realizes that they were the harbingers of a dynamic culture which in later centuries transformed the entire Indian civilization. I cannot imagine that any other European government, let alone any merchant combines, could have undertaken to create a permanent presence in India at so early a time; in one way or another, they all had their hands full elsewhere. But the Portuguese did it, and they also developed in Europe a sizeable distribution system in Lisbon, in Antwerp, and by indirection in Italy. From this cornucopia, all the products of India and the East poured forth, from aloes and diamonds to ginger, pepper, cloves and silks; through them, the attractions of trade with Asia became obvious. The formation of the English and Dutch East India companies early in the XVII century would have been impossible without this example. A Portuguese failure would have made private risk capital on the necessary scale impossible to raise. It was only the successful establishment of Portuguese power over the sea lanes of Western India that allowed further European expansion to succeed.

The trading methods established by the Portuguese in the area endured for two centuries-and-a-half: the armed factory-fort-warehouse, the procurement systems for spices and cloth were all imitated by Portugal's European archrivals, the Dutch and the English, and somewhat later by the French. About the only change in the pattern over the next centuries was the increasing position of textile imports against the original supremacy of pepper.

The other half of Africa

For the purposes of European expansion, Africa in the early modern era was not one territory, but two. The eastern part had of course long been penetrated by Omani Arab traders, but until the Portuguese first rounded the Cape, it might as well have been the far side of the moon so far as European expansion was concerned. Da Gama was the first

European commander to call at such Swahili ports as Kilwa, Mombasa and Malindi, and when the Portuguese founded their own port of call at Mozambique Island, they attached it administratively to the *Estado da India*. Hence it can, if briefly, be considered in this essay.

The station on Mozambique Island was founded after 1507 because it became obvious that there needed to be a refitting and resting place between Lisbon and Goa or Cochin. Whether or not it was properly located, however, has long been subject to question, not only because it proved malaria-ridden, but because a placement nearer to the Cape might (at least theoretically) have better served the transients' needs as more healthful, safer and convenient: the hazards of the Mozambique Channel brought nearly as many ships and their crews to grief as the island base actually benefitted. But the east coast held other attractions for the Portuguese.

Soon after they had settled into Mozambique, between 1512 and 1515, a *degregado*, or convict, one António Fernandes, had been sent out to explore the Zambesi River system, and even before that, the Portuguese had begun to trade for gold in the area. Just as on the continent's western rim, the precious metal was offered them for sale by the indigenes, and just as there, it came from the "mines" whose exact location seemed vague. It is now known that all such production came from sluicing and shaft-digging in the many gravel beds of the Zambesi and its tributaries, an area within the domain of a chieftain known as the Monomatapa.

But when the rich silver mines of Potosi were found by the Spaniards in upper Peru during the 1540s, the Portuguese became convinced that they should become Midases in their own right. Although the crown had early (in 1502) established a *feitoria* and fort in nearby Sofala – which served as a post for bartering the precious metal (in this respect similar in its function to São Jorge da Mina) – by 1571 the temptation on the part of King D. Sebastião's advisers to send a task force into the interior to locate and directly appropriate the mines became too powerful to resist. But although none less than an able former governor of the *Estado da India*, Francisco Barreto, was chosen to lead the expedition, disease, native resistance and internal dissension led to its failure and Barreto's subsequent death.[17]

Nor did subsequent tries prove any more successful; they only served to reveal that the region did not hold one or more big deposits as had hoped. Nonetheless, Portuguese wanderers continued to seek their fortunes there, and some were given grants of land by the Monomotapa. This led in the next century to the crown's extending its suzerainty over the region and the creation of the *prazos*, as they later came to be called, vast estates of semi-feudal nature licensed by the *doação*, or grants of the crown, and extended for the span of three lifetimes. Some of these became vast satrapies – ruled by their *prazeiros*, who while they considered themselves European, became ever more mulatto in racial composition.[18]

The desire for lucre, however, was not the sole motivation of the Portuguese on the eastern rim of the vast continent. Farther north, on the western bank of the Red Sea, the mysterious domain of Prester John in the high massifs of Ethiopia remained a magnet – a purely spiritual one (though it is possible that Bishop Otto of Freising's tales of his fabulous wealth did play a role). In 1512 when an ambassador of the *negus*, or Ethiopian ruler, appeared in Goa and was sent on to Lisbon by Albuquerque, D. Manuel and his advisers determined to return their own ambassador and to make effective contact with the monarch whom they still equated with the legendary priest-emperor. In the XVI century, though, embassies did not travel quickly, and it was only in 1520 that one actually arrived under the trustworthy D. Rodrigo de Lima, set ashore at Massawa by a raiding Portuguese naval force; it discovered the reality of the *negus's* court to be considerably less glamorous than expected, but it found Pero da Covilhã still alive (see page 102), and it provided the world with a unique narrative written by a Franciscan chaplain, Padre Francisco Álvares. The embassy encountered great difficulties in returning to Lisbon via Goa, reaching home only in 1527.[19]

Somewhat over a decade later, in 1540, it was learned in Goa that the *negus*, and with him, Christianity itself, was in grave danger from Muslim invader. The viceroy at Goa, D. Estêvão da Gama, lost little time in responding; the following season, he sent his own brother, D. Cristóvão, with 400 men on a perilous mission which landed at Massawa and marched over the mountains. It found the *negus* dead who had been visited by D. Rodrigo de Lima, but in an act of self-sacrificial heroism was able to save his successor from the "Moors," at the cost of D. Cristóvão's life and those of most of his command. This selfless valor certainly provides one of the most glorious moments of Portuguese overseas history. Subsequent relations, however, may seem less exciting to moderns. The clergymen of the *Padroado*, as the royal rule over the hemispheric church was called, became convinced that the traditional brand of Christianity as practiced in Ethiopia was loose and even bordered on the heretical. D. João III thereupon dispatched Jesuit missionaries to the country, whose job it was to bring the separated brethren into line; unhappily, their criticisms and "reforms" were not gratefully received over the decades; at length, in 1634, the apostles of Rome were roughly expelled.[20]

The intellectual side of a military-trading empire

In an age of sailing ships and the Cape Route, it would surely be expecting too much that Portuguese cultural and intellectual forms would much influence those of such an old civilization as India, or vice-versa, within the term of a century. Commercial and political forms, after all, can be put into effect very quickly, while it takes much more time to accept and assimilate new styles of thinking, especially in the XVI century, when the means of communication were so rudimentary and even intellectuals wore such powerful spectacles in form of religion and prejudice. One can see, aside from Akbar's example, only the slightest glimmer, as in the essays of Montaigne, that other possibilities of thought and action were beginning to pass over to intellectuals on the other side of the *oikumené*, or great Eurasian landmass. Nevertheless, the Portuguese presence in India in the XVI century (or shortly after) did give rise to a few highly significant developments, if ones which had little immediate impact on the subcontinent itself.

Two of these involved cartography and printing. In regard to cartography, the famous and scholarly viceroy, D. João de Castro (1500-1548), became aware during his tours of duty in India that there were no detailed and accurate coastal charts to provide Portuguese convoys and squadrons with reliable navigational data. Of his three *Roteiros*, or routing instructions, two provided the best descriptions made in the XVI century of the stretch from Goa to the top of the Red Sea.[22] Then the first book printed in India was the *Conclusiones Philosophicas*, a theological treatise, produced in 1556 on a press brought from Lisbon by the king, D. João III, and set up at the Jesuit Colégio de São Paulo, in Goa.[23]

In regard to early botany and pharmacology, the Goan physician, Garcia da Orta, was stimulated by the unfamiliar botany of the subcontinent and produced the world's first systematic descriptions of Indian flora and their known uses, in his *Coloquios dos simples e drogas da India*, published at Goa in 1563. His book was noticed, translated and championed as early as 1567 by the French botanist, Charles L'Écluse, or Clusius. It is now recognized as one of the foundation stones of the botanical science.[24]

Then another highly significant chain of developments began, in 1542, with the arrival of Francis Xavier; it led to the birth of cultural anthropology. Though no linguist himself, Xavier recognized immediately after his arrival in India that unless his subsequent missionaries should study and learn the indigenous languages of the peoples among whom they wished to spread the Gospel, they would hardly get off the ground. His beliefs induced his successors to study these tongues and make grammars of them, beginning with Tamil, and extending (geographically speaking) through Chinese and Japanese. The story of the Italian Jesuit, Matteo Ricci, and his Mandarin scholarship may technically go beyond the pale of this volume, but it is more than worth a brief mention that first other Jesuits tried some thirty times without success to gain admission to the Middle Kingdom from Macao before their superior, Alessandro Valignano, in the 1580s, ordered Ricci to begin intensive study of (Mandarin) Chinese, the official language of the court and bureaucracy. Having mastered it, Ricci managed to establish himself first in the Chinese provinces and then in Beijing, where he sent a present of mechanical clocks and other instruments to the Ming emperor. Presently, he was summoned to the imperial court when one or more came in need of winding or repair. All of this occupied the 1580s and 1590s, and by 1601, Ricci, whose diligence, incidentally, enabled him to attain Mandarin status, had become a fixture in the highest circles whence he observed that Confucianism (which the Chinese were not about to surrender for Christianity, anyway) was far less a religion than a social observance. He thus sought to graft Christianity onto it rather than replace it entirely with European norms. Accordingly, he gained tolerance for his teachings as well as a position of great influence. From thence, he not only made many converts among the elites, but was able to protect Portuguese interests in Macao. At his death in 1611, Jesuit influence was firmly established at the imperial center.

While this experiment was in progress, another Italian Jesuit, Roberto de'Nobili, applied much the same lessons in an Indian, Tamil setting. He did not arrive at Madurai until 1607, but he had the benefit of a Tamil grammar and dictionary complied some quarter century earlier by his coreligionist and predecessor, Fr. Henrique Henriques. Ricci's experience in China fitted in perfectly with his own observations that Hindus were not likely to become Christians if it was required of them that they give up living as Indians. He understood that (to him) false pagan beliefs and practices were intermingled with deeply-rooted, but harmless, social observances which converts could hardly be expected to abjure – and that to succeed he must first analyze his subject culture to ascertain what parts must be replaced by Christianity and which were harmless and permissible, *per se*. He himself even adopted Tamil dress and the identity of a *sanniyasi*, or Brahmin guru. Such relativism in the period of the Counter-Reformation inevitably ran him into difficulty both with Rome and his own order, but many descendants of the converts he and his followers baptized still proudly bear their Tamil-Christian baptismal names.[25] It goes without saying that the science he and Ricci created is alive and well.

These intellectual milestones, however, seem more important for the future than for their contemporary impact on Asia; in all other respects, the greatest achievement of the Portuguese empire in India was the building of the empire itself: it became at once the cradle and the anchor of Europe in Asia. Other chapters in this volume will suggest how Portuguese influence flowed on beyond the areas administered by the Goan bureaucracy – or perhaps in some cases, merely trickled. But it is apparent that wherever they went, the Portuguese were harbingers of Westernization and change, whether as bureaucrats, soldiers, traders, advisers, missionaries, or mercenaries.

George D. Winius

Notes

[1] The idea came directly from him, expressed during a joint seminar we gave at Leiden University in 1986. I have not been able to find it among his other writings precisely in this form.

[2] The Samorin was, after all, on the other end of the commercial chain which had long brought pepper to Europe via Alexandria and the Arab world. And although Hindu statues of Parvati were confused by the first Portuguese visitors with ones of the Virgin Mary, there were Thomasite Christians even in Calicut itself.

[3] See *Diário da viagem de Vasco da Gama; fac-simile do códice original, transcrição e versão em grafia actualizada*. With introduction by Damião Peres and transcription by António Baião, 2 vols., (Porto: Livraria Civilização Editora, 1945), I, 36.

[4] See K. M. Panikkar, *Asia and Western Dominance* (London: George Allen & Unwin, 1959).

[5] See Bailey W. Diffie and George D. Winius, *Foundations of the Portuguese Empire, 1415-1580* (Minneapolis: U. of Minnesota Press, 1977), 11-18, 220-22.

[6] See the now famous article by Franklin C. Lane, "The Mediterranean Spice Trade; Further Evidence of Its Revival in the Sixteenth Century," *American Historical Review* 45 (1940): 581-90.

[7] See Diffie and Winius, *Foundations*, 250-51.

[8] On the Indian west coast, only Bassein (today called Vasai), and Goa itself, had more than a few square miles of appended Portuguese territory – and sometimes forts could claim none beyond the range of their guns. In Ceylon, Kotte possessed more, but until deeded to Philip II & I in 1597, the area was not, strictly speaking, Portuguese.

[9] See Jan C. Heesterman, "Warriors and Merchants," *Itinerário* vol. 15, no. 1 (1991): 37-49.

[10] In a long article criticizing the ideas expressed in Niels Steensgaard's Carraks, *Caravans and Companies*. See M.A.P. Meilink-Roelofsz, "The structures of trade in Asia in the Sixteenth and Seventeenth Centuries. A critical appraisal." In *Mare Luso-Indicum*, IV (1980): 1-43.

[11] The convoys and the running warfare are mentioned in all accounts of the Portuguese in India from R.H. Whiteway, in his *Rise of the Portuguese Power in India* (London, 1899) to Michael N. Pearson, in his *The Portuguese in India* (Cambridge: Cambridge U. Press, 1987). But perhaps the best insight is afforded by the XVI-XVII century soldier-turned-tract-writer, Francisco Rodrigues de Silveira, in his *Reformação da milícia e governo do estado da India Oriental*, Ms. 25:419, British Library, fls. 15v-19v.

[12] See Vitorino Magalhães Godinho, *L'économie de l'empire portugais aux XVᵉ e XVIᵉ siècles* (Paris: S.E.V.P.E.N., 1949), 631-632.

[13] See Geneviève Bouchon, *Mamale de Cananor. Un adversaire de l'Inde Portugaise (1507-1528)* (Geneva and Paris: Librairie Droz, 1975).

[14] See Michael N. Pearson, *Merchants and Rulers in Gujarat. The Response to the Portuguese in the Sixteenth Century* (Berkeley and Los Angeles: U. of California Press, 1976).

[15] See Tikiri B. H. Abeyasinghe, *Portuguese Rule in Ceylon, 1594-1612* (Colombo: Lake House Investments, 1966).

[16] After the battle of Plassey, on the Hughli River, in 1759, the Honourable East India Company came to control the *nawab* of Bengal, the *diwani*, and, by 1785 the Northern Circars, lands around Bombay, Madras and Surat. From these nucleii, they came to dominate all India, directly or indirectly. For instances of willing collaboration by Indians in the establishment and maintenance of Portuguese power, see Geoffrey Scammell, "Indigenous Assistance in the Establishment of Portuguese Power in Asia in the XVI Century," in *Modern Asian Studies*, 14 (1980): 1.

[17] Information on Fernandes's explorations are contained in two letters by Gaspar Veloso and João Vaz de Almeida to D. Manual, as reprinted in *Documentos sobre os Portugueses em Moçambique e na África Central (1497-1840); Documents on the Portuguese in Mozambique and Central Africa*, 8 vols. (Lisboa: National Archives of Rhodesia and Nyasaland-Centro de Estudos Históricos Ultramarinos, 1972-1975, II, 180-89 and IV, 282-88. (Note: the author saw a recently-published ninth volume in Portugal in 1990, but was unable to obtain a copy.) A brief account of the incursions into Monomatapa is given in Diffie and Winius, *Foundations*, 347-48, based on Diogo do Couto, *Da Asia, Década IX*, chapter I.

[18] See Alexandre Lobato, *Colonização senhorial da Zambesi e outros estudos* (Lisbon: Junta de Investigações do Ultramar , 1962).

[19] See Francisco Álvares, *The Prester John of the Indies*, ed. C.F. Beckingham and G.W.B. Huntingford, 2 vols. (Cambridge: published for the Hakluyt Society by Cambridge U. Press, 1958).

[20] For the intervention, see Miguel de Castanhoso, *The Portuguese to Abyssinia in 1541-1543*. R.S. Whiteway, ed. and trans., (London: The Hakluyt Society, 1902).

[21] See John Correia-Afonso, S.J., *Jesuit Letters and Indian History, 1542-1773*, 2nd edition (Bombay, London and New York: Oxford U. Press, 1969) and (ed., with intro.) *Letters from the Mughal Court. The First Jesuit Mission to Akbar, 1580-1583* (Bombay: The Heras Institute of Indian History and Culture, 1980).

²² These are the *Primeiro Roteiro da Costa da India desde Goa até Diu* (Lisbon: Agencia Geral das Colónias, 1940), and *Roteiro em que se contem a viagem que fizeram os Portugueses no anno 1541 partindo da nobre cidade de Goa atée Soez que hé no fim Roxo* (Lisbon: Agencia Geral das Colónias, 1940)

²³ See Joseph de Barros, "The First Book Printed in India (A Portuguese Contribution)" in *Boletim do Instituto Menezes de Bragança*, no. 59 (1989): 5-16.

²⁴ See Charles Ralph Boxer, *Two Pioneers of Tropical Medicine: Garcia d'Orta and Nicolas Monardes* (London: the Hispanic and Luso-Brazilian Councils, 1963).

²⁵ See S. Rajamanickam, S.J., *The First Oriental Scholar* (Tirunelveli,Madras: De Nobili Research Institute, 1972).

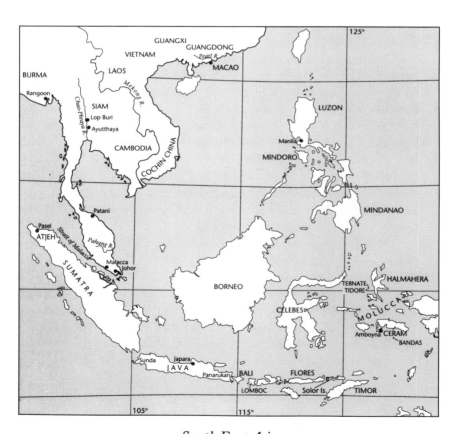

South East Asia

Chapter XI

Portuguese Travel and Influence at the Corner of Asia

W hat has been said earlier about Vasco da Gama once he had reached Moçambique and Sofala holds equally true for the waters east of the Indian subcontinent: one does not speak of "discovery" here, but of "contact" and "connection." All the seaways and all the harbors were known to Asian navigators, and it would be downright Eurocentric to claim that the role of the Portuguese was that of explorer, save in the sense that where they went was new to Europeans. On the other hand, what they accomplished was even more germane to the shape of things to come: their wooden sailing vessels in effect forged steel bonds between the ports and economies of Europe and those of Asia: they were never again to be broken, but destined to grow in our own century into a single world economy.[1]

The ease with which the Portuguese seemed to get about in strange Asian waters need not be considered in any way miraculous or mysterious: Diogo Lopes de Sequeira found Malacca in 1509 and Francisco Serrão the Moluccas by the simplest of methods: they hired native pilots and escorts.[2] And even though Japan in superficial ways resembles a "discovery" in the Atlantic sense, it would appear its seemingly chance encounter by Teixeira, Peixoto, and Zeimoto took place mostly because D. João III and/or any of various viceroys had lost interest and did not continue to hire native pilots and make new expeditions in the usage of D. Manuel I and Albuquerque.[3]

In spite of their minuscule presence during the XVI and XVII centuries, the Portuguese nonetheless enjoyed an influence out of proportion to their numbers. The talented Leiden historian, Leonard Blussé, has remarked that in an isolated non-European kingdom, be it Burma, Pegu, Arakan, Patani, Cambodia, or Siam, the presence of even a dozen or twenty Portuguese traders, mercenaries and their Eurasian families were enough to destabilize its traditional equilibrium and accelerate its change.[4]

Early Portuguese Travels in Southeast Asia

Three years before Afonso de Albuquerque stormed the great entrepôt of Malacca in 1511, its wealth had attracted the royal attention from reports of Gujarati origin gathered in India. In 1508, a trusted *fidalgo*, or nobleman, of the king's household, Diogo Lopes de Sequeira, was dispatched from Lisbon to this hub of southeast Asian trade with four ships and instructions and instructions to visit it and negotiate with its sultan a commercial agreement like those achieved with rulers in Malabar. Sequeira, after a brief sojourn in Madagascar, called in Cochin, where he hired some experienced Muslim pilots, turned Cape Comorin, and sailed under Ceylon and across the Bay of Bengal. After calling briefly on the Sultan of Pasei, in Sumatra, he crossed the straits to his destination.

It was Sequeira's unhappy experience at Malacca which brought Albuquerque there as conqueror in 1511: after an initially cordial reception by the powerful sultan, Muhammed, who allowed Sequeira to establish a *feitoria*, or factory, there, the Muslim merchants from Gujarat convinced him that Portugal was up to no good and prevailed upon him to attack it even before Sequeira's fleet had departed; several Portuguese were killed and the *feitor* and some others taken prisoner. Two years later, Albuquerque as governor liberated them, captured the city and drove Muhammed into exile.

Or at least exile from the city itself, for he merely retreated and set up his capital in Bintan, another part of his territories, later moving to Johore and continuing to oppose the Portuguese where he could. But they had what they wanted: a choke point in the only practical passage between the Indian Ocean and the China Seas. Accordingly, they installed a convoy system in the narrows and obliged native shippers to purchase their passes, or *cartazes*, and to pay port duties. Their intent, however, was hardly to impede the volume and variety of commerce; rather, they sought to disturb matters as little as possible. So far as can be determined, they continued to levy fees in approximately the same amounts as the sultan Muhammed had done. Indians, Javans and Chinese thronged the port as before, whom their new masters administered as per custom, through their own headmen, the *shabandars*. The main changes the conquerors worked were the expulsion of their rivals, the Gujarati Moslem traders and the construction of a powerful fortress, called *A Famosa*, later adding to it a second ring of still mightier walls which enclosed most of the settlement. In addition, they used the city as a jumping off point for the Moluccas and later Macao and Japan – in each case, destinations for which the crown or its viceroys, or in some instances, the captains of the city, claimed the exclusive rights to grant single trading voyages in return for a percentage of the eventual profits.[5]

No sooner had Malacca fallen to Portugal than its diplomats and adventurers set out to penetrate the surrounding regions. In November, only a little over two months after Malacca's fall, Albuquerque sent two of his lieutenants, each in command of a ship, in search of the Bandas and the Moluccas. These were the intrepid António de Abreu, a veteran of all his campaigns, and one Francisco Serrão, the friend of Fernão de Magalhães, alias Ferdinand Magellan.

They were guided by Javanese pilots and accompanied by a wealthy Malaccan merchant, Nehoda Ismael, who had switched his allegiance to the Portuguese when the sultan had fled.[6] In the days of sail, there was only one feasible route to these islands, so highly esteemed as the prime source for cloves, nutmeg and mace (the latter two both parts of the same plant); that was to sail along the northern coasts of Sumatra and Java, keeping to the south of Borneo and Celebes. Through this passage, one round trip per year was made possible by the monsoon winds which alternated from a west-east to an east-west direction. Abreu and Serrão's safe arrival in effect inaugurated a long and eventful association with the region which was terminated only in the next century by the hostilities upon arrival of the V.O.C., or Dutch East India Company.

Abreu returned on the monsoon with a shipful of precious spices, but Serrão's vessel was wrecked on an uninhabited island, from which he escaped only when pirates discovered the castaways' presence, landed, and were in turn surprised by them. Serrão and his men then sailed off to Ternate in their hijacked vessel, but did not return to Malacca. Instead, under Serrão's leadership, they began supporting the Kechil, or sultan, Boleif against his enemy, the sultan of Tidore. Three years later, another Portuguese expedition arrived, but Serrão and a few of his companions elected to remain in this center of the world's clove supply, finding that the usual Christian-Muslim hostility experienced elsewhere in Asia did not prevail here. (In Malacca, by contrast, the rival Gujarati merchants were chased out immediately by the Portuguese together with all but a few of the native Muslim ones.) Thereafter, Portuguese vessels, singly or in groups, were to arrive almost yearly. Portuguese influence soon spread to Amboina and to the Banda Islands, where nutmeg and mace were available in large amounts. The Portuguese constructed small forts in all these places, though for most of the century these were used to discourage illicit trade and guard against the Spaniards rather than to dominate the indigenes. For after the great crossing of the Pacific Ocean by Fernão de Magalhães in Castilian service, a number of new Spanish expeditions followed in his wake, all calling at the Moluccas in hopes that the islands might, after all, lie on the Castilian side of the line. In spite of extended negotiations between Spain and Portugal ending in the Treaty of Zaragoza of 1529 and awarding their usufruct to Portugal, Spanish incursions persisted until the 1540s.[7]

Once thus established in this tropical near-Garden of Eden, however, their Portuguese commanders were all too prone to corruption; the serpent came in the guise of easy money. Shielded from royal retribution by the immense distances from Lisbon, Goa and even Malacca, fortress captains (with the notable exception of the upright António Galvão (1536-1539) could not resist helping themselves in their three-year terms to all of it they could lay their hands upon. And in the process, men like Jorge de Menezes and Duarte de Deça became so drunk with greed that they even murdered two sultans of Ternate, with a regent thrown in. Much of their temptation was inadvertently presented to them on a salver by Lisbon because the crown variously attempted to tax, exclude or otherwise ban traffic in the three spices; the captains, bent on enriching themselves, conceived the regulations as little more than opportunities for accepting clandestine payments. Until 1537, Lisbon tried to enforce a royal monopoly on the condiments; then it turned to free trade with one third sold to the crown at fixed prices or else, when transported in crown vessels, a one-third percentage. After the middle of the century, it resorted to concessionaires, who were awarded or sold the rights to undertake voyages.[8]

But of course no matter what measures the crown in Lisbon proclaimed in order to safeguard its precious monopoly, vessels operated by free-lance Portuguese traders, usually with Malay and Chinese crews, continued to appear in the Moluccas and few of them sailed away with empty holds. Nor was it any wonder (considering the lawlessness and outright criminal behaviour of appointed officialdom) that after a series of such scoundrels, Ternateans revolted against the Portuguese in 1575 and expelled them from their fortress of S. João the following year. But three years later they were invited by the rival sultan of Tidore to ensconce themselves there, where they remained for the balance of the XVI century until expelled by the Dutch early in the next.[9]

Uncivil behavior on the part of the Portuguese secular authorities was partly offset by the gentler priesthood operating under the royal

Padroado, with responsibility for evangelization. In 1546, the great Jesuit missionary, Francisco Xavier, later canonized for his preaching and conversion throughout maritime Asia, arrived at Amboina from Malacca and with the help of other missionaries converted to Christianity a substantial number of the Ambonians who were still Hindus.[10] In later centuries under the Dutch, these same Ambonians, together with the Moluccans and the Bandanese, became their prime colonial troops. Only a cynic might maintain that the proselytization was conceived primarily as a way of creating docile colonial subjects, but it was perhaps natural that contemporaries, both in the Old World as in the New, regarded converts as likely to prove more cooperative.

Presence of the garrisons and the missionaries, of course, constituted one direct form of Western influence, while on the economic level, it can be observed that the Moluccan economy now became directly, rather than indirectly, connected with that of Europe, though monetarization in Portuguese times did not yet take place. Rather, the spices were bartered for cotton cloth and foodstuffs. Just as in Brazil at almost the same era, lands which raised such prime export commodities (whether as in this case, spices, or in Brazil, sugar), were too valuable for food production – while cotton culture required a drier climate. Hence, both rice and cloth had to be imported, giving the Portuguese the opportunity to exchange them for the nutmeg, mace and cloves they desired. This, of course, was more advantageous for them than their acquisition of pepper on the Malabar coast of India, since Brahmin landowners there eschewed barter and demanded only specie from Europe in return for it.[11]

Portuguese influence was not strong in other regions of the Malay archipelago, save for Solor, which possessed saltpetre, and at the end of the XVI century, Timor, with its prime yellow sandalwood. In Timor, missionaries established a permanent station only in 1593 after Portuguese traders had been calling for decades. For the rest, Portuguese vessels en route from Malacca usually called at Hindu Panarukan, at the eastern end of Java near Bali, while Portuguese traders from Malacca obtained rice from the region to bolster that city's own inadequate supply. Private Portuguese traders also ensconced themselves on the other end of the island; in 1562, castaways from a Portuguese shipwreck on the coast of Sumatra scrabbled their way to the nearby Javanese kingdom of Sunda and were pleasantly surprised when they were greeted by a little colony of their countrymen who had settled there![12]

It was persistently rumored that the fabulous gold mines of biblical Ophir were located somewhere on the great island of Sumatra, and naturally, this aroused great interest among the Portuguese; of course all attempts to locate them led nowhere. Otherwise, from beginning to end, relations with the sultanates on Sumatra were invariably hostile, an enmity dating from the days of Albuquerque, when the Portuguese backed the losing pretender to the sultanate of Pasei. Later in the century, Pasei was absorbed into the sultanate of Atjeh, whose origin lay in a pirate community, but which expanded during the century into a trading center and rival of Malacca itself. Together with the exiled sultanate of Malacca's new capital at Johore (near the present-day Singapore), Portuguese Malacca soon had two powerful adversaries for its role as chief entrepôt between East and South Asia. This double rivalry frequently broke into war and blockade, though Portuguese seapower with a few exceptions was able to fend off crippling sieges and restrict fighting to naval battles. It was lucky for Portugal that Atjeh and Johore disliked one another fully as much as they hated the Portuguese; much of their spleen was vented upon themselves. On the whole, however, it would appear that in the course of the XVI century, the Portuguese royal monopoly at Malacca lost ground, not only to these external competitors, but to its own private sector, including its very royal officials – who competed with it by trafficking illegally.[13] Seen in the perspective of four centuries, however, the Portuguese, whether crown monopolists, private traders or *contrabandistas*, all added their strands to the web of Western influence.

What Portuguese migrants meant in Siam

In Siam, to which the remainder of this article is devoted to illustrate the beginnings of Westernisation, Europeans never exercised political control in the sense they did later in India or Indonesia. Nor did they exert their influence directly or even primarily through seapower, though of course it was always in the background as a support and outlet for the Portuguese traders who penetrated inland. Yet, even where European influence was minimal, as was Portuguese penetration into the country during the XVI century, one can still observe the infiltration of Europeans and European ways of doing things. And, nota bene, the process is only observable to historians today because the Portuguese had the peculiarly Western habit of gathering and transmitting back to the metropolis information about faraway events, places and peoples.

While I might have used China, Japan, Cambodia any of the other places just named as my example, I have chosen Siam, if only because in a seminar I gave two years ago, I compared the section about it in a manuscript recently come to light called *La Vida de Jaques de Coutre* with the previously-known and earlier accounts of the country written by Portuguese authors. Aside from this, Siam, or as it is known today, Thailand, was sufficiently remote from other lands that most people, even historians, might not have supposed that either Portugal or the West had played any considerable role there until the XIX century. But the emergent picture went far to suggest that the few Portuguese who penetrated the country three hundred years before acted as catalysts to change by bringing about a certain amount of Europeanization even when the official Portuguese role in that country was minimal and its crown exercised no direct influence.

Reports about Siam from the sixteenth century are fragmentary and second-hand for the most part, and every scrap of evidence from the entire century is needed to enable one to form a picture of how Western ways were inexorably inserting themselves. This is why one can still call an expedition to the Siamese capital Ayuthaya which occurred as late as 1595 as one of "discovery" – since the term "discovery" in Asia really means inauguration of the Westernisation process.

The process was open-ended, of course, and when the Dutch began to assert their influence in Siam after 1602, they also became a part of it. Dutch reports between then and 1660 could easily be added to what I have written here. But of course I am speaking of the Portuguese and the beginning of the process.

Throughout the sixteenth century, Siam remained largely beyond the parameters of Portugal's official empire, touching as it did, neither territories ruled by king and viceroy nor the routes connecting them. At the same time, along with all the contiguous territories, it was penetrated by Portuguese mercenaries and by private traders, who were connected informally either with associates in Malacca, Cochin, or else with another hub of private trading, São Thomé de Meliapur. Incidentally, there was always a certain intrusion into their affairs of the official Portuguese empire from Goa into these regions – very occasionally diplomatic, but more commonly via the *Padroado*, since the missionaries tended to follow the traders and mercenaries on their migrations, if only as a way of making contact with the indigenes, as well as to say masses for the traders themselves. The presence of the clergy in turn tended to give eyes and ears to the crown and, if only indirectly, to keep it mindful of any commercial or military opportunities should they arise.

Both Tomé Pires and Duarte Barbosa had heard of Siam soon after the beginning of the sixteenth century. But though these men are the ones best known to us as the systematic compilers of geographical information about Asia, they reflected no more knowledge than any other Portuguese could have had who might have bothered to inform themselves from the same sources. Soon after the conquest of Malacca in 1511, Albuquerque sent one Duarte Fernandes to the court of Rama T'bodi II, at Ayuthaya. When Fernandes was well received, he sent a mission under one of his *fidalgos*, António Miranda de Azevedo, whose staffmember, Manuel Fragoso, was instructed to prepare a detailed report on the land, including peoples, cities, harbours and the commercial possibilities there.[14]

This report, though it was never published and probably not intended for general consumption, was likely used by João de Barros at a later time for his *Décadas da Asia*. Then in 1518, a third mission was dispatched under a certain Duarte Coelho, who had accompanied the Azevedo mission. A treaty between Portugal and the Siamese king ensued which guaranteed the Portuguese peace with him, gave Portuguese subjects the right to settle and trade in the most important Siamese entrepôts and allowed them the practice of their Christian religion. For their parts, the Portuguese promised, among other things, to provide King T'bodi with firearms and munitions.[15] Both before and after the signing of the treaty, incidentally, Portuguese individuals had begun drifting into the kingdom informally, either to take service as mercenaries or to start private trading operations.

It is hard to assess with any confidence who made the firsthand reports of Siam on which information from the early sixteenth century is based, especially that retailed by Barros. While the chronicler might have had much of his information from Fragoso's report, this is only guesswork. Much of it seems accurate and reasonable in light of later knowledge from other sources, but it was not until the 1550s that any writings appeared whose original author we know and can evaluate. And since these come from Fernão Mendes Pinto, this creates its own problems. Pinto is now believed to be generally truthful, but he seems to have embroidered his facts with fancy whenever memory failed, he wished to make some favourite point, or he wished to claim he had visited an area where he had never been. His most recent translator, Rebecca Catz, even believes that the *"eu"* of his famous *Peregrinação* does not correspond to himself, but only to a fictitious person.[16] While I am somewhat skeptical about this, I admit that it is hard to know exactly how far one can rely on what he writes. In his defense, however, I can say that where Siam and its neighbors are concerned, nothing he reports contradicts what is generally known, but indeed fits and appears to fill it in perfectly. There are, incidentally two Pinto sources dealing with Siam: the chapters 181 through 189 of the *Peregrinação*, and the text of a letter dated 5 December 1554.[17]

Mercenaries, merchants, and information

When one combines all the previously known writings about the country produced by Portuguese writers during the century, two things become clear. The first is that one can gain a reasonable idea of its geography, government, wars, religion and trade, one which cannot be ascertained from any of the country's surviving native sources. As to be expected, anthropologists, students of religion and other scholars, including those who specialise in contiguous regions, have found some gaps, errors and contradictions in their accounts. But these are relatively insignificant because if one assembles all the references, they amount to around fifty pages of solid information which as might be measured by the pages of a modern book. This may not seem much, but the information is indispensable because it allows reconstruction of the complicated political history of the region, shows that a Moslem trading community already existed there, and gives indications how indigenous practices known from a later time may have varied in the sixteenth century. In other words, Portuguese writings not only provide a diversity of data which gave Europeans a true picture of that land during the century, but all this is contemporary information without which our modern knowledge of historical Siam could hardly be so complete if it had had to have been based solely on hearsay gathered in later times.

The second thing to be gained from the early sources seems to me even more important. All of them reveal that a considerable community of free-lance Portuguese traders and mercenaries had appeared in the kingdom (and also in its neighbors, incidentally) and it was precisely these people who slowly but surely upset the old ways of doing things and bound Siam to the West in a variety of subtle ways. We know from João de Barros that these vital "interface" peoples (to borrow a term from the computer world) began to appear almost as soon as the first official Portuguese visitors did. By Pinto's time around the middle of the XVI century, he estimates that there were upwards of 130 Portuguese males resident in Ayuthaya, nearly all of whom were drafted into military service around 1545 to help repel an invasion of Laotians and hill tribesmen. So useful were the Portuguese to the king that, Pinto says, he used them as bodyguards.[18] In fact, they became involved in all the royal activities, not only of Siam, but of all the surrounding lands, and their presence seems to have given rulers an edge over their neighbors. (Conversely, having one's own Portuguese in service kept rivals who also had them from gaining the upper hand – as in neighbouring Burma, Pegu and Cambodia!)

Not only did mercenaries make a decisive difference: frequently they even became powers behind thrones or even petty rulers in their own rights. We know from Pinto, and from other sources, that in adjacent countries, men like Felipe de Brito e Nicote in Burma and Salvador Ribeiro de Sousa in Arakan actually became petty rulers in their own rights, while in Pegu, one Diogo Soares managed to become the most powerful man in the kingdom next to the monarch – until he abused his position and was stoned to death.[19]

Pinto's narrative contains other clues in regard to the role of the Portuguese traders in Siam: he stopped off there, he says, while waiting for a ship and a trading voyage to Japan, manned by other Portuguese.[20] This would serve to indicate how Portuguese traders had forged direct links between lands which had not been joined in direct trading before the arrival of the Lusitanians: Siam with Macau, Japan and Goa itself, and without doubt the resident communities in Ayuthaya and other Siamese port cities inaugurated the Westernisation process which the Dutch of the V.O.C., or United East India Company continued when they founded their first factory there in 1660. One can see that after the Portuguese arrival, king and court and country became irreversibly and permanently changed, woven, as it were into the economic, military, political and technological pattern of the West. The transformations, to be sure, did not take place all at once, but from the arrival of the Portuguese in the Indian Ocean, the way things were done in native kingdoms came more and more to resemble European norms, purely by responding to them.[21]

Until recently, there were no known sources which completed the picture of Portuguese activity in the sixteenth century, for the one difficulty with the Indo-Portuguese trading community is that even though it may have worked a silent influence on Siam's economic life, the traders themselves did not record or transmit information either about themselves or about their host country. But in the 1960s a document written by a Fleming from Bruges was found in the Biblioteca Nacional de Madrid, whose importance was never recognised by the Spanish, no doubt because although it was written in Castilian (though certainly translated from the Portuguese), it dealt entirely with Asia. It seems that the author, the jewel-trader, Jacob van de Coutere, alias Jaques de Coutre or Couto, spent thirty years in Portuguese Asia and among these, his first nine in Portuguese military service. Only after his return from Asia about 1624 did he migrate to Madrid, where he sold jewels to the court of Felipe IV and III until his death in December 1640, in Zaragoza.

The Coutre account of the 1595 expedition

As important as his manuscript was and is, its timing was wrong. 1640 or the years following were hardly favourable ones in Spain for publication of manuscripts on Portuguese Asia. (Perhaps this is even true now, since the C.S.I.C. recently declined to publish the original text!) And so *La Vida de Jaques de Coutre* lay unnoticed until the 1960s, when it was independently discovered by two Flemish- or Dutch-speaking historians, and only because they recognised the name "Coutre" as a variant of the name "Coutere" and called for Manuscript no. 2780 of the *Biblioteca Nacional*. From 1640 until only a few years ago, there had not been a breath of news about it or its author in any of the major or even minor historical sources.

Jaques de Coutre and his brother, Josef, or José, as he was called in Goa, left Bruges at different times around 1590 and met one another in Lisboa before enlisting in the India fleet of 1592 and embarking for Goa. Once there, José settled down to become a *casado* and jewel trader, marrying a Portuguese actually named "Couto," but Jaques went on to Malacca, where he traded jewels on behalf of the captains of Malacca, making expeditions to Pahang, Manila, Johor and Patani, ones which combined diplomatic visits with private trading on the parts of the captain and his officers and retinue. Then, in 1595, the captain, one Francisco de Silva Meneses, was approached by an odd diplomatic couple from Siam, representing the King. One of these was an *"hombre astuto y terrible,"* Frei Jorge da Mota, a Dominican friar, while the other was a Siamese nobleman. Frei Jorge spoke of the plight of Portuguese captives carried off to Ayuthaya after a recent Siamese incursion into Cambodia – and the purpose of his mission was ostensibly to get the Captain of Malacca to ransom them. But Frei Jorge also let it be known that there were plenty of *"rubis, diamantes y safiras"* to be had at very low prices. This prompted Silva Meneses to dispatch a Portuguese embassy to Siam under a retainer, one Simão Peres.[22]

The ransoming of Christian hostages taken in military campaigns to neighbouring regions was not exactly new – Mendes Pinto also tells of it some fifty years earlier, and in this case the hostages had been captured in 1594 during a raid by Prince Naresuen into Cambodia, where he had carried off some religious and a few Portuguese traders. These were ultimately freed, but not before the embassy had taken a few unexpected twists, ones which only go to show that the Siamese were sensitive to European influences. It seems that Frei Jorge da Mota had been one of the friars captured, but that he had insinuated himself into the graces of the king's *privado* and was really more interested in the material than the spiritual. It was he who had invented the story about the cheap jewels, and when the ten Portuguese of the embassy arrived (or really eleven men including Coutre), they found their mission had been grossly misrepresented by Frei Jorge: he had told the king at the presentation of their credentials that they were presents – *paidar*, or military slaves – from his fellow monarch, the king of Portugal. Whereupon the Siamese monarch ordered the preparation of a huge junk, again with twin ambassadors and rich presents for the Portuguese king – and of course plenty of benefits as well for Frei Jorge, who took full credit for having engineered the "donation" of the Portuguese. Ultimately, however, the misunderstanding was corrected, the hostages freed and after some equivocations, the Portuguese were permitted to depart. Frei Jorge thereupon found it prudent to flee.[23]

In addition to this narrative of the embassy, which occupied the Portuguese for the better part of one year, Coutre describes life in the capital and court, providing by far the best firsthand description of the country and its customs written during the sixteenth century. I gather from the whole tenor of his *Vida* that he was not a particularly religious man, and he does not concern himself much with Buddhism, or its spiritual "errors," as practiced in that time and place. He is far more interested in royal justice, in the handling of the royal elephants, and their upkeep and funeral rites, including the voluntary ritual slaying of two keepers of a deceased white pachyderm. He tells of the royal elephant hunts in the forests, the appearances and uses of the palace and the temples of Ayuthaya, and in the nature, outfitting and provisioning of the royal army. His account suggests, when compared with the earlier promise of the 1518 treaty to provide the kingdom with firearms that in the seventy-seven years since, Siam and its neighbors were still dependent on Westerners and their trade in military technology. The Siamese, as Coutre observes, might have manufactured some of their own firearms (via techniques derived from China), but Coutre makes it clear that they were of little purpose because they were too much like popguns – short and small of calibre, both in respect to cannons and to arquebusses.[24] In other respects, Coutre provides much information about the country not previously contained in other European reports.

For example, he reveals that Europeans (there were a few Spanish clergy from the Philippines present and at least one other Fleming) had become fixtures – honored guests and part of the general scene.[25] Most of all, they were beginning to manipulate and manage the kings and nobles for their own convenience. These in their turns proved themselves eager to make use of European capabilities, both military and commercial – so eager in fact that they frequently were deceived by European charlatans like Frei Jorge, as were the kings of Johore and Atjeh at this same period by a renegade Spaniard apparently of Moorish descent who had come from Mexico to the Philippines and portrayed himself as a cousin of the king to gain rich gifts. He was even given, according to Coutre, a ship and slaves by the Sultan of Atjeh![26] Even by this early time, it has become apparent that Asian monarchs and courts were dependent upon both Europeans and the tactics and things they could bring with them.

All of this only serves to illustrate that in Asia, "discovery" really consisted of this twin function of information-gathering and penetration of the infrastructures of society by Western ideas and practices. I have tried to apply this concept to what I have called the last Portuguese expedition of "discovery" (that I know of, at least) before arrival of the Dutch embassy under Cornelius Specx in 1604. Even at this late date, it can be called a "discovery" because it rounds out nearly a century of initial Western contacts with a country which still remained relatively unknown to Europeans until well into the XIX century but which avidly sought after Western ways.

Siam was obviously never quite the same after the Portuguese arrival in 1513. If, almost exactly four-hundred years following Coutre's visit in the Simão Peres embassy, all Asia has become an alloy of it own culture and that of the West, the parade of events leading to this prime reality of our modern world was set in motion by none other than the greatest navigators and adventurers of history. As the world becomes one, it may be increasingly hard to assert that anybody really discovered anybody else, for all members of the human family were already in their places when "discovered" by others of its members.

While the Portuguese may not literally have "discovered" Asia, the truth is undeniable that through their travels and influences, Asia discovered Portugal and Europe. Needless to say, from the moment the Portuguese arrived, neither Europe nor Asia were ever isolated again. When the first Dutch and English embassies arrived a decade after Coutre's visit, they were royally received.

George D. Winius

Notes

[1] I am of course echoing Immanuel Wallerstein here, though perhaps one does not need to depend on his *World Economic System*, 3 vols. (New York: Academic Press of America, 1976-1988) for this insight. One can observe that the moment any trading connection was made between continents which had never exchanged goods or specie, the commercial link was almost never severed. Of course in the XVI century, no intercontinental commerce was significant enough to shape the economic life of either participating area, but merely contributed to it in a lesser or greater way. But the primordial exchanges were significant because the true beginning of a long process.

[2] See Humberto Leitão, *Os Portugueses em Solor e Timor, de 1515 a 1702* (Lisboa: Tip. da Liga dos Combatantes da Grande Guerra, 1948), 39-41; also, Bailey W. Diffie and George D. Winius, *Foundations of the Portuguese Empire, 1415-1580* (Minneapolis: The U. of Minnesota Press, 1977) 245 and 263.

[3] See Georg Schurhammer, S.J., "O descobrimento do Japão pelos Portugueses no ano de 1543", *Anais*, série 2, vol. II, 17-85; also Armando Cortesão, ed., *The Suma Oriental of Tomé Pires and the Book of Francisco Rodrigues*, 2 vols. (London: The Hakluyt Society, 1944) I, 131 and note 1.

[4] Blussé bases this on the presence of the tiny and miserly Dutch garrisons in farflung parts of Java and the Indonesian Archipelago. Even though they may have amounted to only a few soldiers, they were speedily enlisted by local sultans who were eager to involve them in their own games. The Europeans frequently were sufficient to tip the delicate balance of forces. It is quite apparent that the same was true for Siam and its rival powers.

[5] For more information on Malacca, see Luís Filipe F. R. Thomaz, "Malacca, the Town and Its Society during the First Century of Portuguese Rule," in *Revista de Cultura; edição do Instituto Cultural de Macau*, nos. 13-14, "*Os Mares da Asia, 1500-1800; The Asian Seas, 1500-1800*" (1991), 68-79, and *Os Portugueses em Malaca (1511-1580)*, 2 vols., typewritten and reproduced by offset. (Lisbon, 1964).

[6] See João de Barros, *Da Asia*, Decade III, Book 5, Chap. 6.

[7] See Bailey W. Diffie and George D. Winius, *Foundations of the Portuguese Empire, 1415-1580* (Minneapolis: U. of Minnesota Press, 1977), 364-368.

[8] See Luís Felipe Thomaz, "Les Portugais dans les mers de l'Archipel au XVIᵉ siècle," in *Archipel* 18 (1979): 107-109.

[9] Diffie and Winius, *Foundations*, 374-379.

[10] See the three communications of Francis Xavier on the Moluccas written from Amboina, in *Documentação para a história das missões do Padroado Português do Oriente; Insulíndia*, Artur Basílio de Sá, ed.& comp. 6 vols. (Lisbon: Agência Geral do Ultramar, 1954-1986), I, 490-509.

[11] See Vitorino Magalhães Godinho, *L'economie de l'empire portugais aux XVe et au XVIe siècles* (Paris: Ecole Practique des Hautes Etudes, S.E.V.P.E.N., 1969), 631-632; 650-651.

[12] Thomaz, "Les Portugais," 111.

[13] For "Ofir," my colleague, Benjamin N. Teensma, has published an amusing little treatise on the subject, *De roep van Ophir. De Portuguezen op Sumatra in de zestiende eeuw.* (Leiden: Leiden University, 1979).

[14] See Joaquim J. de Campos "Early Portuguese Accounts of Thailand," in *Journal of the Thailand Research Society*, XXXII, pt. I: 83-86; see also Bras de Albuquerque, *Commentários do Grande Afonso de Albuquerque, Capitão Geral que foi das Indias Orientais, etc.*, 4 parts (in any edition, III, chapters XXXV and XXXVI). João de Barros, *Da Asia*, Década III, Livro II, Chapters IV & V, Fernão Lopes de Castanheda, Livro III, Chapter LXII. Gaspar Corrêa, in his *Lendas da India* also describes the embassies, but he runs them together. He also calls António de Miranda de Azevedo "Simão." See the edition of 1858, II, 263 & 264.

[15] This treaty is best summarised in Barros, above, but it does not exist in Biker's *Colecção de tratados e concertos de pazes*.

[16] See Fernão Mendes Pinto, *The Travels of Mendes Pinto.* Rebecca D. Catz, ed. & tr., (Chicago and London: The U. of Chicago Press, 1989), xxxvi-xliv.

[17] It is printed in *Documentação para a história das missões do Padroado português no Oriente.* António da Silva Rego, ed. & comp., 12 vols. (Lisboa: Agência Geral do Ultramar, 1947-1961), V: (1951) 369-372.

[18] In the *Peregrinação*, Chapters 181-189, passim. Siam had no monopoly on Portuguese, either as mercenaries or as bodyguards. In the siege of Ayuthaya in 1548, Portuguese fought on both sides.

[19] *Peregrinação*, Chapters 191-192. For other examples, see George D. Winius, "The Shadow Empire of Goa in the Bay of Bengal," *Itinerário*, 1983-2: 83-101.

[20] *Peregrinação*, at the beginning of Chapter 181.

[21] One can observe the process in many forms. The Mughals, for example, had no navies with which to control European powers or their trading companies which by the opening years of the XVII century

fought one another for access to the lucrative entrepôt harbours of Gujarat and Bengal. By then awakened to the desirability of trade with the Westerners, they cleverly solved the problem and exercised indirect control by putting all European trading groups within their territories on an equal footing and forbidding armament of their factories. In doing so, they developed a form of governance they had not envisioned in the XVI century and in the process increased the complexity of their bureaucracy.

[22] *La Vida de Jaques de Coutre*, Ms. 2780, Biblioteca Nacional de Madrid, fl. 39.

[23] *Vida*, fls. 75-79. The imagination is stirred by the idea of such a junk sailing into the Tagus with its exotic crew and cargo. But unless the Siamese had had an experienced European pilot and extraordinarily good weather, one cannot imagine that it could possibly have reached Europe! When the king learned of the fraud, however, he cancelled the embassy. The king finally lost patience with Frei Jorge, who fled for his life. All this intrigue was lost on Frei Paulo da Trindade, in his *Conquista Espiritual do Oriente*, who merely states that Frei Jorge had been "very favored by the king, and seeing that the great people of the kingdom begrudged the intimacy the monarch had with him, departed secretly for Manila . . ." See Frei Paulo da Trindade, *A Conquista Espiritual da Oriente*, 3 vols., ed. Félix Lopes, O.F.M., (Lisbon: Centro de Estudos Históricos Ultramarinos, 1962-1967), III (1967), 447.

[24] *Vida*, fl. 102. This is not necessarily to imply that the Portuguese were the first to introduce firearms *per se* into Siam, for this possibly was done earlier by the Chinese, who by the XV century had adopted them, probably on example of the Turks or other central Asian peoples. Both Pinto and Coutre speak of varieties of small artillery in their accounts, and these were almost certainly cast in Siam under Chinese inspiration. The same sorts of weapons seem to have been captured in Malacca by the Portuguese under Albuquerque. They also seem to have been too small and light for effective use. In neither Malacca nor Siam does it seem that personnel had been properly trained to use them under battle circumstances or in coordination with other units of their armies.

[25] The other Europeans had come from Manila. When Coutre and his fellows found themselves in their awkward predicament because of Frei Jorge da Mota's misrepresentation, one of the monks based in the Philippines proposed trying to resolve the problem by appealing to the Spanish governor there. See *Vida*, fls. 54-56.

[26] *Vida*, fls. 32-36.

Brazil

Chapter XII

Discovery and Conquest of the Brazilian Frontier

The conquest of colonial Brazil's frontier continues to remain one of the most overlooked episodes in Portugal's discovery of the wider world. Such neglect stems not from any lack of myth provoking experiences – in their daring, difficulties and scope, treks into Brazil's frontier rival any found in early modern overland and overseas explorations. Nor from the lack of importance. Expeditions into the frontier led to the incorporation of over half of South America's land area into Portuguese America and forged the basis of modern Brazil's national identity. Rather, it is the character of the historical process and the groups who conquered the frontier that has shrouded Brazil's frontier history. Portuguese colonists settled on the coast line where they established lucrative plantation and mercantile communities that stamped colonial societies. Unlike the Spanish experience, Brazilian explorers found no exotic civilizations, while discoveries of precious metals did not occur until the eighteenth century. In further contrast to European ventures elsewhere, mixed blooded Americans (*mamelucos*), whose first languages were Indian, led much of the exploration of Brazil. Thus, the penetration into the hinterland produced fewer heroes for Europeans to identify with and fewer written accounts that chronicled their exploits. For contemporaries, the frontier stood as a place outside civilization and the law. It was an environment of violence and godlessness, populated by fugitives, gypsies, New Christians, and *quilombos* (runaway slave communities).[1] For later historians, Brazil's frontier history remains intimately tied up with the destruction of its Indian populations.

For much of the sixteenth century Portuguese America's frontier began at its coastline, where, in the picturesque phrase of Brazil's first historian, Frei Vincente do Salvador, the colonists crawled the coast like crabs.[2] The land enthralled and astonished early Portuguese explorers, most of whom described it as an edenic paradise. They praised its climate, marvelled at the variety colorful animals and wild fruit, and wondered at a verdant palm tree filled landscape that, in Vaz de Caminha's words, extended "as far as the eye can see." Indeed, lush forests covered much of Brazil's northern and southern coastline and would form, along the Serra do Mar mountain range in the center south, an initial barrier to exploration in the hinterland. At second glance, moreover, Brazil's idyllic panorama proved to hide an environment full of difficulties and dangers. Deadly snakes, swarms of mosquitoes and other insects, joined with a searing heat to frustrate attempts at entering the interior.

Brazil's seemingly unlimited territory gave rise to fantastic reports of mountains of gold and resurrected fables about tribes of women warriors and fabulously wealthy white kings. Early expeditions into the interior (*entradas*) proved those tales false.[3] Portuguese explorers found neither advanced civilizations nor mineral treasure. But Spanish encounters with the Incas, and their discovery of a veritable mountain of silver at Potosí, continued to fuel such stories.[4] As a result, bands of Portuguese continued to trek inland searching for a Brazilian El Dorado throughout the sixteenth and seventeenth centuries.

The three decades after Pedro Álvares Cabral's landing on the South American coast witnessed no genuine settlement attempts.[5] Portugal's resources were already thinly stretched in Africa and Asia, areas from which profits had already begun flowing back to Lisbon. Brazil's economic prospects appeared rather dim in comparison. Moreover, it lacked the grandeur and romantic cachet that Portuguese Asia held in the popular imagination. Money could be made in the New World by exporting *d'hote*, called brazilwood, but that necessitated the participation of only a small number of individuals who operated from a group of trading posts scattered along the coast.

The intermediaries

A few Portuguese did arrive to stay, but these individuals, many of whom were castaways and *degregados* (exiled criminals), did not by themselves constitute a significant permanent European presence. From the very beginning of its organized ventures down the West African coast, a standard feature of Portuguese exploration, and common to other nations' ventures as well, had been the deliberate marooning of a few individuals at the furthermost point of travel. Their task was to learn local languages and act as interpreters for following voyagers. Vasco da Gama, for example, carried ten *degregados* to be dropped off on his voyage to India for language purposes. In Brazil, Pedro Álvares Cabral left the first European exiles and subsequent voyages left others as well.[6]

Although few in number such individuals made an important contribution to later colonization through their integration into local Indian tribes. They, together with their mixed-blood offspring, rendered great assistance to the first groups of organized settlers by acting as cultural brokers who cemented ties between Indians and Europeans. João Ramalho, Caramuru, and the Bacharel, the three most famous of those castaways, attained almost mythic stature.[7] João Ramalho along with a lesser known Portuguese, António Rodrigues landed in the area where São Paulo was founded around 1509 or 1510. The pair managed to ingratiate themselves with the native inhabitants to the point where both married the daughters of local chiefs. Ramalho rendered essential assistance to Martim Afonso de Sousa in the highlands around the settlements of São Vicente. In addition to securing an alliance between the Portuguese and local tribes, the pair helped establish the Indian slave trade. Diogo Álvares, O Caramuru, lived around the Recôncavo in Bahia where he fathered a large family of children with Paraguaçu, the chief of a local Tupinamba tribe. By the time Martim Afonso de Souza arrived in March of 1531 Álvares had become so well known that Portugal's king D. João III had sent him a letter to meet the fleet. The Bacharel, a Portuguese castaway most probably named Francisco de Chaves, lived on the island of Cananéia, close to São Vicente, where he helped both Spanish and Portuguese with food and Indian slaves.

Because Portugal lacked the demographic and economic means independently to exploit their new world discovery, Indians proved to be the key to penetrating and occupying Brazil. As in Spanish America, early chroniclers tended to produce romanticized descriptions focusing on the Indians' seemingly ingenuous character. Vaz de Caminha reflected such opinion in his belief that "[the Indians] seem to be such innocent people, that, if we could understand their speech and they ours, they would immediately become Christians...for truly these people are good and have a simplicity. Any stamp we wish may be easily printed on them."[8]

It is not possible to address the role of *bandeiras* or indeed any aspect of discovery in Brazil without addressing the matter of racial mixing. Without the unions between Portuguese and Indians, and the help given to European settlers by their offspring, neither Portuguese America's exploration nor its colonization would have been possible in the manner in which they occurred. Local natives gave Portuguese settlers invaluable assistance during the critical moments of early colonization. They provided Europeans with much needed food and labor. As in Spanish America, early Portuguese pioneers took wives from prominent native families or the daughters of castaways. Diogo Álvares had a large number of children from his several Indian wives, of whom at least two married men in Martim Afonso de Souza's expedition. Moreover, not all the Portuguese who took local brides were of low social origin. Jorge Ferreira, a minor Portuguese noble, married one of João's Ramalho's daughters. Owing to the lack of European women, miscegenation did not shoulder the social disgrace that it assumed in British North America. Duarte Coelho, for example, the donatary captain of Pernambuco, actively supported miscegenation to facilitate peaceful relations with Indian tribes.[9] Coelho's brother-in-law, Jerónimo de Albuquerque, married the daughter of a local chief. Children from such unions provided the Portuguese with an invaluable bilingual liaison with native people as well as military help after serious fighting began between Europeans and Indians.

On the other hand, the Portuguese inclination to associate closely with local Indians also created serious problems. In southern Brazil, where Paulista settlers formed the most extensive fusion with local native groups, colonists found themselves entangled in a constant cycle of bloodshed between rival tribes and clans. Moreover, cultural intermixing between Europeans and natives provoked criticism from religious authorities. Various colonists chose to imitate the Indian custom of taking multiple wives, while some entered common law marriages despite having established families in Portugal.

A variety of difficulties frustrated attempts at systematic exploration in the first half century following Portugal's landfall in the Americas. Brazil's vast size in comparison to the kingdom's rather meager demographic and financial means proved a formidable barrier. Competition for those limited resources furthermore came from Portugal's Asian possessions, which offered far more immediate economic rewards in contrast to the apparent colonial backwater in the Western Hemisphere. In the eyes of many observers Brazil seemed to contain little besides exotic fauna and flora.

In the 1530s two events occurred that changed the direction of Colonial Brazil. First, in December of 1530, king D. João III dispatched Martim Afonso de Sousa firmly to establish Portugal's presence in the Americas. During the 1520s royal officials had become increasingly alarmed about the presence of other Europeans, particularly the French, who had begun arriving in Brazil to acquire brazilwood. D. João III recognized that organized colonizing efforts had to be made if Brazil were to remain in Portuguese hands. He therefore sent Martim Afonso de Sousa with a small fleet and group of four hundred colonists to Brazil. Sousa managed to drive out the French and, in 1532, founded the town of São Vicente. At the same time the crown instituted the captaincy system in which huge land grants were given on the Brazilian coast to twelve *donatários*. These donataries agreed to defend and develop their captaincies at their own cost in exchange for land and future taxing privileges.[10] Although the system failed badly, it did lead to the establishment of permanent coastal settlements. The introduction of sugar cane was the second event. Brazil's northeastern coast immediately proved to have almost the perfect combination of soil, water, and climate for sugar production. Immense profits led to rapid expansion that guaranteed the colony's survival.

Sugar and the frontier

The sugar industry had a direct and enduring impact on the exploration of Brazil's inland frontier.[11] Sugar produced a society based on slave labor, one predisposed to large landholdings and monoculture. Very quickly a profound tension emerged between this commercially organized agricultural society and the largely subsistence settlements that grew outside the central sugar producing zones. Yet the two were never completely separate. Sugar production required an enormous amount of labor. Indians offered an obvious solution to the planters' labor needs, but overwork and European diseases rapidly decimated local tribes. Although slaves imported from Africa eventually became the dominant plantation work force, their high cost, together with recurrent interruptions in supply, meant sugar growers continued to seek Indian laborers.

The hunt for Indian slaves formed the prime attraction for European interest in Brazil's frontier.[12] More than just labor, however, the Indian question lay at the very center of what type of colony Brazil would have become. As in British North America (and later the United States), the entire settlement process was based on the assumption that Europeans and their American-born descendants would naturally displace the original inhabitants. There would be no sharing of a common landscape. Indians would either have to leave the areas Europeans entered or be completely absorbed into European society. Because in sixteenth-century Brazil economic development was synonymous with sugar, absorption primarily meant working as forced plantation labor. As the sugar economy grew, the relationship between Europeans and Indians underwent a fundamental change. Association based on personal service, intermarriage, and mutually beneficial exchanges, (European goods in exchange for cutting down trees for example) transformed into a master-slave relationship. It was that relationship that Brazil's natives found completely unacceptable.

Native resistance to the Portuguese escalated during the 1530s and 1540s to the threat posed by continuing migration and the expanding sugar industry. The ensuing attacks imperiled the entire European presence as at first local natives consistently prevailed over Portuguese colonists.[13] A major problem for the settlers lay in the isolation caused by the initial settlement patterns, but more importantly, by the colony's exceptionally difficult terrain. The already lengthy distances separating settlements grew considerably longer by the dense forests, countless unnavigable streams and rivers, the absence of accessible harbors, and prevailing winds and currents that drove ships far out to sea. Father Inácio de Azevedo hardly exaggerated in claiming that it seemed to him, "easier to go to Portugal and return than to visit the entire province."[14] Indian raids destroyed plantations and slaughtered missionaries and settlers throughout Brazil, causing the abandonment of the São Tomé captaincy in 1545 and the near-abandonment of Espírito Santo.[15] Looking then at great slaughter suffered by both sides, an observer would have been hard pressed to distinguish the eventual winners from the losers.

Mem de Sá's arrival in Bahia as the colony's royal governor (1558-1572) signalled a radical change in Portuguese America. Making Brazil's coastal areas safe for the creation of a sugar-based plantation economy constituted his major accomplishment. Sá launched a series of attacks against hostile natives that succeeded in pacifying local tribes. At the same time he initiated military campaigns along the coastline in support of other settlements. Sá's efforts received critical assistance from the appearance of European disease. Epidemics shattered Indian power through death and famine. As many as one third to one half of Brazil's coastal native populations died as a result of the epidemics of 1562 and 1563.[16] Survivors fled deep into the interior or, among those who stayed, were forced into slavery. Writing in the last years of the sixteenth century, Padre Fernão Cardim observed, "There used to be so many Indians along this coast that it seemed impossible they could be extinguished, however, the Portuguese have given them such pressure that almost all of them are dead, and those [still alive] have such fear, that they have depopulated the coast fleeing as far as three hundred to four hundred leagues into the *sertão*."[17]

By the 1580s Brazil's colonial population numbered over twenty-five thousand, half of whom were white.[18] Although Portuguese America remained a fragile archipelago of coastal communities in which Europeans had yet to establish hegemony over the surrounding wilderness a lasting shift had nonetheless taken place. The colony had passed the stage where Indian raids could truly threaten the entire settlement's existence. Henceforth the triangular relationship between colonists, Indians, and the frontier assumed a different phase. Europeans entered the wilderness either to acquire Indians to augment a growing but not yet dominant African-based labor force or, to proselytize and remove Indians into remote missions to keep them from exploitation by sugar planters. The chief antagonists in those quests were groups of Paulistas known as *bandeirantes*, and Jesuit missionaries.[19]

The *bandeirantes*

Historical leadership in penetrating Brazil's hinterlands has been given to expeditions known as *bandeiras*, the participants of whom became called *bandeirantes*.[20] A *bandeira* was a flag under which quasi-military companies trekked into the frontier. While colonial authorities sometimes instituted official expeditions, private individuals organized most *bandeiras* for the pursuit of profit. Perhaps the most pronounced aspect about *bandeiras* was their multiracial composition. Not only did Europeans usually form a minority within them, the leadership of the company often went to individuals of mixed white and Indian parentage (*mamelucos*). Lack of European women outside the most settled coastal communities facilitated unions between Portuguese and Indians. Thus unlike Brazil's coastal communities, where questions of racial purity became an early social issue, *mamelucos* living on the colonial fringes gained positions of power and responsibility.

The main era of *bandeirante* activity roughly divides into two overlapping phases. The first extended from the 1560s to the middle of seventeenth century during which time southern Brazil became thoroughly explored. In this initial period the *bandeirantes* mainly sought to capture Indians. While colonists had hunted natives for quite some time, systematic expeditions really began during the last decade of the sixteenth century. The small profits realized from Indian hunting never matched the time and danger involved in their pursuit. As the distances grew greater, Indian hunting might have well died out had it not been for the Dutch occupation of Pernambuco and parts of the African coast which drove up the price of native slaves. Demand for native labor began to slacken after Portugal declared independence from Spain in 1640, and precipitously so after 1654 when Caribbean production began depressing Brazilian sugar prices.[21] The search for precious metals accented the second phase of *bandeirante* activity. Tales of mountains of silver and rivers of emeralds lured colonists into the *sertão*, or wilderness. High costs brought about by the war of Restoration stimulated royal authorities to encourage the search for mineral wealth as evidenced by the crown's communication with Fernão Dias Pais for that purpose in 1664. Portuguese officials offered Pais and other colonists rewards of offices and personal honor to venture out into the frontier. The result of those efforts launched *bandeirante* groups to open up the Brazilian west, and led other adventurers to travel up to Peru and throughout the Amazon region.

Demographics and geography made the town of São Paulo the hub for many of the most important and most famous *bandeirante* expeditions into the South American wilderness. The great distance from Brazil's administrative center in Salvador da Bahia, together with the lack of an easily available export commodity, such as sugar, meant São Paulo grew largely unencumbered from interference by royal authority. Yet in searching for the reasons underlying *bandeirante* activity it is essential to banish the traditional assumption the Paulistas sustained a non-capitalistic subsistence-oriented society. Such an economy, the story goes, allowed them time to breach the *sertão* in search of precious metals, or Indian captives to sell to coastal sugar planters. In reality, Paulistas advanced into the *sertão* primarily because of their commercial orientation.

Like the sugar and tobacco regions along the coast, São Paulo's economy and society had slave labor as its foundation. Unlike coastal planters, the agricultural products they produced (wheat and other foodstuffs) did not generate a level of profitability that justified the high cost of importing African slave labor. Paulistas continued to retain Indians as their labor base well after sugar and tobacco planters had made the transition to African slavery, notwithstanding the problematic nature of Indian labor owing to disease and their acquisition. Hence, their primary reason for venturing into the frontier lay in their own labor needs, not simply adventure or supplying coastal plantations.[22]

By the 1580s, war, disease, and slavery had depopulated the area surrounding São Paulo's main settlements. Paulistas, therefore, mounted larger *bandeiras* which, following the Paraíba do Sul and Tietê rivers, ranged increasingly deeper into the continental frontier for captives. By the turn of the seventeenth century, bands of various sizes left the town of São Paulo for plunder and exploration on virtually a yearly basis.

In the main, a small group of whites and *mamelucos* headed such expeditions supported by Indian retainers who made up the majority of the *bandeira*. A continuing shortage of European women meant Portuguese and Indian cultures coalesced to a far more profound degree in São Paulo than the earlier smaller scale encounters had produced along the coast. Many Paulistas spoke Tupi-guarani better than Portuguese. Domingos Jorge Velho, for example, the *Mestre-de Campo* (field master) who led the troops that finally destroyed the great runaway slave community of Palmares, spoke Portuguese only with great difficulty. As often as not, the *mameluco* children from European and Indian unions found little need to speak Portuguese at all. In this hybrid society the European portion remained dominant. Local natives who took part in the expeditions did so on the basis of personal ties to European and *mameluco* settlers. In a real sense, the two groups often had different purposes for forming a *bandeira*. Settlers organized them for commercial profit while Indians joined as personal retainers or went in the traditional pursuit of raiding for prisoners.

As in much of the oceanic exploration during the discovery period, poverty compelled many individuals to embark on distant journeys. The overwhelming majority of Paulistas were dirt poor and acquiring Indian slaves formed one of the few opportunities open to young men seeking to make their fortune. Young men left their families to "buscar remédio para minha probreza" (to seek a cure for my poverty). Representative was Lucas Ortiz de Camargo who joined a *bandeira* to "seek remedies in the *sertão* which is the ordinary business of this land."[23] A glance at sixteenth and seventeenth-century inventories and testaments reveals a population possessing few material goods. Even many of those deemed affluent had a standard of living that thriving European peasants of the time would have considered mean.[24] Yet it is important to point out that not all Paulistas were poor. A number became rich through acquiring Indian labor.

The *Bandeirantes* varied from the familiar pattern of mariners and seamen whom penury propelled out into the unknown. Apart from financial assistance, the leading citizens of Portuguese or other European towns rarely took direct part in overseas exploration; and indeed, only a small minority actually invested in such precarious endeavors. But the magnitude of São Paulo's poverty was so that residents of every station participated in the excursions.[25] Its principal families not only helped equip the expeditions – with weapons, supplies, and slaves – but at one time or another their fathers and sons led them as well. Fernão Dias Pais, to cite one example, a member of the municipal council, and allegedly the richest man in São Paulo, led numerous treks into the frontier in search of human and mineral riches.[26]

Difficult terrain and the mobility of their prey meant *bandeirantes* travelled light, living off the land together with supplies seized from their victims, and carrying with them weapons and as few essentials as possible. It would be mistaken to think that Paulista bands simply plunged headlong into the wilderness; well known trails radiated from São Paulo which *bandeirantes* used to begin their treks. They generally marched about half the day before stopping to set up camp and search for food. Like the ocean mariners of the era, who planted crops and left animals on uninhabited islands, in case they needed supplies on their return voyage, the *bandeirantes* planted crops in places that became supply stations. Not surprisingly, the further they trekked the easier it became to get lost and run out of supplies. In the words of one Jesuit, "lacking all necessities [they] always march on long and difficult journeys...suffering hunger, exhaustion and nakedness while constantly on guard against a thousand ambushes."[27]

The great risks and lengthy distances in such treks produced high casualties among *bandeirantes* and their Indian retainers. A vicious cycle often ensued. Longer treks most often meant smaller bands owing to supply problems involved in maintaining *bandeirantes* and their captives. Smaller bands were vulnerable to attack by vengeful natives. Moreover, they increasingly encountered Indians who spoke languages other than Tupi-guarani, and who were more difficult to control. Profits decreased as losses among *bandeirantes* and their captives escalated with the distances. Anthony Knivet, a marooned Englishman forced to accompany one such expedition in 1590, described dreadful conditions that resulted in the losses on hundreds of men. During one month-long stretch of the journey he wrote of finding "nothing to eate...the Portugals beganne to dispaire, and threw away their Peeces, being not able to carrie their clothes. We were forced to eate...raw Hides of Buffe and likewise we did eate a Cowes skinne...happie was hee who could get a Toade or Snake to eate."[28] Other expeditions thought to have been lost, reappeared years after starting out, during which time their wives at home had remarried and had borne children by new husbands.

Three famous *bandeirantes*

The experiences of Pedro Teixeira, António Raposo Tavares, and Manuel Pires, characterize the breadth of these inland odysseys during the seventeenth century. Teixeira was not a Paulista but rather lived in Maranhão. In 1616 he made his first trip up the Amazon River as a young soldier. By the middle of the next decade, captain Teixeira was leading voyages to "rescue" Indians and attack English and Irish settlements along the Amazon. His most consequential voyage began in 1637 after two Spanish priests, Fray Domingos de Brieva and André de Toledo, with a small group of soldiers left Quito, Peru and descended down the Amazon to Belém. Governor Jacomé Raimundo Noronha immediately sent captain Teixeira accompanied by soldiers together with 1,200 Indian bowmen and paddlers to establish a Portuguese presence in the Amazon region. After arduously paddling up the Amazon, Solimões, and Napo rivers for several months Teixeira reached Spanish territory. Leaving most of his men behind, he pushed up over the Quijos river and eastern Andes to reach Quito in 1638 where he stayed until the following year. During his return down the Napo and Amazon, Teixeira planted a marker claiming most of the Amazon basin for Portugal.

António Raposo Tavares was one of the most audacious and fearsome of the Paulista *bandeirantes*. Throughout the 1620s and 1630s he led raids against Jesuit missions in Paraguay and western Brazil, capturing or killing thousands of Indians. Financial pressures drove Portugal's D. João IV to induce Raposo to launch an expedition in search of silver and jewels but also to ascertain the limits of Portuguese America. His epic trip of 7,000 miles has been called the "greatest *bandeira* of the greatest *bandeirante*."[29] At the advanced age of fifty, Raposo left São Paulo in 1647 accompanied by Portuguese and Indian retainers. He went west on the Paraguay across the Chaco before going up the eastern Andes and travelling via the Guapai, Mamoré, then down the Madeira and Amazon rivers. So arduous was the trip that when Raposo finally returned to São Paulo in 1651, clothes in tatters, covered with mud, he had become so disfigured that his family failed to recognize him.[30] As a quest for mineral wealth, Raposo's expedition failed completely; but in generating geographical knowledge, he succeeded almost beyond measure. For the first time Europeans had knowledge of the navigability of the Rio Grande and its relationship to the Madeira and Amazon. Almost as important, the Portuguese at last realized the width of South America, most particularly between the Paraguay and the Andes.

Fernão Dias Pais personifies the Brazilians ready to lead *bandeiras* in search of wealth. Allegedly the richest man in São Paulo, Dias Pais had led numerous excursions into the frontier in search of human and mineral riches. As early as 1638 he offered to the government to seek out at his own cost the "emerald mines and mountains of silver" which were said to exist in the wilderness. Owing in part to his strong support of the new Portuguese monarchy, Dias Pais obtained royal permission and began what many consider the greatest of all the prospecting expeditions. Accompanied by several well known *bandeirantes* and a large number of Indians, Dias Pais left São Paulo in July 1674 on what would become a seven-year trek through south-central Brazil. The expedition ventured to the headwaters of the Rio das Velhas and down to the São Francisco river valley as far as Serra Frio. The expedition was plagued by difficulties from beginning to end. By the time Dias reached his major campsite on the Rio das Velhas he had "lost a great number of his explorers, and most of his slaves and Indians" from "diseases, hunger, and fighting." The years of fruitless search led his *mameluco* son, José Dias Pais, in an assassination plot against him in order to escape the rigors of the *sertão*. Although José was one of his favorite sons, Fernão Dias hanged him as an example.[31] Although the Serra Frio region would soon prove to possess huge quantities of alluvial gold, Dias Pais failed to discover mineral wealth of any kind. He died in the *sertão* along with a number of his few remaining companions. Nonetheless, his exploration held great importance. It furnished important knowledge about the entire Rio São Francisco valley area. In the 1690s and early decades of the eighteenth century, survivors of his expedition came to play decisive roles in opening up the gold-producing areas in the territory which would become known as Minas Gerais.

The second phase

Exploration through the Brazilian hinterland assumed a new dimension once the *bandeirantes* and other explorers discovered significant quantities of gold and diamonds. No longer did colonists simply voyage into the *sertão* and return to the towns they had left from. Incursions into the wilderness now went in concert with settlement. Pioneers brought cattle and industry with them by which they changed the topographical face of the frontier. Newcomers from Portugal and Brazil's coastal areas quickly displaced Paulistas from the original gold-producing regions. *Bandeirantes* then launched fresh expeditions into the Brazilian west to the frontiers of Mato Grosso and Goiás. There, after the discovery of new mineral strikes became known, the settlement process that had occurred in Minas repeated itself on a smaller scale.

By the 1730s the true era of exploration had come to an end in Portuguese America. To be sure, much of Brazil remained unknown to

Europeans and colonists and would remain so well into the twentieth century. Ventures overland and over water into the interior continued as individuals persisted in their quest for mineral treasure. But the heroic treks of discovery had essentially ended. Brazil's frontier increasingly appeared as a massive unoccupied expanse of territory rather than a alien milieu located at the edge of known civilization populated by mythological characters and holding unimaginable surprises for those venturing within its boundaries.

Although little controversy exists about the *Bandeirantes* efforts in defining Brazil's ultimate political boundaries, a necessary question remains to be answered. Were the *bandeirantes* heroic figures, the soul of the Brazilian nation, as early twentieth century historians and politicians often described them? Did the mixing of Indian, European, and later African races foreshadow the modern Brazilian?

Such an image clearly appealed to a number of competing ideological and political interests within Brazilian society. Ideas then current in Western culture about the racial superiority of Caucasian over non white races, as well as political problems within the Old Republic (1889-1930), strongly influenced the *bandeirantes'* heroic appearance. Because Brazil obviously had a mixed-race population, the Indian-Portuguese origin of the *bandeirantes* served as a counterpoint to pseudo-scientific concepts of European racial superiority. Here, Brazilians could claim, stood a group of adventurers whose exploits compared with any found in the annals of western exploration. The country's newly created republican government, moreover, found the *bandeirante* hero valuable in its search for symbols of national unity. Proponents of such an image maintained that the *bandeirantes* represented a pioneering spirit which continued in the hearts of modern Brazilians. In the search for riches, the *bandeirantes* brought civilization in their trail, and, like the American pioneers, created a continental nation. Paradoxically, the *bandeirantes* also became a symbol of regionalism, particularly in São Paulo, which unsuccessfully attempted to secede from the rest of Brazil in 1933.

Opponents of this popularized heroic image responded with a far different depiction of the historical *bandeirante*. Jesuits and other religious figures had, of course, long condemned *bandeirante* activity.[32] In the main, modern historians have continued their censure. Capistrano de Abreu stands as perhaps the most important of the early critics. His immensely influential works on colonial Brazil undermined the moral ground beneath the *bandeirantes'* changed image by emphasizing their role in Indian slaving, especially in their devastating of Jesuit missions.[33] Clodomir Vianna Moog unflatteringly compared

Brazilian and American frontiersmen, characterizing the *bandeirantes* as predators who created little positive in their wilderness odysseys.[34] Most recently, John Hemming has produced a succession of works that detect no redeeming virtues whatsoever among the *bandeirantes*. Hemming characterizes the entire experience of Indian-European encounters in virtually genocidal terms.[35]. Yet as unfashionable as it might sound, it is important to point out that Brazil before the arrival of Europeans was hardly an Arcadian paradise. Native tribes warred against each other on a constant basis. Much of the permanent population destruction came not from any unique cruelties on the part of the *bandeirantes* or other Portuguese, but from the European and African diseases they unwittingly carried with them which did far more damage to native culture than the Paulistas ever did.

The quincentennial commemoration of Christopher Columbus's 1492 landfall will undoubtedly have created a wider general awareness (and hopefully appreciation) of the Portuguese role in Europe's exploration of the wider world. Celebrating the quincentenary has already generated passionate polemics over the European arrival in the Western Hemisphere and the consequences for the peoples and cultures they found here. To be sure, the *bandeirantes* lacked the loftier motivations found among missionaries and those Portuguese and other European explorers who left their homes out of an intense curiosity about the wider world. Nonetheless, the character of their travails was undeniably valiant, and the scope of their discoveries genuinely valorous. Accordingly, they fully belong among the other pathfinders who voyaged out in the great European reconnaissance.

Bill M. Donovan

Notes

[1] Janaína Amado, "Myths in the Making; Conquering the West in the United States and in Brazil," Paper presented at the 1992 Annual Meeting of the Organization of American Historians, 11-12 for the meaning of *Sertão*. I would like to thank Dra. Amado for kindly letting me borrow her paper.

[2] Frei Vincente do Salvador, *História do Brasil, 1500-1627*, 6th ed. Revised by Capistrano de Abreu, Rodolfo Garcia, and Venâncio Willeke (São Paulo: Edicões Melhoramentos).

[3] For the question of the intellectual reaction to the discoveries see, J.S. da Silva Dias, *Os Descobrimentos e a Problemática Cultural do Século XVI*, Lisbon: Editorial Presença, 1983, and J.H. Elliot, *The Old World and the New, 1492-1650* (Cambridge: Cambridge U. Press, 1970).

[4] One of the most fascinating of those earliest adventurers was the Portuguese Aleixo Garcia, who, with Indian allies, actually invaded the Inca empire years before Pizarro. For a brief sketch of Garcia, see, Charles E. Nowell, "Aleixo Garcia and the White King," *Hispanic American Historical Review* 24:4 (Nov. 1946), 450-66.

[5] H.B. Johnson, "Portuguese Settlement, 1500-1580" in *The Cambridge History of Latin America* 5 vols. (Cambridge U. Press, 1984), I, 253-86, is the best recent summary on Brazil's early colonization. The Bibliographical essay found on pages 588-93 cite all the relevant Portuguese and English literature. Bailey W. Diffie and George D. Winius, *Foundations of the Portuguese Empire 1415-1580* (Minneapolis: Univ. of Minnesota Press, 1977), admirably puts Brazil's early colonization into its imperial context.

[6] Sending criminals, gypsies, and other undesirables to the colonies came to be a common feature of Portugal's empire policy. Brazil in particular became popularly known as being populated by criminals. In a 1546 letter to the king, Duarte Coelho, the donatary captain of Pernambuco, sharply complained of the practice. See, Duarte Coelho, *Cartas de Duarte Coelho a El Rei*, ed. by José António Gonsalves de Mello e Cleonir Xavier de Albuquerque (Recife: Imprensa Universitária, 1967). Carta de 29 de Dezembro de 1546. 49-52.

[7] J.F. de Almeida Prado, *Los Primeiros Provoadores do Brasil*, São Paulo: Companhia Editora Nacional, 1961.

[8] Pero Vaz de Caminha, "The Letter of Vaz de Caminha," in *The Voyage of Pedro Álvares Cabral to Brasil and India, from Contemporary Documents and Narratives* translated and edited by William B. Greenlee (London: Hakluyt Society, 1938), 10.

[9] Francis A. Dutra, "Duarte Coelho Pereira, First Lord-Proprietor, of Pernambuco: the Beginning of a Dynasty," *The Americas* 29:4 (April 1973), 415-41.

[10] H.B. Johnson, "The Donatary Captaincy in Perspective: Portuguese Background to the Settlement of Brazil," *The Hispanic American Historical Review* 52:2 (May 1972), 203-14 is the best statement on the feudal and capitalist aspects of the donatarial captaincies.

[11] Stuart Schwartz, *Sugar Plantations in the Formation of Brazilian Society, 1550-1835* (Cambridge: The U. Press, 1985) is the best study in any language on the history of sugar in Brazil.

[12] Stuart Schwartz, "Indian Labor and New World Plantations: European Demands and Indian Responses in Northeastern Brazil." *American Historical Review* 83:3 (June 1978), 43-79.

[13] John Hemming, *Red Gold: The Conquest of the Brazilian Indians* (Cambridge, Mass., 1978), is currently the most comprehensive source for Indian-Portuguese relations.

[14] Quoted from *Monumenta Brasiliae*, 5 vols. by Serafim Leite, Rome, Archivum Romanum Societatis Iesu, 1956-1960, vol. 4, 373.

[15] Frei Vincente do Salvador, *História do Brasil, 1500-1627*, Livro II, especially pp. 111-13.

[16] Ambrósio Fernandes Brandão, *Diálogos das Grandezas do Brasil*, (1618). Translated as *Dialogues of the Great Things of Brazil*. Translated and annotated by Frederick Holden Hall, William F. Harrison, and Dorothy Winters Welker (Albuquerque, New Mexico: U. of New Mexico Press, 1987), Dialogue II, 107; Pero de Magalhães, *História da Província da Santa Cruz* (1576). Translated as *The Histories of Brazil* by John B. Stetson, Jr., Cortez Society, (NY: 1922), 165; William M. Donovan, *The Native Population of the Americas in 1492*, 2nd ed., Madison, Wis.: The U. of Wisconsin Press, 1992. 211 *et passim*.

[17] Fernão Cardim, *Tratados da Terra e Gente do Brasil* edited by Baptista Caetano, Capistrano de Abreu, and Rodolfo Garcia (São Paulo: Livraria Itatiaia Editora, 1980), 101.

[18] Population figures for the sixteenth century come from a handful of contemporary estimates. Most of these have been summarized by H.B. Johnson, "The Settlement of Brazil, 1500-1800," Table 1, Colonial Brazil: White Population and Engenhos, 1570 and c. 1585. How quickly the colony grew may be gleamed by these figures with those found in the "Rezão do Estado do Brasil, 1612" edited by Engel Sluiter, in *The Hispanic American Historical Review* 24:4 (Nov. 1949), 518-62.

[19] Although the Jesuits established missions in the frontier, their activities can not properly be called exploration and hence will not be dealt with here. The standard source for Jesuit missionary activity remains, Serafim Leite, *História da Companhia de Jesus no Brasil*, 10 vols. (Lisbon-Rio de Janeiro, 1938-1950). See Hemming, *Red Gold*, is the most recent detailed account of Jesuit missionary activity.

[20] A substantial bibliography exists on the *bandeirantes*. Surprisingly, however, little in the way of new work has appeared in recent years. Richard Morse, editor, *The* Bandeirantes: *The Historical Role of the Brazilian Pathfinders* (New York: Knopf, 1965), provides translated excerpts from many of the important studies. His bibliographic essay, while dated, remains useful. See also the bibliographic essays in the *Cambridge History of Latin America*, Vols. I & II, collected in *Colonial Brazil*, (Cambridge: The University Press, 1987) edited by Leslie Bethell. The most original recent studies involving *bandeirantes* are, John Monteiro "São Paulo in the Seventeenth Century: Economy and Society," 1985 unpublished PhD. Thesis, U. of Chicago, and Janaína Amado, "Myths in the Making."

[21] Yet a market for Indian slaves continued into the eighteenth century.

[22] John Monteiro persuasively argues this theme in his, "São Paulo in the Seventeenth Century." Monteiro's thesis is the most original contribution to the topic in the last three decades and deserves to be published.

[23] Quoted from Monteiro, "São Paulo," 227-28.

[24] *Inventários e Testamentos* 48 vols. to date (São Paulo: Arquivo do Estado, 1920-). See for example, the estate of António Pedrozo de Alvarenga probated in 1643, vol. 44, 49-75. The extreme poverty of the Paulistas is the major theme of José de Alcântara Machado, *Vida e Morte do Bandeirante*, São Paulo: Livraria Martins Editora, 1965. For a point of comparison see the description of peasant life found in Natalie Z. Davis, *The Return of Martin Guerre*, Cambridge, Mass.: Harvard U. Press, 1983.

[25] The history of São Paulo's leading *bandeirante* families can be found in the work of an eighteenth-century writer, himself the descendant of *bandeirantes*. Pedro Taques de Almeida Paes Leme, *Nobiliarquia Paulistana Histórica e Genealógica* 3 vols. ed. by Alfonso de E. Taunay (5th ed., São Paulo: Livraria Itatiaia Editora, 1980).

[26] Manoel S. Cardozo, "The Last Adventure of Fernão Dias Pais (1674-1681)," *The Hispanic American Historical Review* 26:4 (November 1946), 467-79.

[27] Jaime Cortesão, ed. *Jesuitas e Bandeirantes no Itatim (1596-1760)* (Rio de Janeiro: Biblioteca Nacional, 1952), 45.

[28] *Hakluytus Posthumus* or *Purchas His Pilgrims*, Hakluyt Society, Extra Series vol. XXIX. (Glasgow, 1906), 213.

[29] Jaime Cortesão, "A maior bandeira do maior bandeirante," *Revista de História* 22:45 (1961), 3-45. An excerpt from this article appears in *The* Bandeirantes: *The Historical Role of the Brazilian Pathfinders*, ed. Richard Morse, (New York, 1965), 100-13.

[30] Jaime Cortesão, *Rapôso Tavares e a formação territorial do Brasil*. Rio de Janeiro: Ministério da Educação e Cultura, 1958; "que foi desconhecida por sua família e parentes," 386.

[31] Pedro Taques de Almeida, *Nobiliarquia Paulistana*, vol. III, 68-69.

[32] António Vieira, SJ, was the most famous proponent of Indian rights. His criticism of the *bandeirantes* can be found in the *Cartas do Padre António Vieira*, 3 vols. ed. João Lúcio de Azevedo, (Coimbra, 1925-28) and *António Vieira: Obras Escolhidas*, 12 vols. ed. António Sérgio and Hernâni Cidade, especially volume 5. C. R. Boxer has written the standard biography of Vieira, *A Great Luso-Brazilian Figure, Padre António Vieira, SJ, 1608-1697*, (London, 1957). Richard Morse has translated excerpts from other missionaries in *Bandeirantes*, chapter four.

[33] João Capistrano de Abreu, *Caminhos antigos e povamento de Brasil*, (Rio de Janeiro, 1930) and *Capítulos de história colonial*, 5th ed. (Rio de Janeiro, 1969).

[34] Clodomir Vianna Moog, *Bandeirantes e pioneiros, paralelo entre duas culturas* (4th ed., Rio de Janeiro: Editora Globo, 1957), translated as Bandeirantes *and Pioneers* (New York: Knopf, 1964). Janaía Amado, "Myths in the Making," is by far the best comparative study of the frontier in the United States and Brazil yet written.

[35] See for example, *Red Gold: The Conquest of the Brazilian Indians, 1500-1760*, (Cambridge, Mass.: Harvard U. Press, 1978); "Indians and the frontier," in *The Cambridge History of Latin America*, 5 vols. (London: Cambridge U. Press, 1984) vol. 2; and, *Amazon Frontier: The Defeat of the Brazilian Indians*, (Cambridge, Mass.: Harvard U. Press, 1987).

Shadow Empire in the Bay of Bengal

When it came to innovating ad hoc imperial structures in what the late John H. Parry called "The Age of Reconnaissance," no European power could hold a candle to Portugal. It had one arrangement for the Atlantic islands, a modification of this pattern for Brazil; then it had another scheme for the African west coast and a different one for the *Estado da India Oriental* (which included the African east coast). Finally, its relations with Macau and the Portuguese stations in Japan were again unique. Thus it did not surprise me particularly when I discovered in 1983 that besides all these systems, there existed yet another variant which nobody had drawn attention to--one which fell somewhere between semi-rule and no rule at all.

This was in the Bay of Bengal, and I only became aware of its special nature little by little. First, I read of runaway *soldados* from Goa escaping to that region in the *Reformação da Milícia e Governo do Estado da India Oriental*, of Francisco Rodrigues de Silveira, while writing a paper on him for the Second International Seminar on Indo-Portuguese History. Later I visited Mylapore and became interested in the Indian east coast. Slowly I began piecing the remarkable story together of how Portuguese presence in the entire bay area must be classified as a separate Portuguese colonial genus, in effect a "shadow empire." It represented neither official initiative nor an extension of royal power to any great degree, but did extend Portuguese commercial, cultural and religious influence in an informal way.

The Portuguese "shadow empire" in the region was neither conquered nor financed by Goa or Lisbon, but settled peacefully by migrant individuals, mostly *casados* – soldiers married and retired from active service – and fugitives. Then its few officers did not follow the usual pattern of salaried, three-year nominations, but were unsalaried and named for irregular terms, sometimes even for life. There was no convoy or port duty system, and in almost all instances, its inhabitants did almost exactly as they pleased at all times. Indeed, for years on end, the most important city, São Thomé de Meliapur, or Mylapore, had no captain at all. The colonial inhabitants' only really infallible ties were with the Catholic Church and the Portuguese *Padroado*, the royal responsibility for the church and its missions within the area of the papal donation.

It is this informal empire that I wish to explore in the following pages. I will suggest how and why the Portuguese presence evolved – or at least how I think it did – how it declined (or perhaps rather how it adapted to circumstance) and what its governmental, religious and commercial parameters were. This article is in effect an update of one I wrote for *Itinerário*, 1983:2. It appeared in the early days of that journal when few libraries subscribed to it; hence copies are extremely hard to locate. Then, as I only later discovered, the Portuguese trading operations in Bengal did not come to quite such an abrupt end as I had believed. As a result, I would like to modify some of my conclusions in the light of subsequent research.

One might alternatively term what I am about to describe the "Bengali Portuguese Presence" to distinguish it from the rest of the *Estado da India Oriental*, for I notice that most maps label as the Bay of Bengal the whole body of water between Nagapattinam on the Indian east coast to Rangoon in Burma, near the site of the old Portuguese fort at Syriam. These places were at the "shadow empire's" extreme limits, while its capital, if it had one, was São Thomé de Meliapur. The sites of other major settlements arced up the coast through Pulicat and Masulipatnam to the Hughli area and then descended again to Pegu. Of these areas, São Thomé probably held the single greatest number of people, while the greatest concentration of hamlets was in and around Hughli – some forty in number.

The heyday of these communities was from around 1570 to 1610, and it corresponds closely with that of the private trading in the *Estado's* west coast heartland, and probably not coincidentally. The private trading on the west coast was carried on by a mixture of Hindu *vanias* and other traders and Portuguese *casado* families, themselves of mixed European and Indian ancestry after the first generation – and thus a part of the general trading picture. Seeing that both Gujarati and Konkani traders traditionally had close trading links, both in cotton cloth and foodstuffs, with Coromandel and Bengal,[1] and that

Goa initially derived much of its foodstuffs from there, it is more than likely that both groups of merchants on the east and west coasts shared in a related and even integrated prosperity. Moreover, Bengal had close ties with Malacca, even before the Portuguese captured that town, and no doubt at least some of the Portuguese emigrants to Bengal seem to have come from there and not from the Portuguese west coast. Much of their trade must have been with that emporium and not with Goa and its satellites on the Arabian Sea.

Semi-official origins

In the beginning, probably the most attractive single thing for the Portuguese about this region on the far side of the Cape of Comorin was the legend of Saint Thomas the Apostle. The quest for Eastern Christians – to borrow a title and phrase from Francis Rogers – was at least as great a magnet for the wide-ranging Portuguese of the discovery era as was trade. As early as 1501, in his letter to the Catholic kings, D. Manuel I wrote them that Pedro Álvares Cabral had sent him "definite information": the sepulchre of St. Thomas was to be found " on the sea coast, in a city which is called Maliapor, of a small population; and he brought me earth from his tomb."[2] By 1507, according to the chronicler, Gaspar Corrêa, Viceroy D. Francisco de Almeida had already sent out a small expedition from Cochin to the east coast of India, with the dual object of discovering the tomb and investigating trade possibilities.[3] But D. Francisco seems to have had too many other things on his mind to act upon the information brought him, though Corrêa says he did report it to Lisbon and it seems to have formed the basis for Duarte Barbosa's description of 1516. Diogo Lopes de Sequeira, who first appeared in Asia en route to Malacca in 1509, also bore instructions in his *regimento* to search for Mylapore.

No further contact appears to have been made, though, until 1517, when a second group of explorers, six in number and travelling in a native vessel, not only found what they believed to be the "*Casa de São Thomé*," the dwelling of St. Thomas, but wrote a letter from it, describing it first hand and giving a new rendition of the legend that the saint had been killed by an arrow on a hill six leagues distant. His bones lay buried in a chapel which formed part of the "*Casa*."[4] The hamlet Mylapore was reported as being adjacent to the dwelling, but the writer, one Manuel Gomes, does not say whether it was presently Christian or Hindu.

While the six men were actually on their way from nearby Pulicat, where it appears that other, nameless Portuguese had already established themselves, the discovery of the long sought-after shrine easily distinguished Mylapore as the preferred place for future settlement. At the same time, or nearly so, another development occurred which favored trade with the already established Portuguese cities on the Malabar and Kanarese coasts. In 1522, the Governor D. Duarte de Meneses named one Manuel de Frias as *feitor da costa do Coromandel*, i.e. business agent of the Coromandel coast, with the idea that he might organize the provision of rice and other commodities from that region for Goa.[5] This all formed a neat conjuncture of God and Mammon, and thenceforward, São Thomé de Meliapor was on its way. Only the next year, in 1523, D. Duarte dispatched a ship with a skilled mason on board and materials for the repair of the tumbledown " house" of the apostle. In the course of excavations, three skeletons were found, one with a spear next to it, which seemed to corroborate earlier legends of St. Thomas's interment.[6] Thus, the finding of the actual relics, or at least the supposed ones, did nothing at all to discourage an already promising situation. It was not long thereafter that a *capitão de Coromandel* was named, with authority over the navigations of the entire Bay of Bengal.

São Thomé grew rapidly during the 1530s, despite citizens' complaints that the captains were too youthful (the post no doubt being considered minor) and only interested in becoming rich.[7] The chronicler, Gaspar Corrêa, passed through on two occasions, in 1531 and 1534, and was amazed to find that all the city's plans for expansion had been realized in so short a time, with empty spaces within the wall becoming "noble streets and rows of houses."[8] In 1537, São Thomé was said to have some fifty households, while seven years later, St. Francis Xavier estimated the number of *casados*, presumably each with a ménage of some sort, at one hundred.[9]

The colonists assert themselves

In 1540, São Thomé appears to have had a narrow escape, one that can most likely be attributed to the plucky attitude of its citizenry. For while the fortresses and towns of the west coast may have been held tightly in reign by the governors or viceroys and their captains, the city of the Apostle Thomas was not about to allow itself to be mismanaged by an avaricious set of whippersnappers bent only on its exploitation. A citizens' letter of 1537 was in fact written directly to none other than the king, D. João III himself, with a plea that a permanent captain be appointed from among their own number, one who would have their own interests at heart. It must have taken about three years for word of this insubordination to have worked its way back to Goa – and when it did, the punishment must have been instantaneous. The viceroy, the irascible D. Garcia de Noronha, seems to have lost hardly a moment in commanding his Captain of Coromandel, Manuel da Gama, to close out the whole operation and bring the Portuguese inhabitants, together with the holy relics, presumably, to the west coast – where they could be kept under thumb.[10] Da Gama indeed seems to have carried out the deportation in part, but Noronha soon sickened and died, apparently sparing both Da Gama and the settlers further inconvenience. Thereafter, the settlers seem to have won their case in part, because São Thomé got its own appointed captain after 1542, or thereabouts, and despite a few bad ones, most appear to have been content to live and let live, being increasingly nominated from among old India hands who sought mostly a pleasant place to retire. A report on Portuguese India compiled for King Philip II and I after 1580 said as much, and the fact that the post was unpaid, did not follow the usual three-year term, and seems frequently to have been vacant, substantiates this. The only other official at São Thomé, also unpaid, seems to have been a scribe.[11] One can only conclude that the government at Goa finally decided that further pestering of the distant Portuguese settlers was not worth the expense and trouble.

There is every reason to believe that the settlers were not overly fond of viceregal central authority. The memorialist-soldier, Francisco Rodrigues de Silveira, reported in his previously-mentioned manuscript, the *Reformação*, that swindling and deliberate mistreatment of the *soldado*, or soldier, class in Goa was what had driven them to escape, especially to Coromandel and Bengal, and other documents imply that the *soldados* and *casados* who had taken refuge there were "criminals" (from the Goan point of view)[12] or simply "tired and worn out" (from their own).[13] All in all, there is every reason to believe that the compromise eventually reached between central authority and the settlers represented a neat balance between centripetal and centrifugal forces.

The role of the *Padroado*

Two factors must have worked together to keep the crown interested in the area. One was no doubt patronage. Having a place to send *fidalgos* (nobles) whose service entitled them to some sort of reward, even if more apparent than real, must always have seemed attractive to both Lisbon and Goa alike – and if one reads between the lines of the report to King Philip II as I just mentioned, one can perceive this.[14] The second factor was the *Padroado*, the Portuguese crown's control of the church in its hemisphere as accorded by the pope. Not only was the discovery of the supposed relics of St. Thomas the Apostle at Mylapore a powerful magnet in those times, but the discovery of the Thomas or Syriac Christians, plus other, immense missionary possibilities along the Coromandel Coast, acted as a spur for the regular clergy. So long as these were involved in the region, the crown had to maintain an active presence. Hence, even though the Portuguese colonists there displayed much of the independent pioneer spirit, the crown was not about to leave them entirely unsupervised and it continued to appoint officers with at least nominal jurisdiction. The colonists may have been quite willing to accept this if only because the local *nayaks* were of two minds about the Portuguese and sometimes threatened their existence in the areas.

In order to suggest how the missionary activity and the hostility of the Vijayanagari *nayaks*, or local governors, seem to have been interrelated, it might be appropriate to take a look at the growing Latin Catholic (as opposed to St. Thomas Christian) activities in the area. This will make it all the clearer why the Portuguese settlers in the area were perpetually in a state of insecurity, and indeed why throughout the entire bay area the "shadow" empire was always in danger from the inland side.

Not until 1539 did the regular orders become involved in the Coromandel area. Or perhaps one should say instead that nowhere in the *Estado da India Oriental* was missionary activity very successful until then. For after the great hope died down that India was already a great Christian nation and after the joy of finding at least a number of Thomas Christians there had begun to wear off, the clergy of the *Padroado* began to consider that their successes were limited to areas within Portuguese jurisdiction, and that their best means of converting Hindus were through intermarriage and material incentive. At the same time, they began to pay more missionary attention to the Thomas Christians themselves.

The St. Thomas Christians at the time of Portuguese establishment in south India were between 80,000 and 200,000 in number and were located mostly in coastal areas which wrapped around Cape Comorin, i.e., from about Mangalore and Cochin in Kerala up to above present-day Madras to Pulicat.[15] Their headquarters, if they can be said to have had any, was wherever their Syriac bishop happened to reside (then in Cochin), for the Thomas Christians had had contact from about the seventh century with the Syrian Christians of the Middle East and received their bishops from them (indeed some authorities believe the St. Thomas legend is no more than legend and that the whole indigenous Indian Christian population is wholly the result of Syrian – Armenian – missionary effort.

However this may have been, the St. Thomas communities were traditionally ruled through Syriac bishops, who until 1597 had the blessing of the Pope, and were thus Catholics not subject to the *Padroado*. Such in itself tended to irritate the adherents of the *Padroado*, who considered the independence of the Syriac church from it as something of an irregularity which ought to be corrected. At the same time, the Syriac administration and service to its Thomasine flocks was considered sloppy and even scandalous. The Latin dislike for the Syriac ritual aside, it was noticed that the St. Thomas clergy, too few in the first place, often sold the Sacraments, that parishioners were horribly ignorant about their faith, that nobody seems to have confessed or done penance, and that thousands of believers had never been baptised because their parents could not afford this luxury.[16] Hence it was that the Latin rite fathers of the Portuguese *Padroado* around Cochin began to devote their best efforts to the Thomas Christians.

Until the coming of the regular clergy to the Coromandel coast, not much in the way of missionary activity was undertaken either among the Hindus or the native Christians. In Mylapore, for instance, there seems to have been only one priest, a certain António Penteado, who managed to get himself appointed as keeper of the "Casa de São Thomé" through connections with the royal family, and had grandiose plans for building it into a monastery. But he was choleric, arrogant and ignorant, or so said his parishioners, and a visiting clergyman complained in the 1530s that he had not baptised a single Indian.[17] This all changed when the Franciscans arrived on the *Costa da Pescaria*, or Fishery Coast in 1538 and baptised perhaps as many as 20,000 Hindu *paravas*, or low caste fishermen.[18] In 1542 they were followed by none other than the Jesuit " Apostle of the Indies," St. Francis Xavier himself. Thereafter, the region became a target area for the two orders, to be joined toward the end of the century by the Augustinians. No doubt after their all-too-modest achievements on the Indian west coast, the east coast successes made it seem that there might be a fair chance to convert India after all, or at least the southern part of it, and at the same time to set the St. Thomas Christians right.

It is not certain whether the attacks the Portuguese settlers experienced periodically in their communities around the Bay were directly due to this proselytization or not. The Hindus of South India are still disturbed when a harijan community converts en masse to another religion, as some have recently been doing,[19] and it would hardly be surprising if this had also been the case four hundred years ago when missionaries began to make inroads. Moreover, the Portuguese, like the contemporary Spaniards in the Americas, regarded pagan temples as structures which virtually begged for treatment with crowbars and sledge hammers. Hence occasionally, even though they were present in the region on the suffrance of the Rajdom of Vijayanagar, they could not resist the holy impulse to pulverize a graven image or three while in the vicinity of some unguarded-looking shrine. Accordingly, the hostile actions of the *nayaks* seem to have depended on their feelings of pique, even though to the north and west, the Goan viceroy and their own raj were united in their struggle against a common enemy, the sultanates of Bijapur and Golconda.

In 1544, for instance, the Badagas, mercenaries of the local *nayak*, attacked the native Christians at Punikkayal, on the *Costa da Pescaria*, intimidating and robbing a number of them. And in 1559, Rama Raya, then briefly the Vijayanagari ruler, swooped down of São Thomé itself and carried off twenty-five of its citizens, along with the relics of the Apostle. The reasons for this incursion are not clear; perhaps it was in retaliation for damage done to temples, as some have alleged, or perhaps he merely needed the money.[20] At any rate, he returned both the captives and the bones after the community had paid a stiff ransom: 50,000 *pardaos*. Once more, in 1577, the *nayak* of Thanjavur angrily approached another Portuguese coastal settlement to the south, Nagappatinam, and threatened the 60 *casados*, 200 Eurasians and 3,000 Indian Christians there, scaring many of them into the available boats before he withdrew. And there were many other such incidents which kept both clergy and settlers in a state of uncertainty. This was no passing phenomenon, for ultimately, the Bengali Portuguese "empire" seems to have declined nearly as much from native Indian attacks as from Dutch and English ones.

Nagapattinam, which I just mentioned, was not far from the *Costa da Pescaria* and about three hundred kilometres south of Mylapore, and it seems to have been settled by the Portuguese almost as early as was the town of São Thomé. In this case, however, instead of being a mere hamlet when the Portuguese arrived, it was already well populated and possessed the best harbor on the entire coast. When the Portuguese settled there, between 1518 and 1530, they merely added their own quarter to the preexistent ones of the Hindus and the Moslems. There seems to have been a *capitão* there by the time Xavier arrived in 1545, and true to the east coast tradition, he also was unpaid.[21] Other coastal settlements, this time to the north of São Thomé, were, as already mentioned, at Pulicat and also at Masulipatam. But neither of these places seem to have had more than a dozen or two Portuguese families until late in the sixteenth century.

Once they had established themselves along the Coromandel coast, one can conjecture that the Portuguese *casados* and fugitive soldiers (who probably soon took wives and considered themselves as *"casados"* as well) opened trading with Bengal and the countries to the east, namely Arakan, Pegu and even Tenasserim, near present-day Thailand. Bengal and Coromandel were famous for their cotton cloths of all varieties and grades, while the countries on the eastern side of the Bay possessed a climate unfavorable for cotton growing and depended on India to supply them.[22] In return, the *casado* traders from Coromandel could obtain gemstones, silver and spices. Thus, the next logical places for Portuguese settlement were in those areas themselves where they had been doing business, though it is far from certain that all the Portuguese who settled in Bengal had first been in Coromandel. That Hindu merchants from the same Coromandel region had not completely preempted this trade is perhaps explained by what some regard as a growing Hindu tendency around 1500 to regard sea voyages as defiling, though there seem to have been many Hindu trading groups in exception. At any rate, the *casados* in Coromandel were in the best trading position, and the opening of Bengal to Portuguese residence provided a golden opportunity for those of them who had not struck permanent roots.

The Indo-Portuguese spread to Bengal and the east

By the second half of the sixteenth century, Bengal was far from a terra incognita for the Portuguese. Even from the days of Albuquerque and Duarte Barbosa, its rich trading potential in cloths, sugar, ginger and spices had been appreciated, but through the years, one expedition after another sent there by the viceroys and governors of Goa had become entrapped in the dangerous maelstrom of regional politics, where Moslems ruled a docile Hindu population and regularly practiced on one another the dirtiest tricks in the book.[23] One emissary, for instance, a certain Martim Afonso de Mello, sent out by Governor Nuno da Cunha from Goa in the mid-1530s, was cordially invited by the Sultan of Gaur, Mahmud Shah, to have dinner with him, then suddenly taken prisoner with his men. All attempts from Goa to free him failed. But when an even more treacherous ruler, Sher Shah, descended upon Gaur from the west and threatened his kingdom, Mahmud freed the Portuguese and enlisted their help. When this indeed proved useful, he rewarded them with charge of his customs houses at the mouths of the Ganges, principally at Satgaon. But then he himself was double-crossed by Sher Shah, with whom he thought he had made peace, and in the fight that followed, Mahmud lost his life. Of course, without his patronage, the customs concession at Satgaon proved nearly worthless, and most Portuguese drifted away.

What Goa and official expeditions had failed to accomplish earlier in the century, Portuguese traders did in 1579-1580. By then conditions were much more auspicious. The crooked Sher Shah was long no more and Akbar was ruling. Moreover, he desired a Bengali trading connection for the profit of his eastern dominions. When a suitably gentlemanly merchant captain, one Pedro Tavares, arrived to do business in the Hughli region, he was invited to visit the capital, then Fatehpur Sikri, and was given several interviews with the Great Mughal himself. Akbar took a liking to him, and Tavares returned to Bengal with *farman*, or patent, permitting him to found a city wherever in the region he liked, with full religious liberty to preach and to make converts. The result was the founding of Ugolim, or Hughli, on the banks of the river of the same name, not far from the site of the earlier customs house at Satgaon. Whether "Partab Bar," as the Mughals called Pedro Tavares, was a *fidalgo* and an ex-appointee of the crown administration in Goa or elsewhere is not known: Frei Sebastião Manrique, writing years later, merely calls him "a respectable man well-versed in politics and affairs of state."[24]

Pedro Tavares is known to have been named as Hughli's first captain, but how long he ruled is not known, or under what conditions from Goa. He and his successors governed with the aid of four assistants elected by the citizenry, and since the names of only three other captains seem to be connected with Hughli during the fifty or so years of its formal existence as a virtually self-governing entity within the Mughal empire, it might well be suspected that, like Nagapattinam and São Thomé, Hughli's chief officers did not follow the usual three-year term of service practiced on the west coast, but were rooted in the community. Certainly, the city did not appear to suffer under their oppression, but grew swiftly: by 1603, a visitor estimated its Portuguese inhabitants at 5000, and it had virtually eclipsed Satgaon, which was soon again in their hands. Just upriver, they founded a second community, Bandel, a few years later, and in 1599, the Augustinians built a large convent there, overlooking the Hughli River. The Jesuits were also active in mission work among the Bengali Hindu population. Increasingly, the Portuguese grew independent of the Mughal emperor, refusing his officials entrance to Hughli without permission and themselves levying taxes on Mughal vessels.[25] Sometime in the early XVII century, they even seem to have stopped paying their annual and rather small tribute to Agra. Yet, curiously, Hughli never seems to have had a real fortress.[26] It should also be noted here that Hughli and Bandel were not the only places in the debouchement of the Ganges where Portuguese established themselves; there were numerous other Indo-Portuguese settlements throughout the delta region, some probably amounting to no more than one or two families and their adherents. Probably none of these ever bothered to seek *farmans* from the authorities to legitimize their presences.

If Hughli took liberties with the rulers under which it operated, the Portuguese to the east and south along the coast were even more independent, if indeed "independent" is the word for it: they tried their hands at empire building and kingmaking. The same Mahmud Shah who had awarded the Portuguese the customs houses in Satgaon in the 1530s had given them another at Chittagong in East Bengal (presently in Bangla Desh) and there the Portuguese customs officers quietly remained in residence while Chittagong slowly grew. By about the 1590s, the Portuguese settlement there rivalled that of Hughli, though it was then subordinate to the King of Arakan, in present-day northern Burma. Relations with him were good until 1602.

Farther south, in Pegu, by that same year, 1602, two Portuguese traders-turned-soldiers-of-fortune, Salvador Ribeiro de Sousa and Felipe de Brito e Nicote, had helped the same King of Arakan, Selim Shah, in some of his campaigns. He rewarded them with customs houses and a fort; meanwhile, the Portuguese flocked to avail themselves of the new opportunities[27] and soon a Portuguese community rose around the new fort, built at a place called Syriam, near present-day Rangoon. One can gather that after one hundred years of residence in Asia, the original Portuguese *casados* had multiplied through their marriages with Indians into a *mestiço* people, though constantly augmented with new white stock from Europe via ex-*soldados* escaping from Goa.[28] There were enough of these floating – literally – merchants available to move in quickly where new possibilities presented themselves.[29]

But, by 1602, it would seem the whole "empire" had reached its zenith. Most of the trade of the entire Bay was in Portuguese hands, and it almost seemed as if the whole east coast might become theirs with a bit of derring-do and political manipulation. One contemporary Englishman, Samuel Purchas, foresaw this and remarks: "...here they might build their fleets and be furnished of sustenance, might send at any time to all places in the south (which in Goa cannot be done but with the Monsoons) and might cause that no ship of Moors should lade pepper, cinnamon or other commodities at Martavan, Reitav, Juncalao, Tanasserim and Queda for Surat or Mecca, but with custom [duty] from them and pass from them."[28]

A time of woes

Instead of achieving this, everything went wrong for the Bengali Portuguese in the next years and decades. Starting in 1602, the capture of the rich, 40 kilometres-long Sandwip Island by Portuguese adventurers from Chittagong caused the Arakanese ruler, the aforementioned Selim Shah to become suspicious that Brito e Nicote (who had nothing to do with it) might show himself to be equally ambitious. He besieged Syriam, while Brito e Nicote tried to raise help at Goa, offering Philip III and II the crown of Pegu. Then Selim attacked Sandwip twice, ultimately forcing the Portuguese to abandon it; meanwhile, he expelled them from Chittagong. In 1607, he murdered hundreds of Portuguese and their adherents who had settled – peacefully – another town within Arakan, Dianga (probably present-day Bunder). By 1604, the Mughals were also beginning to tire of Portuguese independent conduct and built a fort at Hughli to watch over them; instead, the Portuguese wiped it out. The Mughals, slow to anger, did nothing for the moment, but another king, that of Ava, whom Brito e Nicote really did offend, went on the warpath and ultimately ran Brito e Nicote to ground in 1613, impaling him above the entrance to his own fort at Syriam, just as help was on the way from Goa.[29] Then, in 1632, the Mughal, Shah Jahan, apparently was unable to tolerate Hughli any longer and gave orders to capture it, carrying off many of the besieged Portuguese to Agra, whence he later released them and allowed them to return.

But the bloom was off the Bengali "empire," anyway. About the same time, 1608, the Dutch and then the English appeared in the Bay, both settling at Masulipatam and the Dutch at Pulicat, whence the Dutch East India Company set out to sweep the Portuguese from the entire Bay through use of the same kind of pass system the Portuguese had earlier employed on the Indian west coast.[30] Then in 1640, the English planted their Fort St. George a mere dozen kilometers above São Thomé. Only one year later, the Portuguese at Nagapattinam, fearful of Dutch attacks hurriedly swore allegiance to the restored Portuguese monarch, D. João IV, and placed themselves under Goa's protection.[31] Meanwhile, beginning in 1642, São Thomé endured repeated blockades, sieges and plunderings for the remainder of the century.

Survival of the species?

Much additional research is needed in the archives of Portugal, of the Vatican and in the private correspondence of the Honourable East India Company servants at the Tamil Nadu Archives, Egmore, Madras, to determine exactly what happened thereafter to the "shadow empire." It is obvious, of course, that it did not survive all the various blows which rained down upon it in anything like its old glory. But the Portuguese presence does not appear by any means to have been annihilated. In fact there seem to have been two responses, one of the Indo-Portuguese personnel who had formerly served the entrepreneurs in minor capacities, and one of the shipowning and entrepreneurial classes themselves.

If São Thomé de Meliapur itself is any measure, the English at nearby Fort St. George quickly recognized the utility of attracting its residents as their employees – doubtless as stevedores, linguists, soldiers and indirectly as fishermen; even as the fort was being built, company officials offered free land within its walls to those Indo-Portuguese willing to settle there and work for them; before long a considerable community had accepted the offer. In 1642, the English even persuaded an itinerant French priest, Fr. Ephraim de Nevers, to reside there and act as their chaplain; moreover, the first church built there was Catholic and not Anglican.[32] Thereafter, the Indo-Portuguese served their English masters in every possible capacity, from soldiers and militiamen to punch-house keepers. I have not found widespread evidence for such symbiosis between the Indo-Portuguese and the Dutch at such an early date, among other reasons because the *Landmonsterrollen*, or muster rolls, of that company date only from the XVIII century. But if one considers that Goan officials were already accusing the Indo-Portuguese population at Pulicat of doing business with the Dutch enemy in 1622, it would not be surprising if many of the smaller fry among the Indo-Portuguese inhabitants of Masulipatam, Pulicat and other towns had enlisted with them almost at once, even though there is no indication that the Dutch were prepared to be as broad-minded in matters of religion.[33] At any rate, the V.O.C. rolls are full of Portuguese names in the XVIII century.[34]

What became of the Indo-Portuguese entrepreneurs themselves is another matter. Doubtlessly, some were ruined, some took to the bayous of the Hughli and became trader-pirates, and some went to Nagapattinam, continuing to trade in the teeth of the Dutch and English threats, moving after the Dutch captured that city in 1659 to another town nearby, Porto Novo, under the *nayaks* of Senji. Even though the Dutch managed to establish a factory there in 1680, they did not attempt to oust the Indo-Portuguese community, which remained, along with a medley of native trading groups. Moreover, the port's foreign presence was soon augmented by the presence of the English, Danish and Swedes.[35] It is also noteworthy that the Mughals in effect protected the Portuguese communities around Hughli and Bandel through their own policies of deliberately extending equal privileges to all Europeans within their territories while enforcing among them peace and obedience to their laws.[36] Thus the Portuguese were able to exist alongside their stronger enemies for at least the rest of the century, meanwhile maintaining their religion and forms of civil government.[37]

Then there exists another line of inquiry, one uncovered by Leiden University researchers into the Dutch and English companies in the Bay area. This suggests that at least some Portuguese entrepreneurs on the Coromandel coast went into partnership with the English company's servants, who were notorious for their "moonlighting" activities.

It should be recalled that the English and Portuguese were old allies in Europe, an alliance disturbed by the ascension of Philip II of Spain to the Portuguese throne as Philip I in 1580. While peace was made again in 1604 between England and Philip III and II, this did not automatically mean that the Honourable East India Company would follow suit – and in fact, it did not. But, just after the Portuguese *Restauração* of 1640, in 1642, a new peace was concluded between the English crown and D. João IV – and even before this time, the Honourable East India Company found it advantageous to cease hostilities with Goa, in the form of a non-aggression pact made with Goa in 1635. (Significantly, the V.O.C. did not, for it was just then engaged in a protracted battle with Goa over rich cinnamon lands in Ceylon, and it remained on a wartime footing with Portugal on and off for the next generation).

Almost immediately after the peace of 1642 between Portugal and England, V.O.C. commanders began to voice complaints that Portuguese ships were flying English flags and even carrying Englishmen on board in order to ward off their seizure under the Dutch pass-and-patrol system designed to suppress Portuguese competition with the Dutch company in the Bay region. One letter calling attention the practice, written in 1644 by the new Dutch gouverneur of Malacca, Jeremias van Vliet, warns that: "If we allow the English to conduct this back-and-forth trade, it would be an inwardly-eating cancer [for the Company]."[38]

While the V.O.C. integrated this "back and forth" or intra-Asian commerce as an important part of its total operations, the less tightly-organized English company was apparently unable to do so. In fact, in 1674, its directors gave up their last pretenses to profit from such operations and authorised its servants and factors resident in Asia to trade privately in all products of Asia – no doubt because these had already long preempted the profits from their "daytime" employers. It is therefore likely that what the Dutch were complaining about was not the official activities of their then much smaller British rival, but the artifices concocted by ingenious Englishmen to further their extracurricular activities. Merchants like João Pereira de Faria and Cosmo and Luís de Madeiros (or Madeira) and Lucas Luís de Oliveira soon moved from Nagapattinam or São Thomé to Fort St. George, where they became prominent "free merchants" and commanders of the militia; thereafter, until deep in the eighteenth century, there were always Portuguese names prominent among the city's trading community.[39]

Thus it was that by 1680 at least, if not long before, the Dutch East India Company directors had given up all hopes of reserving the intra-Asian trade for their organization – quite likely in the face of just such informal alliances between Englishmen and the old inhabitants of the "shadow empire." For in that year the V.O.C. directors wrote from Amsterdam: "The European competitors make it impossible for the Company to maintain this [monopoly] right, which we thought we had conquered from the Portuguese, employing their flags and servants, or else their passes, allowing them to appear as [English]. Because of the consequences, we dare not put a stop to it."[40]

These quotes might therefore suggest (even before all the letterbooks of the English private traders filed at the Tamil Nadu archives in Egmore, Madras, have been examined) that, adaptable as ever, the Indo-Portuguese merchants, or at least some of them, had found the means to remain in business. If so, one might also twist the idea another way around, and assert that the English private trading networks had in effect absorbed the old Portuguese Bengali country trade. In that case, then perhaps it would be appropriate to speak of an "Anglo-Portuguese Shadow Empire" – if indeed this is not drawing matters out to too fine a decimal place.

The "shadow empire" and the Mughals

One of the several puzzles involving the Indo-Portuguese migrants to Bengal involves their exact relationship to the Mughals. I have already spoken of Pedro Tavares and his visit, while the writings of Edward Maclagan and John Correia-Afonso, S.J. have done much to call attention to the relations between the Jesuits and the Mughal court. But there are many evidences of Portuguese presence in Agra which can be explained by neither Jesuit or other missionary activities, nor by the brief captivity of the prisoners from Hughli. Rather, they seem the result of the continual "leakage" of members of the *soldado* class from unsatisfactory conditions in Goa. This is mentioned either directly or indirectly by a variety of authors, including Corrêa and Diogo do Couto, but it is perhaps best explained by Francisco Rodrigues de Silveira, as alluded to earlier in this article. Silveira was a former soldier in India who turned memorialist after his return to Portugal in 1598, and it is his thesis that neglect and non-payment of soldiers' pay in Goa led to their desertion, especially, he says, to Bengal.[41] From his use of the term, it is probable that he means the area comprising the mouths of the Ganges and not that of the whole Bay.

Given the context in which he writes, it is clear that he is not speaking of *casados* who legally became merchants, but rather of those who merely "took off" for a different life, presumably, as the French visitor, François Pyrard reports, by evading surveillance at the various checkpoints between Goa and Bijapur, or as another writer, Jacques de Coutre suggests, by following the beaches between the palm groves.[42] While a few escapees seem to have had commerce as their goal, probably many more simply practiced what they knew best, or at least were presumed by the Indians to know: they took service as mercenaries with the various sultans of central and south India. We read about their more spectacular exploits in the accounts of Couto and Corrêa, among others.

Of course, through being the biggest and the richest, Agra was the most prominent among the capitals where the adventurers took service; it is known that after the Jesuits established themselves at Akbar's invitation in 1580, there came to be at least two parishes serving the Portuguese community, whose members seem to have represented all occupations – though one gathers that the principal one was still military service with the Mughal.[43] What role Agra played in the migration of *soldados* from Goa to Bengal, however, is not clear. It would seem logical that many of the Portuguese spoken of by Silveira had first been in the Mughal service before drifting on to Hughli – but of course this is only speculation and unsupported by any documentation I have yet encountered. The only certainty is that Portuguese, whether Portugal-born *reinóis* or Indo-Portuguese *mestiços*, lived in nearly all parts of India (not to speak of Arakan or Pegu) and managed to keep informed of one anothers' whereabouts. Hence, their passage from one place to another along the networks, in this case from Goa to Bengal, would hardly have been surprising.[44] One might also suspect that one reason the area around the debouchement of the Ganges was so full of (Indo-)Portuguese pirates is that some of these men were more used to arms than to shipments of salt or bolts of cloth – and that they were quicker to revert to force than were the (Indo-)Portuguese who had entered the region as traders via the maritime route.

The nature of the breed

The phenomenon of the independent, wandering Portuguese entrepreneurs is by no means confined to the Bay of Bengal, of course, for the early settlers of Macao and the discoverers of Japan appear to have been of exactly the same type. Moreover, it also existed in the Brazilian New World, if not in the Zambesi Valley of Africa. And it even recalls the French *coureurs des bois* of early North American expansion history. It is interesting that after 1580, the Philippine kings turned a blind eye to Portuguese trading activities in the Caribbean, and this sea was soon filled with what one imagines to have been the same sort of free-lance activity as in the Bay of Bengal;[45] in fact there is still a suburb of Havana which bears the name "Portugalete." And on land, the activities of the *bandeirantes* in Brazil and those of the *degredados* in Africa bear a suspicious resemblance to the same patterns.

Just what dynamics were behind these have received little attentions from historians, whose primary business it might not be, anyway; only the late Brazilian sociologist, Gilberto Freyre, has offered any partial explanation. He attributes the phenomenon, at least in Brazil, to a kind of hybrid vigor, the hybrid in this case being a mixture of Portuguese, Spanish, negroid and Amerindian strains. But he is wise enough to put some of the onus on experience and environment rather than on biology alone – which in most eyes would be enough to render his argument old-fashioned and unacceptable.[46]

For in its pure form, such a biological theory would not be taken seriously nowadays, save perhaps in that extra skin pigmentation may have provided some useful protection against a tropical sun. Rather, those sixteenth century Portuguese peasants who went to India or Brazil as soldiers or as plantation auxiliaries were hardy, full of folk wisdom (as Freyre himself asserts), and quite capable of surviving with only the barest trappings of civilization. Intermarriage with Indians or Amerindians would have produced children who had accrued knowledge from both cultures, but were completely accepted by neither.

Hence, I suspect that the largely *mestiço* Portuguese in the Bay of Bengal had to seek and follow their own opportunities, while using about as much of the formal Portuguese empire as they found advantageous – its priests, plus an occasional scribe or notary to facilitate their (testamentary) transmission of property. And they might have been willing to acknowledge a captain's authority once in a while if they thought this would help them against their enemies. (On the other hand, they appear to have had no sense of statecraft or diplomatics, and this may have cost them the terrible siege of Hughli in 1632.)[47]

It must have been Portuguese of just this sort that Garcia da Orta had in mind when he wrote: "It is true that the Portuguese are not very curious, nor good writers: they are more friends of action than of speech. They work to acquire through their lawful trading, but they do not treat the Indians badly..."[48]

In any case, these friends of action worked hard, and they made the Bay of Bengal their sphere of influence, indeed a shadow empire of Goa. But during all the intervening centuries, they have paid the price of non-recognition for their achievements. One great drawback of people who lack eloquence is that they do not gain credit half so quickly as those who loudly sing their own songs.

George D. Winius

Notes

[1] Duarte Barbosa, *Livro em que dá relação do que viu e ouviu no Oriente Duarte Barbosa*, ed. Augusto Reis Machado, (Lisbon: Agência Geral das Colónias, 1946), 190.

[2] William B. Greenlee, ed. & comp., *The Voyage of Pedro Álvares Cabral to Brazil and India* (London: The Hakluyt Society, 1938), 49.

[3] Gaspar Corrêa, *Lendas da India*, 4 vols: (Lisbon, 1858), I, 139.

[4] António da Silva Rego, ed. & comp., *Documentação para a história das missões do Padroado português*, 12 vols. (Lisbon: Agência Geral das Colónias Agência Geral do Ultramar, 1947-1958), I, 296-299.

[5] António da Silva Rego, *História das Missões do Padroado português do Oriente* I, 1500-1542 (only volume published) (Lisbon: Agência Geral das Colónias, 1949), 417.

[6] Francisco de Andrade, *Crónica do... Dom João III deste nome*, 4 vols. (Coimbra, 1795), I, 104-109.

[7] Silva Rego, *Documentação*, II, 249-55.

[8] Corrêa, *Lendas*, as cited in Silva Rego, *História das Missões*, 453.

[9] Silva Rego, *Documentação*, III, 165.

[10] Corrêa, *Lendas*, IV, 112 & 157.

[11] "Livro das Cidades e Fortalezas, etc." in *Studia* 6 (1960), fl. 56, located between pp. 352 & 353.

[12] Joaquim Heliodoro da Cunha Rivara, ed. & comp., *Archivo portuguez oriental*, 6 fascicules with supplements (Nova Goa, 1857-1875), fasc. 6, 1131.

[13] Silva Rego, *Documentação*, III, 252.

[14] "Livro das Cidades..." in *Studia* 6, fl. 56, and also section on Negapatão (Nagapattinam), fls. 54 & 55.

[15] Joseph Thekkadath, *History of Christianity in India. Volume II; From the Middle of the Sixteenth Century to the End of the Seventeenth Century (1542-1700)* (Bangalore: Theological Publications in India, 1982), 24.

[16] Thekkadath, *History of Christianity in India*, chapters 2 & 3; see also Silva Rego, *Documentação*, II, 178.

[17] Silva Rego, *Documentação*, II, 197, 356.

[18] Silva Rego, *História das Missões*, 369. In a lengthy quote from the usually reliable *Oriente Conquistado a Jesu Christo*, by Fr. Francisco de Sousa.

[19] Dick Kooiman, "Untouchability in India through the Missionary's Eye," *Itinerário*, 1983:1, 115.

[20] Thekkedath, *History of Christianity*, 201.

[21] "Livro das Cidades..." in *Studia* 6, fls. 54v & 55.

[22] "Livro das Cidades..."in *Studia* 6, fls. 83v-84; also, Barbosa, *Livro*, 184-187, and Garcia da Orta, *Colloquio dos simples e drogas da India*, ed. Conde de Ficalho, 2 vols. (Lisbon: Imprensa Nacional, 1891-1892), II, 30.

[23] An anonymous member of one of these, to Bengal and Burma, left an account which is reprinted with an analytical introduction and note apparatus by Geneviève Bouchon and Luís Felipe Thomaz (jt. eds.) as: *Voyage dans les deltas du Gange et de l'Irraouaddy, 1521* (Paris: Fondation Calouste Gulbenkian: Centre Culturel Portugais, 1988). The visit to the Sultan of Gaur nearly resulted in the loss of the emissaries' lives and resulted in no particular conclusion. It is interesting indeed that already in 1521, there were a number of Portuguese renegades in the region who had abjured Christianity.

[24] *Travels of Fray Sebastien Manrique, 1629-1643*, C. E. Luard and H. Hosten, eds., 2 vols. (London: The Hakluyt Society, 1926-1927), I, 34. It is possible that this was the same Pedro Tavares who traveled to Bengal, on mission there and to Tenasserim and Pegu in 1521. But it is not probable, since the Pedro Tavares mentioned in the anonymous document had to leave the mission because of grave illness; moreover, it would seem the Tavares family alternated the names "Pedro" and "Gonçalo" in every generation. But the Pedro Tavares who founded Hughli was undoubtedly of the same family. See Bouchon and Thomaz, *Voyage dans les deltas*, 78, 389.

²⁵ Joaquim José A. Campos, *History of the Portuguese in Bengal,* with introduction by B. P. Ambasthya (Patna: Janaki Prakashan, 1979. A reprint of the 1919 original), 58-59. It is a pioneering work, if one showing some of the defects of its 66-year age. Unless otherwise cited, all my information about Bengal has this as its source.

²⁶ Manuel de Abreu Mousinho, *Conquista de Pegu pelos Portugueses* (the *Breve discurso em que se conta a conquista do raino de Pegu,* 1617), with introduction by M. Lopes de Almeida (Barcelos: Portucalense Editora, 1936), passim.

²⁷ See Henry Davison Love, *Vestiges of Old Madras, 1640-1800;* 3 vols. (London: John Murray, 1913), II, 148. Other Europeans of the XVII century almost spoke of Portuguese and "*mestiços*" interchangeably. See, for instance, Fr. Norbert's comment on the same page, and I, 34-35 and 388.

²⁸ Quoted in Campos, *Portuguese in Bengal,* 21.

²⁹ See António Bocarro, *Década 13 da história da India,* 2 vols. (Lisbon, 1876), I, 153-159.

³⁰ There is not a great deal of literature on this; I have used the unpublished Leiden University M.A. thesis of M.P.M. Vink entitled: "Pascedullen en protectierechten; de V.O.C. als redistributieve onderneming in Malacca, 1641-1662," (1988).

³¹ On 3 December 1641. See *Documentos remetidos da India* (ms). Lisbon: Arquivo Nacional da Torre do Tombo, Livro 49, fl. 214.

³² Love, *Vestiges,* I, 34-35, 49, and 388; see also Thekkedath, *History of Christianity,* 205-207. The Dutch do not appear to have tolerated Catholic priests in settlements they controlled until the eighteenth century. It was only in 1754 that the Dutch East India Company granted the Indo-Portuguese of Nagapattinam two churches in the city "because the Company cannot do without the support of these people." See V.O.C. 2822, O.B.P. 1754, fls. 805-806, Algemeen Rijksarchief, The Hague.

³³ In 1622, D. António Manuel, in his capacity as the newly appointed *capitão de Coromandel,* reported that the Indo-Portuguese were actively trading with the Dutch at Pulicat and conducting themselves "so far from the interests of Your Majesty that it would almost seem they were not your vassals."The Indo-Portuguese inhabitants, he said, had even ruined any chance of a surprise attack on the town by tipping off the Dutch. See *Documentos remetidos da India, ou Livros das Monções,* 10 vols.-date (Lisbon: Academia Real das Ciências/Imprensa Nacional-Casa da Moeda: 1880-date), VIII (1977), 359. Many Portuguese inhabitants of São Thomé deserted to the Dutch during the V.O.C. blockade of 1642.

[34] Little has so far appeared on the subject. See the unpublished M. A. thesis of Mr. Paul 't Lam, Leiden University. It shows how extensive Indo-Portuguese participation was at a later date. It is entitled: "Indo-Portugees personnel van de V.O.C. Een onderzoek naar de aanwezigheid van Indo-Portugezen in dienst van de V.O.C. in Bengalen en Coromandel," (1989). See also, Frank Lequin, *Het personeel van de Verenigde OostIndische Compagnie in Azie in de achttiende eeuw, maar in het bijzonder in Bengalen,* 2 vols. (Leiden, 1982), I, 108.

[35] See the paper of Dr. Sanjay Subrahmanyam, "The South Coromandel Portuguese in the Late 17th Century: a Study of the Porto Novo-Nagapattinam Complex," presented to the IV International Seminar on Indo-Portuguese History, 11-16 Nov. 1985.

[36] The Mughals, who were not important traders in their own right and possessed no navies, were able to exercise indirect control of their seas through such *divide et impera* tactics.

[37] Books AA 41 & 42 of the Archivio Generale Agostiniano, Rome, illustrate that the Portuguese communities and their missions in Bengal still existed until at least 1714. See especially AA 41, fls. 83-92v and 143-145v.

[38] *Daghregister gehouden int Casteel Batavia, etc., 1643-1644,* H. T. Colenbrander, eds. (Gravenhage, 1899), 127. After the conclusion of their peace in 1642, the English helped alleviate the seasonal blockades of Goa by maintaining communications between the Portuguese settlements, especially Goa and Macau, but also other destinations.

[39] See Love, *Vestiges,* I, 154-156, 197, 433, 444; II, 496-97, among other citations.

[40] V.O.C. 1342, O.B.P. 1680, fl. 1521r & v, Algemeen Rijksarchief, The Hague.

[41] Francisco Rodrigues de Silveira, *Reformação da milícia e governo do Estado da India Oriental,* Add ms. 25:419, British Library, London, fl. 108.

[42] Jacques de Coutre, *Como Remediar o Estado da India?,* B. N. Teensma, ed., Intercontinenta no. 10 (Leiden: Leiden Centre for the History of European Expansion, 1989), 9.

[43] This emerges from Goa 34-I, fl. 226, Archivum Historicum S. I., Rome. See also, Alain Desoulières, "La communauté portugaise d'Agra," *Arquivos do Centro Cultural Português,* (Lisbon-Paris: Fundação Calouste Gulbenkian, 1986), 145-73, but especially 160.

[44] There is no mention in Rodrigues de Silveira of fugitive soldiers living in Coromandel, and so it would seem that they

descended to Bengal via the Jamuna and Ganges Rivers. They must therefore have passed through the Mughal territories to get there.

⁴⁵ Lewis Hanke, "The Portuguese in Spanish America, with Special Reference to the Villa Imperial de Potosí," *Revista de Historia de América*, 51 (1958): 1-48.

⁴⁶ See Gilberto Freyre, *New World in the Tropics; The Culture of Modern Brazil* (New York: Alfred A. Knopf, 1959) Chapter II.

⁴⁷ The Bengali Portuguese do not seem to have understood the importance of good diplomatic relations and protocol. See *Travels of Fray Sebastien Manrique*, II, 395-96. By neglecting to send a delegation to the accession of Prince Khurram to the Mughal throne as Shah Jahan, they may have raised his suspicions and antagonisms to the point where he effected his plans to besiege Hughli.

⁴⁸ Orta, *Colloquio*, II, 248.

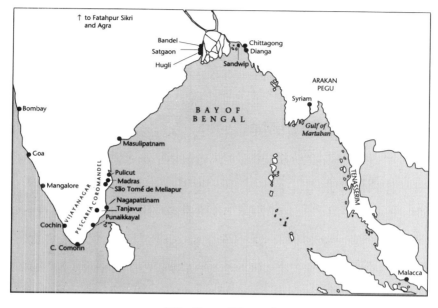

The Bay of Bengal

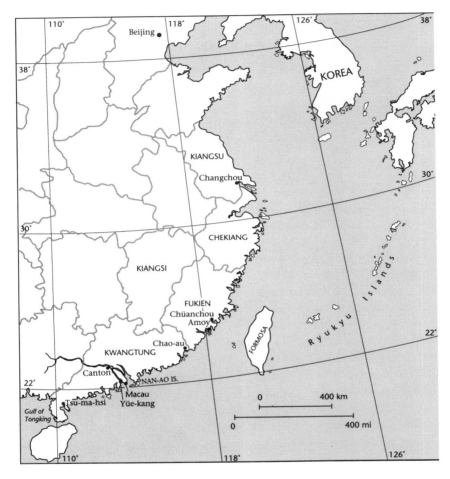

110°

Beijing ●

118°

126°

38°

38°

KOREA

30°

KIANGSU

Changchou

30°

CHEKIANG

KIANGSI

FUKIEN
Chüanchou
Amoy

Chao-au

KWANGTUNG

Canton

NAN-AO IS.

22°

Tsu-ma-hsi

Macau
Yüe-kang

Gulf of
Tongking

Ryukyu Islands

FORMOSA

22°

0   400 km

0   400 mi

110°

118°

126°

China

Ome of the remarkable coincidences in history is that Prince Henry the Navigator was almost a contemporary of Admiral Cheng Ho who, in the early fifteenth century, led gigantic Chinese fleets to Southeast Asia and into the Indian Ocean. In fact, there was a period in history during which the Chinese dominated certain parts of the Asian seas both as a commercial and a military power. In 1411 Ming troops landed on Ceylon, and a little later they intervened to settle an internal conflict on northwestern Sumatra.

Sino-foreign trade in those days was conducted either officially – Chinese government vessels sailed abroad and foreign tribute embassies came to China – or by private merchants. Private trade, though not allowed by the authorities in Ming China, mostly involved "coastal" and some overseas Chinese who, by the early fifteenth century, had already settled in various Southeast Asian places such as northern Java. This picture of two co-existing Chinese trade sectors, an official and a mostly illegal private one, changed in the 1430s when the Ming court decided to discontinue its maritime policy and to withdraw its fleets from Southeast Asia and the Indian Ocean. Hence, after about 1435 we mostly find foreign tribute vessels and illegal private traders sailing in the South China Sea.[1]

The reasons for China's withdrawal of the large government fleets are not yet fully understood and probably will always remain obscure because available documentation is extremely scarce. However, what we can be certain of is that there was no internal factor involved in this development; the Dutch caused much damage to the Portuguese

Sino-Portuguese Contacts to the Foundation of Macao

network of sea routes but Ming government trade was never challenged by an enemy from outside. Its downfall was brought about by internal factors such as cost considerations and the government's general re-orientation in external policies from the sea shore towards China's borders with North and Inner Asia.[2]

It is of course tempting to toy with the question of what might have happened to the Portuguese had the Ming continued to send armadas of one hundred or two hundred sail with a crew of some twenty to. thirty thousand into the Indian Ocean, had China continued to develop its naval technology and its firearms, some of which were aboard her ships, and had she maintained her official network of trade relations spanning from Malindi, Aden and Hormuz to Japan. Probably the Portuguese with their small flotillas and their immense logistical problems would have been halted somewhere in the Arabian Sea or the Bay of Bengal but, needless to say, that is pure speculation; history took a different path.

When the Portuguese captured Malacca in 1511, official Chinese navigation to Southeast Asia was already a matter of the distant past and it was the private Chinese merchants from the overseas Chinese "diaspora" or the coastal areas of Fukien and Kwangtung whom the Portuguese met. These private Chinese traders, disposing of richly laden junks, quickly aroused the interest of the Portuguese in exploring the possibilities of trading to China and it only took a short time until the Portuguese, aided by local pilots, began to search for the route to the Middle Kingdom of which they had heard so much. It is here that our chronological survey of Sino-Portuguese relations begins. We shall follow it up to the 1550s, or, to be more precise, to the point where Macao was founded.

The earliest evidence we have of the arrival of a Portuguese merchant in China refers to the years 1513-14 when Jorge Álvares reached a place called Tamão (T'un-men) somewhere in the Pearl River area. There is some disagreement as far as its precise location and the exact date of Álvares's arrival is concerned but this is of secondary importance.[3] What is more significant, is the news brought back by Álvares to Malacca a few months later: China, he informed, offered rich market opportunities but these could not be fully exploited because the country was closed; it would in fact be extremely difficult, if not impossible, for foreigners to set foot on Chinese soil. Trade could only be done on the offshore islands along the China coast, not in a major port, and it had to be done cautiously and clandestinely.[4]

The reason for this state of affairs on the China coast was that the old laws prohibiting private trade and a free exchange of goods were still valid and that foreigners wishing to trade in China "legally," could only do so by accepting the terms of the tribute-trade system. This implied a formal subordination by the tribute merchants – and their rulers in whose names they would come – to the Chinese emperor's "wise guidance" and "omnipotence." The Ming, mighty as they were, considered themselves superior to all others, physically, culturally and morally; they would not treat foreigners as equals. Such a constellation was new to the Portuguese who, when arriving in the Near East, India or Southeast Asia, had encountered a completely different situation.

Trade: a Chinese puzzle

The case of Ming-China was complicated indeed. In short, China's objection to free sea trade partly stemmed from the Peking government's fear that its coastal subjects might become too deeply involved in smuggling or even piracy endemic to the China Sea. It is also possible that some of the government officials and rich families in the north were concerned over the possibility that the south with all its fertile lands and fine urban centres might become too rich and thereby challenge the position of the north. But the laws and regulations issued to suppress private trade and to "streamline" the south, proved to be a move in the wrong direction. The coastal population depended on sea trade and with population pressure rising in many coastal areas, commercial activities had to continue to ensure the economic survival of these regions. This, however, the government refused to see; instead of removing the trade restrictions which were the chief cause of the malaise – of smuggling and piracy – it continued to fight the symptoms. The subtropical south, in its turn, became increasingly unwilling to accept the inadequate armchair decisions issued in frosty Peking. Quite logically then, the incidence of smuggling and piracy was on the rise. Moreover, some of the local officials and nobility in Fukien and elsewhere became involved in illegal matters as well – which angered the north even more. The local nobility did of course try to play its cards right and make use of its supporters in Peking but it only succeeded in a few cases.[5]

It was under these ill-omened conditions which were to last well into the second half of the sixteenth century that the Portuguese who had completely different ideas about trade and commerce, started their "Chinese adventure." They faced not only the difficulty of finding holes in the "Chinese wall" wide enough to get through, but also the fact that they had to consider every step of action so as not to be confused with "true" smugglers by the Chinese officials. Diplomacy was now required, not warfare – fortunately there were no or only very few Moors out in the China Sea –, and the temptations arising from the average *casado* or *fidalgo's* profit-maximizing instincts had to be carefully balanced against long-term interests in the Far East.

All this must have been exceptionally frustrating to the conquerors of Malacca as the following could not be overlooked: China, in spite of its institutional barriers, absorbed large quantities of Indonesian pepper, precious forest products such as sapanwood or sandalwood, tortoise-shell, medicinal substances, cloves, nutmeg, mace and other things; these commodities were brought by Chinese junks, ships from Japan and Southeast Asia as well as traders from the Ryukyu Islands who maintained an extended network of routes in the South China Sea and who frequently "sneaked in and out." It was even believed that China's import of certain tropical goods, whether legal or not, surpassed the total imports of these goods to India, the Near East and Europe. Moreover, it was reported that huge profits could be made in the China trade – three hundred percent on pepper alone – and, of course, the Portuguese would not want to miss the chance to win a share of this cake.[6]

Misunderstandings

What happened next was logical from the Portuguese point of view. In 1517, Fernão Peres de Andrade captained a small squadron which took Tomé Pires, a botanist, pharmacist and celebrated geographer, to China. Pires had been carefully selected by the Portuguese to undertake this mission – an official embassy to the Chinese court – and it was hoped that in spite of all the obstacles that existed, he would be able to negotiate an agreement which would allow the Portuguese to trade freely in China and perhaps even to set up a permanent base there. But the mission was an inauspicious one from the beginning. When Andrade's ships followed the Pearl River upstream, proceeding to Canton, they fired a roaring round of salute shots. The Chinese, frightened and upset, did not take this as a sign of respect but as a grave insult. The misunderstanding was quickly cleared up but the impression remained that the Portuguese, or the *"Fo-lang-chi"* as they were called by the Ming, were a most "warlike" and "uncivilised" species of "Southern Barbarians" (*Nan Man*). Nevertheless some trade was effected; one ship was even sent to the coast of Fukien, and Pires's request to be granted permission to travel north to Peking was "kindly" reviewed by the authorities. So far, things proceeded in an acceptable way but there was soon another dark cloud on the horizon.[7]

Fernão Peres de Andrade had already left China for Malacca when, in 1519, his brother Simão, a ruffian even by the standards of the time, made his appearance in the Pearl River estuary. Simão did not behave well and later sources, even Barros in his *Ásia*, accused this man of having committed various misdeeds and crimes. Among other things he is said to have sentenced to death a sailor on Tamão without asking the Chinese for their consent. He was also accused of having bought, enslaved and taken some Chinese youngsters to India. The Ming geographers, in utter ignorance of the fact that poor Chinese families often sold their children to the rich, grossly exaggerated this event and went as far as to accuse the Portuguese of having "roasted and eaten" them. This story, depicting the Portuguese as cannibalistic, is quoted in full in the *Shu-yü chou tzu lu* (1574) and was repeated over and over by historians of later generations.[8] Even in our times it appears to have contributed to anti-Portuguese sentiments among some of the Chinese Macao experts.[9] The fact, however, that shortly after the incident Pires was not prevented from leaving Canton for Peking, vaguely indicates that whatever Simão had done wrong, the true or alleged offenses may not have been so heinous in the eyes of the mandarins as was often thought. Nevertheless, the Chinese had some "evidence" at hand now of the "wickedness" of the Portuguese and, if needed, this "evidence" could be turned against them, the innocent Pires and his entourage.

Pires's voyage to the north has been described elsewhere and the Chinese sources were brilliantly analysed by Paul Pelliot and others. What probably harmed the Portuguese most was that an envoy of the expelled Malaccan ruler, the sultan Muhammed, had arrived in China at about the same time as Pires was on the road. This Malay embassy, needless to say, presented the Portuguese in the worst possible light, thereby hoping to gain China's assistance in ousting them from Malacca. The situation was further complicated by the ambiguous role of a certain Huo-ch'e Ya-san, probably a member of the Malay delegation, who appears to have misled and probably slandered the Portuguese on several occasions, and it was also complicated by the fact that the Chinese emperor died in 1521. Under these adverse conditions Pires's efforts to be granted an imperial audience and to present his case ended in failure. He was inappropriately refused and forced to go back to Canton.[10]

Upon his arrival in the southern metropolis things turned from bad to worse. Pires and some other Portuguese who had landed there in 1521 were jailed and their ships surrounded and blocked by Chinese war junks. The Chinese also made it clear that forthwith no Portuguese would be allowed to trade in China. Obviously the mandarins believed that this would stop the "*Fo-lang-chi*" from committing further "atrocities" and even motivate them to restore

Malacca to its former Islamic ruler. But the Portuguese were not as easy a match as the ill-prepared Cantonese had thought. Diogo Calvo and some of his countrymen, aided by Duarte Coelho who, in the meantime, had arrived from Malacca, broke through the Chinese lines and gunned their way out. This was the first major outbreak of open hostilities between both sides and, in fact, between China and a European power.

A second violent encounter occurred in 1522 when another Portuguese squadron arrived at the Pearl River estuary. The men on board at first tried their best to avoid hostilities hoping to be able to pursue some trade, but then were drawn into a full-scale battle in which they lost over forty men and two ships. Details concerning this battle vary in the sources, the only point of interest being that the Chinese side claims to have captured and presented some Portuguese artillery pieces to the authorities for inspection.[11]

The first few Sino-Portuguese encounters having ended in disaster and foreign trade proving a nuisance to many a mandarin, the officials soon decided to close Canton to *all* foreigners. No action to save Pires and his followers could now be undertaken, and the Portuguese decided for the time being to stay in Malacca and hope that conditions in China might improve one day and that trade might become possible in the future. There were also rumors that the Chinese would strengthen their coastal defenses and that they had plans to send a fleet and attack Malacca. While the first was true, in part at least, the latter remained street gossip; the golden days of China's navy were gone; no Ming government war fleet showed up in the Straits. The years that followed the initial period of Sino-Portuguese contacts were thus marked by tense disengagement on both sides with illegal Chinese traders and overseas Chinese probably being the chief carriers of information between the two. This situation prevailed into the late 1520s.

Contrabandistas

In the meantime, smuggling along the China coast continued. In the 1530s and 1540s these activities were particularly apparent in the islands off Kiangsu, Chekiang and Fukien – all to the north of Kwangtung – where trade prohibitions were often handled in a lax way. Of the few foreigners involved in illegal trade, the majority were Japanese but a handful of adventurous Portuguese also took part in it. These Portuguese certainly hoped that Fukien and Chekiang would offer better trade opportunities than Canton, but some evidence also points to a continuation of occasional Portuguese trade in the Pearl River region. In general however, very little is known about this period of Sino-Portuguese contacts and it is only through scattered and often contradictory references in written sources and on old maps that a general picture can be established of where the Portuguese went and what they did.

In Chekiang, to begin with, some Portuguese traded in a place which they called Liampo. This name was phonetically related to the name of a major port in the area, viz. Ningpo, which played a key role in Sino-Japanese relations. However, while Ningpo "proper" was on the mainland, Liampo, where Fernão Mendes Pinto claimed the Portuguese had founded a big settlement of their own, lay on one of the offshore islands – on Shuang-hsü-kang. Other places where the Portuguese met and traded under cover, were situated along the Fukien coast. These were Changchou, Tsou-ma-ch'i (or: -hsi) Ch'üanchou, Yüeh-kang and Amoy. Some trade was also done at Nan-ao, an island between Changchou and Swatou, along the coast of eastern Kwangtung, just at the border to Fukien. Other evidence points to traffic conducted by the Portuguese from Pahang on the Malayan peninsula to southern Fukien.[12] And of course, more is to be found in Mendes Pinto's account which, though semi-fiction, is still useful for the historian as it refers to a number of places along the China coast of which some at least have been identified.

It is also from this book that we know of the fantastic story of Coje Acem, a powerful pirate, whom, if Mendes Pinto is to be trusted, the Portuguese chased all across the eastern seas. This man may have had something to do with Huo-ch'e Ya-san but the phonetical similarity between both names may well be accidental. What is perhaps more important, is that Mendes Pinto clearly indicates that not all the Portuguese behaved well. There is, for example, the story of António de Faria, a freebooter by any degree, who is said to have plundered coastal areas and committed other acts of violence.[13] Supposing that there were more Portuguese in the East now than before, many of whom traded on their own without being adequately supervised by the authorities in Malacca which at that time were more interested in the Moluccas than in China anyway, it is likely that the number of Portuguese freebooters along the China coast had increased in comparison to the 1510s or 1520s. But, of course, there were others as well – those Portuguese who, with an eye for possible long term developments, would certainly try their best to act in a way that would make it plausible for the Chinese bureaucrats to distinguish them from "true" pirates.

One of the important developments in this period was that the Portuguese got in touch with Japan. It is not known when they first began to cooperate with merchants sailing to this easternmost country of the then-known world but it could have been in the late 1530s or in the early 1540s. Once again, it is Fernão Mendes Pinto whose name is associated with this event. In his book he claims to have been driven far off course by a tempest when travelling along the China coast, eventually landing on Tanegashima Island in 1542, thus "discovering" Japan for Portugal. As usual, such claims have to be interpreted with caution. It is possible, however, that illegal traders, "regular" Ryukyuan, or "regular" Japanese merchants introduced the Portuguese to the Japanese market and that some Portuguese had already sailed to Kyushu some time before Mendes Pinto.[14]

Japan, like China or Korea, demanded certain tropical commodities, and it also needed Chinese silk, in particular raw white silk and silk piece goods. Its exports consisted mostly of precious articles and of silver. Silver was particularly important; both domestic silver output and silver exports appear to have increased at around that time. This probably contributed to a growth in Japan's economic power and thereby to a rise in demand for certain imports. In other words, Japan as an expanding market became increasingly attractive, and the Portuguese would not want to miss a good opportunity to gain a share in the profitable, though mostly illegal China-Japan trade which centered on the exchange of silk for silver.

Japan's economic growth probably contributed to a general expansion of sea trade in the Far East – and thereby also to an increase in illegal activities along the coasts of Kiangsu, Chekiang and Fukien. Being faced with this unwanted development, the Chinese officials, instead of liberalizing trade by removing trade restrictions and thereby the most important cause of smuggling itself, once again opted for an even more rigorous suppression of maritime activities, hoping to exterminate piracy and smuggling once and forever. The chief representative of this policy was Chu Wan, Grand Coordinator (*hsün-fu*) and Military Superintendent (*t'i-tu chün-wu*) of Chekiang and also in charge of coastal defenses in Fukien. Chu decided to strike a series of deadly blows against the pirates and smugglers that had infested his province.[15] In 1548 one of his military leaders, Lu T'ang, wiped out the illegal trading base on Shuang-hsü-kang. According to Mendes Pinto, who wrongly dates this event to 1542, several thousand Christians were killed – among them 800 Portuguese! – and more than seventy ships destroyed. However, one Chinese source speaks of only 27 vessels, and that number is certainly more realistic than the numbers found in Mendes Pinto's inflated account of this disaster. It has to be assumed therefore that only a handful of Portuguese were involved in the Shuang-hsü-kang incident and that losses inflicted on them by the Chinese were far from being as grave as Mendes Pinto would have us believe.[16]

Several other clashes between government troops and smugglers or pirates occurred elsewhere, but only two warrant mentioning in the context of Sino-Portuguese relations. Both relate to southern Fukien: According to Chinese sources, a number of Portuguese were among a group of freebooters who attacked the coastal towns of Yüeh-kang and Wu-hsü, but together with the other attackers they were beaten back by the troops of K'o Ch'iao, the local defense commander. Shortly afterwards, in 1549, some "*Fo-lang-chi*" were involved in a raid against Chao-an near the Fukien-Kwangtung border. They were later trapped near Tsou-ma-ch'i and taken prisoner.

While Chu Wan could be satisfied with these and other victories, the local elite which depended on sea trade certainly was not – and sought for ways to remove Chu Wan from his post. This they achieved when, in the aftermath of the Tsou-ma-ch'i incident, some of the prisoners were executed, while the accusations and charges brought against them were found to be incorrect or grossly exaggerated. To the great relief of the local elite Chu Wan and his subordinates were now pronounced guilty of having proceeded unjustifiably and without the approval of the throne. K'o Ch'iao and Lu T'ang were put to death, many other officials who had favoured trade prohibition were discharged from public service, and Chu Wan, knowing that he had no chance to defend his case against the local merchant "mafia," committed suicide ahead of his executioner's arrival in Fukien.[17]

Japan and the return to Kwangtung

With the removal of many important "prohibitionists" from key positions in Fukien and Chekiang, trade restrictions there once again began to be treated in a relaxed way, and illegal trade revived. But the Portuguese, after nearly two decades of trade in that region, now obviously lost interest in Fukien and Chekiang and, once again, began to concentrate their activities on the Kwangtung coast. There are several possible reasons for their return to Kwangtung which marks the beginning of the next period of Sino-Portuguese contacts. One reason may have been that the Portuguese simply had enough of the unstable conditions in Fukien and Chekiang, a second, that fewer "true pirates" who would molest trade were to be found along the Kwangtung coast and that, if a new base could be established peacefully somewhere in the vicinity of the Pearl River estuary, the Malacca-Japan trade could proceed in more predictable ways. The express need to disassociate oneself from pirates was certainly less in the Kwangtung region than in Fukien or Chekiang and this, as we shall see, was to become an important factor in the long run.

It also has to be realized that while many ships sailed back and forth between Japan and Fukien/Chekiang, relatively few appear to have undertaken regular non-stop voyages between Japan and Kwangtung. Hence, chances of grasping a major share in the expanding China-Japan trade were definitely higher in the case of the Kwangtung-Japan traffic than in the case of the Chekiang/Fukien-Japan traffic. Though we do not possess accurate statistics, mid-sixteenth century imports of Japanese silver to the Chekiang-Fukien region probably surpassed imports to the Kwangtung region.[18] In addition to that, Kwangtung depended on Fukienese shipping and re-exports – to some extent at least. Needless to say, the implicit idea here is that China should not be perceived as one market but that it consisted of many "macro regions" – just like India – and that the Portuguese opted for the one region which promised to be most suitable to their endeavours; in the mid-sixteenth century this was Kwangtung and not Fukien or Chekiang.

São João and Lampacau

Thus, at a time when St. Francis Xavier was preaching in Japan and missionary activities had started to expand there, the Portuguese already had begun to use the large island of São João (Shang-ch'uan, St. John) as a trading base. São João, situated some seventy kilometres to the southwest of today's Macao, was considered a remote place by Chinese standards: almost uninhabited, and certainly less frequented by foreigners than Tamão where, during the 1530s, some Portuguese had traded as well. It lay at a respectable distance from major towns and Chinese war junks. In short, hibernating on São João posed few risks, some trade could be conducted on the side and there were almost no pirates in the area to bother the Portuguese. The crews of the first few *naus* sailing to Japan may have wintered there in the late 1540s and early 1550s, and even Mendes Pinto seems to have known the place well. Yet, it was not so much because of the trade between Malacca, China, and Japan that the name of São João was handed down from one generation to the next but rather because of the fact that Xavier had died there in 1552. A church was built on the island to commemorate his death and memories of this great representative of Catholic missionary work in Asia were kept alive in all major Portuguese places within the *Estado da Índia*.[19]

It is not exactly known when the Portuguese presence on São João ended but most likely it only lasted for a few more years after the mid-1550s. While São João was still in use, another place became popular as a trading base in the late 1540s or early 1550s. This was Lampacau (various other spellings, usually Lang-pai-kang in Chinese). The identification of Lampacau has caused much headache to sinologists and historians. Old Portuguese maps vaguely indicate that it was somewhere to the west of present day Macao but for many decades nothing precise could be said about its original location. It was only in recent times that additional references were found in Chinese sources which helped to solve the Lampacau puzzle. Taken together, these sources indicate that in the Ming period Lampacau existed as a separate island. Later the shallow waters surrounding its beaches became silted with sedimentary deposits from the West River and the island disappeared as such. According to Chang Tseng-hsin, it became linked to the neighbouring island of Lien-wan, and the name of the latter came to be used to designate the entire land mass of both islands while the name Lang-pai-ao was more and more restricted to designate a narrow sea passage between Lien-wan and another nearby island, Wen-wan. If true, this would mean that Lampacau was only about thirty kilometers away from Macao.[20]

When the Portuguese first used Lampacau, this island appears to have been completely uninhabited. Luís Fróis, well-known for his work on Japan, and other sources agree in reporting that the Portuguese would put up temporary lodgings there, store merchandise and await fair winds to depart for Malacca or Japan. When a big ship arrived in Lampacau, there were as many as 600 merchants or sailors on the island at one and the same time, as is indicated in a letter by Baltasar Gago.[21] It is not known from where these merchants would receive their victuals and supplies but probably most daily necessities were provided by the local farmers from the nearby mainland. It is also unclear what advantages lay in sailing to Lampacau instead of São João. One possible explanation could be that Lampacau was just at the mouth of one of the major branches of the West River and that by sending merchants upstream in lighters or other small river craft, access to the interior markets where silk could be obtained was easier than from São João which was rather isolated and far away from major river roads.

It is also important to note that when the Portuguese began to sail to São João and Lampacau, their trade between Malacca, China and Japan began to adopt more regular forms. At around 1550, or a little later, this trade was put under the control of a captain-major and it was often done with one big annual carrack instead of many small ships

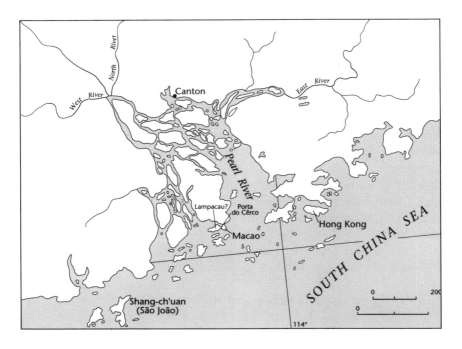

The Pearl River Delta

that would operate without reporting to Malacca or Goa. In a way, then, a concentration of commercial power took place under the guidance and supervision of an authorized person and this probably led to a natural decrease in the kind of free-lance adventurism that had characterized the 1530s and 1540s.

Leonel de Sousa

With the Malacca-Japan trade becoming more regular in this way, the Portuguese, in the eyes of the Chinese, certainly also gained more respect and became more predictable. Yet, while trade between Kwangtung and foreign countries was handled quite liberally since the 1530s and 1540s – it had been interdicted before, in the 1520s, as the reader will recall – trade with the Portuguese remained forbidden and, as before, had to be carried out clandestinely. In 1552, for example, one of the leading Portuguese captains, Leonel de Sousa, had sailed to the China coast without being able to call at the Chinese ports. But, with the Cantonese generally having become more friendly towards foreigners now, the Portuguese revived old hopes that one day permission might also be given to them to carry on their trade more freely. They therefore appear to have made greater efforts than before to refrain from any kind of violence and to prove that they were peaceful traders and had nothing in common with the various groups of pirates infesting the coast. It is possible, though not absolutely certain, that they even helped the Chinese in subduing some of the outlaws.

Be this as it may, Leonel de Sousa, who probably had a "firm grip" on his countrymen and who must have sensed that something could be moved in favour of the Portuguese at this hour, entered into negotiations with the local Chinese administration in 1553 or 1554. The details of these talks are not known but de Sousa eventually succeeded in coming to an agreement with the representatives of the Coastal Defense Commander. This agreement (1554) stipulated that the Portuguese, to their great relief and joy, would now be permitted to trade in Canton. China, after forty years of mutual misunderstandings, had finally opened her doors to the *Estado da Índia*, and all she demanded in return for the permission granted to her former enemies, was the regular payment of custom taxes.[22]

China's demand for taxes indicates that the Canton officials had indeed begun to assess the advantages of cooperation with the Portuguese more realistically than before. There were in fact many benefits that China could derive from this agreement. As already mentioned, Portugal's capacity to furnish certain tropical goods and spices, as well as Japanese silver would make the Cantonese less dependent on the Fukienese who controlled much of the coastal traffic and some of Canton's connections to other countries. Moreover, the agreement came at a time when the situation in Fukien, Chekiang and Kiangsu was about to get out of hand due to a continued rise in piratical attacks against the coastal areas there. It is impossible to assess to what extent this development endangered the Kwangtung-Fukien traffic and thereby the economic well-being of Canton and its environs but by cooperating with the Portuguese, who had excellent arms, the Kwangtung officials certainly took a precautionary step in the right direction: with piracy having already infected the Pearl River estuary, the presence of the Portuguese clearly was a psychological asset which could help to stop the disease from spreading as it had in neighbouring Fukien. Finally, by letting the Portuguese buy silk and sell silver on the Canton market, there would be benefits to the local producers, sales agents, farmers, etc.

Macao

But, of course, some problems remained with the 1554 agreement, the most serious being that no written contract between Leonel de Souza and the Chinese negotiators appears to have survived in the archives. Perhaps even, the agreement was only made orally and never put to paper. This and the fact that there is only very vague allusion to it in the Chinese sources, was used by Marxist historians as a pretext to charge the Portuguese "imperialists" with fraud and to doubt the authenticity of all the relevant Portuguese documentation collected by such authorities as J. M. Braga. Thus, the general tone of the many studies published by most authors from the People's Republic of China is that the Portuguese had "bribed their way in" and that Leonel de Souza and "his kind" had acted in defiance of all the laws and regulations which China had imposed on overseas trade and foreign relations.[23] The annoying as well as ridiculous part of such criticism is, of course, that these same historians, practically none of whom reads Portuguese, tend to portray Ming foreign policy as "suppressive" and "reactionary" while, as soon as the Portuguese and other Europeans are involved, they immediately side with the "prohibitionists" and "suppressors".

Notwithstanding, the 1554 agreement had definitely opened China's doors and during the next few years the Portuguese succeeded in opening them even wider. In short, somewhere in the mid-1550s, perhaps even a little earlier, they began to use the Macao peninsula as a base. Macao, usually written "Macau" in Portuguese, called "Ao-men" in Chinese, and already known to Pires under another Chinese name –

"Hao-ching" in Mandarin or "Hou-keng" in Cantonese –, was closer to the mouth of the Pearl River than either Lampacau or São João and had the advantage of being endowed with an excellent natural harbour, the so-called *Porto Interior*, on its western shore.[24] There were some fishermen, perhaps some Fukienese sailors and a few farmers on the peninsula but otherwise the Portuguese were by themselves. We do not know under what circumstances the Portuguese had been given permission to use Macao and even to settle there but some kind of official permission they must have obtained, since a ground rent had to be paid to the Chinese in return. Marxist historians, failing to see the facts, again argue that the taking-over of Macao by the Portuguese which occurred between 1555 and 1557 was an act of "imperialistic aggression"and that the Portuguese had resorted to illegal means to gain admission. The Portuguese view is different: Macao, it was often claimed in traditional history writing, was given to the Portuguese in reward for their aid in fighting pirates.[25]

Although the details of Macao's foundation remain somewhat uncertain, it is clear that by the late 1550s or early 1560s most Portuguese had already left Lampacau for Macao and that soon after, the first few permanent buildings were set up on the peninsula. It is here that a new chapter of Sino-Portuguese relations begins and where our chronological summary must end. Suffice it to say that Macao grew and that it grew fast and rich, largely deriving its wealth from its position in the silk-for-silver trade between China and Japan, and that it was the first, and in all likelihood will be the last, European settlement along the China coast.

In reviewing what had occurred to the Portuguese in the ca. forty-five years prior to the foundation of Macao, a few things should be summarized here. Early Sino-Portuguese relations can be divided into three stages: an initial phase beginning with Álvares's voyage and ending with the Pires mission and the clashes in the 1520s; a second phase during which individual Portuguese traders and freebooters visited the coasts of Fukien and Chekiang; and a third phase during which Portuguese trade became more regular and switched back to the coast of Kwangtung. Each period was marked by certain developments in China, the general tendency being however that unrest and piracy along the China coast increased and that by the time that Leonel de Souza negotiated the agreement of 1554 the time was indeed ripe for the Portuguese to offer their services as reliable traders to the Canton economy.

It is also worth mentioning here that China's final acceptance of the Portuguese presence on its coast was without precedent and that this acceptance was a remarkable achievement for the Portuguese. In general, as we saw above, foreigners were not treated as equals in China, but the Portuguese having acquired a special status which did not fully comply with the traditional Chinese world order and the system of tribute regulations governing foreign trade, came at least close to being treated as equals by the Kwangtung people.[26]

In Ming and early Qing times all other Europeans failed to obtain a permanent base in China comparable to that of Macao. The fact that they did not "make it" while the Portuguese did, cannot be exclusively attributed to the difficult situation in China. Throughout the later half of the Ming dynasty the Chinese central government was weak and the population living on the maritime "periphery" rarely obeyed Peking. The Portuguese knew how to make use of this peculiar constellation, the others did not. What perhaps accounted more for their failure than China's impenetrability, was that they themselves were unable to adjust to the pace and pulse of the Chinese bureaucrats, or to put it more extravagantly, that they lacked the diplomacy and subtle intuition which the Portuguese displayed in their efforts to come to terms with the moods of an unpredictable dragon.

Having been founded through the persistence of private trade, the Portuguese administration in Macao long resembled more an outpost of the "shadow empire" than it did one of the fortress cities like Diu or Malacca which were subject to the system of three-year offices and royal patronage. Moreover, the Chinese did not regard the city, once founded, as in any way sovereign; Chinese officials remained in residence to collect taxes, while the Portuguese *moradores*, or inhabitants, were said to pay the Cantonese governor large sums to be allowed to stay.[27]

Around 1582, however, it was estimated that the Europeans and their families possessed about five hundred houses, and by that year, these assembled and formed a *senado da câmara*, a municipal governing council closely patterned after those in Portugal. Some four years later in 1586 it was officially recognized by viceregal decree and granted the privileges of Évora.[28] Meanwhile Portuguese vessels from Goa had begun making voyages to Japan, and it was natural for these to stop off en route, first at Lampacau Island and later in Macao itself.[29] The Portuguese viceroy (and only later the crown) had assumed control of these voyages, which originated in Goa, awarding them to individuals for one or more years running and for a variety of reasons, including payment, service or influence.

The nominees would combine visits to China and Japan in a single voyage, for, as noted, Chinese goods, especially the finer silken textiles, were in brisk demand in Japan, while, as also noted, Japan possessed silver mines of which the Chinese had too few. Because the Chinese emperor had forbidden his subjects to trade with Japan and Japanese to make trading voyages to China, this created – literally – a golden opportunity for the concessionaire. By stopping off in Macao to load their vessels with Chinese goods, paid for there and in Canton with silver, pepper, and ivory, and then selling them for silver in Japan, he could next double back to Macao and visit the fairs of Canton on the home voyage to Goa, exchanging this silver for cheap gold – whereas gold was much more expensive in Japan, just as in Europe. It has been estimated that about half of Japan's silver production was thus profitably syphoned off into the Chinese markets by Portuguese traders during the remainder of the sixteenth century – or until the hostile Dutch and English arrived to spoil the game![30]

From almost the time of the foundation of Macao until 1623, it was the practice for the concessionaire to act as the city's captain-general during his stays there. Quite naturally, this led to quarrels with the *senado da câmara*, although the elected body had the decided advantage of continuity and intimate knowledge of the city's affairs. Moreover, in theory at least, the captain-general had real jurisdiction only over the fortresses and defence. For all practical purposes, the *vereadores*, or aldermen, actually were in charge of the city and its affairs, including delegations to the Chinese authorities.

All in all, one might say that Macao was a creation of the informal Portuguese or "shadow empire" but that its very conspicuousness promoted it to a rank beside those of the *Estado da India's* other important cities. And even then, its isolation and its peculiar relationship with the Chinese authorities prevented it from conforming completely to any other model. Yet, as peculiar as were its circumstances, it proved the longest enduring outpost of any European colonial power.

Roderich Ptak

Notes

[1] There is a vast amount of secondary literature on early Ming trade. Some useful English surveys may be found in J.V.G. Mills, tr., *Ma Huan: Ying-yai Sheng-lan, 'The Overall Survey of the Ocean's Shores' [1433]* (Cambridge: Cambridge U. Press, 1970), Introduction, or Joseph Needham, *Science and Civilisation in China*,

IV: 3 (Cambridge: Cambridge U. Press, 1971), 487-535. For comprehensive bibliographical information, see Roderich Ptak, *Cheng Hos Abenteuer im Drama und Roman der Ming-Zeit. Hsia Hsi-yang: Eine Übersetzung und Untersuchung, Hsi-yang chi: Ein Deutungsversuch* }(Stuttgart: Franz Steiner Verlag, 1986).

² On the end of Ming naval policies, see, for example, Lo Jung-pang, "The Decline of the Early Ming Navy," *Oriens Extremus* 5 (1958): 149-68, and the same, "The Termination of the Early Ming Naval Expeditions," in James B. Parsons, ed., *Papers in Honour of Professor Woodbridge Bingham, a Festschrift for his Seventy-fifth Birthday* (San Francisco: Chinese Materials Center, 1976), 127-40.

³ See, for example, José Maria Braga, "The 'Tamão' of the Portuguese Pioneers," *T'ien Hsia Monthly* 8.5 (May 1939): 420-32; J. M. Braga, *China Landfall, 1513: Jorge Álvares's Voyage to China* (Hong Kong: Karel Weiss, 1956); Lo Hsiang-lin, "T'un-men yü ch'i ti tzu T'ang chih Ming chih hai-shang chiao-t'ung," *Hsin-ya hsüeh-pao* 2.2 (1957), 271-300; Luís Keil, *Jorge Álvares, o primeiro Português que foi à China* (Lisbon: Tipografia Beleza, 1933); Albert Kammerer, *La découverte de la Chine par les Portugais au XVIème siècle et la cartographie des portulans*, Suppl. to *T'oung Pao* 39 (Leiden: E. J. Brill, 1944), 48-70; Luís G. Gomes, "Chegam os Portugueses, pela primeira vez, à China," *Boletim do Instituto Luís de Camões* 1.3 (July 1966): 267-73; Artur Basílio de Sá, *Jorge Álvares (quadros da sua biografia no Oriente)* (Lisbon: Agência Geral do Ultramar, 1956); Chang Tseng-hsin, "Shih-liu shih-chi ch'ien-ch'i P'u-t'ao-ya jen tsai Chung-kuo yen-hai te mao-i chü-tien", in Chung-yang yen-chiu-yüan San-min chu-i yen-chiu-so, ed., *Chung-kuo hai-yang fa-chan shih lun-wen chi*, II (Taipei: Chung-yang... so, 1986), 77-88.

⁴ See, for example, Chang T'ien-tsê, *Sino-Portuguese Trade from 1514 to 1644, A Synthesis of Portuguese and Chinese Sources* (Rpt. Leyden: E. J. Brill, 1969), 35-38; Paul Pelliot's review of that book, " Un ouvrage sur les premiers temps de Macao," *T'oung Pao* 31 (1935), 58-94.

⁵ Western monographs on private Ming trade, smuggling and piracy are: *Bodo Wiethoff, Die chinesische Seeverbotspolitik und der private Überseehandel von 1368 bis 1567* (Hamburg: Gesellschaft für Natur- und Völkerkunde Ostasiens, 1963); So Kwan-wai, *Japanese Piracy in Ming China during the Sixteenth Century* (East Lansing: Michigan State U. Press, 1975); Roland L. Higgins, *Piracy and Coastal Defense in the Ming Period, Governmental Response to Coastal Disturbances, 1523-1549* (Ann Arbor, 1981; PhD thesis); Chang

Pin-tsun, *Chinese Maritime Trade: The Case of Sixteenth Century Fu-chien (Fukien)* (Princeton, 1983; PhD thesis).

⁶ On profits in the pepper trade, see, for example, Mansel Longworth Dames, tr., *The Book of Duarte Barbosa*, 2 vols. (London: Hakluyt Society, 1918-1921), II, 215. On China's pepper imports in general: Ts'ao Yung-ho, "Pepper Trade in East Asia," *T'oung Pao* 68.4/5 (1982): 221-47.

⁷ On Fernão Peres de Andrade, see, for example, Gomes, "Chegam os Portugueses," 274-85; Chang T'ien-tsê, *Sino-Portuguese Trade*, 38-46.

⁸ See, for example, Chang T'ien-tsê, *Sino-Portuguese Trade*, 47-48; K. C. Fok, "Early Ming Images of the Portuguese," in Roderich Ptak, ed., *Portuguese Asia: Aspects in History and Economic History (Sixteenth and Seventeenth Centuries)* (Stuttgart: Franz Steiner Verlag, 1987), 145-46; Roderich Ptak, *Portugal in China. Kurzer Abriss der portugiesisch-chinesischen Beziehungen und der Geschichte Macaus im 16. und beginnenden 17. Jahrhundert* (Bammental/Heidelberg: Klemmerberg-Verlag, 1980), 20-21; Stefania Stafutti, "Portogallo e Portoghesi nelle fonti cinesi del XVI e XVII secolo,"*Cina* 19 (1984): 29-51.

⁹ See, for example, Yüan Pang-chien and Yüan Kuei-hsiu, *Ao-men shih-lüeh* (Hong Kong: Chung-liu ch'u-pan-she, 1988), 22-23.

¹⁰ Paul Pelliot, "Le Hoja et le Sayyid Husain de l'Histoire des Ming," *T'oung Pao* 38 (1948): 83 et seq.; Eduardo Brazão, *Apontamentos para a história das relações diplomáticas de Portugal com a China, 1516-1753* (Lisbon: Agência Geral das Colónias, 1949), first chapters; Chang Tien-tse (=Chang T'ien-tsê), "Malacca and the Failure of the First Portuguese Embassy to Peking," *Boletim do Instituto Luís de Camões* 15.1-2 (1981): 149-163 (rpt. from *Journal of Southeast Asian History*).

¹¹ On the battles, see, for example, Huang Hung-ch'ao, *Ao-men shih* (Hong Kong: Shang-wu yin-shu-kuan, 1987), 13-16; Chang T'ien-tsê, *Sino-Portuguese Trade*, 53-61; Chou Ching-lien, *Chung P'u wai-chiao shih* (Shanghai: Shang-wu yin-shu-kuan, 1936), 27-31; Kammerer, *La découverte*, 31-37; Pelliot, "Le Hoja", 98 et seq.; Lin Tien-wei, " An Enquiry into the Portuguese Stay in Hong Kong during the Sixteenth Century," *Chinese Culture* 25.4 (December 1984): 71-77; Ptak, *Portugal in China*, 24-27.

¹² On Liampo and the other places, see, for example, Chang T'ien-tsê, *Sino-Portuguese Trade*, 69-80; Kammerer, *La découverte*, 71-87, 100-105; José Maria Braga, "The Western Pioneers and the

Roderich Ptak

Discovery of Macao," *Boletim do Instituto Português de Hong Kong* 2 (September 1949): 67 et seq.; Charles Ralph Boxer, ed., *South China in the Sixteenth Century, being the Narratives of Galeote Pereira, Fr. Gaspar da Cruz, O.P., Fr. Martín de Rada, O.E.S.A.* (London: Hakluyt Society, 1953); Wiethoff, *Seeverbotspolitik*, 145-65; Chang Tseng-hsin, "Shih-liu shih-chi," 88-94; Ptak, *Portugal in China*, 32-36; Raffaella d'Intino, ed., *Enformação das cousas da China. Textos do século XVI* (Lisbon: Casa da Moeda, 1989); Ch'en Tzu-ch'iang, "Lun Ming-tai Chang-chou Yüeh-kang te li-shih ti-wei," *Hai chiao shih yen-chiu* 3 (1983), 90-97; Hsü Ming-te, "Lun shih-liu shih-chi Che-chiang Shuang-hsü-kang kuo-chi mao-i," *Hai chiao shih yen-chiu* 11 (1987), 14-24.

[13] Fernão Mendes Pinto, *Peregrinação*, chapter 38 et seq.

[14] Much has been written on Japanese-Portuguese contacts prior to the foundation of Macao, particularly in Japanese. I shall only list three Western references here: Georg Schurhammer, S.J., "1453-1943. Descobrimento de Japão pelos Portugueses no ano de 1543" (tr. from German by Francisco Rodrigues, S.J.), *Anais da Academia Portuguesa da História*, 2nd ser., vol. 1 (1946), 17-172; Charles Ralph Boxer, *The Christian Century in Japan, 1549-1650* (rpt. Berkeley, Los Angeles, London: U. of California Press, 1967), chapter 1; Kiichi Matsuda, *The Relations Between Portugal and Japan* (Lisbon: Junta de Investigações do Ultramar and Centro de Estudos Históricos Ultramarinos, 1965), 2-7.

[15] On Chu Wan, see, for example, Wiethoff, *Seeverbotspolitik*, especially, 92-103; So Kwan-wai, *Japanese Piracy*, especially, 50 et seq.; L. Carrington Goodrich and Fang Chaoying, eds., *Dictionary of Ming Biography, 1368-1644*, 2 vols. (New York, London: Columbia U. Press, 1976), I; Frederick W. Mote and Denis Twitchett, eds., *The Camridge History of China. Vol. 7: The Ming Dynasty, 1368-1644, Part I* (Cambridge, etc.: Cambridge U. Press, 1988), 494-95.

16 See, for example, Luís da Cunha Gonçalves, "A famosa cidade de Liampó segundo Fernão Mendes Pinto e a verdade histórica," *O Instituto* (1928): 113-20; Chang T'ien-tsê, *Sino-Portuguese Trade*, 75-80; Kammerer, *La découverte*, 73-76; Braga, *Western Pioneers*, 69-71; Boxer, *South China*, xxvi-xxvii, 192-93.

17 Chang T'ien-tsê, *Sino-Portuguese Trade*, 81-85; Braga, *Western Pioneers*, 72 et seq.; Boxer, *South China*, especially xxvii-xxxii, 194-211.

[18] For silver in and silver imports to mid-sixteenth century China, see, for example, Michel Cartier, "Les importations de

métaux monétaires en Chine: Essai sur la conjoncture chinoise,"
Annales, économies, Sociétés, Civilisations 36.3 (May-June 1981): 457,
458, 461, 462; William S. Atwell, "International Bullion Flows and
the Chinese Economy, circa 1530-1650," *Past and Present* 95 (1982),
68 et seq.

[19] On São João, see, for example, Kammerer, *La découverte*, 88-
95; Huang Wen-k'uan, *Ao-men shih kou-ch'en* (Macao: Hsing-kuang
ch'u-pan-she), 204-07.

[20] On Lampacau, see, for example, Kammerer, *La découverte*,
96-99; Lin Tien-wei, "An Enquiry," 77 et seq.; Chang Tseng-hsin,
"Shih-liu shih-chi," 94-102.

[21] Ajuda Library, Codex 49-IV-49, f. 235, quoted after Braga,
Western Pioneers, 83; Andrew Ljungstedt, *An Historical Sketch of the
Portuguese Settlements in China and of the Roman Catholic Church and
Missions in China* (Boston: James Munroe, 1836), 9; Yin Kuang-jen
and Chang Ju-lin, *Ao-men chi-lüeh* (Taipei: Ch'eng-wen ch'u-pan-
she, 1968; Chung-kuo fang-chih ts'ung-shu ed.), 113; Ptak,
Portugal in China, 38-39.

[22] On the 1554 agreement, see, for example, José Maria Braga,
O primeiro acordo luso-chinês realizado por Leonel de Souza em 1554
(Macao, 1939); Braga, *Western Pioneers*, 84-87, and document pp.
202-08; Boxer, *South China*, xxxiii-xxxv, 190-191; Almerindo Lessa,
*A história e os homens da primeira república democrática do Oriente.
Biologia e sociologia de uma ilha cívica* (Macao: Imprensa Nacional,
1974), 93-95; Caetano Soares, "Assuntos chineses," *Boletim do
Instituto Luís de Camões* 11.1 (1977), 81 et seq.

[23] The worst examples of anti-Portuguese history writing where
such arguments are presented in full probably are the works by Tai
I-hsüan, in particular `Ming shih Fo-lang-chi chuan' chien-cheng`
(Peking: Chung-kuo she-hui k'o-hsüeh ch'u-pan-she, 1984) and
Kuan-yü Ao-men li-shih shang so-wei kan-tsou hai-tao wen-t'i
(Macao: Hsing-kuang ch'u-pan-she, 1987). On the problem of
present day Chinese history writing on Macao, also see Roderich
Ptak and Peter Haberzettl, *Macau im Wandel. Fünf Studien zur
Geschichte und Wirtschaft des Territoriums in der jüngeren
Vergangenheit* (Stuttgart: Franz Steiner Verlag, 1990), 31-32.

[24] Armando Cortesão, tr., *The Suma Oriental of Tomé Pires...and
the Book of Francisco Rodrigues...*, 2 vols. (London: Hakluyt Society,
1944), II, 459, 460; Braga, *Western Pioneers*, 102-03.

[25] See the works of Tai I-hsüan quoted in n. 23, or Fei Ch'eng-
k'ang, *Ao-men ssu-pai nien* (Shanghai: Shang-hai jen-min

ch'u-pan-she, 1988), 14 et seq. For the Portuguese side see, for example, Braga, *Western Pioneers*, 109 et seq.; Benjamin Videira Pires, "0 foro do chão' de Macau," *Boletim do Instituto Luís de Camões* 1.4/5 (1967), 319-34.

[26] K. C. Fok, *The Macao Formula: A Study of Chinese management of Westerners from the mid-sixteenth Century to the Opium War Period* (Honululu, 1973; PhD thesis), provides useful ideas on China's treatement of Westerners and the special status of Macao.

[27] Charles R. Boxer, *Portuguese Society in the Tropics. The Municipal Councils of Goa, Macao, Bahia and Luanda, 1510-1800* (Madison and Milwaukee: The U. of Wisconsin Press, 1965), 43.

[28] Boxer, *Portuguese Society*, 44. On Macao's institutions and businessmen also, for example, George Bryan Souza, *The Survival of Empire. Portuguese Trade and Society in China and the South China Sea, 1630-1754* Cambridge: Cambridge U. Press, 1986), 15-29. On the city's population growth, there, 30-36, and Roderich Ptak, "The Democracy of Old Macao, 1555-1640," *Ming Studies* 15 (1982): 27-35.

[29] Chang T'ien-Tsê, *Sino Portuguese Trade*, 6-8.

[30] Charles R. Boxer, *The Great Ship from Amacon; Annals of Macao and the Old Japan Trade, 1555-1640* (Lisbon: Centro de Estudos Históricos Ultramarinos, 1963), 6-8.

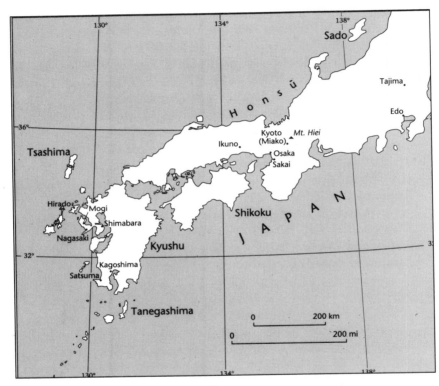

Japan

Chapter XV

Portugal and Japan

By 1529 when the Treaty of Zaragoza awarded the Moluccas to Portugal, the Portuguese were only beginning to move into the northeastern waters of the China Seas, their main goal China, their subsidiary ones unclear. In Malacca, the principal southeast Asian entrepôt, linking the trade routes of the Indian Ocean and China Seas, and the most prized jewel among all the possessions that they had thus far taken, the Portuguese had acquired information about the various countries trading with the former sultanate. These included China and the Ryūkyū kingdom (the archipelago between Japan and Taiwan, present-day Okinawa), then a major trading power whose ships visited China, Korea, Japan and southeast Asia.

The information about Malacca's rich trade was recorded in the *Suma Oriental*, compiled by Tomé Pires between 1512 and 1515, immediately after Albuquerque's seizure of the city in 1511, although the manuscript was not published until 1944.[1] The *Suma Oriental* includes a brief discussion of a place called *Jampon*, a corruption of the Malay words *Japun* and *Japang*, themselves corruptions of coastal Chinese renderings of the Mandarin *Jihpenkuo*, land of the rising sun. Other than Marco Polo's fabled Cipango, this was the first mention of the country in a European language. Pires described it in two vague paragraphs, saying that Japan, located several days sailing to the north of Ryūkyū, was not a major trading nation, having only a limited commerce with China and Ryūkyū, exchanging gold and copper for cloths and fishing nets.[2] Thus a voyage to Japan did not figure on the list of Portuguese priorities in east Asia. China and the Ryūkyū kingdom seemed more attractive.

Pires's sketchy information was wide of the mark, perhaps understandably so, for at this time Japan was in the midst of the *sengoku jidai*, the age of the warring states, which had erupted in 1467 and was to last for just over a hundred years. These civil wars deprived the Japanese polity of any functioning central authority. The powers of the Ashikaga shogunate had shrivelled since the onset of the wars. The shogun had become little more than a ceremonial figure, rather like the emperor. Rival feudal lords battled against each other for local domination and, in shifting alliances, against anyone seeking to rise above the fray and wrap himself in the mantle of legitimacy which the office of shogun – supreme military dictator – and the titles its powers of patronage could still confer. In addition, Pires was wholly wrong in assuming that the Japanese were little inclined to trade and he was misinformed about Japan's trading partners. In fact, Japan had enjoyed an active trade with China and Korea since the ninth century, interrupted by the vicissitudes of dynastic change in both neighbours, at times impeded by the attempts of the Japanese authorities to regulate the trade, and periodically subjected to disruption by pirates who flourished along the relatively autonomous coastal fringes of the three countries.

Trade with China was put on a new footing at the beginning of the fifteenth century by the shogun Ashikaga Yoshimitsu (1358-1408) who established official relations with the celestial empire. The Ming Chinese were amenable to the Japanese overtures for they promised to bring another state into the orbit of the Chinese world of international relations, the tribute system. Protocols were drawn up to govern the ships, men, ports and frequency of the missions that could be sent to China, although in practice the restrictions on the number of visits were not strictly enforced, in the early years at least. Trade was an essential part of these missions; hence they are known as the "tally trade." In 1404 the Japanese were given a number of divided certificates (*kangō*), or tallies, which they had to produce on arrival in China and which had to match the half retained by the Chinese in Peking and in Chekiang. In this way the Ming could distinguish between official missions and ships belonging to pirates (most of whom were Japanese) that had been ravaging the Chinese coast with impunity since the 1350s during the transition from the Yüan to the Ming dynasty. The precise nature of the relationship that Yoshimitsu's arrangement with China defined – whether Yoshimitsu's chosen form of self-address to the Chinese emperor (King of Japan) and his use of Chinese rather than Japanese chronology implied acceptance of an inferior status for Japan in the tributary system – became a matter of controversy, and for some remains so today. But no matter how one chooses to interpret the terminology adopted, the shogun, whose landholdings were limited in comparison with other lords, had much to gain by establishing official relations with China, thereby gaining control over an important source of patronage which he was able to dispose of to his advantage and profit and to enhance his status in the eyes of other lords.

The tally trade between Japan and China lasted until 1547, shortly before official relations between the two empires were terminated. The principal goods that were traded included silk and other fabrics, copper coins, religious images, artefacts and texts, herbal medicines, porcelain and sandalwood from the continent, and gold, wood, copper, sulphur, swords and Japanese craft goods (fans, lacquer-ware, screens, inkstones, testifying to the cultural similarities shared by the countries) from Japan. However, with the emasculation of the shogunate's authority (although not of the prestige of the office itself), during the *sengokou* wars, control of the tally trade with China passed into the hands of the western *daimyo* families of Ōuchi and Hosokawa who each sought to dominate it at the expense of the other and the last two tally voyages to China were fitted out by the Ōuchi, although they themselves were overthrown by a rival clan, the Mōri, in 1558.

A similar arrangement between Japan and Korea was formalised in 1443 but with the one notable difference that the relations and, therefore, the trade were not under the control of the shogunate but of the Sō family on their strategically-located island domain of Tsushima, midway between the two countries in the Korean straits. The Sō, under the determined leadership of Sō Sadamori (1385-1452), had thrust themselves forward to become the sole regulators of the trade which attracted investments from a number of Kyushu lords from whom the Sō could levy a commission. Japanese were given official permission to reside in the ports of Pusan, Naeip'o and Yŏ mp'o where some had been living since 1419 when the Korean king Sejong had decreed that only officially accredited missions with letters of authorisation from Korean and Japanese authorities could enter Korea. The Japanese were interested in importing Korean fabrics, especially cotton, hemp, silk pongee, Buddhist artefacts and texts, rice, dried vegetables, ginseng and exotic items such as tiger skins. The Koreans received much the same goods as the Japanese sent to China, but fewer swords, as well as goods brought to Japan by Ryūkyū ships from southeast Asian emporia and re-exported to Korea, although Ryūkyūan ships also traded directly with Korea.

Trade between Japan and Korea, which was conducted by Japanese (like the Chinese, Koreans were forbidden to travel overseas), outgrew that with China, traditionally Japan's principal trading partner. By the end of the fifteenth century almost three thousand Japanese were recorded in Korean chronicles as trading in Korea. But the Koreans soon attempted to scale down the volume of the trade and to curtail the Japanese presence in their country, moves that provoked Japanese attacks against the Koreans in the three ports. The Japanese overplayed their hand, however, were subdued and in 1512 Naeip'o was made the only port in which the Japanese could reside officially, although Pusan was reinstated in 1523. Thanks to the absence of rival Korean and Chinese carriers, the Japanese enjoyed a favourable trade balance on their overseas trade with their immediate neighbours.[3] Such information had not drifted down to Malacca, or if it had, it had not become familiar to the Portuguese whose first appearance in Japan remained over thirty years distant from Albuquerque's conquest of Malacca.

In their earlier debuts in waters previously uncharted by Europeans, as they proceeded down the west coast of Africa, round the Cape and up the eastern seaboard, across the Indian Ocean and on to the Straits of Malacca, the Portuguese had been able to take advantage of local navigational skills to carry themselves forward and they had benefitted immensely from becoming participants in existing trade flows.[4] Their arrival in Japan was no exception to this pattern.

The Lusitanians appear

The first Portuguese, indeed the first Europeans, are recorded as having reached Japan in September 1543 when a junk en route from the Siamese capital of Ayuthaya for the Fukienese coast was blown off-course in a typhoon onto the island of Tanegashima, just below the southwestern tip of Kyushu. On board were three Portuguese private traders (António da Mota, Francisco Zeimoto, and António Peixoto) and another hundred or so individuals from various parts of the Indies, including a Chinese who could write Chinese characters and was, therefore, able to act as interpreter. The reception was cordial, their junk was repaired and some merchandise was exchanged for silver before the crew departed for Malacca.[5]

Reports of the favourable reception in Japan spread quickly among the Portuguese in the East Indies, and over the next few years the Japanese archipelago, or more precisely Kyushu and some of the islands studding its coastline, became another favoured destination of Portuguese private traders. These traders were among the many who took advantage of the fluid situation on the economically dynamic south China coast where the mandate of Peking was less easily enforceable and which was once again being subjected to attacks by pirates. They were still referred to as *wōk'ou*, or dwarf pirates, *wakō* in Japanese. They were in fact a mixture of Japanese and Chinese, more Japanese than Chinese, according to the most recent analysis. The pirates used various harbours and inlets along the Kyushu coast and among the Gotō Islands as bases for smuggling operations on the south China coast. They resorted to violence to get their way when confronted with uncooperative local officials or to harass debt defaulters.[6]

The Portuguese were made welcome in these troubled waters; after all, they had goods to trade. But this free-booting in the East China Sea was short-lived for the Portuguese traders. By 1550 it was over. In that year the Portuguese viceroy at Goa declared the trade with Japan a royal monopoly under the direction of the *Capitão-Mor de Viagem da China e Japão* (Captain Major of the Voyage of China and Japan), an office originally given as a reward for distinguished service but soon sold off to the highest bidder, who could of course re-sell his allocation.[7] The first, brief, phase of Luso-Japanese relations came to a swift end, at the instigation of the Portuguese themselves. The second, and more lucrative, was about to begin.

After the mid-1550s, when pirate attacks on the China coast reached a peak, the agents of central authority in the Chinese coastal regions were successful in bringing the pirates to heel, it was said, with the help of the Portuguese, although a complete cessation of their activities awaited the emergence of a stronger central authority in Japan. The Chinese eased the restrictions against foreign trade. The one exception was Japan, with whom official relations were broken in 1548. But just as it had proved impossible to seal off the southern Chinese coastal provinces from their natural economic horizons overseas, so too it would turn out to be impracticable, and undesirable, for China to isolate itself economically from Japan. The Portuguese presence in east Asia, cemented by the foundation of Macao in 1557, which became the staging post for the Japan voyage, could not have occurred at a more opportune moment.

Peking's decision to terminate official relations with Japan was unilateral; there was no functioning central authority in Japan to respond to it. The principal victims of the battles of the *sengoku jidai* had been the Ashikaga shogunate which had been quickly stripped of its *de facto* powers but not of its *de jure* ones (it survived as an institution until 1588), and the shogunal and imperial capital Kyoto. But as in Europe, while the upheavals of protracted warfare caused widespread loss of life and senseless destruction of property, their effect on the social and economic order was one of dislocation, not devastation. War, even prolonged warfare, was less of a threat to the survival of human society at this time than the dangers posed by that invisible enemy, the bacterium *Yersina pestis*, which in the form of the pestilence known as the Black Death had levelled the prospects of European economic and demographic expansion in the Middle Ages. During the *sengoku jidai* what Kyoto lost as the cultural centre of Japan, the provinces gained. Culture became more widely diffused. Far from inhibiting cultural pursuits the warlords encouraged artistic expression whether in literature or the visual arts. This helped maintain a sense of national identity. War also stimulated the economy. No matter the accomplishments of new poetic forms or the refinement of the tea ceremony as an art form with wide appeal amongst the warrior classes, wars need money, and when the Portuguese began their trade with Japan the battles of the *sengoku* period were reaching a decisive point as first the warlord Oda Nobunaga (1534-1582) and then Toyotomi Hideyoshi (1537-1598) succeeded in laying the foundations of a restored central authority.

In 1568 Oda occupied Kyoto but instead of installing himself as shogun, which he could easily have done, he made Ashikaga Yoshiaki shogun although he soon found him an ungrateful client, too ready to conspire with his enemies. Nobunaga continued to face enemies until he perished by the sword himself in 1582, assassinated and consumed by flames in his newly-built palace of Azuchi, the most impressive new construction of the age. But he had taken measures to consolidate his rule. He took the first steps towards demilitarising the country by establishing the sword hunt (*katanagari*), introduced the division between the agricultural and military classes (*hei-nō-bunri*), undertook land surveys in the areas under his control (*kenchi*) and began to abolish some of the toll barriers (*sekisho*) which restricted commerce. Hideyoshi, who took over Nobunaga's mantle in 1582, developed these policies and with the successes of his Kyushu campaign he managed to check the ambitions of the most powerful family, the Shimizu of Satsuma, in southwestern Kyushu. The heirs to this formidable achievement were not, as Hideyoshi intended, the Toyotomi family, but those of Tokugawa Ieyasu (1543-1616), one of his most trusted lieutenants, who opportunistically and ruthlessly tore apart Hideyoshi's political testament. After winning the last major battle of the *sengoku* period at Sekigahara in 1600, Ieyasu established the Tokugawa shogunate three years later which proved enduring and carried Japan into the modern era until it was itself swept aside in 1867-68 in the upheavals known as the Meiji Restoration.[8]

A silvery opportunity

If China and Japan could not trade together officially, then economic imperatives in both countries dictated that some other channel would have to be found to enable the exchange of the two commodities each required of the other, gold and silver. The Japanese needed gold, the Chinese silver, the Japanese to finance the military campaigns of the three unifiers or hegemons (and in the case of Hideyoshi, his invasions of Korea in 1592 and 1597) and to pay for the construction of castles, to help maintain order, and the urban development programmes which were started by Hideyoshi, notably the rebuilding of the capital and the expansion of nearby Osaka as a commercial centre. These programmes were intended to serve as metaphors for Toyotomi power and, it was hoped, to symbolise the durability of the regime. In China taxes continued to be paid in silver but existing silver production was declining as mines were exhausted. Conveniently, the Japanese were increasing their production by opening new mines in Tajima, Ikuno and Sado thanks to the introduction of new mining and smelting techniques, especially the *haifuki* cupellation method which was acquired from Korea. But a factor other than mere supply and demand enters the picture, one that was to make the exchange between the two empires one of the most important trade flows in the Indies: the bi-metallic ratio between the two metals. In China the ratio between gold and silver was less than that in Japan, 1:6 to 1:7.50 in 1596, and 1:8 in 1620; in Japan it was 1:7.37 in 1571, 1:10.99 in 1604 and 1:14 in 1622.[9] Until the differentials narrowed almost to parity by the 1620s, the export of gold to Japan and silver to China was a prize of immense profitability to the carrier who had the good fortune to attain it.

The peace dividend stemming from Oda's triumphs and Hideyoshi's pacification of the country created the conditions for further economic growth. In addition to older established imports, there was a sharp rise in demand for Chinese silk, in particular white, raw silk, which the Europeans called "Nanking silk," and other silk wares (silk and cotton mixtures, silk wadding for thicker winter clothing). The Jesuit, João Rodrigues, who worked in Japan from 1577-1610 and who wrote one of the most perceptive accounts of the country, noted that such was the demand and availability of silk that "since the time of Taikō (Hideyoshi) there has been a general peace throughout the kingdom and trade has so increased that the whole nation wears silk robes; even peasants and their wives have silk sashes and the better off among them have silken robes."[10] Silk (and gold while demand continued) was to become the staple Portuguese import into Japan.

Great ships and Nagasaki

From 1550, when the Japan trade was made a royal monopoly, until 1570 the Portuguese *nao do trato*, massive ships by the standards of the day, with some reaching about 1,200-1,600 tons by the end of the sixteenth century, had no regular port of call. They could pick and choose between a number of ports on the Kyushu coast where the local lords, or *daimyo*, welcomed them with open arms, confident of a handsome share in the profits of the trade. The Portuguese were given the sobriquet *namban-jin*, or southern barbarian people, because they came from the south, as had the first Siamese envoys and Sumatran traders who had visited Japan in the fifteenth century. All had come from outside the traditional world of Japan's international relations, a world that took the Chinese one as its model. They were, therefore, outsiders or barbarians. Outsider connoted inferior but it did not imply racially inferior as it is understood in its late-nineteenth century usage. These were people with whom Japan had no official relations and no common culture. Thus they were inferior; a simple and practical construct but a flexible one, unlike the Chinese original from which it was derived.

From 1571 onwards, the *naos* made Nagasaki, in the Ōmura domain on the western coast of Kyushu and a secure natural harbour of outstanding beauty, their preferred destination, sailing from Macao in June or July and arriving in Nagasaki in July or August, and returning sometime between November and January. In short, it was a monsoon trade.[11]

Ōmura Sumitada was a Christian, one of the Jesuits' most important converts. The Jesuits had very quickly followed the merchants to Japan. Francis Xavier arrived in August 1549 and was so impressed by the potential for missionary success that he considered the Japanese "the best [people] who have yet been discovered."[12] The Japan province was established in the same year and the fathers decided that the most likely path to success in a hierarchical society such as Japan was to start with the elite and work down. This policy involved painstaking efforts to familiarise themselves with the language and culture of the country and their linguistic achievement made them indispensible as middlemen for the Portuguese merchants arriving on the *naos*.

But as the financial costs of their ambitious missionary activity in Japan were high, the Jesuits needed to secure for themselves a share of the lucrative trade from the Japan voyage. This they achieved in 1578 when the society signed an agreement with the Maconese authorities allowing them to send fifty peculs of silk on the Japan voyage which they could sell in Japan at the highest prevailing price.[13] The concession was probably granted with the help of one of the most colourful and successful *fidalgos* in the China Seas, Bartholomeu Vaz Landeiro, who arrived in Macao in 1569 and helped build Macao's fortunes. As a participant in the Japan voyages, Landeiro had assisted the Jesuit cause in Japan by carrying the fathers on his vessels and, in the days before Nagasaki became the terminus of the trade, refusing to call at any Kyushu port other than ones where the fathers would be allowed to disembark and proceed with their mission. In 1580 Ōmura made a dramatic gesture. He ceded Nagasaki and the adjacent port of Mogi to the Society. The Jesuits judged that Ōmura's generosity strengthened their position in Japan by providing them with a secure refuge from the shifting local fortunes of the sengoku upheavals not only for themselves but for Christian converts fleeing from domains where Christianity was persecuted. The Jesuit visitor, Alessandro Valignano, the able provincial of the sixteenth-century Jesuit mission in Japan, would have preferred the *naos* to continue visiting many ports of call, acting as bait to hook potential converts, but after much reflection, he judged that the security offered by the cession of Nagasaki far outweighed such potential benefits.[14]

To suggest that the grant of Nagasaki prefigured nineteenth-century extra-territoriality is anachronistic (the Jesuits did not have the desire let alone the right to exercise capital punishment) and to argue that the order was bent on turning Nagasaki into a "military colony" is fanciful. It was, after all, still a time of hostilities and it was only prudent self-interest to build some form of defensive fortifications for a measure of security.[15] Moreover, Valignano stipulated one condition before agreeing to Ōmura's offer – that the donation could be returned at any time. The cession of Nagasaki was an arrangement beneficial to all parties: Ōmura secured a regular income from dues levied on the *naos* and a place of asylum should he be attacked by the neighbouring and stronger domain of Saga; the Portuguese merchants, who were already using it, could readily perceive the advantages of a regular port where they could establish long-term business links with Japanese buyers; the Jesuits for reasons already mentioned. Nagasaki, no less than Macao, which could not survive without the goodwill and cooperation of the Chinese officials and merchants in nearby Canton, existed on sufferance. Unlike Goa or Malacca, Nagasaki was not a fortified enclave and the Portuguese, lacking any motivation for territorial expansion in east Asia, did not harbour the ambition that it should be. The limits of sufferance were soon made clear in 1588 when Hideyoshi, flush with the success of his military campaigns in Kyushu, tore up the grant and, cleverly, appointed the Ōmura and the neighbouring Christian daimyo Arima Harunobu as his representatives to administer the town, which they did until 1592 when Hideyoshi established the post of *daikan*, or deputy, to govern the city in his name, an office continued by the Tokugawa.

These developments had no impact upon the Japan voyage itself which had become extremely profitable. An indication of the scale of the profits can be gleaned from a report on the trade compiled around 1600. The report (probably drawn up by Pedro de Baeza) lists the various products imported by the Portuguese: white raw silk, retros (spun silk made in threads), silk piece goods woven into pictures of birds and other images, gold, musk, cotton thread and piecegoods, mercury, lead, tin, Chinese wood, earthenware, rhubarb, licorice, and white and black sugar. By far the most important imports were silk and gold. The white raw silk was bought for 80 taels per picul in Macao and sold for 140-150 taels the picul in Japan, a profit of over 81 per cent. The cost of gold in Macao depended on its fineness. The purest cost 6 taels 6 mas per tael and was worth 8 taels 3 mas in Japan; less pure cost 5 taels 4 mas and was worth 7 taels 8 mas.[16] The profit margins on other goods were equally high (for example, 142 per cent on cotton thread, 100 per cent on lead).[17]

The report was compiled when the Portuguese trade was in its heyday. But from the early seventeenth century until they were finally expelled from Japan in 1639, the unique position of the Portuguese as carriers in the silk and silver trade from Japan was beset by new challenges. One was the imposition of the *itowapppu-nakama* (silk yarn allotment guild), or *pancada* as the Portuguese called it, in 1604 whereby the newly established Tokugawa shogunate decreed that the Portuguese must sell all their silk at a fixed price to a guild of merchants from the cities of Sakai, Kyoto and Nagasaki (Edo and Osaka were added later) at a fixed price, competition from overseas voyages by Japanese in the early seventeenth century and from the arrival of the Dutch East India Company in Japan in 1609 and the English East India Company in 1613. It should be emphasised, however, that there was nothing inevitable about the eventual Portuguese ouster from Japan in 1639.

So long as the Portuguese continued to sail to Japan, their trade remained profitable. But it was not just through the Japan voyage that Portuguese shared in Japan's overseas trade. In spite of the strict regulations drawn up to tighten the Maconese elite's control over the trade in the 1570s, the *armação* (a corporate agreement detailing how the trade in silk was to be structured and ensure that it remained a monopoly of the *não* thereby cutting out the middle ranking merchants), other Portuguese free-lance traders were involved in traffic with Japan indirectly via Manila, the terminus for the trans-Pacific voyages of the silver-laden galleons from the New World, and a magnate for Chinese traders.[18] Like all black economies, the extent of the informal Portuguese trade linking Macao, Manila and Nagasaki cannot be gauged.

Effects on Japan

But the Portuguese encounter with Japan in the sixteenth century was not confined to trade alone. It touched Japan in other ways and, because of the extensive writings of the Jesuits, some of which were published at the time, it greatly influenced the European perception of the country. Three areas other than trade merit some discussion: weaponry, culture and religion. The muskets introduced by the earliest Portuguese to arrive in Japan attracted immediate attention and Japanese gunsmiths, already familiar with Chinese firearms, were soon turning out first class clones. The date when these Western-style weapons, *tanegashima*, as they were dubbed in Japanese, were first employed in battle is unclear, either 1549 or 1555, but Japanese sources show that their use in the battles of the *sengoku jidai* was widespread. What is most interesting about this transfer of technology between Europe and Japan is not that it prefigures the simplistic reputation that Japan was to acquire in the twentieth century as clever imitators, but rather how sixteenth-century Japanese military commanders put the *tanegashima* to use in the battlefield. Commanders were determined to maximise the accuracy that the *tanegashima* were capable of delivering; speed was, therefore, essential. This led them to line up men in ranks, the first line firing their volleys, then crouching to reload while the men behind them fired. This method was not suggested in Europe until 1594 and was not used extensively until the 1630s.[19]

The impact of Western armaments in Japan proved to be short-lived for their introduction coincided with the last phases of the *sengoku* wars. Both Hideyoshi and Ieyasu introduced measures to reduce the amount of military hardware in circulation in the aftermath of the wars and muskets as much as swords were confiscated in the *katanagari* (sword hunt). In addition, the castle-building programme undertaken from the 1580s at Hideyoshi's instigation made artillery redundant, at least for attacking strongholds. With massive, thick stone walls to act as shock absorbers in any bombardment, the castles were vulnerable only to protracted siege, which in itself required an extraordinary complex mobilisation of resources.[20] The Japanese had little reason to develop firearm technology (their only overseas adventures in this period, Hideyoshi's impulsive, reckless invasions of Korea, became bogged down and were not repeated). Had they done so there are good grounds for supposing that they would have achieved success. They did not, however, and the art of firearm production was lost as quickly as it had been acquired.

The travel literature that appeared from the seventeenth century onwards has a tendency to portray much of Asia as exotic and the drawings with which European publications are illustrated depict the peoples, buildings and dress of east Asia in a uniform but wholly invented *style chinois*. But in the case of the Portuguese in Japan, it is the Europeans who appear as exotic and it was their presence that inspired the marvellous *byōbu* or folding screen paintings of the Keichō era (1596-1615).

The earliest Portuguese merchants introduced the first Western art into Japan in the form of altar tablets (*retablos*) with representations of Christ, the Virgin or other sacred persons painted after the Flemish school. These were generally carried on Portuguese vessels and were used by individuals as amulets. But it is the Jesuits, especially Fr. Giovanni Nicolao, a Neapolitan, who was sent to Japan in 1583 on account of his artistic abilities and talent which he shared with his Japanese pupils, who should be credited with fostering and encouraging the spread of Western artistic techniques in Japan. Exemplary teachers though many Jesuits undoubtedly were, they were not disinterested educators in this or in any other field; they needed decorations for their churches and illustrations for their books, the publication of which became easier after the importation of a moveable press from Europe in 1590. Moreover, given the huge and fundamental linguistic problems of the mission – conversational Japanese was one thing, but how to get across such essential but culture-bound concepts as God, the Trinity, sin, redemption or transubstantiation? – a pictorial entrée into people's minds and hearts, the very approach that many Protestants sought to extirpate in Europe, appeared an attractive, efficacious tool with which to harvest souls. Few examples of Christian art survive (most were destroyed after 1614 when Christianity was ruthlessly outlawed, although the Tokugawa shogunate maintained a warehouse of Christian relics in Nagaski, firmly under lock and key),[21] and none of the early churches. Works that did manage to survive testify to a high level of competence but little originality, perhaps less a consequence of immature talent than of the need to work within the strict confines of a limited genre.

The painted screens depicting the Portuguese, the *namban byōbu* (southern barbarian screens) as they were known, are works of great originality derived from an existing tradition of screen painting depicting scenes of everyday life. The best *namban* screens were painted by artists of the Kanō school in Kyoto and were commissioned by samurai. The most common had six leaves. Their depiction of the Portuguese (both as merchants and missionaries, with Jesuits clad in long black tunics and the mendicants, who arrived in Japan in the 1590s, in rougher-sewn cowls) and their entourage of black slaves as the great *nao* arrives and disembarks its crew and cargo amidst colourful ceremony in Nagasaki, are skillfully executed. They are of immense documentary value, providing information about Portuguese dress unavailable elsewhere and about what the Japanese found curious, odd or striking in the appearance and behaviour of these strangers with their high noses. By way of contrast, the copperplate illustrations of Asia found in contemporary European books, the most notable of which were produced by the De Bry family, while attaining similarly high standards of technical achievement and giving equally free reign to the imagination, resort to invention as a substitute for direct experience. Their value lies in what they tell us about the European image of the people, manners and customs of the Indies; they lack the documentary veracity of the *namban* screens. In other screens different Western subjects were tackled, landscapes, cities, even the battle of Lepanto, but fought on land, and there were attempts to paint Japanese subjects in the Western style, but the examples that survive are competent rather than inspired.[22]

The Lusitanian presence in Japan created a short-lived craze for things Portuguese, and by extension for things European, among the Japanese elite: musical instruments (again used in Churches), clocks, which Japanese crafstmen were soon able to reproduce, and clothes. Christian and Portuguese motifs were used for decoration on garments, helmets, banners, shields, stirrups, even on bottles. But such decoration was simply that: a superficial gloss. It shows no deeper a penetration, no profounder an understanding on the part of its designers or wearers of Christianity let alone of Portugal and Europe than do young Japanese today, dressed in baseball caps and T-shirts emblazoned with "Coca-Cola" or some other icon, of late-twentieth century American culture and society. Japan's cultural encounter with Portugal, and therefore with the West, in the XVI century was skin-deep; with few exceptions, it had not penetrated to the marrow. It was easy to eradicate.

The transmission of knowledge about Japan to Europe was similarly superficial. The first mention of the Portuguese presence in Japan to reach Europe was contained in a letter from St. Francis Xavier written in Cochin on 20 January 1548. Thereafter, much of the information about the country that became available to the European reading public was derived from the published extracts of the Jesuit letters written from Japan. These were much censored in Rome before publication, although the Spanish and Portuguese versions suffered less in this respect than the Italian ones which became the most readily available. The detailed studies of the Jesuits Luís Fróis and João Rodrigues remained unpublished until the twentieth century. There was no source of balance from the Portuguese merchants trading in Japan. As with their fellow-countrymen trading elsewhere in the Indies, Portuguese merchants have left little in the way of letters, diaries or reports recording their impressions of the country or even of their personal affairs, unlike their Dutch and English successors. Nevertheless, both literally and figuratively, the Portuguese presence put Japan firmly on the map of European consciousness.

In the course of the sixteenth century the equation of Japan with Marco Polo's Cipango was suggested and confirmed authoritatively in the early XVII century, by João Rodrigues. Europe also welcomed Japanese to its shores. The first, a convert from a minor samurai background, arrived in Lisbon in 1553 and died in Portugal in 1557. More renowned was the Jesuit-sponsored mission of the four young Kyushu noblemen who reached Lisbon on 10 August 1584. They travelled through Portugal and Spain to Rome where they had audiences with Pope Gregory XIII and his successor and the doges of Venice and Genoa, arriving back in Japan in July 1590. The Portuguese were not alone in promoting such international travel. Two Japanese youths, seized from a Manila galleon off the California coast, were brought back to England by Thomas Cavendish in 1588. Their presence in England was used by Richard Hakluyt to orchestrate his blast to his contemporaries that it was time for England to be playing her part in the "Age of Discovery."[23]

A "Christian Century"?

It is inaccurate to describe the century from the 1540s to the 1640s as Japan's "Christian Century." The forces redefining the Japanese polity in this crucial period of change were shaped little by the Portuguese, whether merchants or missionaries. The three hegemons who restored unity to the Japanese polity did so by wiping out or bringing under control opposition and seeing off threats (real or imagined) to their policy. Christianity came to be viewed as one such threat. In retrospect one can see that the fathers, Jesuit and mendicant alike, became prisoners of their own optimistic belief that, short-term impediments, especially financial ones, notwithstanding, there existed great potential for further success. They overestimated the extent of their achievement in Japan and were unaware of the fragile base on which it was founded. No less than other groups in Japan, the missionaries were hostage to the fortunes of the *sengoku* period and its denouement.

One cannot question the sincerity of the Jesuit mission in Japan or the painstaking efforts put into "this vast enterprise" as Valignano styled the work.[24] Many of the fathers manifested exemplary diligence and patience in mastering the language. The Jesuits published Japanese grammars and dictionaries using Chinese characters and Japanese syllabaries, the most impressive of which are *Vocabulario da lingoa de Japam com a declaração em Portugues*, 1603, and João Rodrigues's *Arte da lingoa de Japam*, 1604, printed in Nagasaki on the Jesuits' moveable printing press.[25] They were extremely circumspect, however, about what European literature they translated into Japanese, not wishing to allow the Japanese to become familiar with the existence or doctrines of the Protestant heretics. One must emphasise that no matter the talent and achievement of the Jesuits, the Japanese were not confronted with a rational, scientific West any more than the Portuguese came face-to-face with a superstitious, backward Japan: the Europeans (Roman Catholic and Protestant alike) and the Japanese believed in a world influenced by spirits, good and evil.[26] Nevertheless, despite Valignano's realisation that unless the fathers established a native church "we shall always be regarded...as suspect foreigners," few Japanese were made priests by 1614, an achievement paralleled in the Philippines and elsewhere.[27]

What ultimately accounts for the banning of Christianity in Japan is not a perceived cultural threat,[28] but the political challenge that Hideyoshi and Ieyasu came to believe nestled in the heart of the doctrine. In 1587 an increasingly capricious Hideyoshi issued a decree expelling the missionaries, but this was not enforced. Ten years later, the arrival of the Franciscans, the storm-troopers of Iberian conquest in the New World, from Manila, shattered the Jesuits carefully laid campaign of presenting the Japanese with a picture of a united Church. Instead, the Catholic mission in Japan gained its first martyrs. To the intense chagrin of the Jesuits, the mendicant presence exposed fundamental differences of approach to missionary activity (the Jesuits, as so often in their history, were accused of focusing almost exclusively on the elite). These differences came to a head in the aftermath of the San Felipe incident, a Manila galleon bound for Acapulco which was shipwrecked on the coast of Shikoku in October 1596. What seemed an easily tractable issue over ownership of the wreck became an issue over which the unfortunate members of the Franciscan house in Kyoto and seventeen Japanese converts plus two Jesuit catechists were put to the stake in Nagasaki in February 1597. (With the exception of the catechists, the Jesuits were able to talk their way out of the death sentence and secure their freedom.)

What triggered this drastic measure was a remark attributed to the ship's pilot that the Spanish king (since 1580 king of Portugal as well, a development which the Japanese had been informed about) had used the friars as the vanguard of conquest in the New World. For Hideyoshi the parallel was easy to see: the armed Buddhist sects and religious *ikki*, or leagues, that had become major participants in the sengoku wars and whose military capacity he sought to emasculate, although without the blood-curdling measures associated with Oda who razed to the ground the armed headquarters of the Tendai sect on Mt. Hiei near Kyoto in 1571, giving no quarter. As foreigners, the missionaries were an easy-target. Yet it would be wrong, even at this date, to argue that the eventual expulsion of the missionaries and the proscription of Christianity in 1614 were a foregone conclusion.

One consequence of the executions of 1597 was to make it clear to the Japanese authorities that there was no link between the fate of the Christian mission in Japan and the continuation of the trade with Macao. Indeed three carracks arrived in Nagasaki the following year. (The imposition of the *itowappu* in 1604 caused more resentment among the Portuguese than the execution of the Christians.) Nevertheless, Portuguese supremacy in Japan's overseas trade, especially, the Sino-Japanese silk-silver trade, was on the verge of extinction. From 1604 Ieyasu, continuing another policy of his predecessor, issued licences (vermillion seals or *shuinjō*), similar to the Portuguese *cartazes*, for overseas trading voyages by Japanese vessels to the various entrepôt of southeast Asia. These voyages spawned a Japanese diaspora which, had it been permitted to flourish, would have become one of the most active and influential in the area. The *shuinsen* or vermillion seal vessels, as the ships were called, often employed Portuguese pilots and made use of Portuguese *portolanos* or navigational maps which were adapted for Japanese use but improved the delineation of the coasts surrounding Japan, captured the lion's share of Japan's overseas trade procuring silk from new markets, such as Tongking, and gave Japan access to a wider range of products for which there was a demand (sappan wood and deer hides from Siam) and which were not included in the manifests of the *nao* to any significant extent.[29]

Rivals

The Portuguese also faced a challenge from the Dutch and English East India Companies, although the extent of this challenge in the second decade of the XVII century when both companies had factories in Hirado, an island domain off the northwestern coast of Kyushu, should not be exaggerated. The Japanese officials and merchants who invested heavily in the *nao* voyages were reluctant to trust their investments to such ill-assorted, untested newcomers whose ships arrived and departed without predictability. Neither the Dutch nor the English made any major inroads into the Japanese market at this time. The Dutch used Hirado as a base from which to pursue their ambition to dominate the spice industry and trade of the Moluccas and their nation's greater struggle of national independence from the Hapsburg monarchy. They even re-exported most of the silk they acquired from attacking Portuguese and Chinese vessels in the China Seas from Japan.[30] It was only in the 1620s, once they had gained access to Persian silk (to satisfy European home demand) and Chinese silk from their factory on Taiwan (with which to supply Japan) that their trade in Japan took off. The English factory was poorly supplied throughout its brief history and was closed down in 1623, a move which the Dutch themselves had once seriously contemplated.[31]

There are several ironies in these developments. One is the failure of both companies to adopt clear policies for their Japanese factories before going to the trouble and expense of setting them up. The extent and profitability of Portuguese trade in Japan had been known in both the Netherlands and England since the early 1590s from Jan Huyghen van Linschoten, whose *Itinerario* was published in 1595-96 and which included detailed Portuguese *roteiros* or rutters for voyages between Macao and Japan, one of the most treasured prizes a trade rival could hope to acquire, and from information brought back to England in 1591 by Ralph Fitch, who had visited Malacca. Fitch estimated that the Portuguese exported 600,000 cruzados worth of silver yearly from Japan in return for their silk imports, making the trade as transparent as anyone could. Another irony is that given that the English did pull out of Japan, deeming their factory there a mismanaged drain on scarce capital, and the Dutch seriously considered doing so, the Portuguese might still have outlasted their Johnny-come-lately European enemies for it should be emphasised that there was nothing inevitable about the emergence of the Dutch as the sole European traders in Japan. Had this occurred, the variables that shaped the shogun's policy towards Japan's overseas trade in the 1630s would have been quite different and the outcome of the policy equally so perhaps resulting in no European presence in Japan had the Japanese still chosen to expel the Portuguese. But the Dutch stayed on and prospered. The shogun Tokugawa Iemitsu, having outlawed overseas voyages by Japanese vessels in 1635, thereby bringing to a sudden conclusion the *shuinsen* voyages, was able to turn to the Dutch from whom the Japanese received a prompt, affirmative reply that the VOC could take up the slack in Japan's overseas trade if the Portuguese were forced out.

The decision to expel the Lusitanians was finally taken in 1639 in the aftermath of Christian-millenarian uprising in Shimabara in 1637-38, and only after much procrastination; the shogunate did not want to destroy overseas trade, but rather to restructure it. The Portuguese were vulnerable because they could not shake off their association with Catholicism in the eyes of the Japanese. By the late-1630s, the *shuinsen* voyages, the presence of the Dutch and English, the involvement of Chinese traders operating from Japan and Taiwan in spite of the continued absence of official relations, the trade with Korea through the Sō domain of Tsushima and the indirect trade of the Satsuma domain in southwestern Kyushu with China through the Ryūkyū kingdom which had become a Satsuma tributary (with the full approval of the shogunate) in 1609, had all shown that Japan could eat the rich cake of foreign trade without having to drink the poison of Christianity.[32]

Trade with Macao was severed and the Portuguese ordered to leave Japan. Almost one hundred years of Luso-Japanese relations came to an abrupt, unsentimental end. A day of celebration was ordered in Batavia, where the governor-general of the VOC resided, when the news reached there. In Macao the panic bells sounded. A mission was despatched in 1640 seeking to have the exclusion order revoked. All members were executed, save for thirteen, who were allowed to return to Macao to bear witness to the terrifying reality that the decree was irrevocable.[33] Yet Macao survived and prospered while in Japan the achievement of those first Europeans became a distant memory.

Derek Massarella

Derek Massarella

Notes

[1] A. Cortesão (tr.), *The Suma Oriental of Tomé Pires*, 2 vols., (London: Hakluyt Society, 1944).

[2] Cortesão, *The Suma Oriental*, I, 131.

[3] For accounts of Sino-Japanese and Japanese-Korean relations see Charlotte von Verschuer, *Le commerce extérieur du Japon des origines au XVIe siècle*, (Paris: Maisonneuve et Larosse, 1988); Kawazoe Shoji, "Japan and East Asia" in Kozo Yamamura, ed., *The Cambridge History of Japan*, vol. 3, (Cambridge: Cambridge U. Press, 1990), 438-45; Jurgis Elisonas, "The Inseparable Trinity: Japan's Relations with China and Korea" in John Whitney Hall, ed., *The Cambridge History of Japan*, vol. IV, (Cambridge: Cambridge U. Press, 1991), 235-62, esp. 248-49.

[4] See Bailey W. Diffie and George D. Winius, *The Foundations of the Portuguese Empire, 1415-1580*, (Minneapolis: U. of Minnesota Press, 1977).

[5] The exact year, whether 1542 or 1543, cannot be settled conclusively. The most reliable of the European sources (António Galvão) gives 1542; a Japanese source, 23 September 1543. After weighing the available evidence Professor Schurhammer concludes that the latter is the most likely (Georg Schurhammer, "O Descobrimento do Japão pelos Portugueses no ano de 1543," *Orientalia*, 21 (1963): 532, 535).

[6] For different interpretations of the *wakō* see Kwan-wai So, *Japanese Piracy in Ming China during the Sixteenth Century*, (Michigan: Michigan State U. Press, 1975) and Elisonas, "The Inseparable Trinity," 250-62.

[7] The purchase price for the office of *Capitão-Mór* was around 20-30,000 xerafines. Profits were estimated at between 70-80,000 pardaos to 150,000 cruzados (C.R. Boxer, *The Great Ship from Amacon*, [Lisbon: Centro de Estudos Históricos Ultramarinos, 1963], 8). George Bryan Souza, *The Survival of Empire: Portuguese Trade and Society in China and the South China Sea, 1630-1754*, (Cambridge: Cambridge U. Press, 1986), pp. 19-20 provide more detail on the evolution of the office.

[8] For developments in Japan during the *sengoku* period see John Whitney Hall and Toyoda Takeshi, eds., *Japan in the Muromachi Age*, (Berkeley: U. of California Press, 1977); John Witney Hall, Nagahara Keiji, and Kozo Yamamura, eds., *Japan Before Tokugawa*, (Princeton: Princeton U. Press, 1981); Jeffrey P. Mass, ed., *Court and Bakufu in Japanese History*, (New Haven: Yale U. Press, 1982).

⁹ See William S. Atwell, "International Bullion Flows and the Chinese Economy Circa 1530-1650," *Past & Present* 95 (1982): 68-90; Souza, *Survival of Empire*, 57-58, 84-85.

¹⁰ Michael Cooper, ed., *This Island Japan: João Rodrigues' Account of 16th Century Japan*, (Tokyo: Kodansha, 1973), 133.

¹¹ Boxer, *Great Ship*, provides the best introduction to the trade.

¹² Derek Massarella, *A World Elsewhere: Europe's Encounter with Japan in the Sixteenth and Seventeenth Centuries*, (New Haven: Yale U. Press, 1990), 24.

¹³ Boxer, *Great Ship*, 42; Michael Cooper, "The Mechanics of the Macao-Nagasaki Trade," *Monumenta Nipponica* 27:4 (1972): 428. This did not restrain some of the fathers from indulging in private trade, which remained controversial throughout the Indies.

¹⁴ Diego Pachecho, "The Founding of the Port of Nagasaki and its Cession to the Society of Jesus," *Monumenta Nipponica* 25:3-4 (1970): 303-23.

¹⁵ C.R. Boxer, *The Christian Century in Japan, 1549-1640*, (Berkeley: U. of California Press, 1951), 101-02, who is inaccurate about the founding of Nagasaki; J.L. Alvarez-Taladriz, ed., *Sumario de las Cosas de Japon (1583)*. (Tokyo: Sophia U. Press, 1953), 78-79; George Elison, *Deus Destroyed*. (Cambridge, Massachusetts: Harvard U. Press, 1973), 96-97, who argues that the Jesuits were intent on establishing a military colony; Massarella, *A World Elsewhere*, 40-41.

¹⁶ Gold figured less among Portuguese imports from the early seventeenth century as the Portuguese faced competition from Japanese and Chinese carriers and also because Japanese production increased (Souza, *Survival of Empire*, 54).

¹⁷ Boxer, *Great Ship*, 179-81; Boxer, *Christian Century*, 425-27. The figures are rated at cost price in Macao, which was higher than in Canton, the source of these goods. There was no customs duty in Japan, although presents to various key officials were de rigueur, but not excessive. The captain of the *nao* was allowed 10 per cent freightage on the silk and given an advance of 500 taels on the other goods plus 60 peculs of the sales price per pecul (Boxer, *Great Ship*, 181).

¹⁸ Souza, *Survival of Empire*, 59, 65-75.

¹⁹ Geoffrey Parker, *The Military Revolution*, (Cambridge: Cambridge U. Press, 1988), 140.

²⁰ Parker, *The Military Revolution*, 143-44.

²¹ Paul van der Velde, ed., *The Deshima Dagregisters: Their Original Table of Contents*, vol. 4, (Leiden: Leiden Center for the History of European Expansion, 1989), 67.

[22] For accounts of the Portuguese influence on Japanese art see Georg Shurhammer, "Die Jesuitenmissionare des 16. und 17. Jahrhunderts und ihr Einfluss auf die Japanische Malerei," in *Orientalia*, 21, (1963): 769-79; C. R. Boxer, Fidalgos *in the Far East. 1550-1770* (Oxford: Oxford U. Press, 1968), 20-26; Fernando G. Gutiérrez S. J., "A Survey of Nanban Art," in Michael Cooper (ed.), *The Southern Barbarians*, (Tokyo: Kodansha, 1971), 147-206.

[23] Richard Hakluyt, *Principal Navigations*, 12 vols., (Glasgow: J. MacLehose, 1903-05), 11, 324-7. On the transmission of knowledge about Japan to Europe see Donald F. Lach, *Asia in the Making of Europe*, vol. I part 3, (Chicago: Chicago U. Press, 1965).

[24] Elison, *Deus Destroyed*, 71.

[25] The press had almost no impact on Japanese printing methods which continued to be dominated by woodblock printing technology.

[26] See Jacques Gernet, *China and the Christian Impact*, (Cambridge: Cambridge U. Press, 1985), 88; Keith Thomas, *Religion and the Decline of Magic* (Harmondsworth: Penguins Books, 1973), 790.

[27] Vincente L. Rafael, *Contracting Colonialism: Translation and Christian Conversion in Tagalog Society Under Early Spanish Rule* (Ithaca: Cornell U. Press, 1988), 185.

[28] The view of George Elison (*Deus Destroyed*, 72, 131).

[29] Hiroshi Nakamura, "The Japanese Portolanos of Portuguese Origin of the XVIth and XVIIth Centuries," *Imago Mundi* 18, (1964): 24-44.

[30] The threat of attack from the Dutch caused the Portuguese to spread their risk and from 1618 to employ smaller *galliota* for the Japan voyage. These vessels proved more adept than the larger *nao* at evading capture.

[31] See Massarella, *A World Elsewhere*, for a fuller exposition of these points.

[32] Massarella, *A World Elsewhere*, 343-46.

[33] Boxer, *Great Ship*, 163-65.

Map of Himalayas

Chapter XVI

Jesuit Explorers in *Padroado* Asia 1541-1721

Between 1541 and 1758 more than 2,100 Jesuits sailed from Lisbon to the Estado da India in service of the Portuguese *padroado*, or royally-controlled church within the papal donation.[1] Most became missionaries, administrators (both for their Order and for the Portuguese crown), confessors, preachers, and educators. Some, like those who served in the courts of the Mughals, Mings, Manchus, and Tokugawas, performed vital diplomatic functions. A few established remarkable records as explorers, becoming the first Europeans known to have seen and to have reported on remote Asian landscapes and their inhabitants. This essay focuses upon the exploits of seven Jesuit explorers in Asia. Four were born in Portugal, one in Spain, another in the Azores, and one in Italy.

The precursor: Francis Xavier

The man who led the way for the Society of Jesus was one of St. Ignatius's original disciples, the Basque-born Francis Xavier (1506-1552).[2] In April 1541 he sailed from Lisbon for Goa as the first representative of the Society of Jesus. Initially he was designated as mission superior and papal legate but in 1549 he became his Order's first provincial in the East. During the remarkable decade that preceded his death Xavier worked ceaselessly to convert pagans and to reform old Christians. He consoled the sick and the imprisoned, remonstrated with unscrupulous royal officials, and chastised and dismissed fellow Jesuits who failed to adhere to his severe ethical standards. His evangelical campaigns took him three times to the Fishery, Malabar, and Travancore coasts, twice to Bassein and Sri Lanka (Ceylon), five

times to Malacca, once to Amboina, the Moluccas, Japan, and ended his ceaseless travels in the Pearl River delta, the stepping stone to imperial China.

Strictly speaking, Xavier was not a discoverer but a follower, for nearly everywhere he went he had been preceded by other Europeans. The most conspicuous exception was the Japanese archipelago, first seen by a Portuguese navigator in 1543. Xavier reached the Land of the Rising Sun six years later. It was during his six-week sojourn in Kagoshima in southern island of Kyushu that he wrote enthusiastically that the Japanese "with whom we have thus far conversed are the best that we have yet discovered; and it seems...that, among pagan nations, there will not be another to surpass the Japanese."[3] While the founder of Jesuit enterprise in Japan was naturally primarily concerned about the possible receptivity of the islanders to Christianity, he did not ignore their economic promise, either. A few months later he wrote the governor of the Portuguese-controlled commercial entrepôt of Malacca that a comparable royal factory should be established in the port that served the capital, Miako, on the large island of Honshu, "for this harbor of Çacay is the richest of Japão, where much and the greater part of the silver and gold of the kingdom is collected." He promised to arrange to send a Japanese embassy to Goa "to see its grandeur and the things there which they lack, so that...the [Portuguese] governor [of India] and king of Japão will negotiate with each other on how the said factory may be established."[4]

Xavier, who died on the island of Shang-ch'uan (or São João), near Canton, China, in 1552, did not live to see the development of the famous silk trade between Portuguese Macao and Japan; nor did he witness the spectacular growth of his Order and its converts in the archipelago. By 1578 there were 44 Jesuits serving in the Japanese isles and they claimed to minister to 100,000 converts. The number of such neophytes grew to 200,000 by 1586 and, despite the temporary banishment of the fathers the next year, to 300,000 by 1592.[5] But what had for a time loomed as the Jesuits' most successful enterprise in eastern Asia ended disastrously for the Society in the early seventeenth century when the shogun expelled its members from Japan (1614) and his successors subsequently brutalized those who stayed behind or continued to enter the islands illicitly during the next three decades. Despite persisting efforts, the Japan enterprise could not be revived and the Society shifted its attention elsewhere in the Far East, primarily to the empire of China.[6]

Bento de Goes and the riddle of Cathay

The demise of Jesuit endeavors in Japan was partially offset by the development of a new enterprise in China. Where Xavier had led, many sought to follow, but until 1583 all were denied entry by Ming authorities. In that year Michele Ruggieri (1543-1607) and a companion succeeded in establishing the first Jesuit mission in China. Within five years Ruggieri was ordered back to Europe and his remarkably talented and discrete companion, Matteo Ricci (1552-1610) would effectively shepherd the Jesuit enterprise there, despite repeated reverses.[7]

Although Ricci's enterprise grew much more slowly than had the earlier Japan ventures, it endured. However, furnishing missionaries to the empire involved long, costly, and always hazardous sea travel from Lisbon to Goa, from Goa to Malacca, and from Malacca to Macao. Hence an alternative land route seemed worth investigating. That was one reason behind the remarkable odyssey of Bento de Goes (1603-1607). But another, more compelling puzzle was the one posed by centuries of reports concerning the existence of the kingdom of Cathay. European travelers had referred to such a kingdom since the mid-13th century. If the Franciscan friars Giovanni de Plano Carpini (1243) and Wilhelmus van Ruysbroeck, or "Roebuck," (1253) were understandably vague as to its location (since neither ever saw it), the Venetian-born merchant-adventurer Marco Polo was far more specific since he based his account of its riches and the power of its rulers upon his long sojourn there (1270s-1290s). Among others, Polo inspired Christopher Columbus, for Cathay was one of the objectives of his first New World expedition.[8]

Although Ricci became convinced that Cathay and China were simply different names for the same polity, Jesuit fathers in India became persuaded that Cathay was actually a separate kingdom surrounded by the Ming empire and by Muslim kingdoms and that it contained lost Nestorian Christian communities.[9] One source of that belief was an old Muslim merchant whom Fr. Jerónimo Xavier, superior of the so-called third Jesuit mission to the Mughal court, met in Lahore in 1598. The old man claimed that he had spent thirty years in the city of Kambalu, Cathay, where some of the inhabitants were followers of Jesus: they supposedly possessed temples and images, including that of the crucified Christ, and were led by priests garbed similar to the Jesuits themselves. Fr. Xavier reported this testimony to Provincial Nicolao Pimenta in Goa with the recommendation that a Jesuit mission seek Cathay via Lahore, Rabul, and points northeastward. Pimenta strongly endorsed the proposal, as did

Clement VIII and Spain's Philip III. The Pope was naturally anxious to enlarge the fold of the Church through the redemption of the peoples "lying between India and Cathay," while the king, who contributed to the expedition's expenses, sought to steal the march on Dutch and English seekers after a Northeast passage between Europe and Asia.[10] But the Jesuits' purposes in undertaking the mission were (1) to determine the true location of Cathay and (2) to establish contact with supposedly isolated Christian communities situated somewhere India and China.

It fell to Provincial Pimenta to determine who was most qualified to lead such a demanding expedition. His choice fell upon a seemingly unlikely candidate, Bento de Goes (Góes, Góis). Goes was born in 1562 in the Azorean town of Vila Franca on the island of São Miguel. Like many young men of his time, he sailed to India as a mercenary soldier to seek his fortune. In 1584 he was accepted as a novice in the Society of Jesus but before completing his novitiate withdrew and sailed off to the Persian Gulf entrepôt of Ormuz, presumably to engage in mercantile activity. Whether he attained material success there is unknown but it is evident that within a few years he became spiritually restless. Consequently, in 1588 he returned to India with a very useful working knowledge of Persian and sought readmission to the Society. He was taken back, an unusual step for the Order at that time. It seems unlikely that he declined to study for the priesthood, as some have written, since the option could never have been his. He, in fact, remained a lay brother, respected for his intelligence, his linguistic skills, his resourcefulness, and his courage. In 1595 he became one of three Jesuits to participate in the third mission to the Mughal court and there made use of his knowledge of Persian to ingratiate himself with powerful personages there. As a result, in 1601, Akbar the Great, the famous Mughal emperor, sent him Goa as his personal emissary with instructions to improve relations between the two governments.

When the provincial became satisfied that Goes was the right man to undertake this difficult assignment, he sent him back to the Mughal court at Agra to make his preparations. With supporting documents supplied by Akbar, the brother left Agra disguised as an Armenian merchant on 6 January 1603, accompanied by two Greeks and a trusted Armenian friend called Isaac. The party traveled to Lahore and from there to Peshawar and Kabul, a major caravan center where the Greeks left Brother Goes. As the accompanying map indicates, he then headed generally east, through the Pamirs to the oasis at Yarkand in western Sinkiang, and then struck northeast to Turfan, where he encountered merchants who had been to Peking (Beijing) who claimed to know Fr. Ricci and showed the brother documents that Ricci himself had written. Their testimony and the evidence they displayed convinced Goes that Ricci had been right all along: Cathay and China were identical. Still, he pressed on since his instructions required him to report before returning to India via a Macao-based carrack. Ultimately, at the end of 1605, he reached Suchau (Sucheu), a gateway to China from Turkestan near the westernmost bend of the Great Wall but still a four-month journey from Peking. He had prospered on his journey, for he then possessed thirteen horses, five paid and two unpaid servants, and merchandise valued at 2,500 gold pieces. But he found himself under what amounted to detention at Suchau and therefore sent two missives to Fr. Ricci to advise him of his arrival and to appeal for relief. His first letter was never delivered and his second did not reach the Peking Jesuits until November 1606. Ricci and his colleagues responded by dispatching one of their young Chinese students to guide Goes and his entourage to the imperial capital.

The would-be guide did not arrive at Suchau until late March 1607. He was shocked to discover the Azorean brother mortally ill, supposedly poisoned by jealous Muslims. Despite his ministrations, Bento de Goes expired less than two weeks after the emissary's arrival, but his death was not the final tragedy, for his enemies managed to seize and destroy his detailed diary, supposedly because it included a list of his debtors. Although Bento de Goes lost his life before completing his remarkable journey, his mission had been successful: he had traversed over 4,000 km of plateau and desert country seen by few previous Europeans; he had convincingly proved that there were no trapped Nestorian communities in Central Asia; and he had seemingly disposed of the notion that Cathay and China were separate entities, though, as will be seen below, there were still some doubters among the Jesuits in India. Well might Yule and Cordier term Goes's trek as "one of the most daring journeys in the whole history of discovery."[11]

The mystery of Tibet

Although Goes had skirted the high plateau of Tibet, he did not make it a primary focus of his endeavors, as did a series of Jesuit explorers during the seventeenth and early eighteenth centuries. They were led by the remarkably determined Fr. António de Andrade, the first European to enter Tibet. The mysterious highlands beyond India had long been the source of intriguing rumors to the Jesuits who had been informed for some decades that communities of Christians resided there. Fr. Andrade became determined to verify such rumors himself. Born in Oleiros in Beira Baixa in 1580, he joined the Society at age 16 and was sent to Goa to complete his studies four years later. After serving for a time as a missionary in the parishes of Goan Salsette, he became successively rector of the colleges of Rachol and New St. Paul's and then superior of the Mughal mission at Agra.[12]

In late March 1624 he and a brother, Manuel Marques, left Agra to follow the Mughal ruler who was making a tour of the northwest province of Kashmir. But when they reached Delhi Fr. Andrade learned that a large number of Hindus planned to undertake a pilgrimage to a temple in the Himalayas some two and a half months' distance to the north. Adopting a Hindu disguise, Andrade and his companion decided to tag along in order to gain an escort to the southern fringes of Tibet. It is presumed that they traveled through the upper Ganges valley via Hardwar, so-called "Gate of Vishnu," the shrine that attracted the pilgrims. At that point they were on the edge of Hindustan and in the territory of the rajah of Srinagar. At the town of Srinagar[13] Andrade and his companion were detained by authorities who recognized that they were neither merchants nor pilgrims. Andrade admitted as much and stated that he simply wished to explore Tibet. After being released he continued on to an important Hindu temple at Badrinath, situated at the foot of a 5,080 m. mountain of that name whose glaciers supply the Vishnu-Ganga. Leaving behind his companion, Andrade pressed on with two Christian servants and crossed the heavily snow-laden Mana pass, beyond which lay the Tibetan plains. He then entered the administrative center of Tsaparang (variously spelled), one of Tibet's leading towns, situated at an elevation of 4,750 m. on the bank of the Sutlej river. There he came to two conclusions: (a) there were no Christian communities nearby and (b) there could be if the Society successfully maintained a mission there. He therefore hastened back to Agra to report and to obtain reinforcements. Before they arrived, he returned to Tsaparang in 1625 and opened the first Christian mission in Tibet. It endured little more than five years, however, and reaped no more than 100 converts before it was destroyed, a victim of a political upheaval. The hoped-for reinforcements never arrived and Andrade experienced a lonely death in the high country. A subsequent attempt to restore the mission in 1640 ended in failure.[14]

Contemporaneously, two other Portuguese Jesuits were seeking to verify the existence of Cathay far to the east of Tsaparang. In the course of doing so they became the first Europeans to travel through the kingdoms of Bhutan, Nepal, and the southern Tibetan province of

Utsang. When Fr. Andrade returned to Tsaparang in 1625, he learned from merchants who had traveled there from China that one and a half month's journey eastward there was a populous kingdom named Utsang. Anxious to expand the Society's presence in the Himalayas, he wrote his superiors suggesting that they dispatch missionaries to Utsang via Bengal. The Jesuits regarded Bengal as part of their Malabar province and had maintained a fledgling (but never flourishing) college at Hughli, near modern Calcutta, since the beginning of the seventeenth century. Consequently it was the provincial of Malabar who detailed two Portuguese fathers and an Italian brother to Utsang.

As is so often the case, few biographical details survive concerning the two fathers, Estevão Cacella and João Cabral, and nothing is known about the background of Bartolomeo Fonteboa, an Italian-born brother who accompanied them.[15] Fr. Cacella was born at Aviz in 1585, entered the Society at age 19, and sailed for India in 1614. His companion, Fr. Cabral, was fourteen years younger, having been born in Celorico in 1599. He joined the Society at age 16 and departed from Lisbon for India in 1624. Two years later he joined Cacella in their remarkable adventure.

That adventure began on 30 April 1626 when the two missionary-explorers left the provincial capital, Cochin, for Hughli. There, according to Fr. Cabral's confident report, they were told that the road to Cathay was well populated, that the ascent was without difficulty, and that its people appeared to conduct themselves as if they were Christians. On 2 August they departed Hughli and reached Dacca ten days later. From there they proceeded to Azo [Hajo], then capital of the kingdom of Cocho but now the northeastern province of Assam. Because of adverse weather, they were unable to cross the mountains to the west until early February 1627. When they did so they traveled in the disguise of Portuguese soldiers in the hope of discouraging attacks by Mughal forces. In the kingdom of Bhutan they became interested observers of the practices of strict lamas but refrained from the sort of censorious comments to which early Christian missionaries so often resorted. As they traveled northward through that kingdom they must have been reminded of their own homeland as they observed that "The country is very rich in corn, rice and cattle, all of which is very cheap. There is an abundance of fruit, many kinds of pears...peaches, apples, walnuts and quinces...peas and very good turnips." Fr. Cacella added that the land was "well provided with Chinese merchandise such as silk, gold and porcelain... From here men go down into those regions, whilst trade is also carried on by them with the people of

[Kashmir]...." Despite the efforts of the local ruler to prevent the Jesuits from leaving his kingdom, the two fathers, traveling separately, managed to reach Shigatse (December 1627; January 1628), situated at an elevation of 3,600 m., a month to six weeks' journey east of Tsaparang. There they obtained authorization to establish a mission and, like Pizarro and Almagro on their way to Peru, they decided to separate: Cacella would stay while the younger Cabral would return to Hugli to report their findings and to obtain reinforcements. Because of the hostility of the ruler of Bhutan, Cabral took a circular route which caused him to pass through the high country of the kingdom of Nepal before descending to Patna (Patam), east of Benares, and following the Ganges down to Hughli. Though he was the first known European to gaze upon some of the world's highest peaks, they made no significant impression upon him. Rather, he was excited about the prospect of the new mission station at Shigatse, "the gate to the whole of Tartary, China, and many other pagan countries." But the mission was doomed to failure: Cacella died there in March 1630 and the provincial of Malabar, recognizing his inability to sustain such a remote base, declined to staff it and recalled Fr. Cabral to undertake another assignment. Until the second decade of the next century no Portuguese Jesuits would find their way to Tibet.[16]

But the memory of the achievements of Frs. Andrade, Cacella, and Cabral remained sources of inspiration to the embattled Jesuits of the provinces of Malabar and Goa. Beginning in 1704 the Portuguese Jesuit inspector (Visitor) to Goa, Manuel de Amaral, expressed a determination to restore the Tsaparang mission but he died before being able to fulfill his ambition. During the ensuing years several others volunteered to undertake the difficult assignment but were diverted to other tasks. The assignment ultimately fell to two men of quite dissimilar character and interests. One was Hippolyte [Ippolyto] Desideri who was born in Pistoia in 1684. He entered the Society at age 16 and upon the completion of his studies became the beneficiary of a special papal audience in September 1712 before sailing to India. Soon after his arrival in Goa the provincial asked him to restore the Jesuit mission to Tibet. It remains unclear whether the provincial was merely carrying out instructions from Father General Miguel Tamburini, known to favor such a move, or was proceeding on his own initiative. Certainly funding for such an undertaking had recently become available because of a large bequest of the Society's special benefactress, the still mysterious Dona Juliana Diaz da Costa.[17] In any case Desideri proceeded to Delhi, having been named superior of the

Jesuit mission to the Mughals.[18] There he encountered Emanuel Freyre, a Portuguese priest born in Ancião in 1679 and a member of the Mughal mission since 1710, assigned to be his companion, but whether as his superior or as his subordinate remains unclear. Some writers, including Fr. Cornelius Wessels, have assumed that since he was the elder, he was the expedition leader but that seems improbable because of his subsequent behavior and because Fr. Desideri was his administrative superior.[19] What is undeniable is that the two did not prove to be happy campers.[20]

Because of the known difficulties of ascending the Himalayas via the routes undertaken by Frs. Andrade, Cacella, and Cabral, the new team decided to approach Tibet via an end run. Accordingly, they proceeded from Delhi to the northwestern province of Kashmir and established their temporary residence in the other Srinagar, a city that the disgruntled Freyre found particularly unappealing.[21] But they remained there from November 1714 until mid-May 1715 awaiting the spring thaw and spending much of their time studying Persian and gathering information about possible routes to the high country. Beginning on 17 May 1715 they proceeded there on foot. For forty days they climbed higher and higher and encountered increasingly miserable conditions. They subsisted on half-cooked rice, were nearly overwhelmed by avalanches and snow-blindness, shivered at night in caves, and negotiated a harrowing crossing of a deep ravine spanned by a twisted willow bridge. It was an unforgettable experience for Freyre who vowed never to repeat it. Accordingly, after they reached the small town of Leh, capital of Ladakh in so-called Little Tibet and a regional herding center, he urged that they continue on to Lhasa, briefly visited in the 1660s by two intrepid Jesuits charged with discovering a feasible overland route from Beijing to Europe.[22]

Although Desideri preferred to establish a mission in Leh, he reluctantly agreed to accompany his colleague. After remaining there for two months they pressed eastward to Tashigong where the senior lama placed them in contact with a Tartar princess, widow of a regional governor and his successor as troop commander. She agreed to include them in her entourage of soldiers returning to their homes in Lhasa. The two fathers remained with her party for the next four months, traveling by horseback over the barren high plateau – land devoid of vegetation, dwellings, or inhabitants, combatting such severe cold that Freyre later confessed he had been provoked to utter curses against the weather, and enduring incessant attacks by body lice. En route they passed a 6,700 m. peak and the town Shigatse, neither of which prompted any comment from Freyre. Having nearly frozen to death on one occasion when he was nearly left behind, his sole ambition seems to have been personal survival. Accordingly, once they reached the holy city of Lhasa he resolved to abandon Tibet as quickly as possible and did so via Nepal. In his brief account of his travels he wrote little about the beauty, appearance or culture of the people of that kingdom but found space to remark on a devastating but unspecified plague that he observed, perhaps influenza, one that he said claimed 20,000 victims.

Freyre never went back to Tibet. Upon his return to Agra he submitted to the Father General a terse, superficial report of his travels in the Trans-Himalayas which demonstrates clearly enough that he had no zeal for missionary toil there nor any inclination to absorb anything of its culture. He soon resigned from the Society and disappeared from the historical record.[23] By contrast, his companion remained in or near Lhasa for the next five years, perfecting his knowledge of Tibetan and his understanding of the principles of the lamas' faith through the study of available religious texts and conversations with the lamas themselves. As a result, he wrote portions of an invaluable account which is partly a travel narrative, partly a history of Jesuit efforts in Tibet, but mainly handbook of the country, its religion, society, economy, and government. Revised and completed years later in Rome, it became the most comprehensive study of Tibet undertaken by any westerner and would remain so for at least a century and a quarter.

Fr. Desideri was compelled to leave Tibet in 1721. His departure was prompted not by local hostility or a coup d'état but by a decision reached in Rome. The Capuchins, rivals of the Jesuits in the Kongo and elsewhere, had taken advantage of the Jesuits' earlier abandonment of Tibet to send their own friars to Lhasa in 1704. They remained there until 1711, when they withdrew to Bengal. However, alarmed by the return of the Jesuits, the Capuchins secured papal authorization awarding their Order exclusive jurisdiction in Tibet. Desideri appealed that decision in vain: both the Capuchins and the papacy, which handed down a series of anti-Jesuit decisions during the first half of the eighteenth century, most notably its decrees condemning Jesuit attempts to reconcile Christian and Confucian concepts in China, remained unrelenting. Consequently, Desideri left Tibet in late 1721 and after serving as mission superior in the Carnatic for a time, he was sent to Rome in 1727. There he completed his remarkable manuscript and expired in 1733.[24]

Retrospect

Frs. Desideri and Freyre were the last Jesuit explorers in Asia prior to the suppression of the Society of Jesus. To be sure, the small contingent of missionary pioneers whose exploits have been summarized in this essay were far from being the only Jesuits to record their travels. Indeed, other Jesuits who served in the East left even more interesting personal accounts of their journeys. Two outstanding examples readily come to mind: first, the remarkable odyssey of Fr. Jerónimo Lobo who survived many misadventures at sea, including a major naval battle, two shipwrecks and capture by Dutch privateersmen and served in India and in Ethiopia (1621-1636), and second, the account by Manuel Godinho of his fascinating overland embassy between Goa and Lisbon via the Persian Gulf and the caravan route between Basra and Aleppo (1662-1663) as a viceregal emissary whose unfilled task was to persuade the Portuguese crown to repudiate the transfer of Bombay to the English.[25] But neither could be termed an explorer in the sense that each person traced here was. To be sure, their purpose was quite different than that of secular explorers who were intent upon gathering spoils or adventuring. The goals of these missionary explorers were to find lost Christians and to convert pagans to what they deemed the true faith. If they disappoint us by their silence upon the beauties of the landscape they traversed and the positive achievements of the peoples with whom they came in contact, that is because their interests and aspirations were quite different than ours would be under similar circumstances. Although some were more praiseworthy in their conduct than others, as a whole they displayed remarkable courage, fortitude, and determination in the face of awesome adversities. While they were the first Europeans to observe many peoples and places and deserve credit for having solved important geographic puzzles, they paid a high price for their achievements in terms of lingering painful infirmities and shortened lives. It is not surprising that these remarkable Jesuits had few imitators during their own lifetimes or, indeed, for generations to come.

Dauril Alden

Notes

[1] Josef Wicki, SJ, "Liste der Jesuiten-Indienfahrer, 1541-1758," in Hans Flasche, ed., *Aufsatz zur portugiesischen Kulturgeschichte, Band* 7 (Munster: Aschendorf, 1967), 252-450. This estimate excludes the French mission to China whose members served at the will of French rulers and in defiance of asserted Portuguese exclusivity in matters pertaining to the Church.

[2] The standard biography remains George Schurhammer, SJ, *Francis Xavier. His Life, His Times,* tr. M. Joseph Costelloe, SJ, 4 v., (Rome: The Jesuit Historical Institute, 1973-1982).

[3] Xavier to his colleagues in Goa, Aug. 1549, as quoted in Schurhammer, *Xavier,* 4:82. The founder of Jesuit enterprise in Japan was not alone in his enthusiasm for the Japanese. His Spanish-born companion and successor, Cosme de Torres, later wrote "These Japanese are more ready to be implanted with our holy faith than are all the other nations of the world. They are as prudent as can be imagined. They are governed by reason as much as, or more than, Spaniards." Schurhammer, *Xavier,* 269.

[4] Xavier to Dom Pedro da Silva, Cangoxima, 5 Nov. 1549, Schurhammer, *Xavier,* 98.

[5] Charles R. Boxer, *The Christian Century in Japan 1549-1650* (Berkeley: U. of California Press, 1951), 242; Josef Wicki, SJ, and John Gomes, SJ, eds., *Documenta indica,* 14 (Rome: Institutum Historicum Societatis Iesu, 1974), 239.

[6] Boxer, *Christian Century,* Chaps. VII-VIII; George Elison, *Deus Destroyed. The Image of Christianity in Early Modern Japan* (Cambridge, MA: Harvard U. Press, 1973).

[7] Louis J. Gallagher, S.J., tr. and ed., *China in the Sixteenth Century: the Journals of Matthew Ricci: 1583-1610* (1942) (Rpr., New York: Random House, 1953); Pascuale M. D'Elia, *Fonti Ricciane [:] Documenti originali concernenti Matteo Ricci e la storia delle Prime relazione tra l'Europa e la Cina (1579-1615),* 3 v. (Rome: Institutum Historicum Societatis Iesu, 1949); Jonathan D. Spence, *The Memory Palace of Matteo Ricci* (New York: Penguin Books, 1984).

[8] Henry Yule and Henri Cordier, comps., *Cathay and the Way Thither...* 4 v. in 2, Hakluyt Society, 2d ser., Nos. 33, 37, 38, and 41 (London, 1914-1915) and separately published.

[9] The Nestorian doctrine, based upon the belief that Jesus Christ represented two natures and two persons, that of God and that of man, spread eastward through Asia to China during the 6th and 7th centuries A. D. Although the numbers of Nestorians in the

Orient was evidently never large, rumors of their existence first came to Europe in the 11th century and intrigued churchmen and others from that time on. Nestorian communities supposedly situated in Cathay, the Himalayas, and elsewhere became associated with the fabled, embattled Prester John whose kingdom was sought by the Portuguese under Henry the navigator. Edward Maclagan, *The Jesuits and the Great Mogul* (London: Burfs, Oates & Washbourne Ltd., 1932), 336-337; Edgar Prestage, *The Portuguese Pioneers* (London: A. & C. Black Ltd., 1933), 349, *s.v.* "Prester John"; and Francis M. Rogers, *The Quest for Eastern Christians. Travels and Rumor in the Age of Discovery* (Minneapolis: U. of Minnesota Press, 1962).

[10] E.g., the instructions issued by the Company of Cathay to Martin Frobisher on his second (1577) voyage called for him to seek a strait to the East and to sail to China with two barks. Samuel Eliot Morison, *The Discovery of America: The Northern Voyages* (New York: Oxford U. Press, 1971), 517.

[11] Much has been written about the Goes mission. The most vital coeval sources include Fernão Guerreiro, *Relação anual das coisas que fizeram os padres da Companhia de Jesus nas suas missões...*, ed. Artur Viegas, 3 v. (Coimbra: Imprensa da Universidade, 1930-1942), 1: 310-314, and 3: 25-30; and Gallagher, ed. *Journals of Matthew Ricci*, 515-521. Leading secondary accounts include Yule and Cordier, *Cathay and the Way Thither*, 1: 154-182, and 4: 169-264; C[ornelius] Wessels, SJ, *Early Jesuit Travellers in Central Asia 1603-1721* (The Hague: Nishoff, 1924), Chap. 1; Maclagan, *The Jesuits and the Great Mogul*, 414, *s.v.* "Goes, Brother Benedict de"; and Vincent Cronin, *The Wise Man from the West* (New York: Dutton, 1955), Chap. 13.

[12] António Franco, SJ, *Ano santo da companhia de Jesus em Portugal* (1718) (Porto: Biblioteca do "Apostolado da Imprensa" Editora, 1930), 151-52.

[13] There were two towns named Srinagar, one in Kashmir, the other, the capital of Garhwal. Graham Sandberg, *The Exploration of Tibet, its History and Peculiarities from 1623 to 1904* (London: W. Thacker & Co., 1904), 23-27, ridiculed Andrade's widely published account of his first visit to Tibet based, in part, upon his assumption that Andrade claimed to have accompanied the Mughal to Kashmir and then proceeded from Srinagar to the destinations mentioned in the text. As Wessels demonstrates (see n. 14), Andrade almost certainly passed through the other Srinagar.

¹⁴ The fullest accounts of Andrade's travels and his abortive mission remains Wessels, *Early Jesuit Travellers*, Chaps. 2 and 3 and Appendix 1, condensed in his "Introduction" to Ippolito Desideri, *An Account of Tibet: The Travels of Ippolito Desideri of Pistoia S. J., 1712-1727*, ed. Filippo de Filippi, Rev. ed. (London: G. Routledge, 1937). See also Maclagan, *The Jesuits and the Great Mogul*, 402, *s.v.* "Andrade, Father Antonio."

¹⁵ The Italian brother, Bartolomeo Fonteboa, played no significant role in the expedition. He was older than the two fathers and sickly and was sent back to Hugli, where he died on 26 December 1626. See n. 16.

¹⁶ The foregoing is based largely on Wessels, *Early Jesuit Travelers*, Chap. V and Appendixes II and III, successive reports from Fr. Cacella, 4 Oct. 1627, and Cabral, 17 June 1628. See also Wessels, "Introduction" to Desideri *Account of Tibet*, 19-26.

¹⁷ Dona Juliana, patroness of Jesuit missions in India (d. 1734), was a Luso-Indian widow who was a lady in waiting at the Mughal court and a prominent convert to Christianity. See Maclagan, *The Jesuits and the Great Mogul*, Chap. XII.

¹⁸ The Jesuit "college" was usually at Agra but its members also accompanied the court to Delhi.

¹⁹ Wessels, *Early Jesuit Travelers*, 210; Desideri, *An Account of Tibet*, 113.

²⁰ On one occasion Desideri tartly noted that Freyre "who had been appointed to accompany me... abandoned me as soon as he arrived [in Lhasa]. *An Account of Tibet*, 112. But he rarely mentioned him by name and usually alluded to him as "the other Father."

²¹ On the two Srinagars, see n. 13 above.

²² Because of the long, hazardous sea journeys between Europe and China, made especially so during much of the seventeenth century because of Luso-Dutch naval rivalry in eastern waters, Jesuit authorities wanted to test the feasibility of an alternative all-land route. Accordingly, in 1661 two Jesuits in China were instructed to undertake such an overland expedition, the Austrian Johan Grueber and the Belgian Albert d'Orville. The two set out from Peking in mid-April 1661 and arrived in Lhasa in early October and remained there for about a month before they resumed their journey via Nepal, reaching Agra the following March. There Fr. d'Orville expired and was replaced by a German father, Heinrich Roth, who made their way via Isfahan, Armenia, Smyrna, and Sicily and arrived in Rome on 20 February 1664. See Wessels, *Early Jesuit Travelers*, Chap. VI, and same, "New Documents Relating to the

Journey of Fr. John Grueber," *Archivum Historicum Societatis Iesu*, 9 (Jul.-Dec. 1940): 281-302. More briefly, see Maclagan, *The Jesuits and the Great Mogul*, 357-58.

[23] An English translation of his report, dated 26 April 1717, appears as the Appendix in Desideri, *An Account of Tibet*. For his resignation and apparently unsuccessful effort to reenter the Order see same, 373, n. 77.

[24] The foregoing relies primarily upon Desideri, *An Account of Tibet*, passim. The jurisdictional dispute between the Capuchins and the Jesuits over Tibet is discussed on 112-13.

[25] *The Itinerário of Jerónimo Lobo*, tr. Donald M. Lockhart with Introduction and Notes by C. F. Beckingham, Hakluyt Society, 2d ser. No. 162 (London, 1984); John Correia-Afonso, SJ, and Vitálio Lobo, tr. and ed., *Intrepid Itinerant: Manuel Godinho and his Journey from India to Portugal in 1663* (Bombay: Oxford U. Press, 1990).

THE
VOYAGES
AND
ADVENTURES,
OF

Fernand Mendez Pinto,

A *Portugal* : During his

TRAVELS

for the fpace of one and twenty years in
The Kingdoms of Ethiopia, China, Tartaria, Cauchin-
china, Calaminham, Siam, Pegu , Japan, **and a
great part of the Eaft-Indiaes.**

With a *Relation* **and** *Defcription* **of moft of the Places
thereof;** their Religion , Laws, Riches , Cuftoms , **and**
Government **in time of Peace and War.**

Where he five times fuffered Shipwrack, **was fixteen times fold,
and thirteen times made a** Slave.

**Written Originally by himfelf in the Portugal Tongue,
and Dedicated to the**
Majefty of Philip King of Spain.

Done into Englifh by *H. C.* **Gent.**

LONDON,
Printed by *J. Macock,* for *Henry Cripps* , and *Lodowick Lloyd* , and are to
be fold at their fhop in *Popes head Alley* neer *Lumbar-ftreet.* **1653.**

Title page from 1st English edition of the Perigrinacam of Pinto

Chapter XVII

Consequences and Repercussions of the Portuguese Expansion on Literature

In his important study, *A Literatura portuguesa e a expansão ultramarina* (1943), the Portuguese critic, Hernâni Cidade, tells us that his people were destined by their geographical location opposite North Africa, and by the crusading nature of the founding fathers, to be the watchdogs or the defenders of the faith. It was this crusading spirit, he says, that determined the national character of the Portuguese and drove them overseas.[1]

Whether or not you agree with this thesis, the fact remains that the spirit of the crusade pervades all the literature produced by the Portuguese throughout the period of Expansion which is under discussion here. It was a rich literature, which in turn, provided the justification for their overseas conquests. There were other impulses for the overseas voyages, as pointed out by the British historian, Charles Boxer, who says that in addition to the crusading zeal, the desire for Guinea gold, the quest for Prester John, and the search for spices were equally important.[2]

Whatever the reasons were that drove the Portuguese overseas, the Age of Expansion was one of the most glorious periods in the history of Portugal. All of Europe was filled with envy and admiration for the achievements of the tiny nation that had added new dimensions to their daily lives. No other nation had given as much eminence to her navigators and explorers to the degree that Portugal had; and she was, indeed, justly proud of them. Those were epic times, and the times produced epic writers who immortalized in poetry and prose the epic deeds of their countrymen. There was an outpouring of "travel literature" in Portugal, which was as much in demand abroad as it was at home. "Travel literature," as it is called

generically, soon replaced the romance of chivalry in the popular taste. The term "travel literature," even when restricted to Portugal alone, is very broad indeed. Strictly speaking, it includes the works of all the chroniclers, travelers, diplomats, navigators, missionaries and poets that have written about the overseas expansion from the XV century to our day. And the list is not complete.

One might say that the opening gun in the Age of Expansion was fired in 1415 with the Conquest of Ceuta, which Gomes Eanes de Zurara immortalized in his *Crónica da tomada de Ceuta por el-rei D. João I.*[3] He completed it in 1440 but it was not published until 1664. It is believed that there may have been precursors of this type of literature in Portugal that must have served as a source for Zurara, but if so, they are lost. Ceuta was taken without too much resistance and with it a vast amount of booty which whetted the appetite of the Portuguese and led them to the wildest hopes that beyond Ceuta were to be found infinite fields for new conquest and unlimited riches. From then on, Prince Henry began to push the frontier of geographical knowledge further and further out until his death in 1460. The results of the expeditions he sent out along the west coast of Africa were chronicled by Zurara in his *Crónica do descobrimento e conquista de Guiné* (1453).[4] During the reign of Afonso V (1438-1481), there was some controversy regarding the legitimacy of the conquest of Ceuta from the religious point of view. But as the court chronicler, it fell to Zurara to justify it ideologically, which he did, by raising the Portuguese military enterprise to the level of a religious crusade. This justification included the capture of slaves and though he expressed compassion for them in his chronicles, he justified their capture by pointing out that their souls would be saved by baptism.

After the death in 1460 of Prince Henry who had held the monopoly of the West African trade, it was awarded by King Afonso V on a monopoly-contract basis to a rich Lisbon merchant by the name of Fernão Gomes, with the Crown reserving the right to monopolize a few valuable commodities. On the expiration of the contract in 1475, Afonso V entrusted the direction of the West African trade to his son and heir, the future King João II, and it became and remained a directly administered Crown monopoly on the latter's accession to the throne in 1481. With João II, gold traffic along the West Coast of Africa for which the factory-fortress of São Jorge da Mina was built, strengthened the position of the Crown, under whose direction, geographic and economic exploration of the newly discovered lands continued.[5] But it was King Manuel (1495-1521) who launched his nation on its spectacular career of militant enterprise in Monsoon Asia.

It may be said that the lyricism of the Middle Ages, the melancholic, repetitious, and simple melodies that distinguished the abundant poetry of Galicia and Portugal, now gave way to a severe and exultant prose, the chronicles of the historians, who found more inspiration in the exploits of warriors, crusaders, explorers, and adventurers, than in the love affairs of peasant girls and shepherds. History and historical evocation were, in fact, the most original forms of expression during the 15th century.

Chronicle as literature

That which is often referred to as the "historiography of the 1500s" appears only in the second half of the 16th century. Its most important representatives are Lopes de Castanheda,[6] João de Barros,[7] Damião de Góis,[8] Gaspar Correia,[9] and Diogo do Couto.[10] With them, the history of the country is now considered to be almost exclusively the recording of its overseas expansion. The nation was living on and for the Orient; that is why it is not surprising that the historians of King Manuel and John III give so much space to the events of those distant places, while paying less attention to the civil, economic and moral life of the country itself.

This preoccupation, imposed by circumstances, goes along with the patriotic enthusiasm motivated by the great deeds of the Portuguese in the Orient. It is in João de Barros (1496-1570) that one notes, more than in any other historian, this sense of the navigation and conquest. The navigation of the ancients – he writes – were as child's play compared to that of the Portuguese, and that the famous Argonauts navigated some 300 to 500 leagues, "dining in one port, supping in another, consuming many refreshments, and stopping frequently for water, with the result that their voyages were more of a pastime than toil."

João de Barros originally conceived of his work as a vast history which would embrace the Portuguese expansion from three different aspects – conquest, navigation, and trade. The first aspect was to be the object of four separate studies devoted to Europe, Asia, Africa, and Santa Cruz (Brazil). However, during his lifetime, only the first three *Décadas da Ásia* appeared in 1552, 1553, and 1563. Since he never visited the Orient, he did not have direct knowledge of the places about which he wrote, but he did have access to the archives of the Casa da Índia. Also, his administrative position as the official chronicler, and his conception of history as a rhetorical and moral construction, prevented him from telling the whole truth, to say nothing of the court censorship to which he was subject, as were indeed all the other historians of the 16th century.

Unlike João de Barros, Fernão Lopes de Castanheda had lived in India. He wanted his *História do descobrimento e conquista da Índia* (1551-1561) to be the first to celebrate the Portuguese expansion. It is composed of a great deal of narrative minutiae which the reader of today would find tiring, but which deals mainly with the human spectacle and the background in which it unfolds. It constitutes direct historiography elaborated by a man who walked on the ground he describes. Eight out of the ten books he wrote were published during the years 1551 and 1561. As they came out they were promptly translated into French, Italian, Spanish and English, and circulated throughout Europe with all the political and psychological consequences that the knowledge of the Portuguese expansion produced in the various European societies of the day.

Damião de Góis's *Crónica do felicíssimo rei D. Manuel* was published in 1566-67. His chronicle is a departure from the usual Portuguese style of the times in that his work is erudite and written in essay form. He criticizes and judges as much as he narrates, his attention given to questions of general interest, such as the expulsion of the Jews, the massacre of the New Christians, the Portuguese expansion, the Ethiopian material, the action of the King which he is not averse to consider severely, like someone who was not bound by Portuguese convention. All this and the unfavorable references he makes to so many protagonists of the drama that was the reign of John II, must have generated a great deal of animosity towards him, which led to his falling into the clutches of the Inquisition, in whose hands he died under mysterious circumstances.

Diogo do Couto continued the *Décadas* of João de Barros by order of Philip II. His historiography is direct and cultured. He was the friend and commentator of Camões. He wrote *Décadas* 4 to 12, and since he told the truth, his books were banned by royal order, his manuscripts lost, stolen, or burned, all of which he re-wrote from scratch.

Gaspar Correia's *Lendas da Índia* were not published until late in the 19th century. His work, which is perhaps the most vigorous literary monument to the Portuguese presence in the Orient, is direct in style. In addition to the careful information it contains, it has a rhythm and a sobriety that appeals to the reader. Correia has neither time nor interest in anything that is not part of the "epic" process. Disagreeing with the responsible local parties for the crisis in India, he made many enemies, and as a result, is believed to have died at the hands of an assassin. The original of much of his work was later stolen or concealed. Since he worked in India as secretary to Afonso de Albuquerque, his books have often been compared with Albuquerque's *Letters to the King*, published in 1884.[11] The few works just mentioned are the most important chronicles of the 16th century. Unfortunately, space does not permit me to say very much about them.

Poetry and the *Lusiads*

Between the middle of the 14th and the middle of the 15th centuries, no literary text is extant that attests to the cultivation of poetry in the Portuguese court. If Garcia de Resende had not undertaken the collection of his famous *Cancioneiro Geral* [12] of the poetry produced in the courts of Afonso V, John II, and Manuel I, we would be ignorant today of a considerable amount of it. However, it seems that poetry did not respond immediately to the "discovery epic" since it was written mainly to entertain the courtiers. The *Cancioneiro* was published in 1516 but it contains poetry from about the middle of the 15th century; and though most of it was written for the pleasure of the court, there are a few examples of poems devoted to the Expansion, but they are not very good. There is one by Sá de Miranda, dedicated to D. Luís, eulogizing his military action in Tunis; and not to be overlooked are the "Poemas Lusitanos" (1598) of his disciple, António Ferreira (1528-69), which are bursting with national pride.

Gil Vicente is also a collaborator in the *Cancioneiro Geral*. His theatre, which depicts the life of the times, also contributes, to a certain extent, to the collective pride in a Portugal that is both conqueror and discoverer. His play, *A Exortação da Guerra*, was inspired by the departure of the Duke of Bragança, D. Jaime, for the conquest of Azamor. It shows that he believes in the ideal of his time – that it is the duty of kings and Christian knights to carry the war to the infidel and maintain the customs that made it possible to expel them from Portugal. The same ideal is present in his *Barca do Inferno* as well as in his *Auto da Fama*. All of which proves that the spirit of the crusade was still very much alive in the early part of the 16th century, which was the most productive period in the life of Gil Vicente.[13]

By the time that Camões appeared on the scene, most of the literature of the Expansion had already been written. It was a literature that went into the creation of his masterpiece. It is that literature that I will attempt to trace here. I have no intention of doing an exegesis of the poem for I don't think it falls within the purview of this essay.

As you may already know, the *Lusiads* tells the story of a small nation which, in the space of a little over a century, carried the flag and its faith across the seas to Africa, Brazil, and as far as Japan.[14] It sings of "heroes who, leaving their native Portugal behind them, opened the way to Ceylon and beyond, across seas no man had ever sailed before."[15] Camões boasted of the "*saber... ganho com honesto estudo*" that went into the writing of his epic poem. For obvious reasons I have limited my discussion to just a few of the best known works that were available to Camões. Of these, the most important was the *Roteiro* or *Relação da viagem de Vasco da Gama*,[16] an anonymous work attributed to Álvaro Velho, who accompanied the Admiral on his momentous voyage. Better known to us are the *História do descobrimento e conquista da Índia pelos Portugueses* of Fernão Lopes de Castanheda, first published in 1551; and the *Décadas da Ásia* of João de Barros, the first of which was published in 1552. These were available to Camões prior to his departure for India in 1553. Also, Gaspar Correia's *Lendas da Índia*, which he probably finished writing soon before his death in Goa in 1565; and though they were not published until late in the 19th century, it is possible that Camões, who was in India at that time, may have read the manuscript. The first edition of Damião de Góis's *Crónica do felicíssimo rei D. Manuel* was printed in 1566, the year before Camões left India. Due to censorship, most of the copies of this edition were destroyed, and the book was reprinted the following year with significant changes; so that in 1569, when Camões returned to Lisbon, it would have been possible for him to read the corrected edition of 1567.

These are, of course, the best known works on the overseas expansion that have come down to us; but who knows how many others Camões may have read that were either proscribed, stolen, or lost – as was the case with the *Suma Oriental* of Tomé Pires,[17] a copy of which was discovered in Paris in 1937 by Armando Cortesão, who translated and edited the English edition for the Hakluyt Society in 1944. There were many others – both published and unpublished, which Camões probably read on his return, such as the *Comentários de Afonso de Albuquerque*, printed in 1557,[18] ten years before the poet's departure for India. And of course, there were the shipwreck narratives[19] which had begun to appear in *cordel* in the latter half of the 16th century, the most famous of which, that of the great galleon *São João* in 1553, that told of the subsequent wanderings and tragic death of Manuel de Sousa Sepúlveda, whose tale was woven into the *Lusiads*. And it is possible that Camões made use of the Jesuit *Litterae annuae*, or Letterbooks, the annual reports of the missionaries to their superiors in Portugal. It is known that João de Barros himself relied on these annual letters for his information on China and Japan. The first collection of these letters was published in 1555, and included a letter written by the then Jesuit Brother Fernão Mendes Pinto.[20] Perhaps Camões had access to António Galvão's *Tratado dos descobrimentos antigos e modernos* which was published in 1563;[21] and in that same year in Goa, he must certainly have read Garcia da Orta's *Colóquios dos simples e drogas da Índia*,[22] since it contains the first poem of Camões to appear in print.

The naturalist Alexander Humboldt and others have proven that Camões's description of the flora and fauna of índia were influenced by the work of Garcia da Orta. When Camões refers to such natural phenomena as waterspouts and St. Elmo's fire, it can be assumed that he does so because they were recorded by João de Castro (1500-1548), author of the *Roteiros de Goa a Suez, de Goa a Diu, de Lisboa a Goa*.[23] Almost every time he describes peoples, landscapes, geography, the exotic features of Africa or the Orient, or incidents during Vasco da Gama's voyage, he bases his account on a chronicle, travelogue, or some other document, in an attempt to achieve strict accuracy. This he combines with the mythological exploits of the heroes of classical antiquity, with whom he compares the exploits of the Portuguese, which he finds superior to those of the ancients.

In an article published in 1972, Luís de Albuquerque tried to establish the historical sources used by Camões for his account of the Vasco da Gama voyage. His study was limited to that portion of the voyage from Mozambique to Melindi. On the assumption, which is quite plausible, that the *Lusiads* were completed in 1569, he examined the works that were available to Camões prior to that date either in manuscript or printed form. He points out that the most important document for the voyage of Vasco da Gama was the *Relação* of Álvaro Velho, whose influence is apparent in the accounts written by Castanheda, Barros, and de Góis. Castanheda, especially, he says, copied whole paragraphs from álvaro Velho's *Relação*. After a detailed comparison of these texts with the *Lusiads*, he comes to the conclusion that Camões consulted both Álvaro Velho and Castanheda directly, as well as other sources. He finds in the *Lusiads* references to facts that only appear in like manner in the *Relação* of Vasco da Gama's shipboard companion, as well as to others that do not appear in any of the other chronicles; in short, he leaves us with the conviction that Camões did not stray too far from the "*puras verdades*" that he found in the texts he consulted.[24]

Wandering as moral truth

If Camões was the greatest poet of the Expansion, then Fernão Mendes Pinto, author of the *Peregrinação*, was the greatest prose writer of the period.[25] Written some time between the years 1569 and 1578, the *Peregrinação* was not published until 1614, some thirty odd years after the author's death. It purports to be an autobiographical account of one man's journey through Asia during the 16th century, a journey that begins in the year 1537 and ends in 1558 when our weary traveler returns to Portugal, after an absence of 21 years. As the title implies, the *Peregrinação* also represents one man's spiritual journey through life, during which he has overcome trials, tribulations, and tests of Christian morality, with only death to separate a man from his ultimate spiritual home and eternal bliss.

There is no doubt that the material that went into the composition of the *Peregrinação* was drawn from the author's own experience of twenty years in Asia, as well as the experience of others, whose tales he heard and borrowed for his masterpiece. But of equal importance were the books that Pinto read about Asia. And very often, the germ of an idea or an episode can be traced to its source.

Albert Kammerer, a French expert on the Near East, doubts that Pinto ever set foot in Ethiopia, and this despite the fact that Pinto's account is fairly accurate. He even concedes that the few mistakes made by Pinto were made as well by other more respected writers on the early history of Ethiopia. Nevertheless, Kammerer regards Pinto's relation as "*d'authenticité douteuse.*" It is highly probable that Pinto based his description of Ethiopia on Father Francisco Álvares's *Verdadeira informaçam das terras do Preste Joam*, written in 1520 but not published until 1540 in Lisbon.[27] It is even more probable that Pinto had purchased the second edition of this work which was translated into Spanish by Thomas de Padilla and published at Saragossa in 1561 under the title of *Historia de las cosas de Ethiópia*. In support of this claim I offer the fact that appended to this second edition was a Jesuit letterbook[28] containing a letter that Pinto had written from Malacca on December 5, 1554, when he himself was a member of the Jesuit Society. Pinto may well have had a copy of this book in his library.

That Pinto read the Jesuit letterbooks is apparent from a comparison between the episode following his departure from Ethiopia (Chap. 5) and a letter by Brother Fulgêncio Freire to the patriarch of Ethiopia. In both instances the Portuguese engage a Turkish man o'war, are beaten and are taken captive to a Red Sea port. And in both instances the circumstances are too similar to be accidental. Brother Fulgêncio's letter of August 1560 was published in Barcelona in 1562, which was just about the time that Pinto was preparing to write his book.

For his description of China, especially for the interior of China, Pinto borrowed freely from Gaspar da Cruz's *Tratado das cousas da China* (1569)[29], as well as from the reports, written and oral, of the

Portuguese prisoners in China who later escaped or were ransomed by their countrymen.

Those are just a few of the examples of the literature of the Expansion which Pinto plagiarized – a perfectly acceptable thing to do at that time.

But Pinto also borrowed from the medieval travel writers who preceded the Portuguese writers of the Expansion. Of all of them, Pinto is most indebted to Odoric of Pordenone[30], who traveled in Asia from 1326 to 1330 and from whose relation he borrowed his description of *suttee*, or the rite of widow burning. To Odoric's *Travels* he also owes his description of the figure he calls the "Talapicor" of Lechune, who is strongly reminiscent of the Dalai Lama.[31]

There is no doubt that the *Peregrinação* is a work of profound moral and religious philosophy. The thesis is "sin and punishment" and the sin is regarded as a crime against God, which receives its due punishment in turn, from the hand of God. Pinto is extremely critical – though never openly so – of the overseas action of the Portuguese, whose self-proclaimed mission to conquer and convert was viewed, from the author's perspective, as a false and corrupt ideal. That is what sets him apart from his contemporaries, Camões included, because he alone, at the dawn of the age of European colonialism, had the courage to question the morality of the overseas Expansion, which he condemns as acts of barbarous piracy. That is what he tries to make clear in the well known António de Faria[32] episode, which is a parody of the overseas action of the Portuguese. And that is precisely what makes the *Peregrinação* a unique document in the history of Western thought.

Pinto's pagans, particularly the Chinese, seem to live in a utopia. They have never heard of Christ, yet they obey the laws of God. They are governed with justice, charity, and mercy by kings who also obey God's laws. That is why they are blessed by God with abundance of wealth and all the good things on earth. They are tolerant of others. They have the freedom to worship God in many different ways and even the freedom *not* to worship God – a daring concept for a man of that age. In other words, Pinto is trying to tell us that there is a morality possible outside the bounds of an established church.

Pinto's criticism of the Portuguese is expressed indirectly, with the utmost duplicity. His book pays full and absolute lip service to the orthodoxy of his day, and is overlaid with the same hypocrisy he charged them with. As long as outward appearances and the proper ritual were observed, he was safe. This was an age when men lost their lives for inattention to form and ritual. The risk he took was a gamble and in the end he triumphed. He gambled perhaps on posterity; but certainly on the select audience that his message was directed to, and was confident that his irony and duplicity would pass – as it did – unperceived, over the head and under the nose of the Inquisition which praised his book warmly. The Censor was satisfied with the surface homage paid to the reigning orthodoxy, for Pinto was careful to cover his indirect criticism with formal protestations of faith. He understood all too well the spirit of the age which laid great stress on the formal observance and outward trappings of piety.

In conclusion, I would like to suggest that a study be done of the medieval travel literature that may or may not have influenced the Portuguese literature of Expansion. I don't think it has yet been considered. Also, I would like to consider – perhaps at some future time – the reverse of the question I have been discussing, with a view to determine not what were the consequences and repercussions of the Portuguese Expansion on the literature of the period, but what were the consequences and repercussions of the literature on the European Expansion. An example that comes to mind is that of the influence that Marco Polo's book had on Columbus's discovery of America.

But I do think it is remarkable that both Pinto and Camões, two literary giants, should appear towards the end of the Age of Expansion, and that they should both constitute, as they do, two precious vessels into which was gathered the essence of the preceding generations.

Rebecca Catz

Notes

[1] Hernâni Cidade, *A literatura portuguesa e a expansão ultramarina.* (Lisbon: Agência Geral das Colónias, Divisão de Publicações e Biblioteca, 1941) vol. I, 13.

[2] Charles R. Boxer, *The Portuguese Seaborne Empire, 1415-1825.* 2nd ed., (London: Hutchinson of London, 1977), 36-37.

[3] Gomes Eanes de Zurara, *Crónica da tomada de Ceuta por el-rei D. João I*, Luciano Cordeiro and Melo de Azevedo, eds. (Lisbon: Editorial da Biblioteca de Clássicos Portuguesas, 1899-1900).

[4] ____. *Crónica do descobrimento e conquista de Guiné.* José de Bragança, ed. 2 vols. (Porto: Livraria Civilização, 1937).

[5] Gaetano Ferro, *As navegações portuguesas no Atlântico e na Índia.* Trad. José Colaço Barreiros. (Lisbon: Editorial Teorema, Ltda., 1989)

[6] Lopes de Castanheda, *História do descobrimento e conquista da índia pelos portugueses.* M. Lopes de Almeida, ed. 2 vols. (Porto: Lello & Irmão, 1979.)

[7] João de Barros, *Da Ásia de João de Barros e de Diogo do Couto.* 24 vols. (Lisbon: Na Regia Officina Typografica, 1778-1788).

[8] Damião de Góis, *Crónica do felicíssimo rei D. Manuel.* David Lopes, ed. 4 vols. (Coimbra: U. Press, 1926, repr. 1949-55.)

[9] Gaspar Correia, *Lendas da Índia.* 4 vols., M. Lopes de Almeida, ed. (Porto: Lello & Irmão, 1975.)

[10] See note 7 above.

[11] *Cartas de Afonso de Albuquerque, seguidas de documentos que as elucidam.* R. A. de Bulhão Pato e Henrique Lopes de Mendonça, eds. 7 vols. (Lisbon: Academia Real das Sciencias, 1884); (Coimbra: Imprensa de Universidade, 1915); (Lisbon: Imprensa Nacional, 1935). (1884-1935).

[12] Garcia de Resende, *Cancioneiro Geral.* 5 vols. (Coimbra: Imprensa da Universidade, 1910-1917).

[13] A. Braamcamp Freire, *Vida e Obras de Gil Vicente,* "Trovador, Mestre da Balança." 2nd ed., Lisbon, Edição da *Revista Ocidente,* 1944.

[14] Vasco Graça Moura, "Luís de Camões," *The Courier* (Unesco), April, 1989, 17-25.

[15] *Canto* I, i.

[16] E. G. Ravenstein, ed., *A Journal of the First Voyage of Vasco da Gama.* (London: Hakluyt Society, 1898). See also *Diario da viagem de Vasco da Gama,* 2 vols. (Porto: Livraria Civilização, 1945).

[17] Armando Cortesão, ed., *A Suma Oriental de Tomé Pires.* 2nd ser., vol. 89, (London: Hakluyt Society, 1944).

[18] Brás de Albuquerque, ed., *Comentários de Afonso de Albuquerque.* 5th ed. 2 vols. (Lisbon: Imprensa Nacional-Casa da Moeda, 1973).

[19] Bernardo Gomes de Brito, *História Trágico-Marítima,* 2 v. (Lisbon: Edições Afrodite, 1971).

[20] *Copia de unas cartas de algunos padres y hermanos de la compañia de Jesus...* [Coimbra] Por Juan Alvarez, MDLV.

[21] António Galvão, *Tratado dos descobrimentos antigos e modernos,* or *Discoveries of the World.* Bi-lingual edition published by the Hakluyt Society, London, 1862.

[22] Garcia da Orta, *Coloquios dos simples e drogas da Índia.* Conde de Ficalho, ed. 2 vols. (Lisboa: Imprensa Nacional, 1891).

[23] João de Castro, *Roteiros de Goa a Suez, de Goa a Diu, de Lisboa a Goa.* 5 vols. (Lisbon: Agência Geral das Colónias, 1940).

²⁴ Luís de Albuquerque, "A Viagem de Vasco da Gama entre Moçambique e Melinde, segundo *Os Lusíadas*, e segundo as crónicas," *Revista Garcia da Orta*, número especial (Lisbon, 1972), 11-35.

²⁵ Rebecca Catz, ed. and trans. *The Travels of Mendes Pinto.* (Chicago: U. of Chicago Press, 1989).

²⁶ Albert Kammerer, "Le problématique voyage en Abyssinie de Fernand Mendez Pinto (1537)," in *La mer rouge, l'Abyssinie, et l'Arabie aux XVIᵉᵐᵉ et XVIIᵉᵐᵉ siècles et la cartoqraphie des portulans du monde oriental.* (Cairo: Société Royale de Géographie d'Egypte, 1947), 21-30.

²⁷ Francisco Álvares, *The Prester John of the Indies.* Rev. & ed. by C. F. Beckingham and G. J. B. Huntingford. 2 vols. (London: Hakluyt Society Publications Nos. 114-115, 1961).

²⁸ See n. 20 above.

²⁹ Gaspar da Cruz, *Tratado das cousas da China.* Aníbal Pinto de Castro, ed. (Porto: Lello & Irmão, 1984), 11-678.

³⁰ Henry Yule, ed.,"The Travels of Odoric of Pordenone," in *Cathay and the Way Thither.* 2d series, Hakluyt Society Publications, vols. 33, 37, 38, 41 (4 v.) (London, 1913-16).

31 See Chapter 127 of the *Peregrinação*.

32 See the António de Faria episode, Chapters 38-79 or pp. 66-153 of the Catz edition.

Aureus numer⁹	litera dominica	Interuallū Concurrentes		februā septuage	martii qdᵗagesi	aplis pascha	maii rogationes	Jūti pentecoste	Jūti corpe xti	beb a pet ad Jo dice superfluī	beb a p ad aduent
		| Residuuz table festoz mobiliuz									
3	e	8	4	9	2	13	18	1	12	3	2	26
	f	8	5	10	3	14	19	2	13	3	1	26
11	g	8	6	11	4	15	20	3	14	3	0	26
	A	9	0	12	5	16	21	4	15	2	6	26
19	b	9	1	13	6	17	22	5	16	2	5	25
8	c	9	2	14	7	18	23	6	17	2	4	25
	d	9	3	15	8	19	24	7	18	2	3	25
	e	9	4	16	9	20	25	8	19	2	2	25
	f	9	5	17	10	21	26	9	20	2	1	25
	g	9	6	18	11	22	27	10	21	2	0	25
	A	10	0	19	12	23	28	11	22	1	6	25
	b	10	1	20	13	24	29	12	23	1	5	24
	c	10	2	21	14	25	30	13	24	1	4	24

Expliciūt table tablaz astronomice Raby abraham zacuti
astronomi serenisimi Regis emanuel Rex portugalie et tc̄
cū canonib⁹ traductis alinga ebrayca in latinū p magistrū
Joseph vizinū discipulū ei⁹ actoris opera et arte viri sole
tis magistri ortas curaqz sua nō mediocri inpresione cōple
te existūt felicib⁹ astris año apma rex etereaz circuitione
1496 sole existēte in 15 g 53 m 35 z piscinz sub celo leyree

From Abraham Zacuto's Almanach

Chapter XVIII

Portugal and the Dawn of Modern Science

Ⅰn *Beyond Objectivism and Relativism* the American philosopher, Richard J. Bernstein, assessing briefly Thomas Kuhn's thesis on scientific revolutions, says:

> The Austrian philosopher, Karl Popper (and others who have made a similar point) correctly note that the line between normal science and revolutionary science is not nearly as sharp as Kuhn sometimes suggests. Normal science is more like revolutionary science, and revolutionary science is more like normal science than Kuhn (at times) leads us to believe. (Bernstein, 1983:70)

Another scholar, John Krige has written along these lines developing, Koyré and Clavelin's views, which agree with Kuhn's on the fact that Aristotelian cosmology and mechanics were rejected and replaced by a new conception of the universe; but, according to Krige, those two historians emphasize that the transition from one world view to the other took time – "it was a process not an event." (Krige, 1980:37)

Krige adduces a feature of Feyerabend's views on scientific revolutions, namely the one of "uneven development of science," and he summarizes his thesis in these terms:

> For Koyré, at least, continuity and discontinuity are not mutually exclusive categories; but they are not equally fruitful ways of understanding the historical process, either.

> My aim... is to defend a conception of discontinuity which, like that of Kuhn and Feyerabend, sees such transitions as involving the complete replacement of one system of thought by another, but differs from theirs in that it emphasizes that such transitions *take time*...(Krige, 1980, 178)

Krige ends his book by insisting that "revolutionary transformations of the human understanding are neither cataclysmic nor do they demolish an existing structure in one blinding flash"; he stresses the fact that rejection of the old system and replacement by the new one do not occur simultaneously; that "science develops unevenly," and that

> discontinuist history is sensitive to differences, seeks to explain them, and to identify the deep structures of which they are the manifest effects. It is patient. It realizes that decades, perhaps centuries, are needed for one universe of discourse or pattern of relationships to replace a rival. (Krige, 1980, 219)

Kuhn would probably agree with all this. Critics may have simply stressed one aspect left out by Kuhn because he was mainly interested in showing the actual shifting of paradigms. In any event, this essay, rather than arguing whether or not Kuhn deserves Krige's criticism, will attempt to support the point made by the latter. I would like to use the generally forgotten case of the Portuguese discoveries during the XV and the XVI centuries. This case study, I believe, will support Bernstein's point and Krige's thesis. If my demonstration is successful, the Portuguese case will enhance A. Ruppert Hall's demarcation boundaries for the first scientific revolution – 1500-1800 (Hall, 1954) – which were recently adopted by Stephen Brush (1988:4). Furthermore, the experimental scientific activities carried out in Portugal will suggest the necessity to stress the spatial-temporal dispersion and discontinuity of the stages of the evolutionary process of the paradigmatic revolution. A corollary supported by a close scrutiny of what took place in Portugal is the question of the thesis defended by Ernan McMullin, according to which "the goal of technical control played virtually no part in the origins of science." (McMullin, 1984, 54) It is supported by a close scrutiny of what took place in Portugal.

The enterprise of the discoveries started in the early 1400s under the leadership of Prince Henry the Navigator. There is a "romantic" view of Prince Henry and his "school" that is still alive in popular accounts of the discoveries. Although the arguments to be presented here will not be based on such accounts, the exaggerated language of the myth will provide a good starting point. The following quotation comes from Daniel J. Boorstin's, *The Discoverers*

> While Prince Henry at Sagres did not actually build a modern research institute, he did bring together all the essential ingredients. He collected the books and the charts, the sea captains, pilots, and mariners, the map-makers, instrument makers, and compass-makers, the ship builders and carpenters and other craftsmen, to plan voyages, to assess the findings,

and to prepare expeditions even further into the unknown. The work Prince Henry started would never end. (164)

This romantic view was born in England (Samuel Purchas, in the XVII century) and it has been divested of its mythical elements by Portuguese historians of this century (Leite, 1958-1960). However, if Prince Henry was not the creator of new ships, a trainer of sailors or an educator of pilots, "he found all this at his command," as the historian Bailey W. Diffie put it. "What he needed to do, and what he did, was to give focus to Portuguese energies" (Diffie and Winius, I, 122). After surveying the available literature, Diffie sums up Prince Henry's legacy to the world in these terms: "No other name has the importance of Henry's in the history of the world's greatest exploring nation – Portugal." (Diffie and Winius, I, 122) It was in this sense that the English physicist Sir George Thomson stated that Prince Henry the Navigator was the "midwife of science." (Hooykaas, 426)

Here, I would like to call attention to an enterprise which, when perceived and analyzed in its total perspective, allows us to conclude that if the Portuguese enterprise did not start with the technologically oriented "school" of Sagres; it progressively moved towards an "invisible college" as the seaborne empire became established some fifty years after the death of Prince Henry. The names of four scientific and technically minded figures excel: Duarte Pacheco Pereira (c. 1460-1533), Pedro Nunes (1502-1578), D. João de Castro (1500-1548), and Garcia de Orta (1503-1568). Their works leave us with evidence that in the fields of nautical sciences, geography, astronomy, mathematics, cartography, tropical medicine, as well as scientific methodology and cooperation among theoretically oriented minds and artisans with technicians, Portugal played a key role in the dawn of modern science. Even though one can find a dozen other authors whose works revealed and contributed to the development of the experimental spirit, it is indeed those abovementioned four authors who were the front runners of such new spirit. Their works are: Duarte Pacheco Pereira, *Esmeraldo de Situ Orbis*, written between 1505 and 1508, which is simultaneously a log book, a navigation guide, and a book of cosmography; Pedro Nunes, mainly the *Tratado em Defensam da Carta de Marear* (Lisboa, 1537); D. João de Castro, mainly in his *Roteiros*, written between 1538 and 1541; and Garcia de Orta, in his *Coloquios dos Simples e Drogas de Cousas Medicinais da Índia*, published in Goa, India, in 1563.

We could summarize the innovative features of these works:
a) Rejection of the authority of the Ancients *per se*;
b) Acceptance of experience as the key criterion of truth;

c) Development of a scientific outlook and methodology;
d) Interface of theory and practice, and of scholars and artisans;
e) Overall awareness of the importance of the new knowledge
   acquired by the Portuguese navigators in the opening of
   new frontiers.

Let us glance quickly at each one of these points:

a) Rejection of the authority of the Ancients *per se*

It is indeed long the list of passages one could quote from the works of Pereira, Nunes, Castro and Orta, where the authority of the Ancients is not only questioned but rejected outright. Here are a few representative samples from *Esmeraldo de Situ Orbis*. The first one is from a description of the Serra de Fernam do Poo:

> This country is very near the Equator, which the ancients declared to be uninhabitable but experience has shown us that this is not so. (Pereira, English Edition, 1937, 134)

Introducing a description of the routes and landmarks from Guabam River to Caterina Cape, he states:

> Experience has disabused us of the errors and fictions which some of the ancient cosmographers were guilty of in their description of land and sea; for they declared that all equatorial country was uninhabitable on account of the heat of the sun. We have proved this to be false...(Pereira, 135)

Duarte Pacheco Pereira introduces his fourth book with general considerations aimed at showing the errors of the Ancients:

> Our own predecessors and those who lived even earlier in other countries could never believe that a time would come when our West would be made known to the East and to India as it now is. The writers who spoke of those regions told so many fables about them that it seemed utterly impossible that the seas and lands of India could be explored by the West.
>
> Ptolemy in his portrayal of the ancient tables of cosmography writes that the Indiana Sea is like a lake, far removed from our western Ocean which passes by southern Ethiopia; and that between these two seas there was a strip of land which made it completely impossible for any ship to enter the Indian Sea. Others said that the voyage was so long as to be impossible and that there were many sirens and great fishes and dangerous animals which made navigation impossible.
>
> Both Pomponius Mela (at the beginning of the second book and also in the middle of the third book of his *De Situ Orbis*) and Master John Sacrobosco, an English writer skilled

in the art of astronomy (at the end of the third chapter of his treatise on the sphere), said that the country on the Equator was uninhabitable owing to the great heat of the sun, and since it was uninhabitable for this reason it could not admit of navigation. But all this is false and we have reason to wonder that such excellent authors as these, and also Pliny and other writers who averred this, should have fallen into so great an error; for they all allow that India is the real East and that its population is without number. Since the real East is the Equator, which passes through Guinea and India, and since the greater part of this region is inhabited, the falsehood of what they wrote is clearly proved, for at the Equator itself experience has shown us that the land is thickly populated. Since experience is the mother of knowledge, it has taught us the absolute truth; for our Emperor Manuel, being a man of enterprise and great honor, sent out Vasco da Gama, Commander of the Order of Santiaguo, one of his courtiers, as captain of his ships and crews to discover and explore those seas and lands concerning which the ancients had filled us with such fear and dread; after great difficulty, he found the opposite of what most of the ancient writers had said. (Pereira, 164-5)

When editing Ptolemy's *Geographia* Pedro Nunes does not even bother annotating his geographical descriptions. The reason he provides is quite obvious to him:

because the thoughts advanced by Ptolemy in this first book, which is the foundation of all his Geography, are so weak: and the reasons that in it he uses have such little strength so much that whoever reads him will be able to understand easily how little information was possessed in his time of the places of the earth...(Nunes, 1940, 176)

Garcia de Orta, who wrote on medicine, uses the didactic style of dialogue between himself, who possesses a "modern" outlook, and his Ruano, a fictional figure whose knowledge is totally based on the authority of the Ancients, for whom he displays a tremendous respect. He points out errors in Averroes and Aristotle, mocks the fanatic followers of the classics, who accept blindly whatever they say even though it may have already been proven wrong by the findings of the navigators and travelers:

because the lands are now more discovered and more known... we now discover more the past errors and people's mistakes. (*Orta*, I, 345)

I do not criticize the Greeks for being the inventors of good letters, as you say; but they are also inventors of many lies. (*Orta*, II, 333)

He feels free to criticize Galen and the Greeks:

> Do not make me afraid of Discorides or Galen, because I will
> say only the truth and what I know. (*Orta*, I, 105)

Orta claims, however, that in Spain he wouldn't dare say anything against them (*Orta*, I, 835) so heavy is the pro-classic humanistic atmosphere. It is his the famous claim that "one knows more in one day from the Portuguese than one could know in one hundred years from the Romans." (*Orta*, I, 210)

D. João de Castro affirms with conviction that the Ancients (St. Augustine included) were ignorant of the existence of the antipodes (Castro, I, 57s). In another passage he states that "nothing is darker and confused in the minds of people and the writings of the Ancients than the cosmography of this / Red Sea / and land" (*Orta*, II, 183) and he criticized or rejected Aristotle when he was in possession of facts which did not support the philosopher's claims.

b) Acceptance of experience as the fundamental criterion of truth

A Portuguese historian labeled what took place in Portugal during the time of the discoveries "the revolution of experience." (Osório, 1947) In one of the above quotations, Duarte Pacheco Pereira justifies his correction of the teachings of the Ancients with the fact that his knowledge was acquired through experience – "experience is the mother of things" – a statement which becomes almost a leitmotif in his book.

In those passages in which the knowledge inherited from the Ancients is challenged, what prompts such challenge is the fact that the new knowledge proceeds from experience – "experience has shown us that this is not so" (Pereira, 1936, 134); "experience has disabused us of the errors and fictions (Pereira, 135); "since experience is the mother of knowledge, it has taught us the absolute truth" (Pereira, 165); "we will proceed with our plan on this toilsome journey, relating truth as we have learned it from experience" (Pereira, 171).

Garcia de Orta criticizes over and over the teachings and "fables" invented without any empirical ground. D. João de Castro's works abound in references to non-verified statements and the importance of first hand experience. A few examples:

> For who can take away from the world this opinion of the
> Ancients? The great experience of the moderns and mainly the
> many navigations of Portugal. (Castro, *Tratado da Esfera* Ed.
> Fontoura Costa, 1940, 305)

It is D. João de Castro who advances further into the analysis of the criteria of truth. As concerned as he is with the data of experience, he assigns, however, an important role to judgment (*entendimento*) in correcting the often deceitful "imagination":

> If one judged only by the senses, all of us would judge that the sun has about the size of a cartwheel, but judgment demonstrates that it is indeed many times larger than the whole earth. (Castro, *Obras*, 55)

Before proceeding, it should be pointed out that Castro, who still functions within the overall classical framework, in spite of the growing transformations he himself brings to it, uses experience as an argument against the alleged motion of the earth. (Castro, I, 60ff) It must be stressed also that the importance of experience had already been recognized by the Greeks themselves. Even Aristotle elaborates on the concept. Galen wrote on experience. So did Robert Grosseteste, Nicolau de Oresme, Theodoric of Friburg and Roger Bacon. (Almeida, 1985, 1179-1186) What is new in Portugal is not the introduction of the concept of experience as a fundamental criterion of truth, but the realization that it is through experience that knowledge must be primarily acquired, as well as the spreading of the belief that a large area of knowledge received from the Ancients must be rejected and replaced by the overwhelming empirical evidence brought forth by the Portuguese discoverers. It is the rooting and the rapid spread of a new outlook, a new mentality, which was to spread with increasing momentum towards the complete revolution and overthrow of the classical world view consummated in the XVII century.

c) Development of a scientific outlook and methodology

Together with correcting the teachings of the Ancients through the new data collected, the "new spirit" reaches further. R. Hooykaas has pointed out that there is a wide gap between Castro's scientific viewpoint underlying his *Tratado da Esfera*, still basically Aristotelian, and his "practical" *Roteiros*, limited in scope to the report of his experience and experiments. Hooykaas writes extensively on Castro's experimental method. In the background of his tasks of noting, as often as possible, the direction of the wind and current, the depth of bays and harbors, and the variation of the needle, "was always the wish to test some accepted rule or to find new rules of nature." (Hooykaas, 355) His awareness of the disturbing factors in observations are summed up by Hooykaas in the following terms:

> Castro's insight in these complications becomes evident almost from the beginning of his journey from Lisbon to Goa, when he

recognizes that the seemingly whimsical behavior of nature may be caused a) by human errors (defects of the senses; lack of skill in manipulating instruments; erroneous calculations which often are a consequence of scanty knowledge of the theory), b) by defects of the instruments, and c) by the influence of the environment on the phenomenon one wishes to single out. (Hooykaas, 355)

Hooykaas provides ample evidence for each of those possibilities from the long and detailed list of Castro's observations, measurements and experiments. Here is an example from Castro's *Roteiros*:

Because I often mention the altitude taken by many persons and intended before hand to do so, it may be that those who read this Roteiro, when finding such a great difference between the altitudes found by the one and the other, could believe that the diversity would ensue from the use of different tables of / solar / declination or from errors of calculation. / Hence his decision to always use the tables of Pedro Nunes / so that the difference will originate only from the judgment of each of them, or from the defects of the astrolabs." (Castro, I, 137)

Hooykaas notes that Castro always mentions meticulously the differences between the observations made by different people and practically always says who they were.

On the instruments, Hooykaas again points to the fact that Castro performed himself practically all measurements of an astronomical, magnetical and hydrographical character, and that before he left for India, besides studying the theoretical aspects of the instruments, under the guidance of Pedro Nunes, he received training in their use. It is Castro himself who states at some point:

for those things that are under the jurisdiction of the mathematical arts, accuracy is of the greatest necessity. (Castro, II, 73)

Serious attention is given to the instruments. Once, when there were serious discrepancies in the readings, one instrument was completely taken apart, cleaned, and the needle was "touched" again with the same lodestone, even though the situation was not resolved. The point was to ensure that all the needles in question were "touched" by the same lodestone.

A few times, when Castro is faced with a problem and he has exhausted all possibilities available to him, he notes that he leaves the problem to Pedro Nunes, the mathematician who stayed behind in Lisbon. (Castro I, 184)

It was through experience that Castro realized and noted that it made no difference whether a needle had been magnetized in Germany by a German lodestone, or in India by an Indian. He concluded that "in spite of the region being so different, the property of the stones appears to be the same."(Castro, I, 74)

It is in this serious problem of variations in magnetic needles that the scientific mind of Castro leads him step by step to the discovery of the fact that the presence of metal objects such as cannon or an anchor "disarranges" the direction of the needle of the compass. The fascinating step-by-step account of this discovery is a remarkable example of scientific methodology and discovery. The late Portuguese mathematician and historian, Luís de Albuquerque has repeatedly claimed for Castro this discovery, which in the history of science is still credited to the French Denis, who rediscovered it in 1666, about 120 years after João de Castro. (Albuquerque, 1983, 115) Albuquerque says:

> Experimentally – but already conducting himself in a critical and modern manner – D. João de Castro could place in question, irrefutably, the false principle of a direct relationship between longitude and magnetic declination. But this result, though significant for its time, was not the only one to which his observations took him. He acted, in truth, as an experimenter situated in the aurora of a science which was to give fruit with its roots in the 16th century. . .
>
> Castro not only proceeded with scrupulous meticulousness in his observations, but also sought always to make them under the best possible conditions, hoping for a calm sea or disembarking on land if possible. Beyond this, whenever he had the opportunity, he would repeat the observations in the same spot or nearby, using various instruments and in successive days, comparing afterwards the results at which he arrived. (Albuquerque, 1983, 113ff)

Then Castro tests hypotheses and laws. In one instance, after successive experiments, he concludes that "the opinion of those who say that on the meridian of these / Canaries / islands the needle points to the true poles of the world, is false." (Castro, I, 136)

On other occasion, his conclusion goes:

> From these operations it is evident that the variation of the needles is not as the difference of the meridian (...) but it seems that there is some other relation, which up until today has not come to my knowledge.(Castro, I, 184)

Looking at the overall picture, Hooykaas is of the opinion that Castro's scientific attitude is rarely met before 1600 and that his was a lonely position in the 1530s and 1540s. He even "reported his failures and mistakes as faithfully as his successes and by doing so he was unique in his own time." (Hooykaas, 392) But the new empirical outlook was not really limited to Castro or Orta even though they may have surpassed their contemporaries, as we can infer from the words of Christopher Columbus:

> The king of Portugal sent Mestre José, his physician and astrologer, to Guinea in 1485, to observe the altitude of the sun in all of Guinea. (Quoted in Diffie and Winius, 141.)

d) Interface of theory and practice, of scholars and artisans

Here Hooykaas again demonstrates the close relations which existed between Castro and the designer and mathematician Nunes, as well as the maker of his instruments, Gonçalves.

But this is almost a leitmotif among Portuguese historians of the period, particularly J. Barradas de Carvalho. If the Portuguese role in the development of science was not one of theoretical breakthroughs, it was a unique example of a close relationship between doers and thinkers. Their problems are the practical difficulties arising in the course of navigation that must be solved. The contribution of the experts is requested, and they interact.

Martim Afonso de Sousa, upon his return voyage from Brazil in 1533, discussed with the court mathematician the difficult problems he encountered in the meticulously recorded observations he himself had made on board. (Nunes, I, 159) D. João de Castro works very closely with the sailors for his readings of the altitudes. When he leaves for India, he brings along an "instrumento de sombras" and the declination tables of Pedro Nunes in order to test their practical use. As J. Silva Dias has pointed out, Castro's utilization of such tools brought him results as well as doubts not foreseen by his teacher and which he, in turn, could not solve, either. (Dias, 145)

Moreover, most of the works of these men are written not for scholars but for laymen immersed in the actual process of the discoveries. Their authors explicitly state such awareness, concerns and objectives.

e) Overall awareness of the importance of the new knowledge acquired by the Portuguese navigators in the opening of new frontiers

Duarte Pacheco Pereira stated it rather bluntly already in the early 1500s:

> We have sailed along the coast and have many years' experience...In this we, the Portuguese, have excelled the ancients and moderns in such wise that we may justly say that, compared with us, they knew nothing. (Castro, 141)

The following sentences from the *Tratado em Defensam da Carta de Marear* of Pedro Nunes are a remarkable example of the awareness these people possessed of the chain of events they had set in motion for the world:

> There is no doubt that the voyages of this reign, for one hundred years now, are the grandest, the most marvelous, of the highest and most discreet conjectures, more so than those of any other people in the world. The Portuguese dared to venture into the great ocean. They went without fear. They discovered new islands, new lands, new seas, new peoples, and, above all, a new sky and new stars. And they so lost their fear that not even the heat of that torrid zone, nor the extreme cold of the far south, with which the ancients threatened them, could hinder them; that losing the North star and finding it returned again, discovering and passing the fearful Cape of Good Hope, the seas of Ethiopia, of Arabia, of Persia, they could arrive in India. They passed the Ganges, that oft-named river, and the great Traprobana, and the most eastern islands. They cleared us of many ignorant ideas and showed us that antipodes did in fact exist there, which even the saints had doubted, and that there is no such region that, because of heat or of cold, is uninhabitable. And that in the same climate and same equinoctial distance there are white and black men and of many different kinds. And they made the sea so plain that today there is nobody who dares to say that he found again some small island, some *baixos* or even some rock (*penedo*) which has not been found already by our navigations. (Nunes, *Obras*, 1940, 175f)

The overall assessment of the advancements made in the various fields of science by the Portuguese is expertly synthesized by Albuquerque in a two-page conclusion to one of his books on science during the Portuguese discoveries. It deserves to be quoted here almost in its entirety:

> Without the pretense of exhausting a theme that merits careful analysis, I sought in this book to show how the development of navigation, starting in the 15th century, demanded, on the one hand, the adoption of new ways of navigating and imposed, on the other, the necessity of recording all conditions under which the maritime voyages in the Atlantic sailed.

This last circumstance required of the navigators careful observation of wind patterns, currents and other phenomena of the physical geography, a posture immediately taken also in relation to the ways and customs of the until-then unknown peoples with which contact was established, in relation to the new flora and fauna of the recently discovered lands, and even to the new stars of the Southern hemisphere. In the beginning of the 16th century this "observation" already had the connotation of "experience" (many times with the restricted meaning of "practice"), claimed in an unclear manner by one Duarte Pacheco Pereira, and even incorrectly by one João de Lisboa; nevertheless D. João de Castro, as well as Garcia de Orta, can already be pointed out as men who regard experimentation in a way closer to the "moderns."

As to navigational technique, one can see that it required the utilization of traditional sciences, such as Astronomy or Geometry (the interference of the latter is above all visible – in naval construction...) However, as the knowledge necessary for the nautical science practiced could be taken from [their] works without great difficulty, this art of navigation never became the impetus for the development of Astronomy, even if it might have contributed to increase the number of stars registered in the celestial catalogs.

Without a doubt it was the first attitude coming out of the Discoveries (that is, the curiosity surrounding all that the voyagers had observed and recorded), the link that most clearly related the Discoveries with the development of science; and the two cases expressly indicated here (Castro, for the study of terrestrial magnetism; Orta, for the study of medicinal plants) constitute, perhaps, the most clear exponents of this relation.

In any case, one cannot fail to recognize that the extent of the Discoveries altered the world's thinking. The more or less impressive reports of. the voyages sped through Europe, were avidly read, and altered traditional schemes of thought. The Atlantic and Indian Oceans, for example, were no longer closed seas, as Ptolemy had taught, known in the West only since the beginning of the 15th century. And as paradigms of those reports we have the *Suma* of Tomé Pires and the *Livro* of Duarte Barbosa (both before 1520), that describe with objective rigor the eastern world cloaked during so many years by fantastic tales. (Albuquerque, 1983, 121ff)

There is a general agreement that the Portuguese advancements did not bring about a major shift of the 16th Century scientific paradigm. Barradas de Carvalho, influenced by a philosophy of history close to Althusser's, has claimed that a pre-epistemological rupture took place in Portugal (Carvalho, 1983), but he himself recognizes that even people like D. João de Castro function within the Aristotelian world view, following his organicist model, as opposed to the mechanicist which replaced it in Newton and Galileo's times.[1]

Hooykaas, who considers Castro a pioneer in experimental physics, aptly calls Castro's work scientific, and with it, the corpus of scientific advancements brought forth by him and the other above mentioned Portuguese as "science in Manueline style," for these works combine "a medieval world view in cosmology and physics with an unprejudiced modern "natural history" (description of lands and living beings) as well as a modern experimental approach in "mathematics" (magnetism). With Castro as the emblematic figure, they represent "an intermediate stage between ancient and modern natural science." (Hooykaas, 421) He explains his borrowing of an architectural term classifying the particular architecture which developed in Portugal in the times of King Manuel I, when the Portuguese discoveries reached their peak:

> The architecture of the Manueline period shows also the remarkable combination of a traditional style together with new, naturalistic elements. In what is nowadays called the "Manueline style" no basically new forms of architecture were introduced, but on the essentially gothic medieval structure was applied an ornamentation which no longer followed the rules of gothic art. The builders borrowed it from what the voyagers described or showed to them of foreign countries, and the representation then was not conventional but realistic. The emblems of imperial power, armillary spheres and globes, and the exotic plants and animals, were no creation of phantasy, like the dragons, unicorns and heraldic lions, but real things. In these ornamental additions the heroic enterprises were immortalized by sails, ropes, cables, pulleys and floats and by naturalistic representations of plants and animals seen in the seas (seaweed, corals) or on the land of Africa and Asia." (Castro, 422)

What conclusions are to be drawn from all this? As it was spelled out in the beginning of this paper, the first scientific revolution appears to have taken longer than Thomas Kuhn seems to suggest. If it is true that one could go endlessly pushing the divisory line further and further back, it seems that the Portuguese case emerges as a complex and intertwined set of events composed of some of the major features (although many in their early stages) which were to characterize the great scientific paradigm shift that operated in the 17th century. As a whole, it announces, points to, and provokes the acceleration to that revolution. As such, it requires the stretching of the boundaries of the first revolution to a longer span of time as well as of space, since Portugal is usually left outside the center stage where the revolution took place. At least, its example should soften considerably the demarcatory limits. Moreover, the Portuguese case seems to constitute a strong proof that: a) science advances through stretches of fragmented efforts, often interrupted or discontinuous both in time and in space; b) that it advances with overlapping of conflicting paradigms; c) that there are parallel creations and recreations at different times without knowledge of the previous ones, d) that there is uneven development of the individual sciences. All these features have been pointed in the debate surrounding Kuhn's thesis, but in that debate the Portuguese case is systematically absent.

On pursuing the history of science

Hence a final remark on these puzzling gaps in the history of science. They exist apparently because many of the above cited documents are written in a language not usually known by scientists. If the historical accounts are deficient, the theoretical inferences built upon them are also likely to be deficient. Let me substantiate my claim that the Portuguese case is not given its due in the history of science, simply because it is not well known. What follows is a corollary that attempts to address this specific question.

Years ago, when I first became interested in the writings of the Portuguese "experientialists," as some people prefer to call them, I used to consult the standard histories of science to check what importance was given to those names. After having consulted them and only rarely finding a reference or two to a Portuguese name, my conclusion was that the role of the Portuguese was not considered important in the universal context. Today, after reading a lot more on the history of science of the times, I realize that I committed the "authority fallacy," for I accepted unconditionally the weight of the words of the historians of science. Understanding a bit more about the modus operandi of research, particularly the natural tendency of taking for granted what has been repeated traditionally by the authorities in a field, as well as the vague and arguable character of many criteria utilized to include or exclude names and to decide on divisory dates. I am now more critical of those general studies.

If the foregoing examples calling attention to the importance of the Portuguese enterprise of the discoveries has any validity whatsoever, one may be impelled to ask why it is not better known. The answer today seems quite clear.

Recently I took a second look at some of the most often cited histories of science and searched for references to the Portuguese, in order to verify the reliability and quality of their sources – to learn whether the references are first hand, and whether they are updated.

Out of twenty-one authors, two of them, Thorndike and Taton, appear to have consulted key Portuguese documents, namely the works of Pedro Nunes and Garcia de Orta. The work of D. João de Castro is mentioned only by Sarton.

In none of those studies does there seem to be any awareness of the existence of works by such reputable Portuguese historians of the discoveries as Joaquim Bensaúde, Duarte Leite, Jaime Cortesão, and Joaquim de Carvalho, Sarton's being the only exception in regards to Bensaúde. The more recent of those books show no knowledge whatsoever of the more contemporary works of Luís de Albuquerque and J. Barradas de Carvalho, nor of the studies of R. Hooykaas.

Taton says of Pedro Nunes that he was "the foremost Iberian mathematician of the 16th Century," "a brilliant and inventive man" who left his mark on more than one branch of scientific endeavor." (Taton, 46) Thorndike refers often to, and quotes extensively from, the works of Nunes and Orta.

As to the role played by the Portuguese sea enterprises in general, the historians of science say very little beyond merely mentioning them, along with the names of Prince Henry, the "school of Sagres," Vasco da Gama and Magellan.

Moreover, there seems to be a clear correlation between the emphasis given to the importance of the Portuguese discoveries and knowledge of Portuguese documents and bibliography. Cases in point are those of Marie Boas, W. P. Wightman, Taton and Thorndike. Acquaintance with the fundamental work of J. Bensaúde, published in French, seems to have weighed considerably in the emphasis given to the Portuguese by Boas and Wightman. Nonetheless, it is still very little, for none of the above twenty-one historians of science shows any evidence of being well informed about the Portuguese case.[2]

An interesting example of how direct knowledge of existing documents as well as good acquaintance with contemporary Portuguese historiography might affect considerably the general outlook of an historian is the case of the Italian historian Carlo M. Cipolla. His familiarity with Portuguese sources is remarkable and not to be compared with that of the historians of science mentioned above. In *Guns, Sails, and Empires. Technical Innovation and the Early Phases of European Expansion, 1400-1700* (Cipolla, 1985) he adopts the expression "Vasco da Gama era" to label the period of European expansion and travels overseas.[3] His bibliography lists some thirty entries on the Portuguese, most of them in Portuguese. Such wealth of information seems almost enough in itself to explain the difference of treatment the Portuguese case receives in his little book.

Our conclusions also seem to be supported by the case of another historian of science, Aldo Mieli, who in his multivolume *Panorama General de Historia de la Ciencia* (1951) reveals a thorough knowledge of Portuguese sources and who, as a consequence, devotes almost a full chapter to the Portuguese voyages.

As one more proof that the more familiar a historian of science is with what took place in Portugal during the epoch of the discoveries the greater is the attention those events receive in his/her overall accounts is George Sarton, who, as indicated in our tables, did possess a considerable amount of knowledge on the matter, at least by comparison with his counterparts. As a result, in his *A Short Account of Scientific Progress during the Renaissance*, it is worth noticing the emphasis and names included in a synthesis of only one paragraph:

> Geographical discoveries were initiated by Henry the Navigator, and in this respect the Renaissance was heralded not by Italians but by Portuguese. Their initiative was followed gradually by other nations. It is hardly necessary to recite those heroic deeds, for everybody is familiar with them. A few names will suffice to awaken your memories: Bartholomeu Dias (1488), Columbus (1492), Vasco da Gama (1498), Amerigo Vespucci (1497-1504), Magellan (1519-22), etc. The Renaissance was truly the golden age of geographical discovery; by the year 1600 the surface of the known earth was doubled. Was not that an achievement of incredible pregnancy? The earth was doubled! It was not only a matter of quantity, but one of quality as well. New climates, new aspects of nature were revealed. (Sarton, 6)

Aquilino Ribeiro, one of the best Portuguese writers of this century, wrote once that the Portuguese language has been the "sumptuous mausoleum" of a great literature written in a language few people know. The same fate has befallen the other writings in that language.

But the Portuguese themselves do not seem to do very much to make their productions available in translation. Many of the best works of the period of the discoveries have never been translated. Those which have been translated appeared only in the last century and exist in some libraries as rare books. Studies written in Portuguese, such as those of Duarte Leite, Jaime Cortesão and Luís de Albuquerque, have still not been translated. But even the exceptions confirm our general conclusion. Joaquim Bensaúde's *Histoire de la Science Nautique Portugaise a l'Époque des Grandes Découvertes*, seems to have been poorly distributed, judging from the absence of references to it even in the works of French historians of science. R. Hooykaas published his remarkable book on D. João de Castro – the leading navigator and experimental scientist of Portugal – as an Appendix to the Portuguese edition of the complete works of D. João de Castro, published in Coimbra, Portugal. J. Barradas de Carvalho's thesis *À la Recherche de la Spécificité de la Renaissance Portugaise* was published in French by a Portuguese Foundation in Paris, a fact that limited immensely its distribution.

Such massive convergence of historical and cultural circumstances may after all explain why the Portuguese role in the early steps of the overthrowing of the classical world view goes largely unacknowledged in the history of science.

One cannot deny that language factors here seem to hamper the historians' perspective as one also cannot fail to notice that some historical events, due to circumstances alien to historical truth, unduly receive more attention than others. One wonders why an enterprise on such a grand scale as the Portuguese step-by-step discovery of the sea route to India has not aroused the curiosity of the historians of science about their scientific knowledge in astronomy, cartography, nautical science, and technology – in ship building, for instance – which allowed for such an accomplishment. One historian at least, Daniel Boorstin, brings it up:

> An organized long-term enterprise of discovery, the Portuguese achievement was more modern, more revolutionary than the more widely celebrated exploits of Columbus. For Columbus pursued a course suggested by ancient and medieval sources...Only the sea was unknown.
>
> By contrast, the Portuguese voyages around Africa and, it was hoped, to India, were based on risky speculative notions, rumors, and suggestions...Portuguese discoveries, then, required a progressive, systematic, step by step national program for advances through the unknown....

The Portuguese achievement was the product of a clear purpose, which required heavy national support. Here was a grand prototype of modern exploration. (Boorstin, 157)

Hence I return to the point I made earlier about, Ernan McMullin's thesis regarding the absence of technical control [4] which, in turn, becomes one more argument in support of the thesis of all those who, like Krige, see the first scientific revolution as a long process full of discontinuities. One of them, in fact, was carried out by the Portuguese, lasted for almost a century, and possessed characteristics which are a miniature of what science would be in the 1700s. If it was an enterprise which did not have direct continuity in Portugal itself, it did have plenty of repercussions in the advancement towards the change of the grand paradigm.

I will close with one more example of the generalized oversight of the Portuguese case. In a recent book of reflections of the state on science, *Paradigms Lost*, John L. Casti writes:

Oddly enough, despite Aristotle's main occupation as an observational biologist, the biggest flaw in his entire world picture was that he advocated no experiments, or even use of observations to serve as a check on the validity of his underlying premises.... It was not until the work of Francis Bacon in the seventeenth century that someone had the courage to challenge the authority of Aristotle and suggest turning the situation around, i.e., trying to infer instances from specific observations. (Casti, 1989, 19)

I will let this example of historical unawareness speak for itself. But the list of similar oversights is a long one. [5]

From the Greeks, and through the Arabs, on its way to Northern Europe, and England in particular, science went through a key transformation in Portugal during the time of the seaborne adventures.

Onésimo T. Almeida

Notes

[1] Yet, J. Maria André calls our attention to the fact that the whole tractatus *De Crepusculis*, by Pedro Nunes, is an attempt at explaining astronomical phenomena in mathematical terms, a trend which, as it is well known, culminated in Galileo's statement that the "universe is written in mathematical language." André quotes Nunes:

> Regarding myself, meantime, that people only answered / the question of the duration of dawns / with things very well known and worn out and, as far as I know, by nobody demonstrated, I was seduced by the intent of explaining clearly this matter through the most certain and most evident principles of mathematics. (André, 42)

[2] This absence of references to the Portuguese pervades all sorts of historical literature. I checked at random two books on navigation (Bathe, 1973 and Robinson, 1938) – and only the first mentions the name of Vasco da Gama.

[3] Adam Smith was of the opinion that "the discovery of America, and that of a passage to the East Indies by the cape of Good Hope, are the two greatest and most important events recorded in the history of mankind" (Smith, 271), but that was from his perspective in economic history. The expression "Vasco da Gama era" seems to have been adopted from the Indian writer, K. M. Panikkar.

[4] Diffie and Winius provide in an Appendix an excellent chronological table of Portuguese expansion, listing 71 expeditions between 1415 and 1502 and indicating the source of their financing. Most of them, it is shown, were of royal initiative. Basically a business enterprise, whose dimension required state support and the collective cooperation of technicians, sailors, and scientists. Such convergence, again, may have lacked continuity in the history of science, but it is indeed a precursory instance of the road science was going to take in the "D-Science" phase of which McMullin speaks. The goal of technical control played indeed a key role in the Portuguese discoveries.

Still against McMullin, their scientific advancements were "pursued because of a hope of technological advantage" (McMullin, 55). Both Hooykaas and Barradas de Carvalho's works support my claim.

[5] The latest example of oversight is Anthony Grafton's *New Worlds, Ancient Texts* (1992), the accompanying volume of an exhibit under the same title at the New York Public Library.

Key to citations within the text

Albuquerque, L. (1983) *Ciência e Experiência nos Descobrimentos Portugueses*. Lisboa: Instituto de Cultura Portuguesa.

_____. (s.d.) *Introdução à História dos Descobrimentos Portugueses*. Lisboa: Publicações Europa-América.

Almeida, O. T. (1986) "Sobre o papel de Portugal nas etapas preliminares da revolução científica do século XVII," in *História e Desenvolvimento da Ciência em Portugal*. II vol. Lisboa: Academia das Ciências de Lisboa, 1173-1222.

André, J. M. (1981) "Os descobrimentos e a teoria da ciência," in *Revista de História das Ideias* 3:77-123.

Bathe, B. W. (1973) *Seven Centuries of Sea Travel*. New York: Leon Amiel Publisher.

Bensaúde, J. (1912) *L'Astronomie Nautique au Portugal a l'Époque des Grandes Découvertes*. Bern: Akademische Buchhandlung von Max Drechsel.

_____. (1914) *Histoire de la Science Nautique Portugaise a L'époque des Grandes Découvertes*. Munich: C. Kuhn.

Bernstein, R. J. (1983) *Beyond Objectivism and Relativism. Science, Hermeneutics and Praxis*. Philadelphia: U. of Pennsylvania Press.

Boas, M. (1966) *The Scientific Renaissance, 1450-1630*. New York: Harper and Row.

Boorstin, D. J. (1983) *The Discoverers. A History of Man's Search to Know His World and Himself*. New York: Vintage Books.

Brush, S. (1988) *The History of Modern Science: a guide to the second revolution, 1800-1950*. Ames: Iowa State U. Press.

Carvalho, J. B. (1983) *A la Recherche de la Spécifité de la Renaissance Portugaise*. Paris: Fondation Calouste Gulbenkian/Centre Culturel Portugais.

Casti, J. L. (1989) *Paradigms Lost*. New York: William Morrow and Co.

Castro, D. J. (1968-81) *Obras Completas*. Coimbra: Academia Internacional de Cultura Portuguesa.

Cipolla, C. M. (1985) *Guns, Sails, and Empires. Technological Innovation and the Early Phases of European Expansion, 1400-1700*. Manhattan, Kansas: Sunflower U. Press.

Cortesão, J. (1978-79) *História dos Descobrimentos Portugueses*. Lisboa: Cículo de Leitores.

Dias, J. S. S. (1943) *Os Descobrimentos e a Problemática Cultural do Século XVI*. Coimbra: Universidade de Coimbra.

Diffie, B. W. and Winius, G. D. (1977) *Foundations of the Portuguese Empire, 1415-1580*. Minneapolis: U. of Minnesota Press.

Grafton, A. (1992) *New Worlds, Ancient Texts. The Power of Tradition and the Shock of Discovery*. Cambridge: The Belknap Press of Harvard U. Press.

Hall, A. R. (1954) *The Scientific Revolution, 1500-1800*. Harlow: Longmans.

Hooykaas, R. (1981) "Science in Manueline Style – The Historical Context of D. João de Castro's Works," in *Obras Completas de D. João de Castro*. Vol. 4. Coimbra: Academia Internacional de Cultura Portuguesa.

Krige, J. (1980) *Science, Revolution & Discontinuity*. Sussex: The Harvester Press.

Leite, D. (1958-60) *Descobrimentos Portugueses*. 2 vols. Lisboa: Cosmos.

McMullin, E. (1984) "The goals of natural science," in *Proceedings and Addresses of the American Philosophical Association*. Vol. 58, Sept.

Mieli, A. (1951) *Panorama General de Historia de la Ciencia*. Vol. 3. Madrid: Espasa-Calpe.

Nunes, P. (1946-60) *Obras*. Lisboa: Academia das Ciências de Lisboa.

Orta, G. de. (1895) *Coloquios dos Simples e Drogas da India*. Lisboa: Imprensa Nacional.

Osório, J. C. (1947) *A Revolução da Experiência*. Lisboa: Edições SNI.

Pereira, D. P. (1937) *Esmeraldo de Situ Orbis*. English trans. London: The Hakluyt Society.

Robinson, G. (1938) *Ships That Have Made History*. New York: Halcyon House.

Sarton, G. (1961) "The Quest for Truth: a Brief Account of Scientific Progress During the Renaissance," in Robert M. Palter, ed. *Toward Modern Science*. Vol. II. New York: The Noonday Press.

Smith, A. (1952) *An Inquiry Into the Nature and Cause of the Wealth of Nations*. Chicago: William Benton, Publisher.

Taton, R. (1958) *Histoire Générale des Sciences*. Vol. II. Paris: Presses Universitaires de France.

Thorndike, L. (1953-59) *A History of Magic and Experimental Science*. New York: Columbia U. Press.

Wightman, W. P. (1962) *Science and the Renaissance*. New York: Hafner Pub. Co.

So much has been written about the life and deeds of Christopher Columbus and so little new documentation about him has emerged in the past century or so that I can hardly claim in this short article to revise, let alone revolutionize, scholarship regarding him. Nevertheless, I think that one valid and interesting point about him remains to be established. My aim here is to call attention to the dire effect upon his career of a parallel event: the discovery of the sea route to India by Vasco da Gama. For notwithstanding all his posthumous fame, during his lifetime the news of Gama's successful return from the spicelands of Malabar seems to have put his rising career into a tailspin after 1499 – from which it never recovered.

Epilogue
Triumph and Disgrace

That this has not previously been understood seems attributable to the almost hermetic sealing of the two historiographical worlds from one another: the Spanish and the American writers have dealt almost exclusively with Columbian voyages, while the Portuguese ones have dealt with their own discoveries and ignored Columbus nearly completely. Moreover, non-Iberian historians of the New World, mostly Italians and Americans, are so engrossed with the latter-day significance of the New World's discovery – something not suspected in Columbus's own lifetime – that they forget the context in which it took place. The result has been that a perfectly obvious conclusion has not been properly drawn.

The most important factor to keep in mind about Columbus and his voyages is that they cannot be understood except in continual relationship to those contemporary ones made by the Portuguese, both immediately before and after them, and directed towards the Cape. And this is true – whether in relation to Columbus in his glory (after his supposed "discovery" of Asia in 1492), or whether in regard to his ruin (the final discredit which fell upon him after 1499, when Vasco da Gama returned from the true "Indies" and it became clear that in the end it was the Portuguese who had won the contest).

Hence the destinies of Christopher Columbus and Vasco da Gama were indissolubly linked. Of these two men, one triumphed and the other failed – failed in that enterprise in which he had apparently gloried so spectacularly, but afterwards was seen to have misrepresented. In fact, in Portugal, Vasco da Gama was later to receive in Portugal precisely those titles which Columbus had been granted in Castile (and afterwards saw withdrawn when the Spanish crown understood that he had failed): those of Admiral and Viceroy of India. They came expressly to be created in Portugal during the opening years of the XVI century in imitation of Columbus's Spanish ones. There could hardly have been a greater irony.

The Race to India

News traveled quickly between Lisbon and Seville – within a few days, as is well known. Afterwards, only a few months were necessary for an investigator to be dispatched, who was to arrest and deprive the new viceroy of his office, without even conceding him a hearing, sending him in chains to the metropolis.

All this was the result of a race, a long one. It had begun long before 1492. Nor did it end in 1493 – its end was not until 1499. A fitting relationship of cause and effect ought to and can be drawn between the two sides of this rivalry. It is this explanation, simple enough after all, which shines through the pseudo-enigmas and so-called explanations over why Columbus fell into disgrace after 1499. Moreover, it explains the muffled manner in which it occurred, the whole affair being hushed-up, the great adventurer being dispossessed of his offices, without even having the right to a public hearing, which from then on he never ceased to request – in vain. (His heirs continued to request this redress after his death, in the celebrated "Columbian Lawsuits.")

It is well known that Columbus had accepted the ideas of such geographical theoreticians as Paolo Toscanelli who based their beliefs on the smaller Ptolemaic earth of only some 18,000 miles in circumference and that the Genoese had even shaved a few thousand from this, perhaps in the belief that the lesser distance would make his enterprise more attractive to royal sponsors, which in fact it probably did. Then, upon his return, he claimed that he had indeed found the

East – and of course was rewarded accordingly by Queen Isabella. Even though this and his second voyage had not positively located the abodes of the Great Khan or of the guardians of the pepper coast, it was still possible to suppose that he had only landed on their outskirts and would soon find his way to those promised lands. Hence there was no reason for his sponsors to be restive.

But in 1497, after many delays, the expedition finally took place which had been prepared from back in the reign of D. João II. It was commanded by Vasco da Gama. Carried in small ships (along routes already well known), his fleet of three ships and a supply vessel left Lisbon in July, 1497. From Sierra Leone, he launched them on their great counter-clockwise sweep through the high seas, which presupposes astronomical navigation and enough knowledge to avoid the belt of southeasterly winds (a route which up to that time had never been practiced by navigators whose rutters are known). In November, he touched land, in South Africa. In that month, he rounded the Cape of Good Hope. From March on, he began to contact the Moslem cities of the Swahili coast of East Africa. Employing a local pilot, he finally arrived at his ultimate destination in May 1498, the city of Calicut, the great center of the commerce in pepper on the Malabar coast, directly in the heart of the so much-desired India – the real India! Vasco da Gama tried to establish contacts and was object of a reception not entirely friendly. He succeeded in disengaging himself and starting his return journey in August of 1498. He made a wretched passage on his return to Portugal with news of his arrival in India – that news which would so bring joy to the Portuguese, but which would also bring about the definitive disgrace of Columbus *vis-à-vis* the Castilians. He occupied a year in this desperate journey, with two ships and a few members of his original crew. From the date of his arrival in August of 1499, the happy days of Admiral Columbus were numbered.

Christopher Columbus parted from San Lúcar de Barrameda in May of 1498, on his third voyage, each time a little more in discredit, although still determined to find a passage more to the west and meanwhile stubbornly identifying the new western lands with India and the Orient he sought (and thereby safeguarding the concessions and titles given him by the Catholic Kings). On this voyage he took six ships, still with royal backing, but now with financial support underwritten by·Italian merchants such as the Berardi (the fleet was accompanied by their commercial correspondent, Amerigo Vespucci). This armada was organized in a spirit of good neighborliness with Portugal, since the treaty of Tordesillas had been signed in the meantime.

In this, his third voyage, Columbus followed a route different from the previous ones, considerably more to the south, making calls at the Portuguese islands of Madeira and the Cape Verdes, and beginning his Atlantic crossing at this latitude, in order, as he himself says, to find out whether there might be any lands in this region which the Portuguese knew about that might lead to India (possibly being the reason D. João should have insisted upon the extra 270 leagues in the treaty of Tordesillas).

He touched upon *terra firme* (which, however, he judged to be a great island in front of Asia) and ran along the coast of Venezuela, reconnoitering the Gulf of Paria and the mouth of the Orinoco, which in a patch of mysticism he considered to be another world, leading to the Terrestrial Paradise. At Hispaniola a hard reality awaited him: there were great problems and a revolt afoot among the Spanish colonizers, who had risen up in great numbers against his brother, Bartholomew (named as governor in his absence). He attempted to alleviate these problems during the rest of the year, but without success.

Back in Spain, the discredit of Columbus now reached massive proportions; not only was he blamed for the predictable failure of his plan to discover the Indies, but for the allegedly unfair way in which he exercised power – as well as for the revolts which were spreading and the traffic in slavery which grew unchecked. The support of the Queen was now much diminished and his enemies had succeeded in turning the minds of the Spanish monarchs against him.

Already in May of 1499, one Francisco de Bobadilla was charged with the duty of sailing to Hispaniola and there to inquire into the conduct of the Admiral. He was also requested to render counsel on the manner by which the spreading rebellion could be ended, as fomented on that island by one Francisco Roldán. But meanwhile, departure of the inquisitor was delayed.

However, when Da Gama arrived back in Lisbon in August 1499 from his discovery of the passage to India, it was made plain to the Castilians that they had lost the game, while the Portuguese had just achieved the coveted goal. The new lands discovered by Columbus continued without positive identification and without giving any indication of appreciable wealth. And if there should there still have been any doubts about the reality of the Portuguese discoveries among the Spanish, these would have been dissipated within a few months, for in April of 1500 when the Portuguese sent their second squadron to India, one which was again to have been commanded by Da Gama, but which ended up under the leadership of Pedro Álvares Cabral (and which took possession of Brazil on the way). Now it was hardly a matter of a few dozen exhausted men returning in two rotting ships, but an ongoing enterprise. Fifteen hundred men departed from a city in celebration, festooned for their departure. In all there were thirteen ships, well armed and provisioned, bound for a precisely known destination, with concrete objectives. Something no longer to be ignored.

Homeward in chains

At this juncture, the investigator Bobadilla sailed, arriving at Hispaniola in August of 1500, with competence both to inquire and to govern. He immediately had Columbus arrested and sent him back to Europe (without even having conceded him an audience). No doubt he was butt of all the animosities accruing from his failure of his plan to discover the Indies, but of course the accusations themselves were inspired by the manner in which he administered with the authority placed at his disposal by the Catholic Kings.

Columbus was sent in chains to Castile, arriving at Cadiz with his brothers in November. Although they were all set at liberty there and the navigator was able to obtain an interview with the monarchs (in Granada, still in December of that year), the truth is that the prerogatives he had enjoyed were all withdrawn from him. He was to retain only some theoretical revenues from Hispaniola, but not the title and the benefits of viceroyalty. He thus fell into a relative disgrace, one which however was not total, since the monarchs continued to protect his son, Diego (upon whom later were to devolve some, but not all, of the benefits which had been taken from his father).

Until his death, Columbus continued to demand a judicial inquest, and to plead that his dignities and revenues be restored and insist eternally (along with his son and other members of his family) that he be exonerated. But the Catholic Kings did not do so, despite the ex-Admiral's lengthy pleas before the crown courts; in fact, the matter was only resolved through an arbitrated settlement and mutual compensations – the habitual procedure employed to rectify differences in matters embarrassing for both parties. One can only say that the attitude of the Catholic Kings was understandable, if only because the concessions defined in the *Capitulaciones de Santa Fé* were to take effect only in case of Columbus's "discovery of India" – which had not occurred.

Once the Catholic Kings had breached the exclusive rights they had conceded to the Admiral, various Spanish navigators departed during the years 1499-1500 to explore to the south of the Antilles and of the coast of the *Terra Firme* out to the limits established by the demarcation line of Tordesillas. Of these, Alonso de Ojeda (who was accompanied by the Italian, Amerigo Vespucci, the commercial correspondent), Diego de

Lepe, and Vincente Yañez Pinzón (who accompanied Columbus on his first voyage) navigated along the northern coast of South America and appear to have passed along the other side of the Amazon River and the Tordesillas meridian, in the last months of 1499 touching upon what is today Brazilian territory, where they found a cross (one possibly left by some previous Portuguese expedition, perhaps one of Duarte Pacheco Pereira). But there is some doubt about all of this, since these navigators operating under license of the Castilian crown describe in great detail only the coasts of Venezuela – which Columbus had already visited during his third voyage.

But the Portuguese also were attempting at this time to explore the new western lands more extensively in conjunction with the Tordesillas line and to take possession officially of those which belonged to them under the terms of the treaty. Thus, the second Portuguese armada which departed for India (led by Pedro Álvares Cabral) made a curious detour. It was a fleet of 1500 men and thirteen ships, with diplomatic and military goals to establish alliances in the Indian Ocean and to make a show of power before Calicut (whose Samorin had seemed condescending and under the impression of Portuguese puniness during the first visit by Da Gama). Cabral carried out his Asian mission successfully, inaugurating the regular *carreira da India*, the Cape route, which assured Portugal of its riches in the first half of the XVI century. But before accomplishing this, after leaving Cape Verde and before heading for the Cape of Good Hope, the fleet of Cabral deviated a bit more to the west from the route followed by Vasco da Gama three years before. He thereupon touched the Brazilian shore, where he remained a week preparing the resumption of his mission, and from which one ship returned to Portugal. In this way the Portuguese took possession and announced officially the finding of a territory included within the hemisphere of Tordesillas.

Lands totally new

During this stopover, the famous letter of Pero Vaz de Caminha was written, in which are related details about the land and its inhabitants, but, as in all Portuguese sources of this era, he does not commit the error of considering these territories as connected to Asia. Nor does he make the mistake of Columbus of calling its inhabitants "Indians."

The great American continent came in the opening years of the XVI century to be recognized as a region in itself by Europeans, and the Portuguese and Castilians rivaled one another in their voyages of exploration as in the news and geographical representations they made. Two great maps, drawn in those years illustrated these processes within the vision of each of the peninsular kingdoms. One is the map of Juan de la Cosa (today in the Museo Naval de Madrid), while the other is the anonymous Portuguese "Cantino Map" (kept in the Biblioteca Estense, at the city of Modena).

The first seems to have been drawn around 1500 by one Juan de La Cosa (probably the same man who was a former pilot of Columbus). But there appear to have been additions on the American side in the course of subsequent years, corresponding to the explorations made by Castilians up to about 1506. It is the expression of the reconnaissances of Columbus, of Vincente Yañez Pinzón and of other navigators in Castilian service both in the Antilles and along the coasts of Central and South America.

The second map, the anonymous planisphere known as the Cantino, was designed in 1502, in Lisbon, by a royal Portuguese cartographer, and spirited off to Italy by an Italian agent of the Este family named Alberto Cantino. It contains the explorations in the Atlantic made by the Portuguese in the years preceding (those of Cabral, Gaspar Corte-Real and possibly Duarte Pacheco Pereira). This map – arguably the most important in the history of cartography – provides the first modern vision of the world as we know it (including, besides Europe and Africa not only the New World, but also the Indian Ocean and the Orient). It does not reflect the slightest confusion over the separateness of the newly discovered lands from Asia; it does not call the lands touched by Columbus "India," but rather "Antilles of the King of Castile."

The initial years of the XVI century, in light of the expectations then unfolding, must have appeared decisive for many and full of hopes. But not for Columbus. The proud Admiral of the Ocean Seas and Viceroy of India would see his star set; there awaited him in the future problems even greater than the ones which beset him. In Castile, embittered and sick, he tried to defend his rights before the sovereigns, he wrote to the Pope and dedicated himself to his *Libro de las Profecias*, full of mystical preoccupations. But all this did him no good. In 1501, the Catholic Kings nominated Nicolás de Ovando as new governor of their occidental possessions, going clean against the concessions they granted Columbus in the *Capitulaciones de Santa Fé*. Ovando departed for Hispaniola in February of 1502.

Around two months later Columbus sailed on his fourth and last voyage. In great discredit and now without the support of the crown, he nevertheless succeeded in obtaining authorization for this new voyage to the Western lands, but financed by his own slender means, without his former honoraria and concessions as viceroy. He went with the object of discovering the so much sought-after westerly passage which would permit access to India – and even hoped to encounter Vasco da Gama, who was on his way there, since he had departed on his second voyage in that same year, 1502, via the Cape of Good Hope (Columbus even bore letters from the Spanish kings in case he should encounter the Portuguese!).

He sailed from Seville with four ships, putting to sea in April of 1502, as just said, almost following upon the track of Ovando, who was voyaging to succeed him in the governorship of the Indies. He carried express orders not to call in Hispaniola, but he did not heed them and tried to visit it, alleging navigational difficulties. He was impeded in his departure by Ovando. From there he set a southerly course, reconnoitering the coast of Honduras and the shoreline of Panama. He beat a return passage with great difficulty and ran aground in June 1503 in Jamaica, where he was isolated and menaced by the indigenes. He experienced difficulty in obtaining relief from the Castilians in Hispaniola, and only in June of 1504 did it finally arrive. In September of the same year, again by his own means, he finally managed to depart for Europe, destined never to return to the lands he had discovered. After that, there awaited him only death. His end was not so destitute and abandoned as the romantic historiography of the past century would lead one to believe, but in any case, he was certainly embittered and defeated.

In the last years of Columbus's life, the Castilian colonial enterprise was to assume new directions under the direct initiative of the crown. In 1503, there was created in Seville the *Casa de Contratación*, to centralize Spanish commercial and overseas activities and assure their royal control. In 1504 Queen Isabella the Catholic died, who in spite of everything had been the protectress of Columbus (at least she had been that in greater measure than her husband, Ferdinand of Aragon).

In Seville, and afterwards in Valladolid during the year 1505, Christopher Columbus suffered from arthritis and other health problems, but continued to insist upon his rights as forgotten by the Castilian crown, and in this vein wrote frequently to his son, who lived at the court. He died in 1506 in Valladolid, at the very same time the Portuguese achieved their victories in the Indian Ocean, regulating commerce and shipping there and beginning to install themselves in its strategic port cities. Afonso de Albuquerque was already in the Orient, who would soon become the great architect of Portuguese power in Asia.

Enter Vespucci

The lands of the western Atlantic thus became for the Portuguese secondary in importance; only the island or mainland to the southeast remained to them, of which Pedro Álvares Cabral had taken possession under aegis of the Tordesillas treaty. (This is not to count the more shadowy claims to the *Terra Nova*, in the northeast, where fisheries continued to be developed.) Meanwhile, it was essential to identify the extensions to the north and south of the southeastern territory, which Cabral had called *Vera Cruz* and which would come to be known as Brazil.

Between 1501 and 1503, in two or three expeditions, the Portuguese initiated the first explorations of the Brazilian shoreline, along the eastern coasts of South America, to southerly latitudes unknown with any exactitude. The commerce of the new land was leased to the merchant, Fernão de Loronha, but there are great disputes about these voyages of the opening years of the XVI century, both in regard to their geographical scope and their commander. This must almost certainly have been the Portuguese Gonçalo Coelho (the father of a future captain-donatary of Brazil), but on board was also the Florentine, Amerigo Vespucci, who combined his experiences with Gonçalo Coelho aboard Portuguese ships in 1501 with those he had had with Castilian ships in 1499, sailing with Alonso de Ojeda along the shores of the Spanish *Tierra Firme*, to draw the conclusion that one was dealing with a New World, in contradistinction to the "Indies" of Columbus. And this conclusion was expressed in two letters which he wrote to this effect, and which came to enjoy an enormous editorial éclat.

The Vespucian letters with these affirmations that Europeans were dealing with a New World and that Vespucci was its discoverer – whether these were made by him or due to interpolations for which he was not responsible – circulated throughout Europe in printed editions, and thus his name came to be associated with the new land masses. In 1507, these came to be baptized as "America" in his honor by the German cartographer, Martin Waldseemüller. The widespread diffusion of Vespucci's name was due to the celebrated map of that year, printed as the *Cosmographiae Introductio*. There are quite naturally those who perceive in this an injustice and an irony of fate, and certainly in some measure this is justified. For Vespucci hardly participated in the great discoveries in any measure commensurate with the honor of having his name assigned to them. By contrast, Columbus – who fought all his life with unbreakable force of spirit for the realization of his dream – never came to have his name linked with the new lands which he effectively discovered (although one might say by mistake!)

But destiny is like this – not always just – and in this case, it chose that Waldseemüller, influenced by the widely circulated letters of Vespucci, gave the name "America" to the new lands of the West, thus conceived as separate from Asia. Had Christopher Columbus not been so imprisoned in the *idée fixe* of his own making and had his contract with Castile not stipulated discovery of Asia a precondition of his titles' legitimacy, he might have (openly) drawn Vespucci's conclusion for himself. But in a way, the fates have been kind to him, after all. For among the vast majorities of the world's population, the irony is veiled by historical ignorance. Today, everyone knows – without perceiving the oxymoron – that "Columbus discovered America!"

Alfredo Pinheiro Marques

Bibliographical Essay

A Printed Treasury

Although in every European country the reservoir of documentation from the XV and XVI centuries is scanty (and in Portugal the earthquake of 1755 destroyed a good bit of that), there still remains a trove of information about the discovery and expansion period. Moreover, no nation has made greater efforts to transcribe and publish the records of its eventful past. So after the essays in this volume were completed, it occurred to me that rather than my merely appending to them a bibliography consisting of the previous citations, readers might better appreciate being provided with a guide to the great variety of primary printed materials on which they are largely based.

Many of these titles surround me on my bookshelves as I write, and nearly all will be found not only in a specialist's library, but also in a good-to-excellent university collection. Of course, most of these are exclusively in the Portuguese language, but wherever there are English translations, I will mention them. My aim is to emphasize items centering on the XV and XVI centuries, just as do the essays in the *Pathfinder* itself, but in history there is a certain continuity which makes it artificial to be procrustean about arbitrary divisions in time. Some books and manuscripts written in the course of the XVII century refer in whole or in part to the history of the XV and XVI centuries and utilize materials no longer extant. Besides this, some exclusively XVII century documental collections provide an idea of the mechanisms and routines which also prevailed in the XVI century – for which documents are lacking. Such is true, in spirit, for example, of the series pertaining to the deliberations of the Goan viceregal council.

My idea in featuring printed primary accounts and documents is to aid history enthusiasts and university students who are ready to progress from modern, secondary books about Portuguese expansion history, ones which give a general idea about it, into something more ambitious – for instance an M.A. thesis. If they stick with the subject beyond that point, they will certainly have to study the language in order to inform themselves sufficiently. And I have often discovered to my surprise that amateur historians – history buffs – will often go to lengths to acquire a necessary foreign language after they have done a certain amount of reading and wish to know more. Hence my essay is directed to these, and not really to the specialists. There may be something for them in the footnotes to the *Pathfinder* articles themselves, but my remarks here are not really intended for my colleagues already in the field.

Contemporary written records: collected and printed

Original documents are the lifeblood of historiography, and they fall into two categories. First, there are the narrative accounts, in our case, of an exploration, a travel, or some other experience involving the early contacts between Europeans and non-European peoples. These make interesting reading in and for themselves. The second category comprises documents relating to the deliberations of councils, the taxing of cargoes or partnership agreements, transfers of property or of testaments, and these tend to appeal exclusively to researchers, if because understanding them demands a good deal of background knowledge combined with some sort of investigative topic into which they can be woven. Documents of both sorts may be perfectly neutral in themselves, but because they must be interpreted by modern scholars who tell what *in their opinions* they mean to our own times, these original materials can easily be enlisted by modern historians to illustrate a particular viewpoint or argument, whether nationalistic, anti-colonial, Marxist, missionary, or simply as links in a chain of events. Other scholars may use the same documents to argue for a completely different synthesis.

Hence, these contemporary sources must remain the bedrock of historical reasoning, in that all modern interpretations must be judged upon how plausible they are perceived to be when compared to the accounts and facts recorded by our distant European ancestors. Historians of the *sigilo* school, mentioned in several of the essays in this volume, have been attacked, and I believe with excellent reason, simply because the few XV century passages upon which their thesis of secrecy is built are counterweighted by so many others which testify to very many foreigners being parties to Portuguese geographical exploration in the same age. Were all these pertinent documents hidden, or inaccessible, the distortions might prove extremely hard to detect and remedy. Readers would have little choice but to lend their credence to what the "experts," so called, had asserted.

This can only underline the importance of collecting and printing for distribution throughout the world's libraries as many as time and money permit of the important narratives, letters, council deliberations, receipts, inventories, bills of lading, and testaments surviving from the past. Such work is basic, both to democracy and to internationalization, for it at once helps to remove historiography from the realm of the elite, and it aids the process of universalizing what once were purely national histories. In the case of Portugal, I would hardly seek to discourage anyone from going there to study the documents in manuscript, for the pleasantness of its land and people are well known, nor is there any immediate danger that every document one needs for a study will soon be printed and put into the world's libraries. On the other hand, to make the best and most economical use of one's time in the actual archives, free access to what has already been printed on a subject and deposited closer to home might reduce a stay in Lisbon to a duration one can afford or gain a grant to undertake. Over the past two centuries Portuguese historians have spent at least as much of their time transcribing and printing primary documents (or in the case of early printed materials, reprinting them) as they have in preparing and writing studies of their own, and it is only logical to take advantage of their labors.

The West is virtually unique in having both made and saved such records, and in the case of early European expansion, the information the early Portuguese have recorded does double duty. For in most cases, Portugal alone is the bridge between Europe, Africa, Brazil and the East in regard to preserving the knowledge of a distant past, even one anteceding Portugal's arrival. We would know precious little of places like primordial Brazil, of Vijayanagara, early Ethiopia, the Congo or Siam, much less about something as recent as the Mughal empire, were it not for Portuguese written records. The Lusitanians, as was true of the Dutch and English after them, always and everywhere set out to discover and record the history and backgrounds of the places and peoples they encountered. For instance, in the case of Vijayanagara, an important, but relatively short-lived empire in South India, were it not for the abovementioned chroniclers, including Bocarro, and for three other accounts, those by Domingos Paes, Fernão Nuniz and Manuel

Barradas, it would be absolutely impossible to reconstruct its dynasties and the events transpiring there during the three centuries from its rise to its abrupt decline. It is thus hardly a coincidence that one always finds Asian and African scholars, not to speak of North and South Americans and other Europeans, in the archives of Lisbon, Coimbra and Évora. A great many are far less interested in European history, *per se*, than in their own.

Incidentally, before proceeding, I should say that in deciding which titles to include and which to omit in this essay, I was guided by the prospect of reasonable availability. By definition I have omitted manuscripts not (yet) printed and to be found only in Portuguese and European archives (including libraries with manuscript collections) and restricted myself to printed materials. Please note that I have not included rare books printed in the XVI or XVII centuries *unless they have been reprinted in more recent editions* and hence might be found in many, if not most, good libraries.

The classic chroniclers

Leaving aside for the moment shorter accounts on specific topics, Portugal possesses an unparalleled wealth of historiography on its expansion written by chroniclers, both official and self-appointed, which affords a panorama of Portuguese African and Asian discoveries. One thinks not only of João de Barros, Fernão Lopes de Castanheda, Gaspar Corrêa and Diogo do Couto, but also including lesser lights like António Bocarro and Manuel de Faria e Sousa, who comprise perhaps the most important single group of proto-historians writing in the XVI and early XVII centuries. Of their likes Portugal can justly be proud. The Portuguese pioneers, as their Spanish neighbors and after 1492, co-expansionists, were fully aware that something extraordinary was transpiring as they were making their contacts with the non-European world, and their writings testify to at least as important a facet of Renaissance Europe as that of Italian art or English drama. The Portuguese, as reflected in their chroniclers, display the same curiosity, inventiveness and restlessness in another dimension, and their contributions to European civilization have been of equal, but different value. If, as Arnold Toynbee remarks, Western civilization has been the first in history to cover the globe, it was the Portuguese who initiated the process and, equally importantly, so faithfully recorded what they witnessed and how they felt about it.

João de Barros (1496-1570), Fernão Lopes de Castanheda (c. 1500-1559), Gaspar Corrêa (c1490-1565), and Diogo do Couto (1542-1616) were all writers concerned primarily with Asia, and in

Barros's and Couto's cases, peripherally with Africa. Most had dissimilar backgrounds. Barros, the bastard son of a nobleman, was an official court chronicler and never visited Asia, but he had access to all returning personnel and documentation and he also possessed an unusual feeling for accuracy and source materials, as well as a clear and elegant writing style; before his death, he wrote four decades in imitation of Livy, which he called the *Décadas da Asia*. More than a generation after him, an ex-soldier living in Goa, Diogo do Couto, who had received a classical education in his youth, set out to continue Barros, and he completed eight more, though the twelfth has been lost. He did not quite command Barros's gift for elegant and polished prose, but he had another advantage perhaps even greater: he lived in and had wide experience of Asia. Moreover, he had the same regard for accuracy and balanced judgment. As, for that matter, did the two non-official chroniclers, Corrêa and Castanheda. Like Couto, both were soldiers and officials with wide experience in the Orient and, together with an equal eye for anecdote and detail, they displayed an equal sense of recording the epochal times they witnessed for posterity. They comprise two very welcome alternative sources for our understanding of what transpired.

Faria e Sousa (1590-1649) and Bocarro (d. 1649) both wrote in the XVII century and their work is considered less useful than that of the abovementioned quartet but it can hardly be neglected entirely. For our purposes, since the *Pathfinder* is centered on the XV and XVI centuries, Bocarro may even be considered as too late, for by his intent, though not always in his digressions, he covers only the viceroyalty of D. Jerónimo de Azevedo, between 1612 and 1617, while Faria e Sousa, who writes in Castilian (living as he did during the Union of Crowns), treats the entire XVI and the first decades of the XVII century. Faria e Sousa is worth reading because he sometimes fills in details and viewpoints not found in the earlier chroniclers. For though he never traveled outside the Iberian Peninsula and mostly employed their writings, especially those of Barros, he did possess some sources not now extant. A late XIX century author on the Portuguese in India, Frederick Charles Danvers, lifted practically his whole book, *The Portuguese in India*, long a standard work, from Faria e Sousa. Bocarro should also be mentioned as the author of a compendium of Portuguese fortresses and cities in the East, called *O Livro das plantas de todas as fortalezas, cidades e povoações do Estado da India Oriental*. This was published in three volumes at Goa in 1937 as part of the *Arquivo Português Oriental (Nova Edição)*, though its modern editor,

A.B. Bragança Pereira, did a thoroughly sloppy job in transcribing and proofreading it.

It is always an extra pleasure to employ the original editions of these chronicles, and American libraries like the John Carter Brown, on the Brown University campus at Providence, the Houghton in the Harvard University Yard, the James Ford Bell in Minneapolis, the Newberry in Chicago, will have all of them. But the originals, while subjectively rewarding, are hardly necessary for scholarly purposes. A large number of other university libraries from Florida to Washington have the 1778 Régia Officina Typográfica 24-volume edition of the *Da Asia*, the complete compilation of Barros and Couto, while the 1924-29 4-volume edition of Castanheda by the Coimbra University Press is also widely distributed. There have also been subsequent reprints of this work, as well as a modern edition of Barros, that was edited by Manuel Múrias in 1945-46 in four volumes and published by the Agência Geral das Colónias. Faria e Sousa has been translated into Portuguese and published by the Livraria Civilização, of Porto, and it is maintained in print to this writing. To my knowledge, Bocarro's *Década 13 da Historia da India* has only been published once, in 1876, by the Academia Real das Sciências de Lisboa, but, surprisingly it was still in print in Lisbon until the 1970s. It seems to have gained wide distribution and I have encountered it in almost every library I have visited. Corrêa, the earliest of the writers, was also one of the last to appear in print. To have an original edition of his *Lendas da India* is to go back no further than 1858, since his manuscript lay unpublished for four centuries before the Academia Real das Sciências de Lisboa did so in that year. It has recently been republished in a "bible-paper" series, called *Tesouros da Literatura e da História*, of Lello & Irmão, Porto. Incidentally, before going on to the other wealth of primary material dealing with Portuguese overseas history, I should perhaps say that I hesitated, but save for this mention of them, have ultimately decided to leave out (save for this mention) the illustrious chronicle of the reign of D. Manuel I by the humanist Damião de Góis, because it is not *exclusively* devoted to the *ultramar*. It is perhaps sufficient to say that it contains useful insights and has received modern editions from the University of Coimbra Press. Góis wrote elegant Latin and Portuguese and pulled no punches if he disagreed with official policy. It was his dangerous independence of mind, no doubt, which led to his arrest and demise at the hands of the Inquisition.

Shorter chronicles and accounts

To cite only the famous chroniclers of overseas Portugal is but to scratch the surface when surveying the wealth of primary reference matter available. I might commence my survey of it in the Infante, Prince Henry's, own time with the chronicle of his life and exploration, as written by his courtier, Gomes Eanes de Azurara (or often Zurara), called the *Crónica de Guiné*. It is widely available in a modern edition of the *Livraria Civilização*, of Porto, edited by José de Bragança. Readers need not know Portuguese to utilize the chronicle, however, for it appears in the Hakluyt Society's edition by Raymond Beazley and Edgar Prestage, called *The chronicle of the discovery and Guinea*, written by Gomes Eanes de Azurara, 2 vols., issued in the First Series for 1896 and 1899. Of subsequent importance are the chronicles of Rui de Pina (1440-1521) and of the poet, Garcia de Resende (1470-1536), who wrote in passing about the discoveries under D. João II. Pina's is by far the most factual and Resende obviously cribbed from him extensively. But Resende was an amusing gossip and his work has its place as well. Pina, however, remained much longer in manuscript, and his *Crónica do muy excellente Rey Dom Joam de gloriosa memória* only found its publisher in 1792-1796 in an edition of the Real Oficina Tipográfica. More recently, this has been reprinted in the Colecção de Clássicos Sá da Costa. Resende had already been published in 1545 and again in 1554, but joins Pina both in an edition of the Real Oficina (1778) and most recently in an edition of the *Tesouros da Literatura e da História*.

Along with these, two other works which were written at about the same time deserve attention, and happily for those who do not read Portuguese or Italian, both have received English translations. The Venetian merchant, Alvise da Cadamosto, twice voyaged under Prince Henry; he visited the African coast and discovered the Cape Verde Islands; his account, written after his return to Italy first appeared in Fracanzano da Montalboddo's *Paesi nuovamente retrovati*, of 1507 and subsequent editions, and it was translated for the Hakluyt Society by G. R. Crone, appearing in 1937. The other work is the *Esmeraldo de Situ Orbis*, of Duarte Pacheco Pereira, an explorer and servant of both King D. João II and of D. Manuel I, who spent many years in Africa, and this work, among other things, describes navigation along its western coast. It was not published in Portugal until 1892, but has received several subsequent editions, including an English translation for the Hakluyt Society by George H. T. Kimble, in 1937. While speaking of explorers, I should also mention a small volume which contains transcriptions of all the known documents pertaining to

Bartolomeu Dias, the discoverer of the Cape of Good Hope. It is called *Bartolomeu Dias. Corpo Documental-Bibliografia*, and was published in Lisbon in 1988 by the Comissão Nacional para as Comemorações dos Descobrimentos Portugueses.

For readers who might like to penetrate further inland into Africa, there is a work by the papal chamberlain, Filippo Pigafetta, who acted as the emanuensis for a Portuguese, Duarte Lopes, who lived in the Congo for many years before being sent on a mission to Rome, where he met Pigafetta. The result of their collaboration was the *Relazione del Reame di Congo*, published in the Eternal City in 1591; it is the best XVI century description of West Africa. Though highly esteemed in earlier centuries, it did not receive a Portuguese translation until 1949, published in two volumes by the Agência Geral das Colónias.

Speaking once again of the Hakluyt Society, one should mention two or three other publications which continue the story of maritime exploration and bear on the first Portuguese visits to India and the discovery of Brazil. There is, first of all, the English version of the codex often called the *Diário da viagem de Vasco da Gama*. While I strongly recommend that readers consult the facsimile edition of the original manuscript published in 1945 by the Livraria Civilização, the English text has long been available as published in 1898 by the Hakluyt Society: *A journal of the first voyage of Vasco da Gama, 1497-1499*, and translated by E.G. Ravenstein. Vasco da Gama's voyages, incidentally also were featured in an earlier publication of 1869, where one E.J. Stanley translated those passages of the chronicler, Gaspar Corrêa, which dealt with all three of them. Then, the principal documents bearing upon the discovery of Brazil by Gama's successor in India, Pedro Alvares Cabral, were also translated, edited and published by the Society in the same year, 1937, as were the Cadamosto voyages. The compiler and translator was William B. Greenlee, and he conveniently assembled all the important narratives, including the Pero Vaz Caminha letter, the first description of the land and its inhabitants, plus some from Italian sources. The volume is called *Cabral's Voyage to Brazil and India*. Those, incidentally, who wish to pause in Brazil longer than Cabral did should supplement these papers with the chronicle of Pero de Magalhães, also called "Gandavo," entitled *História da Província Sancta Cruz*. This received a Portuguese edition in 1875, published by the Academia Real das Sciências. Then, in 1922, the American, John B. Stetson, provided it with an English translation, in two volumes published by a New York-based scholarly body, the Cortés Society. It was entitled, *The Histories of Brazil*. Before leaving Brazil, one might also include the

Tratado descriptivo do Brazil, of Gabriel Soares de Souza, edited by the famous Brazilian historian, Francisco Adolfo Varnhagen, in 1865. To my knowledge, however, this has never received an English translation.

Accounts with focus on Portuguese India

Although Portuguese expansion in India was well covered by the great narrative chronicles already mentioned, several important early sources describing the lands as first encountered should not be neglected. There is the account by an anonymous Portuguese in the Cabral fleet of 1500 who provides an interesting description of the port Calicut and its trade. It exists today only in Italian originals, as reprinted both by Montalboddo and later by Giovanni Battista Ramusio in his great mid-XVI century collection, *Delle navigazioni et viaggi*, published in three volumes at Venice in 1550-59. While Ramusio has recently been reprinted in Italy, the text has been translated into English by Alvin E. Prottengeier and may be found in an edition by John Parker, published in 1956 by the University of Minnesota Press and called *From Lisbon to Calicut*. Both the foregoing and a fuller account by one Thomé Lopes, a member of Vasco da Gama's second fleet, were combined in a book by Christine von Rohr, called *Neue Quellen zur Zweiten Indienfahrt Vasco da Gama*, as published at Leipzig in 1939. (The Thomé Lopes text is also in Ramusio, incidentally.) Another early description, one covering Portuguese activities from the years 1506-09, was written by a contemporary, Valentim Fernandes, to an acquaintance in Nuremburg; among other things, it reports possibly the first Portuguese contact with Ceylon. It is to be found in vol. XXIV (1960) of the *Boletim da Biblioteca da Universidade de Coimbra*, on pp. 338-58. Then there is an account of the voyage of Viceroy Francisco de Almeida to India in 1505. It exists in an early XVI century book with only one surviving copy and relates the adventures of a Spanish officer in Almeida's service. It has been edited by James B. McKenna, as *A Spaniard in the Portuguese Indies: the Narrative of Martín Fernandez de Figeroa* (Cambridge: The Harvard University Press, 1967).

Two works of lesser value on the overseas expansion which also have received modern editions are the chronicles of the reign of D. João III, by Francisco de Andrada and Frei Luís de Souza. They are worth mentioning mostly for this reason. Andrada was official chronicler and was supposed to have written a complete account of the period, but instead devoted his volume exclusively to the Portuguese in Asia. The quality of his *Crónica do muyto alto e muyto poderoso rey Dom João o III deste nome*, first published in 1613 is extremely patchy, for in places he plagiarizes whole pages from Correa and Couto. In others, he earns his salt by divulging facts, especially ones concerning the economic status of the Estado da India not found elsewhere. His work was republished in the XVIII century and again in 1976, by the *Tesouros da Literatura e da História*, of Porto. When Philip IV and III during the Union of Crowns had his work reviewed, it was found wanting, ostensibly because of its exclusive concern with Asia, and he appointed a Dominican, Frei Luís de Souza, to write a more suitable one. Frei Luís, however, died before he came further than the year 1542; his work was rediscovered only in the XIX century. Frei Luís's style and sly comments on the reign are amusing enough, though his recital of Asian affairs, like Andrada's, are taken from other chroniclers. What makes him worthwhile are his notes of material collected in preparation for the years 1542-57, which he did not live to complete. The famous historian, Alexandre Herculano, came across them together with his fragmentary manuscript and had them published with it, as the *Anais de D. João III*, in 1844. The notes are highly interesting, because, among other things, they have some revealing financial summaries, showing how D. João III foolishly wasted his moneys on dynastic marriages, amounts which eclipsed those invested in his infrastructure and empire. The work was reprinted in two volumes by the *Colecção de Clássicos Sá da Costa* in 1954.

Regarding Portuguese India proper, no tour of source materials would be complete without paying homage to the compendium of letters written by or about the great governor, Afonso de Albuquerque, published in seven folio volumes by the Academia (Real) das Sciências between 1884 and 1935. It has not been translated *in extenso*, but one can obtain an idea of Albuquerque's prose from a recent book, *Albuquerque, Caesar of the East. Selected texts by Afonso de Albuquerque and his son*, edited and translated by T. F. Earle and John Villiers (Warminster, Aris & Phillips, 1990). The (natural) son in this case is Brás de Albuquerque, who at D. Manuel I's own request also took his father's Christian name, Afonso, the possible cause of some modern confusion. The book he wrote about his illustrious father, the *Comentários do Grande Afonso de Albuquerque*, was first published in 1557, and has received several new editions through the centuries, including two in the twentieth. It has also been translated by Walter de Gray Birch for the Hakluyt Society, in four volumes of the First Series between 1875 and 1885, as *Commentaries of the Great Afonso Dalbuquerque, second viceroy of India*.

Moving along toward mid-century, there are two bodies of collected letters which afford interesting insights into the thoughts and doings of a pair of famous men associated with Goa and Portuguese Asia (who, incidentally, were personal friends): D. João de Castro and Francisco Xavier, the saint. On D. João there are the *Cartas de D. João de Castro*, collected and edited by Elaine Sanceau and published in Lisbon in 1954, by Agência Geral do Ultramar, while Xavier is represented by the two-volume *Epistolae S. Francisci Xaverii aliaque eius scripta*, compiled and edited by Georg Schurhammer, S.J., and Josef Wicki, S.J., and published by the Monumenta Historica Societatis Jesu in Rome between 1944 and 1945. I am not including D. João de Castro's famous *Roteiros* here, if because they are more of geographical and specialized nautical interest than his *cartas*, but Professor Almeida has featured them in his essay, "Portugal and the Dawn of Modern Science" (Chapter XVIII). To my knowledge, the three *Roteiros* have not been translated.

I might say in passing that there were several biographies of St. Francis Xavier written and published in or before 1600 – those of Manuel Teixeira, Horatio Tursellinus and João de Lucena – but I would not counsel their uncritical use. It would be wiser to read a modern author's, Fr. Georg Schurhammer's, works on the great missionary beforehand.

In addition to the letters of such famous men, the correspondence of others less well-known is also interesting. For instance, there are the *Cartas de Simão Botelho*, as contained in a series known as the *Subsídios para a história da India Portuguesa*, edited by R. J. de Lima Felner in 1868 and published by the Academia Real das Sciências. Other texts included in it are interesting, too. Botelho was a fiscal troubleshooter who visited the various Portuguese installations in India and found plenty of trouble to shoot at, but perhaps not hit.

If one enjoys sieges, one can read about one of the great defenses of all times, that of the second beleaguerment of Diu, in 1546. It received a vivid account in Latin by one Diogo de Teive, published in Coimbra two years later. More recently, this little book was given an English translation by R. O. W. Goertz, in 1973, and printed in Lisbon by the bookseller Afonso Cassuto, of R. B. Rosenthal. It employs the original Latin title, *Commentarius de rebus a Lusitanis in India apud Dium gestis anno salutis nostrae MDXLVI*. Some other narratives of the same siege, including one by Leonardo Nunes, who participated in it, were collected and printed by António Baião, in a book called *História quinhentista inédita do segundo cerco de Dio*, as published in 1925 by the Coimbra University Press.

While I am on the subject of sieges, I should also mention the *História da India no tempo que a governou o visorei Dom Luís de Ataíde*, written between 1572 and 1578 by one António Pinto Pereira, but not published until 1617. Its author was seemingly a diplomat, who through his intimate knowledge of Asia must have served there at one time or another. His subject was twice viceroy, in the years 1568-71 and 1578-81, but Pereira's narrative covers only the earlier term. It, however, was the busy and important one: in 1570, an alliance of south Indian sultanates, the Samorin of Calicut and the Sultan of Johor all attacked Goa, Malacca, Chaul and other parts of Portuguese India, but were beaten off through the courageous and skillful efforts of Ataíde. The *História* has been reprinted (1987) in a facsimile edition by the Imprensa Nacional-Casa da Moeda, with introduction by Manuel Marques Duarte. On the viceroys who ruled from Goa between D. João de Castro and Ataíde, there is also Duarte de Eça's *Relação dos Governadores da India*, from 1571, a manuscript from the Archivum Romanum S. I., published in Calgary in 1983 and edited by R.O.W. Goertz.

Finally, if one wishes a view of how things (mis-)functioned in India after Ataíde's time, I can recommend the memorial by a common soldier, Francisco Rodrigues de Silveira, based upon his experiences between 1586 and 1598. It is called *Reformação da milícia e governo do Estado da India Oriental*, and it is part chronicle and part critical analysis of Goan policies in general and military mismanagement in particular. The manuscript somehow worked its way into the British Museum in the XIX century, where it was discovered by a lawyer and adviser to the Portuguese monarchy, one A. de S. S. Costa Lobo, who copied it out, but published it at Lisbon in 1877, in a despicably mangled form. This was called *Memórias de um soldado da India*. More recently, Benjamin N. Teensma, of Leiden University, has prepared a proper critical edition from the British Museum text, and it will soon be printed by the Fundação Oriente. For another glimpse of the seamier side of the Portuguese viceroyalty, Silveira can be supplemented by the little work of Diogo do Couto, called the *Dialogo do Soldado Prático*. Perhaps for obvious reasons, it was not published during Couto's lifetime, but ultimately did make it into print in 1790. It consists of two dialogues, of which the second received a modern edition, edited by M. Rodrigues Lapa and published in 1937 and subsequently in the Colecção de Clássicos Sá da Costa series.

Church and missionary history is best covered in the great series of printed documents discussed below, but I might mention two titles here which touch upon ecclesiastical activities in Goa proper. The former director of the Arquivo Nacional da Torre do Tombo, António Baião, published in 1930 a volume of correspondence by the

Inquisitors in Goa to the Inquisitor General and others in Lisbon, entitled *A Inquisição de Goa; Correspondência dos Inquisidores da India, 1569-1630*. This was volume II, published by the Coimbra University Press in 1930. Volume I, interestingly enough, was published by the Academia das Ciências de Lisboa, and in the year 1949. It is a monographic introduction to the earlier volume of documentation. The other work was published in 1969 by the Centro de Estudos Historicos Ultramarinos and is called *O Livro do Pai dos Cristãos*. It was introduced and annotated by Fr. Josef Wicki, S.J. The *Pai dos Cristãos* was a secular office purely indigenous to Portuguese Asia and its occupant was in charge of cathecumenizing those converted to the Christian faith, and with the care and baptism of native children who had no next of kin. The *Livro* is a collection of documents, most of them from the XVI century, which legislate and regulate its functions.

Before leaving Portuguese India, one is almost obliged to mention the *Colóquio dos simples e drogas he cousas medicinais da India*, of the physician Garcia da Orta, whose description of Indian flora counts as the first of its kind in the world. It was originally published in Goa in 1563 and was one of the very earliest books printed in Goa, and hence in India. It has received numerous subsequent editions in Portugal and has received translations into most European languages. Much less known, but a worthy companion to it is the *Tractado de las drogas y medicinas de las Indias Orientales*, of the Portuguese, Cristóvão de Acosta, originally published in Spanish at Burgos in 1578, after the author took service in Spain. Although the book is based upon Orta, whom Acosta knew in Goa, it contains many original things, including the first woodcuts illustrating Asian flora. It has been translated into Portuguese by Jaime Walter and issued as the *Tratado das drogas e medicinas das Indias Orientais*, published in 1964 by the Junta de Investigações do Ultramar.

The focus on Asia and its peoples

Although it is difficult to divide the documentation left by the early Portuguese in Asia into neat categories, some works depart from a primary emphasis on the activities of the Portuguese themselves and display a wider geographical and ethnic interest in geography and peoples. Among the earliest and most famous of these is the *Livro em que da relação do que viu e ouviu no Oriente Duarte Barbosa* (1516) and the *Suma Oriental* (1512-1515) of Tomé Pires. Both were first printed in whole or part by Ramusio in the XVI century, but subsequent manuscripts in the original Portuguese have appeared and been given their own editions. Both authors undertake to describe the ports, peoples and commerce from the Red Sea or East Africa to Malacca, Sumatra and the Moluccas, while Pires also includes China, which he only later visited; in general, he writes more of the Far East than did Barbosa. Both men had personal experience of most they describe and were keen observers of the geography and the peoples whom they encountered. It is interesting that the Hakluyt Society was the first modern publisher of both writers, beginning with a translation of Barbosa in 1866 from a Spanish manuscript. But this was superseded by a more definitive one from a Portuguese original, as *The Book of Duarte Barbosa*, translated and edited in two volumes by Mansel Longworth Dames (1918-1921). Pires received one of the Society's few bilingual editions in 1944, as *The Suma Oriental of Tomé Pires*, as translated and edited by Armando Cortesão. Incidentally, the preferred Portuguese edition of Barbosa was edited by Augusto Reis Machado and published by the Agência Geral das Colónias in 1944.

A Portuguese work unique for its time in that it did not concern itself solely with national discoveries was the *Tratado dos descobrimentos, antigos e modernos*, written around the middle of the XVI century by the former governor (1536-1540) of the Moluccas, António Galvão, and first published in 1563. Galvão, who also wrote a history of the Moluccas which may have survived in its final draft (see below) concerned himself here with compiling a narrative comprising all the maritime voyages of world discovery made until his own time. It hardly makes for entertaining reading, but it has been shown highly reliable and often supplies information found in no other source. It has had various subsequent editions, ranging from one translated by Richard Hakluyt and included in the original *Principall Navigations* to a popular one of the Livraria Civilização, first published in 1944, but the one most used in the English-speaking world is the Hakluyt Society first series version as edited by C.R.D. Bethune in 1862. It is called *The Discoveries of the World*.

As several essays in this volume indicate, the Portuguese presence in Asia was hardly confined to a few enclaves ruled from Lisbon and Goa; instead, Portuguese traders and adventurers penetrated the entire Orient, where besides carrying on legitimate commerce, they soldiered, advised kings and even pirated. Many were too busy to write anything (even if they were literate) but what they did write about themselves and the peoples and lands they encountered is extremely revealing and important. Without any doubt, the most famous writing by any of these wanderers was the *Peregrinaçam*, of Fernão Mendes Pinto, a work first published in 1614, thirty years after its author's death in 1583. Pinto had so many nonstop adventures after his arrival in Goa in 1537 that his stories were not readily believed by contemporaries, but scholars today perceive that he was essentially truthful, even if he did not set out to make his every word represent literal fact; it is even possible that, back in Portugal many years later, his fantasy and even his satirical intent filled in where his memory failed. Certainly, this is true of some place names. But he did indeed wander through the backlands of Arabia and southeast Asia and even reached Japan soon after its discovery. As one of the first Europeans there, and in places like Burma and Siam, he testifies to the initial role Europeans played in these places – as advisers, gun runners, mercenaries, and, of course, as missionaries. He even tried his hand briefly at this latter activity, in Japan.

Fernão Mendes Pinto has had many Portuguese editions through the centuries, the most recent being by the Imprensa Nacional-Casa da Moeda in 1983, not to speak of Spanish, French, Dutch, German and English ones, but he did not receive a complete, accurate and annotated English edition until that by Rebecca Catz, published in 1989 by the University of Chicago Press. It is called *The Travels of Mendes Pinto*. Dr. Catz has also edited a volume called *Cartas de Fernão Mendes Pinto e outros documentos*, published in 1983 by Editorial Presença, Lisbon, in which she discusses five letters alleged to be from hand and attempts to add to what little is known for certain about his life outside the *Peregrinaçam*.

The *Peregrinaçam* not only introduces its readers to lands beyond the direct pale of Portuguese administration, but to communities of traders and mercenaries dwelling in small communities from the Coromandel coast of India through Bengal and along the east coast of its bay as far as Pegu and Tenasserim; others lived in Sumatra, Siam, Cambodia, Macao and Japan. This miscellaneous community is not well represented by any other single book or manuscript of the era, save perhaps the *Breve discurso em que se conta a conquista do Reino de Pegu na India Oriental*, by Manuel de Abreu Mousinho, published in 1613 and recounting a freelance military campaign of 1600 in Burma by the adventurers, Salvador Ribeiro de Sousa and Felipe de Brito e Nicote, which resulted in the overthrow of its king. It was reprinted in 1990 in Mem Martins, by the Publicações Europa-América, together with an introduction and notes by Maria Paula Caetano.

Tracing other activities of the other wandering Portuguese in print is not easy, if because they meander in and out of many historical narratives and collections of documents. But one can obtain glimpses of them, among other places, in the Lusitanized Fleming, Jaques de Coutre's, *Andanzas Asiáticas*, as a modern Spanish publisher (Historia 16) has titled his *Vida*. Coutre, alias Jacob van de Coutere, or often in

Portuguese documents, Couto, was a soldier-turned-jewel trader who spent some thirty years in the Orient, traveling first out of Malacca and then from Goa between 1592 and 1623; in addition, he made two trips overland from India through the Middle East to the Mediterranean. The *Andanzas* were published in Madrid in 1990, for although the memoir was originally written in Portuguese, Coutre came to reside in Madrid, where his son had the manuscript translated into Castilian. One must also resort to a XVII century manuscript in Spanish for further glimpses of the extra-Goan world of Portuguese traders and mercenaries in the *Itinerario da las missiones orientales*, of Frei Sebastião Manrique, S.J., a Portuguese whose work was translated by Col. C. Eckford Luard as *Travels of Fray Sebastien Manrique, 1629-1643*, and published in 1927 by the Hakluyt Society. Here I am cheating on my 1600 chalkline somewhat, but materials affording glimpses into the world of the itinerant Portuguese are suitably scarce.

One other traveler who voyaged from India through the Middle East to Europe – and nearly a century before Coutre – was António Tenreiro, who around 1528 journeyed through Persia to Tabriz and thence across the Mesopotamian wastelands to Aleppo. His *Itinerário* has never been translated into English, but it is noteworthy for the unique information it provides on Asian peoples and trading routes at this early date. It was originally published in 1565, but perhaps the most accessible edition of it is that of António Baião, in a volume called *Itinerários da India a Portugal*, and printed by the Coimbra University Press in 1923. The same route, incidentally, was also taken by one Pedro Teixeira in the first years of the XVII century and his account is a detailed and valuable supplement to Tenreiro's. Fortunately, this one has been translated by Donald Ferguson and published by the Hakluyt Society in 1902, as *The Travels of Pedro Teixeira*.

Some materials for the historiography of native cultures

One dimension common to all descriptive writings by Portuguese or those associated with them during the discovery era is the information and insights they provide into the history of regions hitherto unknown, or almost so, to Europeans. One can say this equally of the works of Pero de Magalhães on Brazil, those of Coutre on India or Siam, of Barbosa and Tomé Pires, or in another sense, even of any writings by the Portuguese in the East who were themselves creating history by their activities. But the works I especially mean to emphasize in this section are the works of primarily historical nature which are either unique in their casting of light on regions hitherto virtually unknown, or which excel in historical scholarship and have afforded a window on worlds now lost which would otherwise be virtually without written history save for them. One can almost point in any direction from Goa and find an important work on the subject. Not surprisingly, many, if not most, were written by clergymen, literate men trained in observation and inclined to bookishness, and ones who necessarily had to possess a great deal of patience.

To the west of Goa, in Ethiopia for instance. There is the *Ho Preste Joam das Indias*, of Padre Francisco Álvares, chaplain to the Portuguese on the Rodrigo de Lima expedition from Goa to the Abyssinian *negus*, or emperor in 1520; his is the first detailed eyewitness description of the country and was published at Lisbon in 1540; its Hakluyt Society edition in two volumes by C. F. Beckingham and G. W. B. Huntingford dates from 1961. On Ethiopia there are also several other works of varying utility. Best among them is the voluminous *História da Ethiopia*, of the Jesuit Pedro Paez, written in that country in the first decades of the XVII century, where he served as a missionary until his death in 1622. He was able to read Amharic and used native sources for the XVI century; his work is a compendium of ethnological, political, religious and geographical information. It has not been translated into English, but is available in four volumes from the Livraria Civilização, as edited by Elaine Sanceau in 1945-1946. There are also two other works, one by Miguel de Castanhoso and the other by João Bermudes, both encompassed in the same work issued in 1902 by the Hakluyt Society and translated by F. C. Danvers. Castanhoso was an officer in the expedition of 1541-1543 under D. Christóvão da Gama, sent to rescue the *negus* from his Moslem enemies; he was an excellent observer and has provided a good picture of the Ethiopian peoples and religion, together with an account of the dramatic events in which he took part. Bermudes came to the country with the same Lima expedition which brought Álvares in 1520, but he stayed on and claims to have been made Patriarch by a *negus*, an assertion which was disputed by others. The value of his narrative is patchy because he is suspected of deliberate invention at times.

One excellent early book with the name Ethiopia in its title, is not about Ethiopia at all, but about Mozambique. This is the *Ethiopia Oriental e varia historia de cousas notaveis do Oriente*, of Frei João dos Santos, a Dominican who lived there for eleven years at the end of the XVI century. It describes the people, their customs, and the politics of the region from first hand knowledge. It was originally published in 1609, in Évora, and has been republished only once, in Lisbon, in 1891, by the Biblioteca dos Clássicos Portugueses. But it has been summarized by the XVII century successor to Richard Hakluyt, Samuel Purchas, in *Purchas, his Pilgrimes*. Part of it has also been translated by George M. Theal, in his *Records of South Eastern Africa* (London, 1898-1903).

Just as the history of Ethiopia was well served by the labors of the Jesuit, Paez, and that of Mozambique by Frei João dos Santos, a work of equal, or even superior merit was composed by another priest, this time about Ceylon. This was the scrupulous *Conquista Temporal e Espiritual de Ceylão*, a work written late in the XVII century. It was compiled from original sources by Father Fernão de Queyroz, S.J., who lived much of his life in Goa. It provides rich material for historians, and even anthropologists and geographers. It was not printed until 1913. Thereafter, it received a good English translation in 1930, from Bishop Simon G. Perera, S.J., where it was published in Colombo by the government printer. It is the basis for practically all Sri-Lankan historiography, since Queyroz probed far into the distant native past of the Island consulting sources and traditions no longer extant.

Nearer to Goa, I have already mentioned the Portuguese accounts of Vijayanagara, and these do the same for it on a much smaller scale. They were conveniently translated into English by Robert Sewell and published in 1900, as *A Forgotten Empire* from a Portuguese edition by David Lopes published in Lisbon in 1898 and called *Crónica dos Reis de Bisnaga*. This book has been reprinted several times, most recently in 1983 by the Asian Educational Services, of New Delhi.

And finally, still in the south of India, there was a fascinating mission at Madurai, in present day Tamil Nadu, where Jesuits under the leadership of a remarkable Jesuit priest, the proto-anthropologist, Roberto de'Nobili, attempted to fuse the Christian religion to what he interpreted as purely a religious local customs. This story properly belongs to the XVII century and not to the discovery era *per se*, but I cannot resist mentioning a work of 1616, written there by one Padre Gonçalo Fernandes Trancoso, S.J., who had worked in South India with his order since the 1570s. His treatise, as edited by Father Josef Wicki, S.J., and published by the Centro de Estudos Históricos Ultramarinos, Lisbon, in 1973, is called the *Tratado do Pe. Gonçalo Fernandes Trancoso sobre o Hinduismo*. It is certainly the earliest systematic analysis of the Hindu religion as practiced in the area, and for its time, it is remarkably objective.

The Moluccas, producer of mace and cloves, two of the Orient's most sought-after spices, have received two good XVI century descriptions, one by Gabriel Rebelo, between 1543 and 1554 a factor and officer of the Portuguese fort on Ternate and a second, anonymous one, which I will discuss presently. Rebelo's *Informação das cousas de Maluco* is a valuable and detailed description of the islands and their surrounding peoples, their religious beliefs, customs and society, including a history of the Portuguese activities between 1539 and 1552, as well as the rivalry with Spanish interlopers. It was not printed until 1856, and then as only a section in vol. VI of a more general work, the *Collecção de notícias para a história e geografia das nações ultramarinas*, which, incidentally did not reproduce the best version in manuscript, that of the Arquivo da Casa da Cadaval, in Muge, the Ribatejo.

Concerning the other anonymous work mentioned above, it chronicles the period 1512-1539 and usefully supplements the *Informação* of Rebelo. Since it is known that the illustrious António Galvão, mentioned above as author of the *Tratado*, wrote a history on much the same subject and would have necessarily covered the identical period in his account, it is quite possible that the manuscript, which turned up in the Archive of the Indies, Seville, is his. At any rate, Fr. Hubert Jacobs, S.J., of the Jesuit Historical Institute in Rome, who translated and edited it has cautiously identified it as a probable first draft of Galvão's work. But whether or not it is by the former governor, it is of considerable value. Not only does it provide another description of the islands' inhabitants and their surroundings, but it neatly describes political events not covered in Rebelo's writings. The edition provides both the Portuguese text and an English translation. It was published by the Institutum Historicum, S.I., in Rome and St. Louis in 1971.

China never received a full-scale history based upon early Portuguese contacts, no doubt because until the foundation of Macau and well afterwards, life there was too impromptu. But there is one interesting description, the *Tratado das cousas da China*, by Padre Gaspar da Cruz, first published in the 1560s and recently reprinted (1984) by Lello & Irmão in Porto. Then, many shorter relations of travels, observations and experiences in China exist from the XVI century, and of these three interesting ones have been selected and translated with an introduction by Charles R. Boxer. They were issued by the Hakluyt Society in 1953 as *South China in the Sixteenth Century*. The narratives are that of Galote Pereira, part of the *Tratado das cousas da China*, of Padre Cruz and one of Padre Martin de Rada, the latter a Spaniard. Of course my previous point can hardly be applied to China that without Portuguese sources many nations would have no recorded history, for it is well known that China has its own chronicles. Hence the value of these narratives lies rather in the realm of observation of Chinese life and customs by early European visitors.

Nor was Japan exactly in dire need of having its history written by Europeans. Even so, the Portuguese arrived there at a crucial time, when the islands were ravaged by a great civil conflict, and they, or at least their Jesuit associates, played a considerable part in the drama by converting some of those actively engaged. Hence the *História de Japam*, of Father Luís Fróis, S.J., fills in many details which might otherwise certainly have been lost of the complicated political scene and its protagonists. Padre Fróis, more than his confreres Queyroz and Paes, focused his history as much on the comings and goings of Jesuit personnel as on the country itself, but in any narrative of this length and detail, much of Japan is bound to show through. Moreover, since the Jesuits themselves were actors in the Japanese history of that epoch, what he writes is extremely valuable. The Jesuit scholar, Georg Schurhammer, S.J., first made use of the work by publishing in 1937 a history of the Jesuit missions there which was based upon it, but more recently, Father Josef Wicki, S.J., edited and annotated the text itself, which was published by the Biblioteca Nacional de Lisboa in five volumes between 1976 and 1984. A shorter work by a Jesuit, but a useful and perceptive one, is the account of Fr. João Rodrigues, S.J., which has recently been edited by Michael Cooper and published as *This Island Japan: João Rodrigues's Account of Sixteenth Century Japan* (Tokyo: Kodansha, 1973).

There are three more works by clergymen which are primarily ecclesiastical in intent, but which merit attention here, not only from historians of Catholic missions in Asia, but from more general ones of Portuguese Asia, especially those interested in Portuguese settlements in places outside the areas controlled by Goa, which I have dubbed the "shadow empire." The first of these is Padre Francisco de Souza's *Oriente Conquistado a Jesus Cristo*, originally published in Lisbon in 1710 in two volumes, but reprinted in 1978 with an introduction by M. Lopes de Almeida, in the *Tesouros da Literatura e da História* series of Lello & Irmão, Porto. The author, who was born in Brazil in 1648 or 1649, served for many years as Jesuit superior at St. Paul's College and the Professed House in Goa and was official historian of his Order's missions in Asia. That part of his opus which survives as the *Oriente Conquistado* covers the years 1542-1585. It abounds in references to the Asian scene as well as constituting an authoritative regional history of his order.

Much the same can be said of another Jesuit, Padre Sebastião

Gonçalves's *Primeira parte da história dos religiosos da Companhia de Jesus*, whose three volumes edited by Josef Wicki, S.J., and published by Editorial Atlántida between 1957 and 1962, contain competent religious history, but also abound in asides concerning economic and political life. Gonçalves, who served as an assistant to the Provincial at Goa for many years, died there in 1619, apparently without completing the second and third parts.

The final work of the religious trio is the *Conquista Espiritual do Oriente*, by the Franciscan, Frei Paulo da Trindade (1570-1651), whose equally lengthy manuscript also lay unpublished, in this case until 1960-1967, when edited by M. Felix Lopes, O. F. M. and brought into print by the Centro de Estudos Históricos Ultramarinos. Frei Paulo was primarily concerned with defending his order's missionary record and lards his account with miracles, but his work is highly detailed and has considerable value for historians, especially since the Franciscan Order was not centralized like that of the Jesuits and (part of) the Augustinians and is not well represented by surviving historical documentation. The work also contains much useful political information, much of it about regions subject to native kings.

Some printed documental series

Narratives or at least documental collections with a single theme, such as the collection of an individual's letters, have a self-evident thread running through them that large collections of documents tend to lack, and this makes them suitable for reading as well as for researching. But the bigger collections are rather for research purposes than for general reading; they are more suitable for those seeking a certain type of evidence. I have lumped them into a separate category for that reason.

For anyone interested in the discoveries of the XV century involving the African coast in the reigns of Prince Henry and D. João II, there is no substitute for the large and thick five-volume series called the *Descobrimentos Portugueses*, assembled and introduced by João Martins de Silva Marques and published between 1944 and 1971, by the Instituto de Alta Cultura. This contains all the pertinent documents from the entire period and is a formidable archive in itself. The first volumes were long out of print and fetched hefty prices until the whole series was reprinted and generously subsidized by the Instituto Nacional de Investigação Científica, in 1988. At this writing, the whole series is available at a price which will fit almost any purse and must be counted as one of the best bargains on the bookseller's horizon. The years covered are 1147 – the founding of modern

Portugal with the capture of Lisbon – to 1500. I should only remark that the enumeration of the volumes is somewhat confusing, if because what is really volume II is called *Supplemento ao Volume I*, while II is in two tomes, which might be counted as III and IV, while V, completing the chronological sequence, is called III. At any rate, it is today sold as an entire set, and it would be ill-advised to buy single volumes of the original series, unless, of course, one is merely filling in a broken set. If one is especially interested in the life and activities of Prince Henry, the Silva Marques volumes can be supplemented by the *Monumenta Henricina* (1960), produced in twelve volumes by the commission, *Comemoração do V Centenário da Morte do Infante D. Henrique.* These volumes contain, besides some documents also to be found in the Silva Marques volumes, other patents, letters and other documents of the Prince not directly related to the discoveries themselves.

If the documentation of the Middle Ages is neatly taken care of by the Silva Marques *Descobrimentos Portugueses*, that on the XVI century is far messier. There is, however, one great, but confusing and even cabbagelike, source of documentation on XVI century Portuguese Asia in existence, one which only the cognoscenti tend to know about – or dare to use. This is the original *Archivo Portuguez Oriental*, of Joaquim Heliodoro da Cunha Rivara, formerly archivist of the Arquivo do Estado da India Oriental, as well as director of the Biblioteca Pública de Évora. (It is not to be confused with the much later series called the Arquivo Português Oriental, edited by A. B. Bragança Pereira in the 1930s with entirely different content.) It contains documents of all categories, *regimentos, álvaras, cartas régias* and *patentes*, as well as others, and was published at Goa in unbound fascicules between 1857 and 1875, some of them not even the same page size as the others; few people or institutions had the patience to stick around and collect them all. Besides which, Cunha Rivara was a perfectionist and in the course of his own searches would come across more documents from time to time which he would then insert into reprintings of a fascicules previously given the same number, something which might lead the unwary to believe that they had a complete set when they did not own another copy of the same fascicule with the subsequent *aditamento*. Moreover, the contemporary practice of selling the fascicules as without binding and hence, adequate means of keeping the pages in place (in an era when buyers were supposed to take them to their own binder for suitable covers to fit their own purses and tastes) led to the frequent peeling off of some outer pages when the fascicules were not promptly put between boards, which they seldom were. I found some still circulating in this condition in Lisbon during the 1960s and 1970s, and all of them lacked pages.

The result of this is that I have found only one copy in a major library which is absolutely whole and complete – at the British Library; I was told by a colleague years ago that even the copy in the Biblioteca Nacional de Lisboa misses pages. Hence, unless one goes to London, one can never be certain that the evidence one seeks has not been peeled away. The paper is poor and fragile; no copies are ever lent by libraries and must be used *in situ*. To conclude this somewhat discouraging discussion, I will list in general what each volume contains, but take no further responsibility save to recommend a one-year stay in Goa. In brief, leaving aside the question of additions, Fascicule I, documents from 1529 to 1611; Fascicule II, privileges of the City of Goa; Fascicule III, instructions to the governors and viceroys during the XVI century; Fascicule IV, Councils of Goa; Fascicule V, more administrative documents of the XVI century; Fascicule VI, documents of the XVII century, with a supplement of documents from the XVIII century. There is also another XIX century publication of documents from the Goan archives, the *Arquivo da Relação de Goa*, which as the title suggests, pertain to the law courts. They are in two volumes, published at Goa between 1872 and 1874, as assembled by José Inácio de Abranches Garcia, but these begin only with the year 1601 and fall just outside our strict purview. They do, however, afford some idea about how things were done in the previous century.

The same can be said for the series called the *Documentos Remetidos da India, ou Livros das Monções*, the royal correspondence to the viceroys and governors of Portuguese India at Goa. Unfortunately, it does not begin until 1605, and does not belong to the discovery epoch, proper; it would seem that prior to the Philippine period in Portuguese Asia, outgoing viceroys and governors simply packed their records with their other baggage and brought them home as souvenirs. The Hapsburgs put an end to this and required their deposit with the government. What of viceregal correspondence survives from earlier periods, or rather, what of it can presently be found in printed documents is virtually all to be found among the fragile pages of the *Archivo Portuguez Oriental*. Since writing this passage, I have learned that the venerable collection has been photomechanically reproduced by Asian Reprints, of New Delhi. One can only hope that its proprietor, Mr. J. Jetley, has obtained a complete copy of the original.

To date, the post-1605 *Documentos Remetidos* series so far available in print comprises ten volumes and extends to the year 1624 – but the series is open-ended and has been appearing in fits and starts since

1885 from the Imprensa Nacional. In any event, the series still has a very long way to go if it is ever to reach the XVIII century. Please take note if interested in it that it comprises (almost) entirely the India-bound correspondence, i.e., that from Lisbon to Goa, because viceregal replies to the chancery and king came to rest in Lisbon and were destroyed in the great earthquake of 1 November 1755 – which is the reason the documents are called *remetidos da India* – "remitted from India": the Pombaline government ordered the part of the correspondence housed in Goa sent back to Lisbon to fill the gap. In any case, what went on in Goa can partly be reconstructed without the viceregal letters to the king, since the king usually repeats what the viceroys have said in the beginning of his letters; besides this, the viceregal council's deliberations at Goa have been preserved at Goa since 1618, and are available up through the XVIII century, as published by Bastorá, Goa. The series is called the *Assentos do Conselho do Estado*, in five volumes (1953-1957), plus two supplementary ones from 1972, both containing documents not included in the first five, published as parts I and II. I only mention this in passing, if because documents of the XVII century really do not pertain to the discovery period.

For those with interest in the economic side of the *Estado da India*, two recent studies, one by Vitorino Magalhães Godinho and the other by Artur Teodoro de Matos, are devoted to budgets, instructions, receipts and disbursals pertaining to the Indian viceroyalty. Both reprint *in extenso* original fiscal documents such as they still exist, mainly from the XVI century. The book of Magalhães Godinho is called *Les finances de l'état portugais des Indes Orientales (1517-1635)* and reprints in its second part 242 pages of fiscal documents. The work by Teodoro de Matos, entitled *O Estado da India, nos anos de 1581-1588*, reprints documents containing line items from these years, concentrating on a station-by-station summary of revenues and expenses. Both works have long interpretive introductions. A third, and older, work along the same lines, but without an interpretive study is the *Regimento das Fortalezas da India*, of the former Goan archivist, Panduronga S. S. Pissurlencar. It was published at the Tipografia Rangel, Bastorá, Goa, in 1951. Together, the trio of books provide a fair assortment of primary material to help one understand the *Estado's* finances.

Pissurlencar's other documentary volume, *Agentes da Diplomacia Portuguesa na India*, published by Bastorá in 1952, shows how the viceroys often used native subjects on diplomatic missions to surrounding native rulers, but few of its documents are from the XVI century. More appropriate to the study of diplomatics in the Goan viceroyalty is the older *Collecção de tratados e concertos de pazes que o Estado da India fez com os Reis e Senhores com quem teve relações nas partes da Asia e Africa desde o princípio da conquista até ao fim do século XVIII*, collected and edited by Júlio Firmino Júdice Biker in 14 volumes and published in Lisbon between 1881 and 1887. As the title indicates, it prints texts of all the treaties the compiler could find in Portuguese archives and in the chronicles. It is extremely useful and can be found in a surprising number of libraries.

Before I turn from collections of political documents to some extremely useful series of ones on ecclesiastical and missionary activity, I would like to call attention to a unique joint venture which resulted in a bilingual collection of documents on eastern Africa. It was originated by Padre António da Silva Rego and his Centro de Estudos Históricos Ultramarinos in collaboration with E. E. Burke, director of the National Archives of Rhodesia and Nyasaland; their efforts resulted in the first eight volumes of an ambitious project called *Documentos sobre os Portugueses em Moçambique e na Africa Central 1497-1840; Documents on the Portuguese in Mozambique and Central Africa, 1497-1840.* As the title would suggest, it is a mirror-image Portuguese-English text, and it combines all the known documents, official, semiofficial, ecclesiastical and private from the areas, and not only constitutes an extremely useful compilation from the Portuguese archives, but a help for Anglophones learning to read documents in the Portuguese language. The original eight-volume series comprised the years 1497-1588. With the demise of Father Silva Rego and the disappearance of Rhodesia, one might have surmised that the series was defunct, but in 1989, a volume IX, covering the years 1589-1615, was published under the rubric of the National Archives of Zimbabwe and what remains of the old Centro of Silva Rego, now amalgamated with other institutions and called the Centro de Estudos de História e Cartografia Antiga do Instituto de Investigação Científica Tropical. This ninth volume disappeared almost as soon as it was published, and those responsible for its distribution never seem to have put it on public sale – which is a pity for historians and research libraries, unless they were lucky enough to be on the mailing list.

Finally, Father Silva Rego also had a hand in creating two other series of printed documents, all published by the Centro de Estudos Históricos Ultramarinos, one exclusively on the *ultramar,* and the other containing many overseas documents in it, which ought to be included in any roundup of overseas documents generated in the XVᵛ and XVI centuries. The first is the series called the *Documentação Ultramarina Portuguesa,* in five volumes between 1960 and 1967. The original idea behind it was to print documents pertaining to the Portuguese expansion from other European archives, and of these, the first three contain ones from the XV and XVI century, together with some of the early XVII century. For example, there are descriptions of Brazil and letters of the Jesuits written from the court of the Great Mughal. Then the fourth and fifth are from later centuries. After this, the series was continued in an entirely different direction with volumes VI, VII, and VIII (this latter published only in 1983) – and called the *Colecção de São Lourenço*, as edited by Elaine Sanceau. It should be considered as a separate publication since it does not conform to the earlier idea of Portuguese documentation assembled from foreign archives. This former monastic collection is now in the Torre do Tombo, and all documents it contains date from the reign of D. João III. Volume VI(I) contains correspondence of the Count of Castanheira, his *de facto* secretary of state, and also deals with the administration of the fortresses in North Africa; vols. VII(II) and VIII(III) comprise documents pertaining to the Indian administration of D. João de Castro during the years 1545 - 1548. Hence, most of this bears directly and indirectly on the overseas empire.

The other series referred to above is the *Gavetas da Torre do Tombo*, apparently still continuing and which has now reached twelve volumes at this writing and completes *gaveta XX*. The *gavetas* are drawers, in this case full of manuscripts. They are not differentiated into domestic, European and overseas categories, but are all jumbled in together, and from one document to the next, one might leap from the XIII century to the Council of Trent to the Inquisition of Évora to the Moluccas. Fortunately, volume XII contains a good index and virtually all of the documentation is bracketed from the late Middle Ages to the XVI century. It is therefore a research tool to be considered in this essay.

Whether the two-volume *Registo da Casa India* has much real value as a research tool is debatable. It was published in 1954-1955 by the Agência Geral do Ultramar, as edited by Luciano Ribeiro, and its entries range from 1508 to 1633. If it were really what its title suggests, the complete register kept by the Lisbon clearing house of *all* people sailing to and from India during the period included, and *all* grants made to them, it would obviously be invaluable, but in fact the official and complete *Registo* was lost in 1755, and this one is no more than an extrapolation from it of royal grants made to *fidalgos*. It may be of use to someone seeking collateral information about a personage under study in another context, allowing for the fact that Portuguese names are frequently similar, and that the Simão da Silveira or Diogo Taveira da Cunha one might be studying at a certain period could have a *doppelgänger*. Its validity for administrative study obviously depends upon its completeness, and, lacking that, knowing what the original criteria were for inclusion or exclusion actually were. Aside from its original subtitle, *"de todas as mercês, governos, fortalezas e viagens que os reys Dom Manuel, Dom Joam o 3°, Dom Enrique e os três Phelippes, fizerão e derão a diverças peças desde o anno de 1512 ate o de 1629,"* there is no way of determining. So I offer the title mostly for the sake of completeness.

I have now cleared the way for some ecclesiastical series, beginning with three, one completed and the others conceived by the late Father Silva Rego, although none were published by his Centro de Estudos Históricos Ultramarinos, but by the Agência Geral das Colónias, subsequently called the Agência Geral do Ultramar. The one he himself assembled is called *Documentação para a história das missões do Padroado Português do Oriente; India*, and it is complete in twelve volumes of various thicknesses, appearing between 1947 and 1958, and encompassing the years 1499-1582, at least formally so, for I have also found in the last volumes many documents of later date. Silva Rego did not hesitate to include documents which had appeared in other series, which is a great help when one is using it, and when so, he invariably identifies their provenance. Moreover, he prints secular documents where they help elucidate the political climate and circumstances surrounding the missionary activity. So indeed the work has great value for historians working outside the strict parameters of the title. I have found it useful, for instance, in pursuing information about the Portuguese of the "shadow empire."

The second work was to be paired with his and begins with the identical words, *Documentação, etc.*, but it ends with: *Insulíndia* and embraces the years 1506-1595 (-99). It was compiled by Father Artur Basílio de Sá, in 5 (6) volumes, and printed by the same agency between 1954 and 1958 (-88). From the title, one can perceive that it deals with Indonesia rather than India, and all the good things said about the work of Silva Rego apply here; the series is much sought after by workers in all fields of Indonesian history, anthropology and mission work. In 1988, a sixth volume appeared, though no one seems to know how to acquire it, including myself. It seems to represent work done for the series by the late Father Sá, but not published at the time of the other volumes.

The third series, or rather, double series, was by Father António Brásio and was called the *Monumenta Missionária Africana – Africa Ocidental,* and of the volumes which have appeared to date, only about the first eleven need concern us. Practically speaking, they begin with the XV century, and I have designated 1630 as the cutoff period. The series' existence is especially welcome to Africanists specializing in the western coast because this area is not represented by other historical series. Following the pattern of the Silva Rego-Basílio de Sá *Documentação* series, this one includes a generous cross section of Portuguese documentation, including many descriptive *relações* concerning the region and does not restrict itself to ecclesiastical documents alone. It has been widely employed by those in many fields of study. The first series, of nine volumes, began with its volume I (1952), covering the years 1471-1531, and reached my arbitrary cutoff date, 1620, with volume VI (1955), though note that volume IV (1955) contains documents from 1469-1599 and acts as a supplement to the first three. The second series, beginning with volume I (1958) is apparently still alive, despite Father Brásio's death in 1991. Volume I covers the years 1342-1499, while volume IV (1968) embraces the years 1600-1622.

I should mention as a kind of footnote to Father Silva Rego's creation of the *Documentação* projects and the reprinting of many documental books by his Centro de Estudos Históricos Ultramarinos, that a serial publication he originated, *Stúdia*, also contains printed documents in places, along with some useful secondary articles and documental calendars. It has been taken over by other hands and is still appearing regularly. One of the reprints of great value to me has been the late XVI century photocopy of the *Livro das cidades, e fortalezas, que a coroa de Portugal tem nas partes da India, e das capitanias e mais cargos que nelas ha, e da importancia deles* – a compendium of the whole command, logistical and concessionary structure of the empire as it came under the Spanish kings after 1580. At this writing, *Stúdia*, which began publication in 1958, is approaching fifty numbers, including a few double ones.

To end this long bibliographical excursion, I should call attention to the publications of the Institutum Historicum S. I., the Jesuit Historical Institute, in Rome. Since 1931, the order has maintained this body in a house near the Archivum Romanum S. I. in order to transcribe, annotate and publish the historical records of their order in their activities throughout the world. During this time, the fathers, especially Schurhammer, Leite, Wicki and Jacobs have worked in the area of the Portuguese empire, or more specifically, the *Padroado Português*, the hemisphere of missionary responsibility assigned to the Portuguese crown by Pope Alexander VI and his successors. This has resulted in three important series which students of the Portuguese empire would do well to consult: the *Monumenta Braziliae*, in five volumes covering the years 1538 to 1565, as edited by Serafim Leite, S.J., the *Monumenta Indica*, in sixteen, as edited by Fathers Josef Wicki, S.J. and J. Gomes, S.J., covering the years 1540-1594 and the *Documenta Malucensia* (on the Moluccan Islands), in three volumes, dealing with the years 1542-1682, as edited by Father Herbert Jacobs, S.J.

These are all meticulously prepared and annotated by their editors, and the documents are all in the languages in which written. Most are in Portuguese, though a portion are in Latin and a few even in Spanish. The only drawback to those whose Latin is absent or rusting is that until the early 1980s, when it changed to English, the notes and annotations are in that language, though I assure you that it is nowhere as taxing as Cicero or Ovid. The documents I found particularly interesting were the *litterae annuae*, the annual reports from the provincials to Rome. These are usually in Latin, although frequently, the original Portuguese version is printed, too, or else is the only one surviving. (It is comforting to moderns that the Latin of many of the Portuguese fathers on mission was too rusty for composition of the reports and that after an annual letter had been prepared in Portuguese, it usually was given to one of the fathers for translation who was known to be a good Latinist.)

No American library outside perhaps the Widener at Harvard University, the Newberry at Chicago, or the New York Public Library, is likely to have all the publications I have named, but most should be available from one institution or another on interlibrary loan. I have, as explained in the beginning, trespassed occasionally on the XVII century in my roundup of publications, but it is often genuinely difficult to halt at a chronological frontier. In many cases, knowledge of the slightly later period will serve to increase one's feel for the workings of the earlier one, and as it was, the only real change wrought by the turn of the XVI century was the coming of the English and Dutch competition which held such dire consequences for the Portuguese establishment.

About the Authors

Dauril Alden has been Professor of History at the University of Washington in Seattle since 1959. He is author of the classic study, *Royal Government in Colonial Brazil, with Special Reference to the Administration of the Marques de Lavradio, Viceroy, 1769-1779* (California, 1968) as well as of numerous articles on Brazil and on the Jesuits. He has recently completed the first volume of an extensive two-volume work, *The Establishment of an Enterprise:the Role of the Jesuits in Portugal, her Empire and Beyond, 1540-1750*, forthcoming from the Stanford University Press.

Onésimo T. Almeida is Chairman of the Department of Portuguese and Brazilian Studies, Brown University, Providence, Rhode Island. He is a specialist in intellectual history and the history of science. He is the author of numerous articles on the subject and his book on the rise and fall of science in Portugal will be published by Grádiva, Lisbon.

Rebecca Catz is a Research Associate at the Center for Medieval Studies, University of California at Los Angeles. She is translator and editor of *The Travels of Mendes Pinto* (Chicago University Press, 1989), for which she has been decorated by President Mário Soares with the Order of Prince Henry the Navigator.

William Donovan holds the Ph.D. degree from The Johns Hopkins University and is currently associate professor of history, specializing in Latin America, at Loyola College, Baltimore. He is author of several articles on Brazil and of the forthcoming book, *A Merchant of Lisbon, Francisco Pinheiro; Commerce and Society during the Brazilian Gold Rush.*

Francis A. Dutra, a Brazilianist, is professor of history at The University of California, Santa Barbara. His *A Guide to the History of Brazil* is the standard bibliographical work. He has recently expanded his interests to Portugal, where he has been studying its social institutions, especially the Order of Christ.

Felipe F.R. Fernández-Armesto is reader in medieval history at St. Antony's College, Oxford, and has written *Christopher Columbus, 1451-1506* (Oxford, 1992) a book which has corrected many of the myths surrounding the famous navigator. Another of his books is titled *Before Columbus: Exploration and Colonization from the Mediterranean to the Atlantic* (U. of Pennsylvania, 1987). He has also edited the Times *Atlas of World Exploration.*

Luís Adão da Fonseca is professor of medieval history at the Universidade do Porto, director of the Fundação Luís de Camões and a member of the Comissão Nacional para a Comemoração dos Descobrimentos Portugueses. He has written many articles and books, among them, *O essencial sobre Bartolomeu Dias.* (Lisbon: Imprensa Nacional/Casa de Moeda, 1987).

Harold V. Livermore, professor, emeritus, of Jesus College, Cambridge, and longtime secretary of Canning House, Belgrave Square, London, was for many years head of the Department of Romance Languages at the University of British Columbia, Vancouver. He is the author of numerous books, including: *A History of Portugal, A New History of Portugal, A History of Spain, The Origins of Spain and Portugal,* and of a host of learned articles.

Alfredo Pinheiro Marques, lecturer at the University of Coimbra, was closely associated with the late Luís de Albuquerque and is a former member of the Comissão Nacional para a Comemoração dos Descobrimentos Portugueses. He has been working for years on an electronic bibliography of the Portuguese discoveries and has written many works on the subject, including three in English: *Portugal and the Discovery of the Atlantic* (1990), *Portuguese Cartography and the Making of the World Picture* (1991), *and Portugal and the European Discovery of America* (1992), all published in Lisbon by the Imprensa Nacional/Casa de Moeda.

Derek Massarella is professor of history at Chuo University, Tokyo. A graduate of Worcester College, Oxford, he specializes in the history of European expansion and has most recently written a study of early contacts, *A World Elsewhere. Europe's Encounter with Japan in the Sixteenth and Seventeenth Centuries* (Yale,1989). In 1992 he was in residence at the Institute for East Asian Studies, Princeton.

Roderich Ptak is professor of Sinology at the University of Munich and interests himself particularly in contacts between Europeans and Chinese during the expansion era. Among other works, he is the author (with Dieter Rothermund) of *Emporia, Commodities and Entrepreneurs in Asian Maritime Trade 1400-1750* (Stuttgart: F. Steiner, 1991).

Carmen M. Radulet is professor of Portuguese language and literature at the Università della Tuscia, Viterbo. She is author (among other books) of *Os descobrimentos portugueses e a Italia* (Lisbon: Vega, 1991) as well as of many original and respected articles on the Portuguese discoveries.

John K. Thornton is an Africanist and professor of history at Millersville University, Pennsylvania. His most recent book is *Africa and the Africans, the Making of the Atlantic World, 1400-1680* (Cambridge, 1991). He is also known for his *Kingdom of Kongo* (Wisconsin, 1983).

Charles Verlinden is professor emeritus of history from the University of Ghent. He is among the most renowned authorities in the history of late medieval and early modern navigation, cartography and trade. He has written several books in French and Flemish, of which his *Beginnings of Modern Colonialism* (1979) has appeared in English. He may have set a modern record by publishing over seven hundred articles in his field! Most recently, he served on the faculty of the Maritime History Institute, held at the John Carter Brown Library in 1992-1993.

George D. Winius has taught at the University of Florida, at Leiden University, and most recently, at Brown. Most of his publications are on the Portuguese and Dutch in Asia, the most recent (1991) being *The Merchant-Warrior Pacified; the Changing Political Economy of the VOC in India* (Oxford, 1991,with Marcus P. M. Vink). He is president of the new Forum on European Expansion and Global Interaction and a corresponding member of the Academia Internacional da Cultura Portuguesa.

THE INDEX

A

Abreu, António de, 215
Abreu, Capistrano de, 241
Adil Shahi, of Bijapur, 198-199;Yusuf Adil Shah, of, 194, 198; Ali Adil Shah, 199-201
Adorno, Ieronimo, 201
Affaitati, of Cremona, 77; Giovanni Francesco de A., 151, 157
Afonso Henriques, 31, 34
Afonso, (prince), 111
Afonso I (of Kongo), 123-124; attacks Munza; letter to Manuel I, berates Portuguese, 127
Afonso III, 32-33
Afonso V; his regent gives Prince Henry permission to colonize Madeira, 73; Braganças gain dominance over, 85; farms out African concessions after d. of Prince Henry, 89; marries Infanta Juana, 92; defeat at Toro, 92-93; dies, 93; lavishly endows nobility, 111; sends Diogo Gomes on diplomatic missions, 122; letter to Christian of Denmark, 172
Afonso, Diogo (squire of D.Fernando), 75
Agra, 202-203, 256, 258; Portuguese in, 261-262

Ahmadnagar (Nizam Shah of), 201
Akbar, 201, 202; his dealings with the Jesuits, and his *Din-I-Ilahi*, 203, with Bento de Goes 315; accords *farman* to Tavares, 256
À *la recherche da la specifité de la Renaissance Portugaise*..... 357
Albergaria, Lopo Soares de, 141, 201
Albuquerque, Afonso de; leads fleet and ordered to build fortress, 140-141; storms Goa, 194; poisons Samorin, 198; captures Malacca, 206; sends Serrão & Abreu to Moluccas, 214; sends missions to Siam, 220; his letters, 332-333
Albuquerque, Francisco de, 141
Albuquerque, Jerónimo de, 232
Albuquerque, Luís de, 103, 335, 349, 351-352, 357
Alcáçovas, treaty of, 93, 134
Alcobaça, Cistercian monks at, 32
Alenquer, Pedro de, 96, 107
Aleppo, 323
Alexander VI (pope), 103, 107, 134-135
alfândega, 197
Alfarrobeira, 85
al-Mansur, 25-26
Alfonso I (of Aragón, "the Battler), 29

Alfonso V (of León), 26
Alfonso VI (of León), 27-29
Alfonso VII (Raimúndez), 29, 31
Alfonso XI (of Castile), 35
Alho, Afonso Martim, 34
Ali Raja (of Cannanore), 198
Aljubarrota, battle of, 36
Almeida, Francisco de, 141, 198, 201, 249
Almeida, Lourenço de, 140, 201
Almeida, Onésimo T., 173
Almoravids, 29
Álvares, Francisco, 102, 206, 336
Álvares, Diogo (O Caramuru), 231, 232
Álvares, Jorge, 270
Álvaro, D. (of Bragança), 139
alvazil, 26
Amaral, Manuel de, 320
Amazon (R. and region), 239
Amboina (Ambon), 215, 217
Amoy, 275
Ancião, 321
Ancients, 346
Andes (Mtns.), 239
Andrade, António de, 317-319
Andrade, Fernão Peres de, 272
Andrade, Simão Peres de, 272-273
André, J.M., 359, n.1
Angra de S.Braz, 136
Annobón Is. (*Ilha do Ano Bom*), 96

"Antilia," 53, 59, 170, 173
Ao-men (Macao), 281
Arakan, 255, 257
aratchis, 202
Arguim, bay and island, 85, 93
Arima Harunobu, 300
Aristotle, 345, 347
armação agreement, 300-301
Armas, Rumeu de, 64
Armazém de Guiné, 100
Arquivo Nacional da Torre do Tombo, 147
Ascensão (Ascension Is.), 152, 154
Ashikaga (shogunate), 292, 295; A. Yoshimitsu, 292-293; A.Yoshiaki, 296
Ataíde, Luís de, 201
Atjeh, 201, 218, 225
Ava, king of, 258
Aveiro, João Afonso, 101
Averroes, 345
Aviz, 319
Ayuthaya, 219, 221, 223-224, 294
Azambuja, Pedro de, 94
Azevedo, António Miranda de, 220
Azevedo, Fernão Lopes de, 92
Azevedo, Inácio de, 234
Azo (Hajo), 319
Azores, 53; evidence for early cartography of, 54; first stage in identification, 55-57; second stage, 58; third stage, 59-61;

consideration of evidence, 61-65; pairing with Canary exploration, 63-64; in Catalan Atlas, 72; early development, 84

Azuchi, 296

B

Babur, 202

Bacharel (Francisco de Chaves?), 231

Bacon, Roger, 347

Badrinath, 318

Baeza, Pedro de, 300

Bahadur Shah, of Gujarat, 200

Bahia de Todos os Santos, 157

Banda (archipelago), and route to, 215

bandeiras, bandeirantes, 231, 235ff.; 263

Bandel, 256, 260

Barbosa, Duarte, 79, 219, 249, 352

barca & barinel, small sailing vessels, 85

"Barcellosa de Sam Bordão," 188, n. 27

Barcelos, Pedro Maria de, 175

Bardes and Salcete, 199

Barreto, Francisco, 205

Barros, João de, 100, 102, 112, 146, 154, 220, 221, 273; discussion of his *Décadas,* 331, 334

"Bartolozzi Letter," 148, 158

Basra, 323

Bassein, 195

Batavia, 308

Beazley, Raymond, 81

beeswax, 34

Behaim, Martin, globe of, 99

Belém (Portugal), 145; (Brazil), 239

Belmonte, 145

Bemoi or Bemoim (Wolof King), 101, 123

Bengal, 202, 248, 255-257

Benguela, 129

Benin, king of, 123

Benincasa chart, 63

Bensaúde, Joaquim, 86, 355

Berardi, Gianotto, 147

Bergamo, Matteo da, 78

Bernard (primate and papal legate), 28

Bernard, Saint, 31

Bernstein, Richard J., 341

Bertran chart, 63

Bezeguiche (Dakar), 148, 156

Bhutan, 319

Bianco, Andrea, chart of 1448 (Milan), depicts *"ixola otinticha,"* 53, 54; interpretation of Azores, 59-60. Chart of 1436, 60

Biggar, H.P., 169

Bijapur (see Adil Shahi)

Bintan, 214

Black Death *(Yersina pestis),* 296

Blanco (Cape), 74

Blussé, Leonard, 214-215

Boas, Marie, 355

Boccaccio, Giovanni, 46-47

islands; mentioned by Petrarch, 44; by Pliny (?), 45; first authenticated visit, 46; and Majorcans, 47-49; interest by Aragon, 49-50; by Portugal, 50; and Castilians, 51; in Dulcert map, 51; Portugal abandons claims to, 93

Cannanore, 138, 141, 198

Cantino, Alberto, 152; the C. mappemonde, (of Modena), 151, 152, 154; place names on, 157; shows voyage of G.Corte-Real, 175

Cão, Diogo; lack of background information, 94-95; theories of Carmen Radulet on voyages, 95-97; reaches Congo R., his *Rio do Padrão*, 95; made *cavaleiro*, embassy to Manicongo, takes natives hostage, 96; exchanges hostages for embassy, reaches Cape Farilhões, inscription at Ielala, 97-98; death (or disgrace)? 98-99

Cape Verde Islands, insufficient evidence for early discovery of, 54; sighted by Cadamosto, 74; Portuguese presence, 125; visited by Vasco da Gama, 136

"Cape Verde Letter," 148

capitão de Coromandel, 250

Capitão-Mor da viagem da China e Japão, 295

captaincy system, 233

Capuchins, 322

Caraci, Giuseppe, 150, 151

Caramansa (Bantu chief), 94

Caramuru (Diogo Álvares), 231

Cardim, Fernão, 234-235

Carpini, Giovanni de Plano, 315

cartaz (maritime pass) system, 196, 214; compared to *shuinjo*, 306

Cartier, Jacques, 175

Carvalho, Joaquim Barradas de, 350, 353, 355

Casa de Guiné e Mina, 94

casa de São Thomé, 249

casados, 197, 248, 251, 254-255

Castanheda, Fernão Lopes de, 146; discussion of his chronicle, 332, 334, 335

Casti, John L., 358

castle-building (of Toyotomi Hideyoshi), 300-301

Castro, João de; his *Roteiros* and *Tratado*, 207, 335, 343ff.

"Catalan Atlas," (of 1375), 41; identifies Canaries, 52; and Madeira, Porto Santo, Desert Islands, and Savage Islands, 53; dating, 55; features in common, 56

Catalan portolan charts, of Paris & Naples, 56

"diaspora" (of Chinese trade), 274-270
"Diego de Silves" (on Vallseca map), 60-61
Diffie, Bailey W., 103, 192
Dighton Rock, 181
Diogo, Duke of Viseu, 111
Din-i-Ilahi ("true light"), 203
Diniz (king of Portugal), 33; creates fleet and hires Pessagno, 71
Diu, 194, 200-201
donatórios, 233
Doria, Joan, 49
Dudum siquidem, Eximiae devotionis, Pius fidelium (see Alexander VI)
Dulcert, Angelino, map of, 47, 72
Dulmo, Fernão (see: Olmen, Ferdinand van)
Dutch, on Gold Coast, 94; effect of invasion on Brazil, 236 (see also V.O.C.)

E

Eanes, Gil, 85
Earthly Paradise, 45
Edward, the Black Prince, 35
Egmore (Tamil Nadu archives), 258
Elmina (see S.Jorge da Mina)
Empoli, Giovanni da, 78, 150, 154
English, of Hon. East India Co., 258-261; 300; in Hirado, 307

English, private traders, 260-261
Enrique IV (of Spain), 92
entradas, 230
epidemics; in Brazil, 234; in Japan, 296; in Tibet, 322
Esmeraldo de Situ Orbis, 100, 113-114, 343, 344-345
Espirito Santo (captaincy), 234
Este, Ercole d' (Duke of Ferrara), 152
Estreito, João Afonso, 76
Eugenius IV (pope), 92

F

Fagundes, João Álvares, 178-179
(A) Famosa, 215
Faria, António de, 275
Faria, João Pereira de, 261
Farilhões, Cape, 97
Fatehpur Sikri, 256
feitor da costa do Coromandel, 250
Ferdinand I, king of Castile, 26-27
Ferdinand (k. of Aragon), 92, hears of Brazil's discovery from Manuel I, 146, 154
Fernando, Duke of Bragança, 111
Fernandes, António, 205
Fernandes, Duarte, 220
Fernandes, Francisco, 177
Fernandes, João ("O Lavrador"), 175, 176-178
Fernandes, Valentim, 75, 156

chronicle of D.Manuel, 332, 334

Gomera, identified with "Gumeyra" 50; on Pizigani chart (?) 52

Gomes, Diogo, 75, 122

Gomes, Fernão; royal concessionnaire, 89; farthest point reached by, 95; 330

Gomes, Manuel, 249

Gonçalves, André, 153

Gonçalves, Antão, 85

Gonçalves, João, 177

Gonneville, Paulmier de, 160

Good Hope (Cape), 100-101

Goto (Is.), 295

Granada, 37

Grán Canaria, 49

Grand Banks, 174, 178

Greenlee, William B., 150

Gregory VII (Hildebrand), pope, 28

Grosseteste, Robert, 347

Grueber, Johan, 326, n.22

Guanabara Bay, 157

Guapai (R), 239

Guedes, Max Justo, 156-157, 159

Guimarães, 24

Gujarat (Cambay), and Gujarati, 194, 199-201, 202, 214, 215, 248

guns; breech-loading swivel, 185-186; in Japan, 301

gun-slave cycle theory, 126-127

Guns, Sails, and Empire, 356

Guyenne, 34, 35

gypsies, 243, n.7

H

Haeghen, Willem van der (Guilherme da Silveira), 77

haifuki cupellation method, 297

Hall, A. Ruppert, 342

"Hao-ching" (or "Hao-keng") = Macao), 282

Hardwar ("Gate of Vishnu"), 318

Harisse, Henry, 175

Heesterman, Jan C., 191, 195-196

Hemming, John, 242

Henriques, Henrique, 208

Henry II (of Castile), 35

Henry VII (of England), 89, 174, 176

Henry of Burgundy (count of Terra Portucalensis), 28, 30

Henry, Prince (Infante D.Henriques), member of the *ínclita geração*, 37; deference to traditions of discovery, 42; receives authorization to colonize Madeira; monopoly on Guinea navigation, 73; granted allowances; fights at Ceuta; gains titles and power, 82; capitalistic interests, 82-83; African interests vs. insular ones, 86; evaluation, 87; proposes crusade, 91; persistent "romantic view," 342-343

Kyushu, 293ff.

L

Lahore, 315
lamas, 319
Lamego, 26
Lampacau (Lang-pai-kang), 279
Landeiro, Bartolomeu Vaz, 299
Landmonsterrollen, 259
"Lansarote da Framqua"(to be identified with Lançarote de Malocello?), 50
Lanzarote, island of; tower, 50
Larsen, Sofus, 171
lateen sail *(vela latina)*, characteristics, 106- 107
Leh (capital of Ladakh), 321
Leite, Duarte, 103, 149, 355, 357
Lemos, Gaspar de, 153, 154
León, house and city of, 2
L'Ecluse, Charles (Clusius), 207
L'Espoir, 160
Lettera di Amerigo Vespucci dellle Isole Novamente Trovate (the *Quatour Navigationes)*, 147-150
Levillier, Roberto, 156
Lhasa, 321, 322, 326, n.22
Liampo (Shuang-hsü-kang Is.), 275, 276
Libro del conoscimiento, 41, 52, 56
Lien-wan, 279
Lima, Rodrigo de, 102

Linschoten, Jan Huyghen van, 307
Lisbon, nature and location of, 20; title bestowed by Julius Caesar upon, 21; Raymond incapable of holding, 28;
first voyage of discovery from, 30; captured by Afonso Henriques, 31; receives *Casa de Guiné e Mina,* 94
Litterae Annuae, 334
Llull, Raymond, and missionaries, 48, 49
Lobo, Jerónimo, 323
Lobos, Isla de, 51
Lopes, Fernão, 34, 37
Loronha, Fernão de, and dyewood, 158-161 (see also Quaresma [São João] Island); summary, 160
Luanda (Is.), 129
Lucena, Vasco Fernandes de, 98, 133-134
Lucira Bay (*Bahia de João de Lisboa*), 96
Lucira Grande, 98
Lukala (R.), 129
Lusitania, province created by Augustus Caesar, 21
Luso-Chinese relations, stages in, 282; reasons for Portuguese success, 283
Lu T'ang, 276-277

M

Macao, circumstances of agreement with Chinese, 280-282; *senado da câmara,*

Maranhão, 239

Marchioni (Florentine firm), 73; Bartolomeo M., in Brazil & African trade, 77, 139; finances ship, 150

Margre, Pere, 48, 49

Markham, Clements R., 149

Marques, Alfredo Pinheiro, 109

Marques, João Martins da Silva, 169

Martellus, Henricus (Heinrich Hammer); *Insulario* of, 97; map of 1479, 100; map of 1489, 101

Massangano, 129

Massari, Leonardo, 151, 158, 159, 160

Masulipatam (Machilipatam), 248, 259

Mato Grosso, 240

McMullin, Ernan, 342, 358

Meale Khan, 199

Medeiros (or Madeira), Cosmo and Luís de 261

Medici, Lorenzo di Pier Francesco de', 147, 148, 158

Medici Atlas (Laurentian Library), 54, 56, 72

Meiji Restoration, 296

Meilink-Roelofsz, Marie Antoinette P., 196

Mello, Martim Afonso de, 255

Mendes Pinto, Fernão (see Pinto, Fernão M.)

Meneses, Duarte, 250

Meneses, Francisco de Silva, 223

Merlin legends, 45, 46

mestiços, in Bengal area, 257, 263

Miako, 314

Mieli, Aldo, 356

Minas Gerais, 240

Ming dynasty, politics, 269, 270; reasons for restriction of trade, 271ff.; as seen by historians of P.Republic, 281; "tally trade" with Japan, 292

Miranda, Sá de, 333

Moluccas (archipelago), and route to, 215

Mombasa, 205

Monomatapa, the, and region, 205

Montalboddo, Fracanziano da, 148

Montemor, 25-26

Monte Pascoal, 145

Moog, Clodomir Vianna, 241-242

Mora, Joan, 49, 64

morabatino (maravedí), 29

Mori, 293

Morison, Samuel Eliot, 62, 103, 105, 148, 150, 172-173, 175, 177-178

Mossel Bay (*Bahia dos Vaqueiros?*), 100

Mota, António da, 294

Mota, Avelino Teixeira da, 103

Mota, Jorge da, 223-225, 228, n. 23

Mozambique, 115, 136

mudaliyars, 202

confinement in West Africa to slaving enclaves, 128; pro-blems with trading in Ming China, 276 ff.

"Portugalete," 263

Portuguese language, 124

Porto Seguro (Baía Cabrália), 145, 157, 159

Pothorst & Pining, 171

Povoa de Varzim, 25

prazos, prazeiros, 205-206

Prester John, 91, 101-102

Priuli, Girolamo, 150

Promontorium Prassum, 98-99, 133-134

Ptolemy and Ptolemaic geographers, 91, 344

Pulicat, 248, 249, 252, 259

Punikkayal, 254

Purchas, Samuel, 257

Pusan, 293, 294

Pyrard de Laval, François, 262

Q

Qtb-al-Din al-Nahrawali, 119, n.39 -120

Quaresma (Is., now Fernão de Noronha), 157

Quatro Ribeyras, 75

Quijos (R.), 239

quilombos, 229

quincentenary, Columbian, 242

Quito (viceroyalty of Peru), 239

R

Ramalho, João, 231, 232

Rama T'bodi, 220

Rangoon, 248

Raposo (see Tavares, António Raposo)

Raymond of Burgundy (count of Galicia), 28-29

Recco, Nicoloso da, 72

Reconquest (Reconquista), 25-35

Reinel, Pedro; Bordeaux map of, 95

Resende, Garcia de, 110; his *Cancioneiro*, 333

Restauração, 260

retablos, in Japan, 302

Ribeiro, Aquilino, 356

Ricci, Matteo, 208, 315, 317

Rio das Velhas (R.), 240

Rio de Janeiro, 157, 160

Rio de Oro, 85

Rio do Padrão (see Congo R.)

Rio Grande (R.), 239

"river of gold," 49

Roderic, king, 22

Rodrigues, António, 231

Rodrigues, Francisco, chart of, 152

Rodrigues, João, 297, 304; *Arte da lingoa em Japam*, 305

Romanus pontifex (see Nicholas V)

Rondinelli, Piero di Nofri di Giovanni, 151, 157, 158

Roteiros (of D.João de Castro), 343, 347ff

Roukema, Edzer, 145

Round Tower (of Newport), 181

Ruggieri, Michele, 315

Ruysbroeck, Wilhelmus van

Tsaparang, 318, 320
Trastemires, Gonçalo, of
    Maia, 26
*Tratado....de Todos os
    Descobrimentos*, 148
Tratado da Esfera, 346ff.
*Tratado em Defensam da Carta
    de Marear*, 343, 351
Trevisan di Bernardino,
    Angelo , 151
Tristão, Nuno, 85
Tsou-ma-ch'i (or -hsi), 275, 277
Tsushima (Is.), 293, 308
Tupí-Guaraní, language, 237,
    238
Turfan, 316
Tuy, 25

U

Urban II, 30
urcas (large medieval round
    ships), 77
Urraca, 27-29
Uso di Mare (Usodimare),
    Antoniotto, sails to
    Gambia, 73; meets
    Cadamosto at Senegal R.;
    later sails with him, 74
Utsang, 319

V

Valers, En, 48
Valignano, Alessandro, 208,
    299, 305
Vallseca, Gabriel map
    (Barcelona), 59, 60
vanias (Banyans), 248
Varnhagen, Francisco Adolfo
    de, 149
Varthema, Lodovico de, 78-79

"Vasco da Gama Era" (of
    K.M. Panikkar), 192, 203-
    204; (of Carlo Cipolla),
    356
Vaz Dourado, Fernão, atlas
    of, 172
Velasco, Pedro de, 171
Velho, Álvaro, 136, 334, 335
Velho, Domingos Jorge, 237
Vera Cruz ("Is."), 146
Verlinden, Charles, 42, 64
"vermillion seals" *(shuinjo)*,
    306; and the *shuinsen*
    vessels, 306
Vermoim, 25
Vespucci, Amerigo, 114;
    voyages of and letters
    attributed to, 147-150;
    describes 1501
    expedition to Brazil, 154-
    155; 156; returns to
    Seville(?), 157
Vicente, Gil, 333
Vida de Jaques de Coutre, 218,
    223-224
Vijayanagar (Narsinga), 199,
    254
Vikings, 24-26
Vishnu-Ganga (R.), 318
Visigoths, 22-23
Vivaldi, brothers, 44
Vliet, Jeremias van, 260
V.O.C. (Dutch East India
    Company), 215, 222,
    258-260, 261, 300; in
    Hirado, 307; retained by
    Iemitsu; Dutch
    celebrations, 308
*Vocabulario da lingoa de
    Japam*, 305

Vogt, John L., 153, 158, 159
volta do largo, 138

W

Waldseemüller, Martin, 148, 152
Wad Draa, 49, 51
wako, 295
Williamson, J,A., 169, 177
Wilton Codex (Huntington Library), 91
Windsor, treaty of. 36-37
Warri, state, 123
Wen-wan, 279
Wessels, Cornelius, 321
West River, 279
Wightman, W.P., 355
wine, 34, 37
wo k'ou, 295
wool, of Castile, 37
Wu-hsü, 277

X

Xavier, Francis, 207-208, 250, 253, 254, 278, 298, 304, 313-314
Xavier, Jerónimo, 315

Y

"Yale Map of 1403"(by Francesco Beccario), 60
Yarkand, oasis of, in W.Sinkiang, 316
Yo mp'o, 293
Yoshimitsu (see Ashikaga)
Yüeh-kang, 275, 277
Yule, Sir Henry, and Henri Cordier (in *Cathay and the Way Thither*), 317

Z

Zaccaria, family, 44
Zambesi (R.) system, 205
Zaragoza, treaty of, 216
Zarco, João Gonçalves, 73, 83
Zeimoto, Francisco, 294
Zuane Pizzigano map, 173
Zurara, Gomes Eanes de, 81, 83; paints heroic picture of Prince Henry, 85-86; justification of conquest, 330

Ysopete-Zaragoza, 1489

hic liber confectus est
madisoni .mcmxcv.

946.902   Portugal, the pathfinder
POR